The Colonial Divide in Peruvian Narrative

The Colonial Divide in Peruvian Narrative
Social Conflict and Transculturation

Misha Kokotovic

sussex
ACADEMIC
PRESS

BRIGHTON • PORTLAND

2 4 6 8 10 9 7 5 3 1

First published in 2005 in Great Britain by
SUSSEX ACADEMIC PRESS
P.O. Box 2950
Brighton BN2 5SP

and in the United States of America by
SUSSEX ACADEMIC PRESS
920 NE 58th Ave.   Suite 300
Portland, Oregon 97213–3786

British Library Cataloguing in Publication Data
A CIP catalogue record for this book is available from the British Library.

Library of Congress Cataloging-in-Publication Data
Kokotovic, Misha.
   The colonial divide in Peruvian narrative : social conflict and
   transculturation / Misha Kokotovic.
      p. cm.
   Includes bibliographical references and index.
   ISBN 1-84519-029-7 (hardcover : alk. paper)
   1. Peruvian fiction—20th century—History and criticism.
   2. Social conflict in literature.   3. Group identity in literature.
   4. Literature and society—Peru.   I. Title.
   PQ8407.S6K65 2005
   863′.6093552—dc22
                                                         2004020670
                                                         CIP

Typeset and designed by G&G Editorial, Brighton.
Printed by MPG Books, Bodmin, Cornwall.
This book is printed on acid-free paper.

Contents

Acknowledgements   vi

Introduction   Social Conflict and Narrative Form   1

1   Modernity from the Margins: Narrative Form and   32
    Indigenous Agency in *Broad and Alien is the World*
    and *Yawar Fiesta*

2   From Development Theory to *Pachakutiy*: José María   65
    Arguedas's Anthropology and Fiction in the 1950s

3   Between Feudalism and Imperialism: Indigenous Culture   96
    and Class Struggle in *All the Worlds* and *Drums for Rancas*

4   The *Criollo* City Transformed: Andean Migration in   124
    Urban Narrative

5   Mario Vargas Llosa Writes Of(f) the Native: Cultural   163
    Heterogeneity and Neoliberal Modernity

Epilogue   More than Skin Deep? Social Change in Contemporary   195
               Peru

Notes   202
Bibliography   257

Acknowledgements

This book got its start in the early 1980s, long before I ever imagined I would write it. For those unconscious beginnings, I am indebted to Mary Weismantel, who first showed me the Andes, and to the people to whom she introduced me there, in particular the *familia* Chaluisa of Yanatoro, Ecuador (with apologies for my initial and at times churlish incomprehension). Thanks are also due to Kay Candler, who has no doubt forgotten giving me my first copy of *Yawar Fiesta* over twenty years ago. Though I did not get around to reading it for more than a decade, and though it was several more years before I began to understand its significance, Arguedas's novel ultimately provided a re-encounter with the Andes of which the present book is a product.

I am grateful to the University of California, San Diego for a Faculty Career Development Award, a Chancellor's Summer Faculty Fellowship, and a Hellman Fellowship, without which this book would have been more difficult to complete. In addition, the UC San Diego Office of Graduate Studies and Research generously supported the publication of *The Colonial Divide in Peruvian Narrative*.

I inflicted early versions of some of the arguments that appear in this book on my undergraduate and graduate students, who rewarded my efforts with more interest, good humor, and thoughtful feedback than a teacher might reasonably expect. They were instrumental in helping me to elucidate my ideas, and such clarity as may be found in the pages that follow is due in no small part to my students.

Writing is a solitary task made possible only by the friendship and solidarity of many, and in this respect I have been very fortunate. From nearby and afar, the following individuals contributed in one way or another to seeing me through to the end of the manuscript: María Bernath, Carlos and Iris Blanco, Charles Briggs, Terri Cain, Jaime Concha, Greg Dawes, Claire Fox, Kenia Halleck, Nancy Hesketh, Gretchen Hills, Sara Johnson, Ksenija Kokotovic, Neil Larsen, Mike Murashige, Eduardo López-Gibson, Yajaira Padilla, Max Parra, José Ruiz, Rosaura Sánchez, Marta Sánchez, Colleen Smith, Jacki Stanke, Cyndi Trupin, Patricia Valiton,

Acknowledgements

Don Wayne, and León Zamosc. In addition to their encouragement and support, Priscilla Archibald, Jody Blanco, Susan Fitzpatrick, Brian Gollnick, Petar Kokotovic, Nancy Postero, and Mary Louise Pratt read parts or all of the manuscript and offered valuable insight and suggestions. Susan Kirkpatrick read several chapters and provided a crucial jump start when the writing stalled about halfway through. Christine Hunefeldt shared her historical knowledge of the Andean region and provided excellent suggestions for reworking key parts of the manuscript. Jorge Mariscal read the entire manuscript and proposed much needed revisions, while his ironic take on the profession helped me keep things in perspective. Though everyone mentioned here provided sensible advice at every turn, it was not in their power to compel me to act upon it. I am therefore solely responsible for any errors and omissions that plague the following pages.

My editor, Tony Grahame, has been a model of efficiency and understanding. I am also indebted to the two anonymous readers to whom Sussex Academic Press entrusted my manuscript. The readers' exemplary professionalism and constructive critique helped strengthen my arguments and improved the readability of the book.

Finally, and unfortunately for her, Carrie Sakai shared with me the drudgery and occasional despair of academic writing. I can only hope to make up the lost hours, and moments, in the years to come.

The author acknowledges with thanks Confluencia: Revista Hispánica de Cultura y Literatura for permission to reproduce "Vargas Llosa in the Andes: The Racial Discourse of Neoliberalism," originally published in *Confluencia,* vol. 15, no. 2 (spring 2001): 156–67; and Revista Canadiense de Estudios Hispanicos for permission to reproduce "Mario Vargas Llosa Writes Of(f) the Native: Modernity and Cultural Heterogeneity in Peru," originally published in *Revista*, vol. 25, no. 3 (2001). These two articles form the basis of Chapter 5 of this book.

INTRODUCTION

Social Conflict and Narrative Form

This book explores narrative representations of ethnic and class conflict in twentieth-century Peru, a culturally heterogeneous society built on the colonial divide between indigenous Andeans and their Spanish conquerors.[1] From the Conquest through to the nineteenth century, the divide was geographical as well as social: the descendants of the conquered lived mainly in the Andes, those of the conquerors primarily, though not exclusively, on the coast. Twentieth-century modernization, however, would bring the two groups into a renewed confrontation rivaling that of the Conquest.[2] The resulting intrusion of indigenous Andeans into a national consciousness monopolized by *criollo* (white) elites transformed Peruvian intellectual life, provoking intense debate over who would define the cultural contours of the nation's nascent modernity. As the eminent Peruvian historian Jorge Basadre observed in 1931, "the most important event in twentieth century Peruvian culture is the growing awareness among writers, artists, men of science, and politicians of the Indian's existence."[3] Through a study of narrative fiction and non-fiction (novels, short stories, memoirs, anthropological and political essays) spanning the second half of the twentieth century, I examine the forms such awareness would take among Peru's literary intellectuals since Basadre first noted its importance.

Between the 1940s and the 1990s, changing class relations in the countryside, massive rural-to-urban migration, indigenous peoples' struggles for land, education, and effective citizenship, and a decade-long war between the *Sendero Luminoso*, or Shining Path, insurgency and government security forces changed the face of Peru, but not in the way that the country's *criollo* elites anticipated. Peru's elites had long argued that national development and progress required integration, understood as a one-way process through which the indigenous Andean population would be assimilated into the Western culture of the *criollo* minority. What actually happened is considerably more complex. Indigenous peoples

1

organized to defend their land, attended university, joined leftist political parties and revolutionary movements, and migrated from the Andes to coastal cities without acculturating to *criollo* norms. Many maintained their indigenous identity, while others developed an urban Andean, or *cholo*, identity distinct from and in opposition to that of the dominant *criollo* minority.[4]

These changes, particularly rural-to-urban migration and the consequent growth of the urban, *cholo* population, tended to blur the boundary between the two sides of Peru's colonial divide. The terms Indian and *criollo*, along with others like *mestizo* or *cholo*, do not mean exactly the same thing today as they did in the colonial period (when the word *cholo* did not yet exist) or even in the mid-twentieth century. Likewise, their meaning is dependent on the context in which they are used, by whom they are used, and to whom they are addressed. However, this does not mean that social divisions and the conflicts to which such divisions gave rise have disappeared. Although the cultural identities of the two primary social groups have evolved over time, they have done so in opposition to each other, reproducing the divisions between them in new forms.

The term colonial divide, denoting a social division of colonial origins, is still justified even in late twentieth-century Peru, but the nature of that division has changed in the five centuries since the Conquest. Rather than a rigid boundary between two clearly demarcated social groups, in the second half of the twentieth century the colonial divide in Peru has taken the form of hierarchical opposition between two poles, indigenous Andean and *criollo*-Western, in which the former is negatively valued and the latter positively. Between these two poles extends a continuum along which individuals and groups position themselves and/or are located by others according to context. Such positioning is an integral part of a struggle for power, since cultural (or ethnic, or racial) superiority is asserted by reference to another individual or group's greater relative proximity to the indigenous Andean pole of the continuum, which marks them as inferior. Tellingly, this is one meaning of the verb *cholear*, to treat someone as a *cholo*.[5] In contemporary Peru, cultural (or ethnic, or racial) identity is fluid and relational, but this has not necessarily attenuated social divisions and antagonisms.

Over the last several decades, rural indigenous peoples and urban Andean migrants have challenged the hierarchical nature of the opposition between the two poles of Peru's colonial divide, particularly the *criollo* elite's equation of modernity with its own Westernized culture and backwardness with indigenous Andeans and their cultural traditions. In place of this, rural and urban Andeans have posed the possibility of alternative, culturally heterogeneous forms of modern life at least partly rooted in Andean traditions. In the chapters that follow,

I examine literary intellectuals' representations of and responses to these developments at key periods in twentieth-century Peruvian history: the aftermath of a frustrated series of popular challenges to oligarchic rule between 1915 and 1932; the Odría dictatorship of 1948 to 1956; the indigenous land struggles of the late 1950s and early 1960s, which precipitated the breakdown of the semi-feudal system of land tenure and hierarchical social relations known in Peru as *gamonalismo*; the transformation of Lima and other coastal cities by mass Andean migration from the 1950s through the 1980s; the Shining Path war of the 1980s; and the turn to neoliberalism inaugurated by the watershed presidential elections of 1990.[6]

During this period, authors such as Ciro Alegría, José María Arguedas, Manuel Scorza, Julio Ramón Ribeyro, Alfredo Bryce Echenique and Mario Vargas Llosa exposed the unfulfilled promises of modernization in the Andes and attempted to imagine a modernity compatible with their nation's cultural heterogeneity, or, conversely, portrayed the latter as responsible for the multiple inadequacies of Peru's emerging, peripheral modernity. Moreover, they developed new narrative techniques to write across Peru's colonial divide. In analyzing the narrative forms these authors used to represent class and ethnic conflicts in their rapidly changing society, I draw on the related concepts of heterogeneous literatures and narrative transculturation developed by Antonio Cornejo Polar and Ángel Rama, respectively.[7] Though the terms are frequently invoked in theoretical debates, the concepts have rarely been brought to bear on a corpus of texts in a systematic fashion, as I do here in this regional and historical case study.[8]

Heterogeneous Literatures and Narrative Transculturation

Cornejo Polar and Rama developed their theories in the 1970s, in the context of an escalating confrontation between Latin American national liberation movements and a resurgent US imperialism.[9] In these years dependency theory dominated Latin American social science, and its influence is apparent in both Cornejo Polar's and Rama's efforts to construct a literary criticism rooted in Latin American social reality and independent of metropolitan cultural theory.[10] As Cornejo Polar notes, his notion of heterogeneous literatures was a contribution to a broader critical effort underway during the 1970s to "adapt the principles and methods of our critical practice to the distinctive characteristics of Latin American literature."[11] Through such efforts, Cornejo Polar, Rama, and others hoped to produce "a truly Latin American criticism."[12]

The project of an independent Latin American literary criticism arose in the wake of the phenomenal international commercial success of and critical acclaim for the 1960s "Boom" novels of Julio Cortázar, Gabriel García Márquez, Carlos Fuentes, and Mario Vargas Llosa, whose formal innovations were derived primarily from European and North American literary modernism. Against this powerful current, Cornejo Polar and Rama focused on the autochthonous, regional sources of literary renewal in the works of an earlier generation of authors marginalized by the critical and commercial apparatus associated with the Boom. Without rejecting theoretical contributions from metropolitan centers, Cornejo Polar, Rama and others sought to fashion a criticism capable of addressing the social divisions exacerbated by Latin American nations' dependent, peripheral role in the capitalist world system.

In developing their key theoretical concepts, both Cornejo Polar and Rama drew on earlier Latin American traditions of cultural criticism. Cornejo Polar, for example, begins his discussion of heterogeneous literatures by invoking the figure of José Carlos Mariategui (1894–1930), the founder of the Peruvian Socialist Party who in the 1920s adapted Marxism to the study of Peru's distinctive social and cultural history. Mariátegui had argued in his *Seven Interpretive Essays on Peruvian Reality* (1928) that Peru's deep cultural divisions, a legacy of the Conquest, imposed special requirements on literary study: "The Quechua-Spanish dualism in Peru, still unresolved, prevents our national literature from being studied with the methods used for literatures that were created and developed without the intervention of the conquest."[13]

Cornejo Polar's concept of heterogeneous literatures is explicitly an attempt to respond to this need for a critical method for the study of literature in Peru and other culturally fragmented Latin American societies.

Cultural Heterogeneity and Literary Form

Much Latin American literature, Cornejo Polar notes, is as internally divided, or culturally heterogeneous, as the societies in which it is produced. To define heterogeneous literature, he distinguishes between four elements, or "instances", of the literary process: "production, the resulting text, its referent, and the system of distribution and consumption."[14] A homogeneous literary work is one in which all four elements fall within a single sociocultural order. A heterogeneous work, by contrast, is the result when one or more of these elements belong to one sociocultural order and the rest are derived from another.

Cornejo Polar's principal example of the former are the 1950s urban narratives of Sebastián Salazar Bondy and Julio Ramón Ribeyro in Peru and of José Donoso and Jorge Edwards in Chile. Their works, he argues, "put into play perspectives characteristic of certain sectors of the urban middle classes, . . . refer to the problems of this same group and are read by a public of the same social status. Literary production then circulates within a single social space and acquires a high degree of homogeneity: it is, one could say, a society which speaks to itself."[15] However, it would be difficult to find a Latin American literary work which could not in some respect be considered at least partly heterogeneous. This is true even of the works Cornejo Polar uses as his examples of homogeneous literature. It may well be that he exaggerates the dichotomy between heterogeneous and homogeneous literatures for heuristic purposes. Whatever the case, it is more useful to think of the difference between homogeneous and heterogeneous literatures as a matter of degree rather than of kind.

Though heterogeneous literature could in principle take a variety of forms, depending on the distribution of the elements of the literary process among different sociocultural universes, all of the examples Cornejo Polar offers are of the sort in which "production, the text and its consumption correspond to one universe and the referent to a different and even opposed one."[16] This pattern, he argues, describes the sixteenth-and-seventeenth century chronicles of the Conquest, the early nineteenth-century poetry associated with the anti-colonial struggle for emancipation from Spain, and the twentieth-century social realist, *indigenista* genre of works by predominantly *mestizo* provincial writers about and usually in defense of the indigenous population. For Cornejo Polar, moreover, there are two distinct variants of this type of heterogeneous literature. While in most such texts a native referent is represented through the Spanish language and Western literary forms imposed upon it, in some cases the referent produces a kind of interference with the norms of the established Western genre to which the text nominally belongs.

In some heterodox chronicles of the Conquest by indigenous and *mestizo* writers, Cornejo Polar notes, "one may detect deviations in form that can only be explained by the action of the referent upon its means of enunciation."[17] If in more orthodox chronicles, "the production process smothered the referent", in heterodox ones "the referent is able to impose certain conditions and generate a modification in the formal structure of the chronicle."[18] Such is the case, for example, of Felipe Guaman Poma de Ayala's use of drawings in his early seventeenth-century indigenous chronicle *Nueva Corónica y Buen Gobierno*, in which he denounces abuses by colonial officials in the viceroyalty of Peru. As critics have shown in recent years, Guaman Poma's chronicle is not fully comprehensible unless one attends to the indigenous cultural traditions and world-view that partially structure the text.[19]

A similar example is the independence era poetry of Mariano Melgar, who wrote both overtly political, patriotic verse as well as love poems, which are relatively unknown outside of Peru. In his political poetry, "the accusations against Spain or the praise for independence and liberty are processed literarily according to the values that governed the literature of the era", namely neoclassicism.[20] The love poems, by contrast, draw on a popular song form descended from pre-Columbian traditions and known as the *yaraví*. Ironically, the overtly political poems dedicated to Peru's struggle for independence from Spain are formally dependent on the literary conventions of the very colonial power they denounce, while the love poetry, though lacking in overt political content or intent, is more independent in its literary form and more representative of a potentially national popular culture. For Cornejo Polar,

> Melgar's yaraví represents a more consistent act of liberation than the neoclassical poems about the independence of our nations: if the latter display an external correspondence to the historical process of independence, a process which they in a sense betray because of their adherence to metropolitan models, the yaraví, by contrast, though not about political events, realizes at a literary level the ideal of liberty and independence that the other poems, because of their dependence, can only announce.[21]

The dependence of patriotic poetry on Spanish models at the very birth of the Peruvian nation may be taken as a cultural expression of the subsequent persistence of colonial forms of domination in the newly independent republic.[22] By contrast, Melgar's *yaraví* hints at the possibility of a more democratic and inclusive national culture.

Late nineteenth-and early twentieth-century *indigenista* authors, too, were dependent on Western literary forms for the representation of the indigenous referent of their works. *Indigenista* literature, as Mariátegui pointed out in 1928 and as Cornejo Polar emphasizes, is not indigenous literature, but rather the work of provincial *mestizos* seeking to represent indigenous interests.[23] Though most *indigenista* works took the side of the indigenous population, they did so from within the boundaries of the Western literary genres of the novel and the short story (in their successive historical variants: romanticism, bourgeois realism, social realism). Like the chronicles of the Conquest, these works addressed "a distant reader foreign to the universe presented in the text."[24] That is, they represented indigenous peoples to an implicitly non-indigenous reader. In the cultural split between indigenous referent and Western literary form and reading public, Cornejo Polar argues, *indigenista* texts express in their very structure the divisions and conflicts of the societies in which they were produced, divisions and conflicts which more homogeneous literary works tend to elide. For Cornejo Polar, the significance of *indigenista* narrative is not limited to the realist representation of an indigenous referent. In the cultural heterogeneity of their very form, he suggests, *indigenista* works undermined the *criollo* elite's illusion of a unified, Hispanic national culture.

The best *indigenismo*, moreover, "not only takes up the interests of the indigenous peasantry; it also incorporates, to varying degrees, timidly or boldly, certain literary forms organically derived from its referent."[25] In such works, particularly those of the bilingual (in Quechua and Spanish) Peruvian novelist and anthropologist José María Arguedas (1911–69), indigenous cultural traditions serve not only as referent but also as an element of narrative structure. According to Cornejo Polar, even the best *indigenista* fiction does not resolve the structural split characteristic of heterogeneous literatures. Rather, it creatively deploys it to modify the Western novel form and give indigenous culture a greater role in the production of meaning and the literary representation of social conflict in deeply divided Andean societies.

Narrative Transculturation

Ángel Rama's term narrative transculturation designates a similar formal modification of the Western novel by indigenous and other regional cultural traditions. Like Cornejo Polar, Rama draws on the contributions of an earlier generation of Latin American cultural critics. He borrows the concept of transculturation from Cuban sociologist Fernando Ortiz, who coined the neologism in 1940 as an alternative to the already established term acculturation.[26] In 1936, North American anthropologists Robert Redfield, Melville J. Herskovits, and Ralph Linton had published the "Memorandum for the Study of Acculturation" as a guide to anthropological research on culture contact and change, in which they defined acculturation as "those phenomena which result when groups of individuals having different cultures come into continuous first-hand contact, with subsequent changes in the original cultural patterns of either or both groups."[27] Acculturation, in its original sense, left open the possibility of mutual cultural influence and did not simply mean the assimilation of one group to the culture of another. Indeed, Redfield, Linton, and Herskovits were careful to distinguish acculturation from assimilation, noting that though the latter was "at times a phase of" the former, it was only one of several phenomena comprehended by the term acculturation.[28] Processes of acculturation, they argued, could have several outcomes, ranging from assimilation, to social groups' combination of their own culture with elements from another, to one group's rejection of another's cultural's influence.

In practice, however, the term was rarely used in this broad sense. The field of applied anthropology, in particular, tended to reduce the meaning of acculturation to the one-way influence of the West on other cultures. For this it drew sharp criticism from Herskovits, who argued that by focusing almost exclusively on contacts between Western and non-Western cultures, applied anthropology ran the risk of falling into an "uncritical tendency to see native cultures everywhere forced out of existence by the overwhelming drive of European techniques."[29] In Herskovits's view, such an approach displayed "a type of ethnocentrism that should be absent from the scientific studies of an anthropologist."[30] In spite of this warning, acculturation nevertheless became virtually synonymous with assimilation.

It was against this sense of acculturation and the teleology it implied that Ortiz proposed the term transculturation to describe the complex, mutual influence that results when cultures come into contact, even (or especially) under conditions in which some cultures are subordinate to and dominated by others.[31] Ortiz was interested not only in how subordinated groups select elements from the dominant culture imposed upon them and adapt those materials for their own purposes, but also in the influence subordinated groups exert on the dominant culture. His paradigmatic example of transculturation at work in conditions of domination was his native Cuba, where extreme inequality was born of the Spanish Conquest of the indigenous population and the subsequent enslavement of African peoples. Though the indigenous and African cultures of the subordinated had not survived intact, they had nonetheless influenced the expressive forms and practices of everyday Cuban life (music, dance, food, religion). By revealing and legitimating this influence, Ortiz helped redefine and democratize Cuban national culture, rooting it in the popular culture of the subordinated.[32]

In the essays collected in his highly influential *Transculturación narrativa en América Latina* (1982), Rama adapts Ortiz's concept to the study of twentieth-century Latin American narrative. While Ortiz focused on subordinated groups' direct influence on the dominant culture, Rama was interested in how such influence is mediated by local or regional intellectuals through literature, a "high" cultural form associated with dominant groups. He used the term narrative transculturation to describe the work of novelists from relatively isolated rural regions where indigenous and other traditional cultures maintained a high degree of coherence and autonomy in the face of the centralizing, modernizing force of both national capitals and transnational capital. To varying degrees, such authors occupied, at least initially, a space between subordinated and dominant cultures. Writers like Juan Rulfo (1917–86), João Guimarães Rosa (1908–67), Gabriel García Márquez (b 1928,), and especially José María Arguedas were so immersed in the rural cultures of marginalized regions of Mexico, Brazil, Colombia, and Peru, respectively, that their search for adequate means of literary expression for such regional cultures led them to transculturate the Western novel form. They not only introduced new languages or folkloric content into a pre-existing narrative form, but also restructured the form of the novel itself according to traditional cosmologies. The resulting works were intended as a means of contesting elite definitions and domination of the Latin American nation-state.

Unlike the more cosmopolitan Boom novelists of the 1960s, whose world-renowned literary innovations were inspired primarily by European and North American models, the regionally rooted writers of the 1940s and 1950s who interested Rama drew on rural popular cultures to renew Latin American narrative. In *Transculturación narrativa* Rama in effect constructs and defends a kind of regionalist counter-canon to the Boom.[33] Though it might be objected that García Márquez is one of the most famous of Boom authors, and that even Guimarães Rosa is sometimes included in the Boom, Rama was interested in them as regionalist writers rather than as representatives of the Boom. Rama in any case doubted that the Boom existed as anything more than a commercial phenomenon (as opposed to a genuine literary-political movement).[34]

Cornejo Polar and Rama in Contemporary Perspective

By focusing on Cornejo Polar's analysis of how the indigenous referent of certain literary works influences the literary form by means of which that referent is represented, I have emphasized the complementarity between this theoretical approach and Rama's. In doing so, I do not mean to suggest that there are no differences between them. Cornejo Polar's concept of heterogeneous literatures emphasize a state, that of the division of Latin American societies as it is manifested in Latin American literature. Rama's narrative transculturation, by contrast, refers to a process of cultural change and literary renovation or innovation produced by dominant and subordinate cultures' interaction and mutual influence upon each other. As Raúl Bueno has observed, processes of transculturation occur only where there is cultural heterogeneity, and narrative transculturation produces a particular kind of literary heterogeneity, the kind exemplified for Cornejo Polar by the works of José María Arguedas.[35]

My focus on the complementarity of these two theorists' approaches runs against the grain of much recent criticism, which has tended to stress their differences. Some have criticized Rama's theory of narrative transculturation as yet another attempt to absorb subordinate cultures into the dominant one, while counterposing Cornejo Polar's concept of heterogeneity as an early acknowledgement of the autonomy of subordinate cultures from dominant ones, and of the antagonism between the two. Friedhelm Schmidt, for example, argues that while Cornejo Polar's concept of heterogeneous literatures is derived from the actually existing cultural heterogeneity of Latin American nations and emphasizes the conflicts among those nations' constituent social groups, Rama's concept of narrative transculturation, by contrast, tends to erase such antagonism. Moreover, Schmidt claims that "the processes of transculturation described by Rama imply changes exclusively in dominated cultures. . . . transculturation at no time affects the dominant culture."[36] However, the claim that narrative transculturation leaves the dominant culture intact fails to describe Rama's discussion of an Arguedas or a Rulfo, the whole point of which is that such authors' works change Latin American literature by drawing on subordinated regional cultures. According to Rama, regional cultures, mediated by provincial intellectuals like Arguedas or Rulfo, modify official national cultures.

For Schmidt, nevertheless, Rama's theory of narrative transculturation ultimately derives from the ideology of cultural *mestizaje*, to which Cornejo Polar's concept of heterogeneity is explicitly opposed. Cornejo Polar, for example, has argued that "the ideology of *mestizaje* is in anthropology what the ideology of class reconciliation would be in sociology. . . . *mestizaje* understood as a non-conflictive synthesis . . . is a form of imagining reconciliation by ignoring real conflicts."[37] Though in earlier years he had considered transculturation complementary to his own ideas, near the end of his life Cornejo Polar came to lament the conversion of transculturation into "the most sophisticated cover for the category of *mestizaje*."[38] However, here Cornejo Polar refers not to Rama's use of the term but to the meaning it had acquired in some quarters by the 1990s. There *are* certainly moments in Rama's work when he seems to express a desire for a synthesis of cultural differences that would produce an integrated national (or Latin American) culture. However, the primacy Rama accords to the conflictive, antagonistic nature of processes of transculturation is ultimately more important than his occasional references to a synthesis in any case rarely presented as harmonious. As Patricia D'Allemand observes,

> while this wish for a synthesis is present in Rama's discourse, at the same time it does not cancel his own emphasis upon the permanence of conflicts and differences of socio-cultural origins in the new forms generated by transcultural literatures. The ideal of harmony is absent from his description of the new forms whose gestation is presented through images which emphasize confrontation and tension. Rama's analysis favors the field of processes

of cultural production and, more specifically, that of production of artistic forms as the arena for confrontation between the various cultural formations within Latin America.[39]

To equate transculturation with *mestizaje* is to simplify and misrepresent Rama's nuanced theorization of Latin American narrative responses to modernization. While it is possible that the term has become virtually synonymous with *mestizaje* in recent years, for Rama it designated more complex, multidirectional processes of cultural and literary change.

John Beverley, too, has recently criticized narrative transculturation as a form of *mestizaje*. He begins by claiming that Rama's idea of narrative transculturation was "exemplified for him by the novels of the 'boom,'"[40] which Rama supposedly saw as a vehicle for the integration of indigenous and other traditional cultures and peoples into a more inclusive Latin American nation-state. Through literature as well as other forms of intellectual work, subordinated social groups would be incorporated into the cultural and economic modernity emanating from metropolitan centers, and the task of "developing new cultural and political forms in which their formative presence in Latin American history and society could be made manifest" would be the "providential role of a 'lettered' vanguard."[41] In Beverley's view, for both Rama and Ortiz (though Ortiz is praised for addressing everyday practices rather than just the more elite literary ones) "transculturation functions as a teleology, not without marks of violence and loss, but *necessary* in the last instance for the formation of the modern nation-state and a national (or continental) identity that would be something other than the sum of its parts, since the original identities are sublated in the process of transculturation itself."[42] Beverley argues, in effect, that transculturation is still an elite project, an updated version of *mestizaje*, which leaves intact the unequal power relations between intellectuals and subordinated social groups.

This reading, however, misrepresents Rama's argument, principally because the Boom novels *did not* exemplify transculturation for him. Beverley identifies Rama with the Boom in order to claim that, like the Boom, transculturation was an elite leftist-nationalist project which failed to represent subordinated groups adequately. At stake in this misidentification of Rama's project with the Boom is the theoretical-political viability of the idea of transculturation. Beverley argues, for example, that "from the perspective of transculturation, Rama can not conceptualize ideologically or theoretically movements for indigenous identity, rights, and/or territorial autonomy that develop their own organic intellectuals and (literary or nonliterary) cultural forms."[43] This, too, is inaccurate, for Rama devotes some twenty pages of *Transculturación narrativa* to a discussion of *Antes o mundo não existia*, the Portuguese translation of a collection of oral traditions by Umúsin Panlõn Kumu and Tomalãn Kenhíri, a father and son team of organic intellectuals from the Desâna indigenous group of the Brazilian Amazon concerned with preserving their people's indigenous identity.[44]

While it is true that Rama did not directly address the sort of indigenous movements Beverley mentions (in part because they barely existed or were at least much less visible in his day), it was not the concept of transculturation that prevented him from doing so. Indeed, transculturation describes well the ways in which contemporary indigenous movements (the CONAIE indigenous federation in Ecuador, the Maya cultural rights movement in Guatemala) have adapted modern technologies (video, computers, fax, e-mail, internet) and modes of political organization (NGOs, political parties, research institutes), the Spanish language, and Western cultural forms (the novel, for instance) for their own purposes. This adaptation of selected elements of the dominant culture has facilitated such groups' assertion of indigenous identity and political rights in both national and international political arenas. Transculturation does not necessarily produce cultural homogenization or synthesis. Rather, it can be a means for the refashioning or reinvention of difference.

Beverley also interprets Rama's posthumously published essay *La ciudad letrada / The Lettered City* as a repudiation of narrative transculturation.[45] In this last and unfinished work, Rama examines the complicity between writing and power in Latin America through a study of the historical evolution of what he calls the "lettered city": the set of institutions that have used their monopoly on literacy to exclude illiterate majorities from the elaboration of official histories and collective identities. Beverley finds in Rama's essay a confirmation of his own view that literature has historically been little more than "a form of class, gender, and ethnic violence."[46] Literature, he has argued, "was implicated in the colonial formation of Latin America itself and subsequently in the construction and evolution of Latin American nation-states . . . Literature . . . not only had a role in the self-representation of the upper and upper-middle strata of Latin American society; it was one of the social practices by which such strata constituted themselves as dominant."[47]

Literature in Latin America has, it is true, played all of the oppressive roles Beverley attributes to it, but it has also been capable of a reflexive critique of its own relationship to power. Indeed, this is the case with transcultural narrative, which not only attempts to represent the subordinated and their interests but also draws on subordinated cultures to modify the inherited literary forms that have played a role in constituting the cultural dominance of Latin American elites. Transcultural narrative, that is, undermines from within elite literary forms' pretensions to universality, demonstrating their inadequacy for representing the lives and perspectives of those excluded from the dominant culture. This, it would seem, is not so different from the self-critical role Beverley advocates for North American academic intellectuals, that of "working against the grain of our own interests and prejudices by contesting the authority of the academy and knowledge centers at the same time that we continue to participate in them and to deploy that authority as teachers, researchers, administrators, and theorists."[48] If contesting the dominant culture from within is possible in the academic sphere, then why not also in the literary one?

Beverley seems not to perceive this parallel. Moreover, his attempt to draft the later Rama of *The Lettered City* as a precursor of his own pessimism regarding the progressive potential of literature is dubious at best. In this posthumously published essay, Rama focuses on the role of the Latin American lettered city from its origins in the colonial period through the first two or three decades of the twentieth century. He says little or nothing in this work about either the 1960s Boom or the regionalist writers of the 1950s treated in *Transculturación narrativa*. Indeed, *The Lettered City* traces a growing democratization of Latin American society and culture in the 1920s and 1930s (a result, in part, of the emergence and growth of a labor movement), and there is scant evidence here to justify the conclusion that Rama had come to view the work of narrative transculturators like Arguedas or Rulfo as anything but a continuation and extension of the cultural democratization which had begun earlier in the century.

As Jean Franco has recently observed, "popular culture did succeed in breaching the walls of what Ángel Rama termed 'the lettered city'; through this breach, indigenous languages and cultures entered into productive contact with lettered culture. . . . Describing this as 'transculturation' . . . Rama argued that the writing of José María Arguedas, . . . exemplified the potentiality of a cultural counterpoint in which one culture did not dominate the other." [49]

Indeed, Rama's two most influential works complement rather than contradict each other. *Transculturación narrativa*, notes Françoise Perus, was "expressly conceived by its author as a counterpart to the idea that animated *The Lettered City*."[50] Beverley, however, downplays the nuances of Rama's argument regarding literature's relationship to power in Latin America in order to strengthen his own claims that writing itself is not only constitutively incapable of representing interests of subordinated groups, but is also irremediably hostile to them.

Against such an assessment, I argue for the complementarity and continued usefulness of Rama's and Cornejo Polar's theories of heterogeneous literatures and narrative transculturation, respectively. My understanding of the two terms is informed by Perus's helpful articulation of the relationship between them:

the heterogeneity of spaces, times, and movements that reproduces within the sphere of literature the discontinuities, the internal ruptures, and the disorder of processes of modernization in the periphery . . . is what Ángel Rama attempts to understand by means of the application and adaptation to narrative of the anthropological notion of "transculturation."[51]

Dependent modernization has helped to perpetuate in Latin American nations a cultural heterogeneity born of the Conquest, a heterogeneity that all writers confront, and which some have attempted to represent and incorporate into the very form of their works. The concept of narrative transculturation "focuses attention on the artistic responses and solutions . . . found by literature for the difficulties posed by this same *cultural heterogeneity*."[52] Narrative transculturation, that is, refers to the creative process through which some writers have rendered the contradictions and social conflicts of dependent modernization in their works. Heterogeneous literatures in which the indigenous referent makes itself felt in the Western form of a work are the result of that process. Used together, the two concepts provide a means for tracing through literary works the class and ethnic conflicts generated by modernization in Peru.

Indigenous Peoples, Intellectuals, and Representation

This book examines the influence of indigenous Andean culture on Peru's literary intellectuals, who responded in their essays, short stories, and novels to the periodic emergence of rural indigenous movements and the transformation of urban centers by Andean migration. These developments affected not only what writers wrote about but also how they wrote about it, and in some cases it led them to modify the Western novel form by drawing on indigenous Andean cultural patterns. Such transcultural narratives did not directly alter the subordinate status of the indigenous population. They did, however, suggest the possibility of intellectual decolonization and cultural democratization, neither of which a modernization synonymous with Westernization has achieved in Peru or other dependent, peripheral societies.

As Mary Louise Pratt has observed, "the structure of power between center and periphery is in open contradiction with the emancipatory project of modernity. In the very imposition of its ideas, in other words, modernity stands in contradiction with itself, even though this is systematically invisible in the center."[53] The imposition of a Western version of modernity on Latin America through modernization driven from abroad, in which a dependent elite has played a key role, has not produced the promised emancipatory effects. Rather, it has perpetuated not only metropolitan nations' domination of peripheral ones, but also the subordination of popular majorities to national elites within Latin America. By drawing in part on autochthonous sources for their formal innovations, transcultural narratives challenge such subordination and dependence, and pose the possibility of an alternative modernity rooted in Latin America's subordinated popular cultures. Though such works have not had direct "emancipatory effects for the subordinated majorities represented in them", as Pratt notes, they are nonetheless significant in that they constitute "encounters with non-metropolitan reality and history in terms not dictated by the metropolis. . . . Their emancipatory power, as critics have frequently noted, resides in their rejection of the self-alienated position of imposed receptivity."[54]

It has become fashionable in certain quarters of the US academic community to claim that intellectuals are irremediably complicit with existing power structures and incapable of writing about subordinated social groups without reproducing the relations of domination and subordination between themselves and those they write about. John Beverley, for example, considers it an "inescapable fact that [elite] discourse and the institutions that contain it, such as the university, written history, 'theory', and literature, are themselves complicit in the social construction of subalternity."[55] To get around this dilemma, Beverley advocates a project of subaltern studies that "registers rather how the knowledge we construct and impart as academics is structured by the absence, difficulty, or impossibility of representation of the subaltern."[56] However, this self-deconstructive gesture only displaces the subordinated from the center of the academic attention they briefly commanded back to the margins. Declaring the subordinated unrepresentable in academic or literary discourse leaves politically committed intellectuals little to do but write about themselves, and it is not at all clear how this is supposed to benefit those in whose name the self-deconstructive gesture is made.

The Colonial Divide in Peruvian Narrative starts from the rather different premise that although intellectual representations of the subordinated may well be complicit with and reinforce the prevailing distribution of power, there are varying degrees of such complicity, and it is worth distinguishing among them. To be sure, academic study and the writing of literature are elite cultural practices, all the more so where inequality is as extreme as it is in Peru. I do not claim that narrative transculturation is a means of speaking for or giving voice to, much less liberating, the indigenous Andean population. Rather, as Martin Lienhard points out, "by simulating the existence of radically alternative voices", transcultural narrators "were able to suggest the richness of discursive universes that develop outside the jurisdiction of the lettered sphere."[57] Jean

Franco goes even further in defining ethnopoetics, her synonym for what Rama called narrative transculturation, as "a form of translation that negotiates the meeting of disparate epistemologies and transforms their energies in the cause of justice and hence of political action."[58] By alluding in their very form to the vitality and creative potential of subordinate cultures, transcultural narratives suggest not only the survival of those cultures, but also their capacity for both self-transformation and the transformation of the social structures responsible for their subordination.

All of the works analyzed herein are, to varying degrees, examples of heterogeneous literature, but not all of them are transcultural narratives. While most of the writers discussed relied on the literary forms of Peru's dominant *criollo*, Westernized culture to represent the role of indigenous peoples in the social conflicts generated by dependent modernization, only José María Arguedas did so by drawing on indigenous Andean culture. An extended engagement with Arguedas's work is inevitable in a study of the sociocultural contradictions and conflicts of twentieth-century Peru, for as Alberto Flores Galindo has suggested, "Arguedas is one of those exceptional individuals who in his linguistic trajectory and his work as a writer condensed the tensions and concerns of a society."[59] Born to a provincial *mestizo* family, raised in part by an indigenous community, Arguedas grew up bilingual in Quechua and Spanish and felt within himself the linguistic and cultural divisions of Peruvian society, an internalization of his nation's social and cultural conflicts that likely contributed to his suicide in 1969.[60] Though he would spend most of his adult life in Lima, he returned to the Andes repeatedly, as both teacher and anthropologist, and remained in close contact with indigenous Andeans in both the countryside and the city. Arguedas dedicated his entire life's work, both fiction and non-fiction, to exploring the role of indigenous culture in a rapidly changing Peruvian society, and his short stories, novels, and anthropological articles provide a unique vantage point on the twentieth-century transformation of that society.

In addition, Arguedas is of more than regional interest, for as Jean Franco points out, he was part of a generation of Latin American writers for whom "the redemption of indigenous and black cultures and the valorization of oral culture as a bond of community amounted to an affirmation of values specific to the Americas that were an alternative to those of the dominant West."[61] In the work of writers like Arguedas and the Guatemalan Nobel Prize winner Miguel Ángel Asturias, she notes, the songs and words of oral tradition "are physical carriers of memory that still resonates in print culture."[62] This attempt to breach the lettered city through the privileged gates of literature was ultimately frustrated not by the lettered city's impermeability to democratizing popular currents, but rather by its decline in the face of what Franco calls "the global remapping of the urban and rural world"[63] begun by the mass media even while Arguedas and Asturias were still carrying on their democratizing literary projects. However, though the rise of the mass media may have displaced literature from its traditionally privileged relationship to power and thereby deprived it of its former influence, this very displacement has perhaps made literary representation more available to counter-hegemonic projects. Though clearly lacking the audience and therefore the influence of the mass media, literature remains a medium, perhaps more unfettered now by its more distant relationship to power, for the imagining of alternative worlds and social orders, one which should not be dismissed. Attempting to duplicate the example of an Asturias or an Arguedas would make little sense under today's very different conditions, but this does not mean that there is nothing to be learned from their works.

Though all of the works examined here are critical of Peruvian society, the transcultural form of Arguedas's narrative constitutes the most radical challenge to the inequalities of Peru's traditional socio-cultural hierarchy as well as the variation of it produced by dependent modernization. This is so because Arguedas's transcultural narrative requires readers to engage with indigenous Andean culture, thereby challenging a predominantly elite potential readership's longstanding resistance to such an engagement with, and recognition of, its Andean other. Through the transformation of literary and academic genres according to indigenous Andean cultural patterns, Arguedas helped decolonize and democratize the elite spheres of literature and the academy, opening a space within them for an indigenous voice. His representation of indigenous Andeans was a "speaking about" intended to facilitate the dominant culture's ability to hear the subordinated "speak for" themselves. The following chapters make this case through a series of contrasts between Arguedas's works and those of Ciro Alegría, Manuel Scorza, Julio Ramón Ribeyro, Alfredo Bryce Echenique, and Mario Vargas Llosa. Before exploring these contrasting approaches to the representation of modernization and its consequences in a deeply divided society, I will first review the historical determinants and significance of the 1920s intellectual awakening to the existence of Peru's indigenous population, an awakening that historian Jorge Basadre, writing in 1931, considered the most important event in twentieth-century Peruvian culture.

Political Power and Modernization in Early Twentieth-Century Peru

As in other parts of Latin America, in Peru the first two decades of the twentieth century were characterized by oligarchic rule and a free-market, export-oriented economy. This period in Peruvian history is known as the "República Aristocrática", or Aristocratic Republic, a not entirely accurate designation for, as Contreras and Cueto point out, "the ruling class of early twentieth century Peru shared ideals and social origins that were more bourgeois than aristocratic."[64] However one characterizes the Peruvian elite of the period, under the Aristocratic Republic, economic power was highly concentrated, and the majority of the population was excluded from political participation.[65] Nevertheless, the concentration of power did not imply monolithic unity among the elite. Rather, the Aristocratic Republic rested on a sometimes uneasy partnership between two groups whose interests did not always coincide: a modernizing commercial and financial elite on the coast, represented by the ruling Civilista Party, and the semi-feudal, landowning elite of the Andean interior, known as *mistis* or *gamonales*.

The export-oriented coastal elite depended on foreign, especially US, capital and markets as well as on the *gamonales'* ability to maintain social control in the countryside, where a weak central state had little authority.[66] As Flores Galindo and Burga note, the oligarchic system of rule characteristic of the Aristocratic Republic "was sustained by the support it received from imperialism and the violence the *gamonales* imposed in the interior of the country."[67] Though the semi-feudal landowners' interests were at times opposed to those of the commercial and financial elite on the coast, the *gamonales'* membership in the ruling oligarchy could be tolerated because they provided a valuable service, and because the conflicts that often strained the alliance between the landowning class of the Andean interior and coastal bourgeoisie were minor compared to those that divided both groups from the indigenous majority.

The relative political stability of the Aristocratic Republic, combined with increased world demand for Peruvian raw materials, particularly during the First World War, led to an economic expansion that in turn fueled the growth of urban middle and working classes. The effects of economic growth were felt in the countryside, too, as a boom in wool exports stimulated the expansion of haciendas in the southern Andes, often at the expense of indigenous communities. The effects of such economic expansion in both the countryside and the capital would begin to undermine the political stability of the Aristocratic Republic toward the end of the century's second decade. For example, after years of losing their lands to neighboring haciendas and fruitless legal struggle against such unlawful dispossession, many indigenous communities turned to more militant means of defending their property, resulting in a series of indigenous rebellions in the southern Peruvian Andes between 1915 and 1924.[68] Though put down by military force, the rebellions increased the visibility of the indigenous population and had a significant impact on *mestizo* intellectuals from the Andean interior, both those who had migrated to Lima and those who remained in their home provinces. The intellectual and cultural consequences of this wave of indigenous rebellion will be discussed below.

Rural indigenous movements were not the only form of resistance to the social inequalities of the Aristocratic Republic. In 1919, the disruption of Peru's export-dependent economy by the end of the First World War triggered a successful strike for an eight-hour working day by a growing and increasingly militant labor movement, which quickly gained the support of a parallel university student movement for educational reform. The combination of such labor unrest, ongoing indigenous resistance in the countryside, and mounting demands for change from the middle classes, set the stage for the fall of the Aristocratic Republic and the beginning of the *Oncenio*, or eleven-year rule, of Augusto B. Leguía (1919–30).

Leguía had been Finance Minister and President (1908–12) during the Aristocratic Republic, but had gone into exile after a falling out with the Civilista Party in 1913. Returning to Peru in 1919 as an independent, anti-Civilista candidate, he campaigned for President on a populist, anti-oligarchic program directed at the new middle and working classes. Though it seemed likely that he would be elected, Leguía staged a coup that gave him more control over the state than he would have derived from an electoral victory.[69] During his subsequent eleven years in power he implemented a project of modernization aimed at constructing what he called *La Patria Nueva*. Under Leguía, the state grew rapidly and played a greater role in the economy, sponsoring, for example, the construction of new roads, railroads, and irrigation works in the provinces as well as new avenues, plazas, and other urban infrastructure in Lima. However, Leguía's modernization program remained heavily dependent on foreign, particularly US, capital, and Peru's foreign debt grew significantly between 1919 and 1930.[70]

Striking a reformist, populist pose in the early years of the *Oncenio*, Leguía courted the working and middle classes as well as indigenous communities in order to defeat the Civilista establishment and consolidate his power.[71] For example, he formed a commission to investigate the causes of indigenous unrest in the southern Andes, gave legal recognition to indigenous communities in the new Constitution of 1920, and created an indigenous affairs section in the Ministry of Development.[72] Nevertheless, Leguía's measures on behalf of the popular classes and the indigenous population were often merely symbolic. In addition, the overall posture of his government toward those it claimed to represent could be quite contradictory. For example, while he was promulgating the above-mentioned measures in favor of the indigenous population, he also approved the *Ley de Conscripción Vial* of 1920, which authorized the conscription of adult males for twelve days of unpaid road construction work each year. Though in theory the law applied to all adult males between 18 and 60 years of age, in practice indigenous men made up the majority of those compelled to work on the state's road construction projects.[73] As in the past, under Leguía roads continued to be built with involuntary indigenous labor.

In the later years of the *Oncenio*, once he consolidated his power, Leguía gravitated away from popular sectors and toward the plutocracy that soon formed around him. Though the *Oncenio* produced significant changes in Peruvian society—the expansion of the transportation network to link formerly remote Andean regions to coastal cities, the beginning of rural-to-urban migration and the consequent growth of those cities, the expansion of the state and its bureaucracy, the growth of the urban middle class, and the subordination of formerly autonomous regional elites to central government authority—these did not include a significant democratization of the nation's political system. As Julio Cotler has noted, "the traditional mechanics of domination, a result of the political articulation of the bourgeois and landowning sectors that made up the República Aristocrática, was re-established under Leguía, but on a new foundation, without affecting the pre-capitalist condition of rural areas."[74]

Indigenism, Socialism, Populism

Despite these limitations, "Leguía's populist policies encouraged the formation of various movements that ended up escaping the control the regime had hoped to wield over them."[75] Perhaps the most significant of these was the cultural and political movement known as *indigenismo*. In its broadest sense, *indigenismo* refers to an emphasis on Peru's indigenous, Andean heritage (in opposition to its Spanish one), and a redefinition of regional or national identity as rooted in indigenous culture, variously interpreted. Such an emphasis was not unprecedented, for as early as 1888, in the wake of Peru's disastrous loss to Chile in the War of the Pacific, Manuel González Prada had proclaimed that "the groups of *criollos* and foreigners who inhabit the strip of land between the Pacific and the Andes are not the real Peru; the nation is made up of the masses of Indians scattered across the eastern side of the [Andes] mountains."[76] Clorinda Matto de Turner, too, had denounced the exploitation and abuse of the indigenous population in her 1889 novel *Aves sin nido / Birds Without a Nest*. In the early years of the twentieth century, moreover, the *Asociación Pro Indígena* (1909–17) of Pedro Zulén and Dora Mayer de

Zulén, had "aimed to educate the public about the abysmal conditions of Indians [in order] to stimulate reforms."[77]

By 1920, such intellectual and political interest in indigenous Peru had become widespread. In literature, Enrique López Albújar's *Cuentos andinos / Andean Stories* (1920) inaugurated the twentieth-century tradition of *indigenista* narrative. In the visual arts, José Sabogal launched a new, *indigenista* style of painting with a 1919 exhibition in Lima of his work, which featured the landscapes and human types of the Andes. Under Sabogal's leadership, *indigenismo* would dominate Peruvian painting for the next three decades.[78] In the nascent social sciences, Julio C. Tello carried out archeological research into Peru's pre-Columbian past, while Hildebrando Castro Pozo's *Nuestra comunidad indígena / Our Indigenous Community* (1924), Luis E. Valcárcel's messianic *Tempestad en los Andes / Storm in the Andes* (1927), and José Carlos Mariátegui's *7 ensayos de interpretación de la realidad peruana / Seven Interpretive Essays on Peruvian Reality* (1928) focused on the nation's indigenous population, Andean cultural traditions, and their relevance for the present. *Indigenista* groups formed in the southern Andean interior as well and published short-lived, but influential, vanguardist journals such as *Kosko*, *Kuntur*, and *La Sierra* in Cuzco and the *Boletín Titikaka* in Puno.

As Ángel Rama has observed, *indigenista* intellectuals, many of them *mestizos* from the provinces, came from "a new social group produced by the imperatives of modern economic development . . . one which demands certain rights from the society of which it is a part. Like every group that has acquired mobility, as Marx pointed out, it demands those rights on behalf of all oppressed social sectors, making itself their representative and interpreting their demands as its own."[79] As an emergent social group, the *mestizo* intellectuals of the *indigenista* movement considered the indigenous population they sought to represent crucial to their aspirations of breaking the *criollo* elite's monopoly on political power. So did Leguía. Seeking to capitalize on the new prominence of the indigenous question and attract allies in his struggle against the civilista elite of the Aristocratic Republic, Leguía proclaimed a policy of "official" state-sponsored *indigenismo* and declared himself the "Protector of the Indigenous Race."[80] In 1921, he appointed the distinguished sociologist and *indigenista* Castro Pozo to head the new Section for Indigenous Affairs in the Ministry of Development.[81] The same year, Leguía even supported the First Indigenous Congress of the more militant successor organization to the *Asociación Pro Indígena*, the *Comité Pro Derecho Indígena Tahuantinsuyu*, founded in 1920 with participation from indigenous Andeans themselves.[82]

As the existence of an official, state-sponsored variant of it suggests, *indigenismo* took on different ideological forms and served various ends.[83] It was a broad and rather heterogenous current of thought rather than a single, unified movement. Indeed, there were several versions of *indigenismo* in the 1920s: "the 'indigenismo' of landowning sectors themselves, that of enlightened Right-wing thought, that of the radicalized petty bourgeoisie, whether from Lima or the provinces, and, finally, the marxist indigenismo of José Carlos Mariátegui and of the young communists of Cuzco."[84] *Indigenismo* did not always imply the defense of the existing indigenous population, which some regional elites considered merely a degraded remnant of a magnificent, but extinct, Inca empire in need of resurrection. These elites could defend their own interests and autonomy against the centralism of Leguía's regime and the regional indigenous population alike by casting themselves as the true inheritors and redeemers of a glorious indigenous past.[85]

The new social actors and anti-oligarchic struggles that helped to propel Leguía into power also produced two radical critics of Peruvian society—José Carlos Mariátegui (1894–1930) and Víctor Raúl Haya de la Torre (1895–1979)—whose work would shape Peru's intellectual and political life for generations to come. Both men had been strongly influenced by Manuel González Prada's polemical critique of the *criollo* elite and defense of the indigenous population, and their analyses of Peruvian society coincided in many respects, at least initially.[86] However, their positions subsequently diverged, leading to their founding of rival political parties which would compete for the allegiance of the popular classes they sought to represent: Haya de la Torre's populist APRA (*Alianza Popular Revolucionaria Americana* / American Popular Revolutionary Alliance) and Mariátegui's Peruvian Socialist Party (renamed the Peruvian Communist Party after his death).[87]

Prior to the indigenous rebellions and labor movement of 1915–24, Mariátegui had been a self-taught journalist and writer whose rejection of the *criollo* elite's nostalgia for the colonial period expressed itself in a bohemian, avant-garde aestheticism.[88] However, the Peruvian social movements triggered by the economic disruptions of the First World War, along with the advent of the Mexican and Bolshevik revolutions, would politicize the nonconformist journalist, who would write in support of both the indigenous rebellions in the countryside and the worker's movement in Lima. His active participation in the latter would run him afoul of the newly installed Leguía regime, which in 1919 rid itself of Mariátegui by offering him a choice of jail or a government stipend to go to Europe. Mariátegui chose Europe, eventually settling in Italy, where he witnessed the worker's struggles of the *biennio rosso* (1919–20), the founding of the Italian Communist Party (1921), and the rise of fascism.[89] He remained in Europe for four formative years during which he came into direct contact with Marxism and observed with great interest the political debates and social struggles occasioned by the triumph of the Bolshevik revolution. Upon his return to Peru in 1923, he would attempt to adapt the Marxism he had learned in Europe to analyze economic, social, and cultural conditions in Peru. Mariátegui and *Amauta*, the widely-respected journal he founded in 1926, would become the center of gravity for many of Peru's *indigenista* intellectuals and would influence political and cultural debates throughout Latin America.

In his analysis of Peruvian society, Mariátegui developed a rather heterodox Marxism; the historical development of Peru, he proposed, did not fit the orthodox marxist scheme of a progression from feudalism through capitalism to socialism. In Peru, the bourgeoisie had failed to liquidate feudalism and construct a truly national economy because of its dependence on foreign capital. Moreover, under such conditions of dependence, capitalist economic development could only serve foreign interests at the expense of Peru's national interest. As Flores Galindo and Burga note, "for Mariátegui, Peru was a semi-colonial society and this condition would only get worse with the expansion of imperialist capital. There was no way of achieving national independence within the capitalist system."[90] For this reason, Mariátegui argued that an effective nationalist resistance to imperialism had to be anti-capitalist and could only take the form of a class struggle against a dependent bourgeoisie that represented foreign interests rather than those of Peru. Moreover, because Peru lacked a large proletariat, the working class would have to ally itself with the nation's indigenous majority, whose surviving traditions of collectivism would facilitate the construction of a modern, yet uniquely Andean socialism. Peru, thanks to its indigenous traditions, would be able to leap from feudalism directly to socialism, bypassing the capitalist stage of development.[91] For Mariátegui, the solution to the problem of imperialism and to the "problem of the Indian", synonymous in his view with the persistence of a semi-feudal landownership pattern in the Andes, was the same: a revolution made by indigenous peoples themselves with the help and leadership of the organized working class and radical *mestizo* intellectuals. As a means of achieving this goal, Mariátegui founded the Peruvian Socialist Party in 1928.

Haya de la Torre, for his part, had gained political prominence as a leader of university student support for the workers' movement during the strikes of 1918–19. His subsequent opposition to Leguía led to his deportation in 1923. From his exile in Mexico, where he absorbed the populist nationalism of the Mexican revolution and for a time received a stipend from José Vasconcelos's Ministry of Education, Haya de la Torre would announce in 1924 the formation of the APRA, initially conceived as an international front against US imperialism in Latin America. For

Haya de la Torre, Peru was an essentially feudal society in which capitalism had not developed organically but rather had been implanted by British and US imperialism. Imperialism, that is, was the first rather than the highest stage of capitalism in Peru.[92] Consequently, and unlike Mariátegui, Haya de la Torre advocated resisting the dependence and subordination associated with imperialism without rejecting capitalism, for in his view Peru required capitalist development before it could hope to construct a socialist society. In addition, the resistance to imperialism would have to take the form of a broad nationalist struggle which, though waged by an alliance of classes, would be centered on and led by the growing middle class. Though Haya de la Torre also invoked Peru's indigenous traditions and talked of constructing an "Indoamerica" free of US imperialism, his references to indigenous culture were primarily symbolic and, unlike Mariátegui's, did not constitute the core of his political program.

Initially, Haya de la Torre and Mariátegui had been allies and collaborators. Mariátegui, for example, had published Haya de la Torre's articles in *Amauta*.[93] However, their increasingly contrasting analyses of Peruvian society ultimately strained the relationship. The two would part ways in 1928 after Haya de la Torre announced from Mexico the formation of the *Partido Nacionalista Libertador*, a Peruvian front of the APRA intended as a vehicle for his presidential ambitions. Taking advantage of the popular unrest produced by the economic depression contracted from the US in 1929, Mariátegui and Haya de la Torre's rival parties renewed the anti-oligarchic struggle initiated more than a decade earlier. However, though Leguía fell in 1930, he would not be overthrown by the Peruvian Communist Party or the APRA, but rather by a military rebellion backed by a dissatisfied fraction of the elite. The new cycle of popular, anti-oligarchic struggle would be brought to a close in 1932 by the massacre of thousands of APRA rebels who had staged an insurrectionary uprising in the northern coastal city of Trujillo. The popular agitation of the early 1930s was followed by more than a decade of military and conservative civilian rule, during which the prospects for radical social change were not encouraging. In spite of the changes effected during Leguía's *Oncenio*, the alliance of coastal bourgeoisie and gamonal landowners in the Andean interior forged under the Aristocratic Republic would not be fully liquidated until the advent of a new wave of indigenous land movements in the late 1950s and the agrarian reform promulgated in 1969 by the populist military dictatorship of Juan Velasco Alvarado.[94]

For much of the twentieth century, the Peruvian Communist Party and the APRA would compete for a mass following, a rivalry in which the latter would generally have the upper hand. In spite of Haya de la Torre's opportunistic shifts of ideological position, including the abandonment of anti-imperialism in the 1940s, the APRA would become a highly organized and disciplined mass party capable of winning national elections (though such victories were routinely denied it by the military). The Communist Party would develop a much smaller following, in large part because of the growing sectarianism of Mariátegui's successors and the party's subservience to Moscow from the 1930s through the 1950s. Both Mariátegui and Haya de la Torre would maintain a strong presence in Peruvian intellectual and political life for decades to come, the former posthumously through his essays on Peruvian society and culture, the latter primarily through his leadership of the APRA over the next half century.

In the chapters that follow, the focus will be on the socialist *indigenismo* theorized by Mariátegui, for it has had the greatest and most enduring influence on subsequent writers, including Alegría, Arguedas, and Scorza.[95] All three are commonly considered *indigenista* authors, though not all of them accepted their classification as such. Henceforth, this book adopts Mariátegui's more restricted definition of the term *indigenista*, for it serves as a good starting point for the study of such writers: "Authentic 'indigenistas', who should not be confused with those that exploit indigenous themes for mere 'exoticism', collaborate, consciously or not, in a political and economic effort to assert [indigenous] rights."[96]

Literary Representation, Modernization, and Indigenous Culture in the Peruvian Andes

Chapter 1 contrasts the narrative form of two novels written and published in the aftermath of the frustrated popular struggles of the early 1930s: Ciro Alegría's epic *El mundo es ancho y ajeno / Broad and Alien is the World* (1941), perhaps the paradigmatic *indigenista* work, and José María Arguedas's *Yawar Fiesta* (1941). Both authors were provincial *mestizo* intellectuals from the Andes who had participated in these struggles, Arguedas as a sympathizer of the Communist Party and Alegría as a founding member of the APRA.

Alegría's novel chronicles an indigenous community's struggle for survival in a rapidly modernizing nation. Written in an anachronistic, nineteenth-century realist style, *Broad and Alien is the World* is structured around a pair of heroic individual characters who embody the novel's utopian alternative to *gamonalismo* and capitalist modernization alike: a modern Andean collectivism. However, the bourgeois individual of nineteenth-century realism makes a poor vehicle for representing Andean communal values and ultimately undermines the novel's alternative vision of modernity. Because of its inability to imagine Andean culture in anything other than Western terms, *Broad and Alien is the World* ends on a pessimistic note, with the massacre of the indigenous community. By contrast, *Yawar Fiesta* is a transcultural narrative that modifies the Western novel form by crossing it with elements of Andean cosmology. The result is a complex representation of a multi-sided struggle over the course and cultural form of modernization in Peru. Positing culture as both a site and a means of the struggle for power, *Yawar Fiesta* ends not in a massacre, but in what may be interpreted as at least a partial victory for indigenous Andeans, who are depicted as agents of, rather than obstacles to, modernization. Though neither work offers a clear solution to Peru's persistent inequalities, *Yawar Fiesta* expresses greater faith in indigenous Andean culture as a source of an alternative modernity modeled in the very transcultural form of the novel itself.

Chapter 2 focuses on the works José María Arguedas produced during and immediately after the military dictatorship of Manuel Odría (1948–56). Odría intensified the pace of modernization and deepened Peru's economic and ideological dependence on the US, and this chapter examines such ideological influence and Arguedas's resistance to it in his anthropological essays and the only novel he published in the 1950s, *Los ríos profundos / Deep Rivers* (1958). Arguedas began his doctoral studies in anthropology in the early years of the Odría dictatorship, at a time when postwar US development theory dominated Peruvian social science. The main premise of development theory, that modernization required the acculturation of indigenous peoples to Western norms, appears throughout his essays from this period. Arguedas's use of this idea, however, is inconsistent. At times he seems to embrace it uncritically, while on other occasions he appears much more ambivalent. The frequently incongruous form of his essays, I suggest, is a product of Arguedas's attempt, carried out against the grain of the developmentalist anthropology in which he was trained, to carve out within it a space for indigenous culture and agency at a time of extremely limited prospects for the kind of struggles that were the subject of his early fiction.

Arguedas was never able to contain his ideas within the framework of development theory and began to distance himself from it when more radical approaches to social change presented themselves. The fall of the Odría dictatorship in 1956 and the consequent resurgence of indigenous land struggles in the late 1950s, along with the triumph of the Cuban revolution in 1959, broadened the horizons of the possible and helped revive in Arguedas the more radical politics of his youth. The early signs of this process can be located in *Deep Rivers*, his best known and most celebrated work of narrative transculturation. The novel is permeated by Andean beliefs, which serve as a means of imagining more radical remedies than capitalist development for the inequalities of Peruvian society.

In the late 1950s and early 1960s a new wave of indigenous land move-ments, even more numerous and widespread than those of the 1915–24 cycle of rebellion, signaled the decay and weakened position of *gamonal-ismo* in the Andes.[97] Chapter 3 explores José María Arguedas's and Manuel Scorza's contrasting representations of these movements in *Todas las sangres / All the Worlds* (1964) and *Redoble por Rancas / Drums for Rancas* (1970), respectively. *All the Worlds*, Arguedas's most overtly political novel, describes the changes produced in an Andean community by the collapse of a semi-feudal social order under the impact of capitalist modernization. Written in a social realist style, *All the Worlds* was consid-ered obsolete in the context of the 1960s Boom. The novel's outdated realism left literary critics unimpressed, while social scientists concerned with class exploitation attacked its author for what they perceived as his retrograde attachment to anachronistic Andean traditions. This, they suggested, had led him to write a confusing novel that misrepresented modern Peru. However, Arguedas's least appreciated novel combines an Andean mythological world-view with the Western novel form in order to represent indigenous Andean culture as a resource and not an obstacle in the struggle against both feudalism and imperialism.

Manuel Scorza (1928–83) described *Drums for Rancas* as an "infuri-atingly true account" of a 1958–63 struggle by indigenous communities of the central Andean department of Cerro de Pasco to defend their lands against both local landowners and a US-owned mining company. Scorza had participated in this struggle and concluded that a conventional social realism was inadequate for faithfully representing the indigenous commu-nities' response to the oppression they suffered. In order to produce a sufficiently infuriating and true account of what he had witnessed, he experimented with new literary forms. In *Drums for Rancas*, and in four subsequent novels about the Cerro de Pasco indigenous movement, Scorza renews the *indigenista* genre by introducing irony, humor, and narrative techniques associated with the Boom (fragmented, non-linear narration and magical realism). He deploys these techniques to construct a complex representation of the relationship between modernity and indigenous Andean culture, in which the latter functions as both a means and an obstacle to the former. However, Scorza ultimately concludes his five-novel cycle by attributing the indigenous movement's definitive defeat to the persistence of a mythological Andean world-view, thereby implicitly calling for indigenous Andeans to renounce their cultural traditions in the interest of the class struggle against both feudalism and imperialism. Unlike Arguedas, Scorza reduces indigenous Andeans' subordination to a question of class exploitation, and portrays culture and ethnicity as unhelpful distractions.

In reality, the Cerro de Pasco movement and other indigenous land struggles of 1956–64 were not as much of a failure as Scorza's novels imply. Though many of these movements were violently repressed, some managed to hold on to the land they had seized from large landowners. The unrest in the countryside, moreover, increased pressure on the government to enact a meaningful agrarian reform. However, the government of president Belaúnde Terry (1963–68) proved incapable of more than timid half-measures, and the emergence of Peruvian guerrilla movements, albeit short-lived ones, soon threatened a revolutionary explosion. Seeking to head off such an outcome, the military, now dominated by a new generation of nationalist, reform-minded officers, seized power in October 1968. Led by General Juan Velasco Alvarado, the armed forces implemented a series of radical measures, including the expropriation and nationalization of key industries and communication media, reform and expansion of the educational system, one of the most far-reaching redistributions of agricultural land in Latin American history, and the adoption of an official *indigenismo*, albeit one which redefined the indigenous population in class terms as peasants, deemphasizing their cultural identity. These measures, particularly the 1969 agrarian reform, would finally destroy the *gamonal* landowning class in the Andes.

The countryside was not the only scene of dramatic social change, however. By the late 1940s, the rural to urban migration facilitated by Leguía's road construction boom of the 1920s had reached massive proportions. Andean migrants swelled the population of coastal cities, especially Lima, and remade hostile urban environments in their own image. Lima, which for centuries had been a *criollo* stronghold, was Andeanized within one or two generations. Chapter 4 examines literary representations of rural to urban migration from the 1960s and 1970s, beginning with Julio Ramón Ribeyro's short story "La piel de un indio no cuesta caro" / "An Indian's Hide is Cheap" (1961), a relatively conventional, yet highly accomplished social realist representation of the relationship between *criollo* elites and Andean migrants in the newly Andeanized coastal city. The experience of urban life in a suddenly multiethnic metropolis also gave rise to new forms of literary expression, and the rest of the chapter contrasts Ribeyro's realism to the more experimental writing of Alfredo Bryce Echenique's *Un mundo para Julius* / *A World for Julius* (1970) and José María Arguedas's *El zorro de arriba y el zorro de abajo* / *The Fox from up Above and the Fox from Down Below* (1971), arguably his most transcultural work. Both Bryce Echenique and Arguedas developed new narrative techniques to depict the transformation of coastal cities by migration from the Andes and to capture the experience of urban life from the perspective of *criollo* elites as well as Andean migrants.

Though *A World for Julius* and *The Fox from up Above and the Fox from Down Below* are innovative works, the transcultural form of Arguedas's narrative challenges the reader to imagine a new, more democratic Peru in a way that Bryce Echenique's affectionately satirical portrait of Lima's aristocratic *criollo* elite simply does not. In the northern coastal town of Chimbote, a cultural cauldron that attracted migrants from all over Peru during the anchovy fishing boom of the 1960s, Arguedas distinguished the emergent face of a new nation. In *The Fox from up Above and the Fox from Down Below*, set in Chimbote, he embarked on an anguished search for a narrative form capable of representing the complexity of the economic and cultural changes Peru was undergoing. Drawing on pre-Columbian Andean mythology and contemporary indigenous culture, Arguedas chronicles the struggles for survival and dignity of Andean migrants and poor *costeños*, of fishermen and fishmeal factory workers, of prostitutes, priests, and even an Andeanized Peace Corps volunteer and the emergence of new, transcultural forms of solidarity and collective identity.

Unfortunately, Arguedas's tentatively hopeful vision of a new Peru would not be realized. Instead, in the 1980s the country descended into civil war between the maoist Shining Path insurgency and government security forces. Many in the *criollo* elite interpreted the Shining Path's violence and brutality as an expression of the indigenous culture they had long blamed for Peru's backwardness. Chapter 5 examines the representation of indigenous peoples in several of the works MarioVargas Llosa wrote and published during the Shining Path war. His earlier works, most notably *La casa verde / The Green House* (1966), had expressed sympathy for an indigenous population victimized by a capitalist form of modernization represented as brutal, exploitative, and destructive. However, by the late 1980s, with the Shining Path war as a backdrop, Vargas Llosa had come to share the view of many of his fellow *criollos* that indigenous cultures are an obstacle to a capitalist modernization now depicted as virtually synonymous with progress, freedom, and social justice. This change, I argue, is the product of his ideological evolution from the 1960s, when he considered himself a socialist, through to the 1980s, by which point he had become a champion of free-market economics and a fervent neoliberal. By 1990, he had drifted so far away from the leftist leanings of his youth that he ran a well-publicized campaign for President of Peru as the candidate of a resurgent Right.

Vargas Llosa's changing views on indigenous culture are explored through readings of the essays "Informe sobre Uchuraccay" / "Report on Uchuraccay" (1983) and "Questions of Conquest" (1990), the novels *El hablador / The Storyteller* (1987) and *Lituma en los Andes / Death in the Andes* (1993), and the memoir of his presidential campaign, *El pez en el agua / A Fish in the Water* (1993). The first three of these works were published before the 1990 elections, during Vargas Llosa's gradual entry into Peruvian politics, while the remaining two were published afterward and reflect, both directly and obliquely, the author's frustrating experience as a politician.

In the first three works, Vargas Llosa addresses, respectively, the Shining Path war, the legacies of the conquest, and the fate of the Machiguenga, an indigenous group of the Peruvian Amazon whose cultural survival is threatened by modernization. In each case, he attributes his nation's underdevelopment and extreme social inequality to indigenous peoples' isolation from Peruvian society and their incomplete assimilation to the modern, Westernized culture of the *criollo* elite. These texts rehearse what would be the core themes of Vargas Llosa's 1990 presidential campaign: individual initiative unleashed by the free market as the only possible form of modernization, and the incompatibility of Peru's indigenous cultures with this neoliberal vision of modernity. They also suggest that Vargas Llosa's unexpected electoral defeat, in which the indigenous and *mestizo* majority's vote against him was decisive, was due at least in part to his fundamental misreading of class and ethnic conflict in contemporary Peru. Drawing on anthropologist Carlos Iván Degregori's revealing analysis of the role of cultural and ethnic divisions in the 1990 elections, I examine Vargas Llosa's own account of his unsuccessful campaign for the presidency in *A Fish in the Water,* and analyze the novel *Death in the Andes* as an expression of the writer-candidate's frustration with Peruvian politics in the wake of his electoral defeat. As if in retaliation against those who failed to elect its author president, *Death in the Andes* returns to the theme of the Shining Path war only to attribute the brutality of the conflict to atavistic Andean barbarism.

Since Vargas Llosa's defeat in 1990, the *criollo* elite he represented has found more effective means of perpetuating its dominance of Peruvian society. It has relied on unconventional populists like Vargas Llosa's victorious opponent Alberto Fujimori, Peru's first President of Japanese descent, and Alejandro Toledo, Fujimori's successor and the nation's first elected *cholo* Head of State. Though the *criollo* political and economic establishment initially opposed both men, it subsequently found their demagogic manipulation of indigenous identity a useful mask for policies benefitting national and global elites rather than popular sectors who, at least at election time, felt themselves and their interests represented by such "outsiders." However, the majority of the population eventually became disenchanted with both men. Though it proved an effective means of winning elections, Fujimori's and Toledo's opportunistic use of Andean cultural symbols was no more than an illusion of the democratization that indigenous and *mestizo* voters sought. *The Colonial Divide in Peruvian Narrative* concludes with an assessment of the current prospects for overcoming Peru's cultural and class divisions and of the contribution, albeit symbolic, of Arguedas's transcultural narrative to the democratization of Peruvian society.

1

MODERNITY FROM THE MARGINS

Narrative Form and Indigenous Agency in
Broad and Alien is the World and
Yawar Fiesta

Ángel Rama once noted that 1941 may be considered a key date in the history of Latin American literature "because it marks the appearance of twenty narrative works, including several of fundamental importance, that permit one to draw a literary cross section of the continent, one which provides an overview of the different narrative directions, diverse generations, and multiple literary areas of America."[1] Around 1941, he argues, "the paths of [Latin American] narrative diverge, without, however, producing an opposition between the old and the new, but rather separating within the new, broader and richer than is generally recognized, a multiplicity of creative lines."[2] For Rama, this key year inaugurates a period of regional and formal differentiation in Latin American narrative which runs through the triumph of the Cuban revolution in 1959. Drawing on a variety of both local and international sources, the innovations of the 1940s and 1950s anticipate the more widely recognized renewal of Latin American narrative commonly attributed to the 1960s Boom authors.

Among the 1941 novels Rama mentions, two are from Peru: *Broad and Alien is the World*, by Ciro Alegría (1909–67), and *Yawar Fiesta*, by José María Arguedas (1911–69). Both works address early twentieth-century social change and conflict in the Peruvian Andes by denouncing the landowning elite's abuse of the indigenous population and chronicling indigenous communities' struggles against projects of modernization imposed from above. *Broad and Alien is the World*, which would be the

32

last of Alegría's novels published in his lifetime, treats the period 1912–28, while *Yawar Fiesta*, Arguedas's first novel, takes place in the 1920s and 1930s. Because of their defense of indigenous rights, both novels are usually considered orthodox *indigenista* works.[3] Rama, however, uses them as contrasting examples of two divergent currents in Latin American narrative.[4]

He calls the first current "Andean social narrative" and includes in this group *indigenista* and other realist works concerned with social conflict in the Andes. Inaugurated in the 1930s by novels such as César Vallejo's *El tungsteno* (1931) and Jorge Icaza's *Huasipungo* (1935), this current achieved international recognition in 1941 with the phenomenal success of *Broad and Alien is the World*. Andean social narrative, according to Rama, is characterized by a "passive acceptance of models developed for other circumstances and contexts."[5] Works like *El tungsteno* and *Huasipungo*, for example, apply the formulas of socialist realism to Peruvian and Ecuadorian contexts, respectively, while *Broad and Alien is the World* draws on nineteenth-century European bourgeois realism. Rama associates *Yawar Fiesta* with the second current, which in this early formulation of his argument he refers to as "narrative acculturation", but which he would soon rename "narrative transculturation", adapting Fernando Ortiz's useful neologism to the analysis of literary texts. Though *Yawar Fiesta* is inspired by the same literary models as *El tungsteno*, *Huasipungo* and *Broad and Alien is the World*, it adapts those models for the expression of an Andean world-view by refracting them through the lens of indigenous traditions, transculturating the narrative form of the *indigenista* novel in the process.[6]

Broad and Alien is the World and *Yawar Fiesta*, published in the same year, approach their common theme with very different narrative strategies which, moreover, account for their subsequent histories of reception. The accessible and accomplished realism of *Broad and Alien is the World* earned Alegría instant international renown, while Arguedas would not be recognized as a major Latin American novelist until the publication of his second novel, *Deep Rivers*, in 1958. In 1941, both authors entered their novels in a literary contest sponsored by the New York publishing house Farrar & Rinehart. *Broad and Alien is the World*, which Alegría had written expressly for the contest and submitted in Chile, was chosen as the Chilean entry and went on to win, while *Yawar Fiesta*, which Arguedas submitted in Peru, never made it past the Peruvian pre-selection committee. Thanks in part to the Farrar & Rinehart prize, by 1950 *Broad and Alien is the World* had been translated into fourteen foreign languages, including English, and went through twenty authorized (and several pirate) editions in Spanish between 1941 and 1961.[7] It was among the most widely read works of pre-Boom Latin American literature.[8]

Yawar Fiesta attracted a much smaller readership and would wait seventeen years for a second edition, made possible only by the success of *Deep Rivers*. Rather than a measure of the relative quality of *Broad and Alien is the World* and *Yawar Fiesta*, the difference in the initial critical reception and commercial success of the two novels reflects the complexity and difficulty of Arguedas's transcultural narrative, which relied on Andean cultural forms its contemporary critics and readers were ill-equipped to understand. *Yawar Fiesta*'s nuanced representation of the role of culture in social conflicts was, in short, ahead of its time.

Since the death of both authors in the late 1960s, interest has faded in Alegría's works, and *Broad and Alien is the World* is virtually ignored today.[9] Arguedas's novels, by contrast, have drawn growing critical attention. Scholars have recognized the relevance of his work for contemporary debates over the relationship between modernity, cultural difference, and narrative form, and there is now a large critical bibliography on Arguedas.[10] However, aside from the obligatory chapter in book-length studies of his narrative fiction, *Yawar Fiesta* does not figure prominently in this bibliography. Rama, for example, makes no mention of *Yawar Fiesta* in *Transculturación narrativa en América Latina* (1982), focusing instead on *Deep Rivers*. Several other studies have examined the influence of indigenous Andean culture on the form of Arguedas's later novels, but critics have yet to analyze *Yawar Fiesta* as a transcultural narrative.[11]

In this chapter I examine *Broad and Alien is the World* and *Yawar Fiesta* in order to explore the implications of their divergent narrative forms for the representation of social conflicts in the Andes during a period of rapid modernization between 1910 and 1940. The two works' contrasting narrative strategies are rooted in the somewhat different regional contexts with which they engage and with which the two authors were most familiar. Alegría was born and raised on his family's haciendas in the northern Andes, where little Quechua was spoken, even in indigenous communities. Arguedas, on the other hand, was from the more indigenous southern Andes of Peru, where Quechua was, and still is, widely spoken not only by the indigenous population, but also by *mestizos* and the *misti* elite. *Broad and Alien is the World*, consequently, is set in the fictional northern Andean village of Rumi, while *Yawar Fiesta* takes place in the real southern Andean town of Puquio, in and around which Arguedas spent much of his youth.

Both writers would draw attention to these regional differences in order to avoid having their works pitted against each other by critics eager to determine who had produced the more "authentic" representation of the indigenous Andean population. As Arguedas, for example, explains in an interview:

Scholars, even important ones, have often erroneously considered my narratives as more authentic interpretations of the Indian than those of Ciro [Alegría]. No. Both are equally authentic. The fact is that Ciro interpreted the life of the Peruvian people of the northern Andes, where the Indians do not speak Quechua, which means that they were much more culturally subjugated than the peasants of the central and southern region. Ciro's Indians are, in reality, less Indian.[12]

In his memoirs, Alegría concurs by noting that "my Indian is northern: an Indian who does not speak Quechua ... Arguedas's Indian is southern and, more specifically, from Apurímac: more silent and lyrical".[13] Intended to disarm one kind of comparison, based on a spurious notion of authenticity, these statements nonetheless enable another, based on narrative form.

Because *Broad and Alien is the World* is set in the north, Alegría did not confront as great a linguistic and cultural divide between his potential readers and his indigenous characters as did his compatriot from the southern Andes. Consequently, Alegría was not overly troubled by the problem of how to represent indigenous Andean culture using a language, Spanish, and a narrative form, the novel, alien to it. He could assume that the language and cultural forms of the conquerors were adequate to the literary and political project of defending the conquered. In writing *Yawar Fiesta*, Arguedas, by contrast, struggled to fashion a form of Spanish capable of representing Quechua speech and expressing an indigenous Andean-world view.[14] What enabled such formal experimentation was his immersion in indigenous culture during his youth. Due to family circumstances, Arguedas grew up not only bilingual in Quechua and Spanish, but also bi-cultural. His mother died in 1914, when he was less than three years old. His father soon remarried, but the young Arguedas was never accepted by his stepmother and stepbrother. During don Víctor Manuel Arguedas's frequent and prolonged absences from home (after losing his job as a judge in Puquio, he was compelled to travel the Andes in search of work), his new wife and stepson treated the young Arguedas like one of the household's indigenous servants. To escape their abuse, the future writer fled to the nearby hacienda of a relative, where, from 1921 to 1923, he was raised by an indigenous community in which he came to identify closely with indigenous Andean culture.[15] The fate of such communities and the values Arguedas associated with them would be his lifelong concern. Alegría, by contrast, had not had as intimate an experience with indigenous communities and had not experienced the world through the Quechua language and indigenous Andean culture.

Though their early years were rather different, the two authors' trajectories would converge in the decade leading up to the publication of *Broad and Alien is the World* and *Yawar Fiesta* before diverging again after 1941. Both were *mestizo* intellectuals from the Andean interior who moved to coastal cities in the 1920s, an experience millions of Peruvians would share in the following decades and one emblematic of Peru's peripheral modernity.[16] In their new urban environments they not only studied, wrote their first works of fiction, and began to publish, but were also attracted to and participated in movements for radical social change. Alegría went to secondary school and briefly attended university in Trujillo, where he also worked as a journalist and was one of the founding members of the APRA in Peru. Arguedas studied in Ica from 1926 to 1928 and arrived in Lima for the first time in 1931 to attend the University of San Marcos, where he became a sympathizer and collaborator, though never officially a member, of the Peruvian Communist Party founded by Mariátegui a few years earlier.[17]

Their radical politics would land both authors in jail. While organizing an armed APRA uprising in northern Peru in 1931, Alegría was arrested, tortured and imprisoned in Trujillo. He was freed during the July 1932 APRA rebellion in that city and, unlike many of his comrades, escaped the military's subsequent suppression of the uprising and massacre of *apristas*. As he fled toward the Ecuadorian border, however, he was arrested again. Saved from execution by the opportune intervention of a family member, he spent the next year in a Lima prison. Upon his release thanks to an amnesty decreed by General Oscar Benavides in 1933, Alegría immediately plunged back into journalism and politics, which led to yet another arrest and, ultimately, his deportation to Chile in 1934, where he would write *Broad and Alien is the World* seven years later. After traveling to New York in 1941 to accept the Farrar & Rinehart prize, he stayed on in the US until 1949, then spent much of the next decade in Puerto Rico and Cuba. He would not visit Peru again until 1957, and would not return to live there until 1958.[18]

Arguedas's experience in Lima was not quite so dramatic, but he, too, supported efforts to rid Peru of oligarchic rule. Though he never formally joined the Communist Party, he participated in student movements affiliated with it, taught workers' study groups organized by the Party, and contributed articles to its newspaper, *Democracia y Trabajo*.[19] In 1937, for example, Arguedas took part in a student demonstration at San Marcos University against the campus visit of an Italian General sent by Mussolini to train Peru's police.[20] His participation in the protest would cost Arguedas a year in jail, from 1937–8, an experience about which he would publish, many years later, his prison novel *El Sexto* (1961).

Both authors would subsequently break with their respective political parties. Alegría formally and publicly resigned from the APRA in 1948 over its authoritarianism.[21] Arguedas drifted away from the Communist

Party at about the same time, in part due to his dismay at its growing sectarianism and the defection of some of its high level leaders to the Right.[22] Both writers distanced themselves from their parties out of disillusionment, but neither renounced his belief in the need for social change in Peru. Attempts to bring about such change had been repeatedly frustrated in the turbulent period between 1915 and the early 1930s. Indigenous movements in the Andes and labor movements in Lima in the wake of the First World War, Leguía's populism in the early years of the Oncenio and his project of rapid modernization, Mariátegui and Haya de la Torre's activism and founding of the Socialist Party and the APRA, respectively, the APRA rebellion of 1932; all failed to wrest power from the oligarchy. Alegría and Arguedas had come of age in these turbulent years and had participated in the late stages of the popular challenge to the oligarchy.

However, the 1930s were a period of conservative reaction, which both Alegría and Arguedas experienced first hand in prison. By the time both authors were released, and Alegría deported, the hopes for revolutionary change in the short term had become much harder to sustain. Writing in 1941, Alegría from exile, Arguedas from Sicuani in the Andes, they looked back on more than two decades of defeat for popular struggles, led since the late 1920s by the APRA and the Communist Party. *Broad and Alien is the World* and *Yawar Fiesta* reflect on the recent history of defeat and explore forms of popular agency rooted in indigenous culture and independent of outside leadership. While both authors remained affiliated with their respective political parties in 1941, the beginnings of their gradual separation from them can already be observed in the two novels' exploration of alternative forms of agency and paths to social change. Alegría and Arguedas sought such alternatives using different narrative forms rooted in their contrasting regional backgrounds.

Modernization and the Defense of Community in *Broad and Alien is the World*

Broad and Alien is the World is a vast *indigenista* epic. Written in a nineteenth-century style anachronistic even in the 1940s, this paradigmatic *indigenista* narrative has been described as a "synthesis of Víctor Hugo and Zola."[23] Its brand of realism, as Peter Elmore has observed, "demands didactic clarity" and leaves nothing unexplained.[24] The novel's didactic tone is facilitated by the use of what Mario Vargas Llosa has called "an intrusive narrator" who intervenes frequently to orient the reader, interpret and supplement characters' thoughts and statements, fill in gaps in the narrative, and tie up loose ends.[25] As the narrator himself

37

explains, "in urgent instances we have intervened in order to clarify some confusing thoughts and feelings as well as certain incomplete reminiscences."[26] With little room for ambiguity, Alegría's novel casts its central conflict between the indigenous community of Rumi and the *gamonal* Alvaro Amenábar as, simply, a struggle between good and evil.

Broad and Alien is the World relies on such antiquated narrative techniques that Gerald Martin has called it one of the most accomplished nineteenth-century novels of twentieth-century Latin American literature. For all that, Martin recognizes that though it is "unwieldy, poorly organized and erratic in style", *Broad and Alien is the World* is nonetheless "majestic despite its unevenness and moving despite its sentimentality."[27] Moreover, unlike earlier examples of the *indigenista* genre, Alegría's novel treats its indigenous characters as fully formed human subjects capable of comprehending and resisting the forces that oppress them, and not, as in César Vallejo's *El tungsteno* or Jorge Icaza's *Huasipungo*, helpless victims so degraded and reduced to such a brutish state by centuries of exploitation that they are barely capable of rational thought, much less of organized resistance.

Though far from modern in its own narrative form, *Broad and Alien is the World* is a novel about modernization. It chronicles the relationship between the independent indigenous community of Rumi and a rapidly modernizing nation from 1912 to 1928.[28] The central conflict in the novel, the struggle for land between Rumi and the *gamonal* Amenábar, is motivated by the latter's desire not only to expand his already vast properties but also to develop a nearby mine, for which he requires indigenous labor. Through the figure of Amenábar, *Broad and Alien is the World* registers two of the most prominent early twentieth-century manifestations of capitalist modernization in the Andean countryside: the expansion of haciendas at the expense of indigenous communities and the growth of a mining industry dependent on indigenous labor. Moreover, the novel's central conflict gives rise to several secondary plots in which Rumi's loss of its best lands propels dispossessed *comuneros* across much of northern Peru, from rural areas to urban centers and from the Andes to both the coast and the Amazon jungle, in search of new ways of making a living. On coca plantations and other haciendas, in the Amazon rubber boom, in the mines, and in Lima, the displaced former *comuneros* of Rumi encounter the peripheral, dependent modernity of a nation that turns out to be not only a broad and alien world, but also one hostile to the indigenous and the poor.

The profusion of secondary plots, which repeatedly interrupt the main narrative about the land conflict between indigenous community and *gamonal*, has often been interpreted as poor organization. Alegría completed *Broad and Alien is the World* in four months in order to meet the deadline of the Farrar & Rinehart literary contest, and the novel's apparently rambling structure is sometimes attributed to the haste in which it was produced.[29] However, as Tomás Escajadillo has shown, *Broad and Alien is the World* is not as poorly organized as it seems.[30] The frequent digressions from the main narrative about the land conflict serve to draw a sharp contrast between life in the indigenous community and the *comuneros*' fate in the rapidly modernizing nation outside it. Indeed, it is through such a contrast that *Broad and Alien is the World* articulates what Escajadillo takes to be its central theme: "The community is the only habitable place for indigenous Andeans."[31]

Indeed, Alegría's novel portrays the indigenous community as more than merely habitable, for Rumi is idealized in *Broad and Alien is the World* as a happy realm where justice and the common good prevail. It is everything the rest of the nation is not and, implicitly, a model for what the nation could be. However, at the end of the novel this Andean utopia is destroyed, and along with it the only dignified form of life available to the *comuneros*. Indigenous tradition, though idealized, is unsustainable, while modernization, though degrading and even fatal, seems inevitable. There would appear to be no alternative. Nevertheless, the matter is not as simple as it seems, in spite of the novel's aspirations to didactic clarity. Rather than forcing a choice between modernization and the preservation of tradition, *Broad and Alien is the World* leaves room for a different process of modernization, one carried out from within the indigenous community by the *comuneros* themselves.

This process is initiated by Rumi's traditional indigenous mayor, Rosendo Maqui, and continued by Maqui's adopted son and successor as mayor, Benito Castro. The two mayors of Rumi have often been interpreted as representing indigenous tradition and Western modernity, respectively. However, the contrast between Rosendo Maqui and Benito Castro should not be exaggerated. The former, though a traditionalist, undertakes some important changes in the community, while the latter, though more modern and worldly, remains loyal to the community and at least some of its traditions. Both leaders combine elements of Western modernity with indigenous tradition, though in varying proportions, in order to better defend Rumi from the expansion of neighboring haciendas.

Rosendo Maqui is a wise patriarch who has never traveled very far from Rumi and has presided over the community as mayor for much of his adult life. Both he and his community are initially associated with immutable tradition. As the narrator is careful to note, Rumi means "stone" in Quechua, and in the opening pages of the novel Rosendo Maqui contemplates his community while seated on a stone, motionless, "like an ancient idol."[32] His immobility "makes him one with the rock, and both seem fused into a monolith."[33] The references to stone and idols suggest a persistence of the Inca past in the present. A cliché of the *indigenista* genre, the comparison of the indigenous community to stone suggests its enduring, timeless nature, but also an incapacity for change. There could hardly be a more static image of either Rumi or its mayor.

The petrified image of Rosendo Maqui turns out to be deceptive, however, for he does not remain fused to the rock for long, and even as he sits on it he thinks of the school the *comuneros* are building at his instigation. Rosendo Maqui, it turns out, has already attempted to hire a teacher and petitioned the authorities for school supplies. He has done so because he believes that tradition alone will not be enough to defend a community increasingly vulnerable to *gamonales* like Amenábar. The *comuneros*, he decides, need schooling in the ways of their adversaries in order to understand and protect themselves from the law, which serves only the wealthy and is perceived by Maqui as "a shady, criminal sleight-of-hand."[34]

The school, as it turns out, will not be built in time to help the *comuneros'* in their legal battle against Amenábar, and will be abandoned along with the rest of the town before a single class is held in it. Nonetheless, Rosendo Maqui's efforts to provide the next generation of *comuneros* with a school demonstrate his understanding that the community must change if it is to survive. Though Rumi may be a refuge from an unjust world, it is nonetheless part of that world, and the *comuneros* cannot isolate themselves from it completely. By building a school, Rosendo Maqui attempts to take control of change, rather than see it forced upon the community. Ultimately, he fails and ends his days in prison, falsely accused of directing an attack on Amenábar as the *gamonal* took legal possession of Rumi's land. Despite the failure, his efforts to obtain a school for his community belies the narrative's initial, static representation of Rosendo Maqui and links him to Benito Castro, who also undertakes the construction of a school as mayor of Rumi.[35]

Benito Castro, however, is not as completely identified with indigenous tradition. He is a *mestizo* fathered by an outsider to Rumi, a soldier in the transient army of one of the caudillos who vied for power in the aftermath of Peru's disastrous loss to Chile in the War of the Pacific (1879–84). Like other children of indigenous women raped by members of such armed bands, Benito Castro is never fully accepted by the whole community, and is particularly resented by his mother's indigenous husband. After an altercation in which he kills his stepfather in self defense, Benito Castro is compelled to flee Rumi to avoid prosecution by both the community and the state. His long exile – which begins in 1910, before the novel's central conflict commences, and lasts until his return in 1926 – takes him throughout northern Peru. He works as a peon on various haciendas, takes a succession of jobs in Lima, and serves several years in the army.

He hears about or witnesses the most important historical events of the period, such as the 1885 indigenous rebellion of Atusparia in the northern Andes, the birth of the labor movement in Lima, and the 1918–19 strikes which led to the establishment of the eight-hour workday. He encounters political agitators and anarcho-syndicalist labor leaders, learns to read and is exposed to *indigenista* journals such as *Autonomía*, published by Pedro Zulen, the founder of the Asociación Pro Indígena (1909–17).[36]

Though Benito Castro is at least partly an outsider to the indigenous community, his very existence is a product of forces and events external to Rumi, and he is absent from the community for much of the novel, he maintains his allegiance to Rumi during his long exile and dreams of returning to the place he considers home. With more experience of, and success in, the outside world than any other *comunero*, he concludes nonetheless that Rumi offers a better life. Haciendas, he learns, are all the same: "they pay enough to exist on, but not to live on."[37] Work in the community, carried out for the collective good, he concludes, is qualitatively different from work done for an hacendado: "And what a difference between the work on the ranches and the work they did in the community. In Rumi the Indians worked willingly, laughing, singing, and the day's duties were a pleasure. On the ranches the men worked sadly, laggingly, and they seemed stepchildren of the earth."[38]

Even in Lima, where fellow workers try to interest him in the labor movement, anarchism, and marxism, he compares everything (unfavorably) to his community: "Santiago was interested in the labor movement and had read a great deal on the subject, but whenever he tried to talk to Benito about it, the latter would say: 'Yes, it's somewhat like my community, but my community is better.' He compared everything to the community."[39] Despite his sympathy with leftist political doctrine and socialist values, the indigenous community is Benito Castro's model of a just society. In Peru, according to *Broad and Alien is the World*, a more egalitarian social order will have to be constructed, in part at least, from native materials.

Upon his return to Rumi, Benito Castro is quickly reintegrated into the community despite initial opposition from traditionalists. Because of the many ways in which exile has changed him, he is perceived as a *mestizo* at first, but nonetheless ultimately reclaims his place in Rumi as a *comunero*. He marries, has a son and carries on Rosendo Maqui's legacy as mayor. Like his predecessor, he persists in the legal defense of the community against Amenábar's renewed efforts to acquire its remaining land. However, when legal measures fail, Benito Castro abandons Rosendo Maqui's strategy of peaceful resistance. Relying on his military experience instead, he leads the community into armed struggle and attempts to spark a region-wide indigenous uprising in the northern

Andes. Though the *comuneros* manage to repel the army's initial attack, Benito Castro is ultimately no more successful than Rosendo Maqui. The hoped for regional rebellion never materializes, and an isolated Rumi is eventually overwhelmed and destroyed by army reinforcements which arrive by truck on a road recently built by involuntary indigenous labor. To Amenábar's expanding haciendas and his mine, the novel adds, at the very end, another key feature of modernization in the 1920s, a road, which deals the community a fatal blow.

Both Rosendo Maqui and Benito Castro promote the transformation of their community from within in order to ensure its survival in a rapidly modernizing nation. In both cases, the changes they initiate are motivated by their commitment to the preservation of Rumi's collectivist traditions. The two mayors, of course, are not identical. However, the contrast between them does not constitute a binary opposition between indigenous tradition and Western modernity. Rather, Rosendo Maqui and Benito Castro represent modernizing projects that differ in the pace rather than the kind of change they envision. If the former is somewhat more gradualist and relies on formal schooling and a legal system in which he nonetheless has little faith, the latter does not reject these measures, but rather adds to them a "pragmatic" revision of indigenous beliefs and armed struggle when legal means fail to yield results. Both confront a capitalist modernization imposed from above with a collectivist form of modernization initiated from within the indigenous community.

Alegría's merit in *Broad and Alien is the World* is to have represented indigenous peoples as capable of intervening in processes of modernization. Rosendo Maqui and Benito Castro, unlike the virtually inert *comuneros* and hacienda peons who populate works such as *El tungsteno* or *Huasipungo*, are agents, and not merely objects or victims of modernization. However, the changes they initiate in Rumi are exclusively reactive, a response to threats from outside the indigenous community. Moreover, though intended to defend indigenous cultural values, mainly of collectivism, against those of the world beyond Rumi, such changes nonetheless do not arise from within indigenous Andean culture. Their provenance, rather, is the very world against which they are supposed to defend indigenous Andean collectivism. In addition, there is little notion in Alegría's novel that the ideas and methods derived from *criollo* or *mestizo* Peru are to be adapted to indigenous Andean culture. Their introduction to Rumi, on the contrary, requires the sacrifice of at least some indigenous beliefs. In didactic fashion, Alegría's novel proposes to do away with only those indigenous beliefs rendered as "pernicious" for the community, but one might well ask whether the Western schooling desired by both of Rumi's mayors would make such distinctions. Would the indigenous pupils' collectivism survive a curriculum based, no doubt, on the liberal individualism espoused by Peru's oligarchy? *Broad and Alien is the World*, in effect, is about a process of *mestizaje* initiated by Rumi's first mayor and accelerated by its last. It is no accident that leadership of the community passes from the indigenous patriarch Rosendo Maqui to his adopted *mestizo* son Benito Castro. Though raised a *comunero*, the latter nonetheless is exiled from Rumi and undergoes a sixteen-year apprenticeship as a *mestizo* before returning to take charge of the community and initiate new and more far-reaching changes. The aim of such *mestizaje*, of course, is to defend and preserve the collectivism that the novel holds to be the core value of Peru's indigenous population. But one might well wonder about the status of collectivism itself in *Broad and Alien is the World*.

In keeping with the nineteenth-century realism on which he draws, Alegría relies on an intrusive narrator and a handful of heroic individual characters to represent and defend the collectivism of indigenous communities. While the narrator repeatedly attributes a collectivist tradition to the indigenous community, either directly or focalized through principal characters such as Rosendo Maqui and Benito Castro in their occasional indirect interior monologues, there is very little evidence in the novel of such collectivism at work in Rumi. Though often invoked and spoken about, it is rarely shown. There are a few scenes of community meetings and of course the final collective defense of Rumi. Missing from the novel, however, is a sense of how communal identity and values are sustained and reproduced. Rumi as such has little existence in the narrative apart from its two mayors, whose personal qualities seem to imbue the community with what identity it has. After Rosendo Maqui's death, for example, Rumi falls into a decay from which only Benito Castro's return saves it.

The rituals, festivals, oral traditions, or labor practices through which community is constructed are rarely mentioned in *Broad and Alien is the World*, and when they do appear they play a minimal role. One gets the sense that the collectivism the narrator so earnestly and movingly defends is more a projection of his (and Alegría's) values onto Rumi, or rather its heroic leaders, than an autochthonous feature of the community itself. This is nothing new in the *indigenista* genre, of course. As Antonio Cornejo Polar has pointed out, *indigenismo* is a heterogeneous literature which relies on the narrative forms of a dominant culture to represent and defend a subordinate one. The latter is merely the referent and is not understood in its own terms, for its meaning is overdetermined by other elements of the narrative. This is not the only form of literary heterogeneity, but it appears to be the operative one in *Broad and Alien is the World*, where the indigenous community serves as a model for the utopian objectives of an alternative nationalist project, which, however much it invokes indigenous Andean tradition, remains external to it.

Modernization From Above and Modernization From Below in *Yawar Fiesta*

Like *Broad and Alien is the World*, *Yawar Fiesta* is about the social conflicts of modernization in the Andes in the early decades of the twentieth century. However, it approaches this theme in a very different manner. As Peter Elmore has observed, *Yawar Fiesta* "appears anomalous when compared to the crystallized image of what supposedly defines *indigenista* writing."[40] In this, his first novel, Arguedas departs from *indigenista* literary convention in several respects. While *Yawar Fiesta* opens with an initial clash over land, its primary focus is a bullfight, or rather, a struggle over the form and meaning of a bullfight, which Arguedas uses to represent the conflicts generated by modernization in the Andes. The novel is set in the southern Andean town of Puquio, where an Andean-style bullfight known as the *turupukllay* serves as the centerpiece of the annual *Yawar*, or blood, fiesta of the title, a local festival which doubles as a celebration of Peru's national independence day, July 28. *Yawar Fiesta*'s central conflict is set in motion when, in an unspecified year during the 1930s, the national government attempts to replace the *turupukllay* with a purportedly more "civilized", Spanish version of the bullfight. As its association with national independence suggests, and as the state's attempt to control it makes evident, far more than the fate of local tradition is at stake in the form of the bullfight. Rather, the *turupukllay* functions in *Yawar Fiesta* as the symbolic condensation of a larger struggle over the power to determine the contours of Peru's modernity.

That struggle, moreover, is not reducible to a clash between *comuneros* and *gamonales*, for it involves not only Puquio's four indigenous communities, known as *ayllus*, and its white *gamonal* elite, known as *mistis* or *principales*, but also local *mestizos*, government authorities from the coast, and Andean migrants to Lima. The government ban on the *turupukllay* propels these groups into alliances one does not ordinarily encounter in the *indigenista* genre. The most retrograde *gamonal*, for example, sides with the *comuneros* he exploits mercilessly, while the migrants to Lima collaborate with a national government they otherwise oppose. In addition, unlike other *indigenista* works, *Yawar Fiesta* does not culminate in the massacre or defeat of an indigenous community. As Antonio Cornejo Polar has noted, "the traditional *indigenista* novel repeats a scheme based on the accumulation of dispossessions, usurpations, and abuses to such a point that it produces either the destruction of the Indian's capacity for resistance or a violent and heroic, but always unsuccessful, response."[41] *Yawar Fiesta*, by contrast, concludes with the *ayllus*' subversion of the national government's attempt to control the bullfight.

To an extent greater than in other *indigenista* novels of the period, Puquio's social groups serve as *Yawar Fiesta*'s main characters, for the ethnographic manner in which the town's social structure is described identifies groups, rather than individuals, as the novel's principal protagonists. Unlike *Broad and Alien is the World*, which begins with Rosendo Maqui's contemplation of his village and filters its description of Rumi through his consciousness, *Yawar Fiesta* opens with the narrator's direct description of Puquio, which he divides into its constituent social groups before introducing any individual characters. The individual characters who subsequently do appear are even more closely identified or merged with the groups they represent than is common in the genre, while the *ayllus* are never differentiated into individual characters at all and always act as collectives.

One social group, however, is virtually absent from the novel: the world of *Yawar Fiesta* is almost exclusively masculine, and women, particularly indigenous women, play a very limited role in it. They speak only once in the novel, in reaction to the sound of the *wakawak'ras*, the trumpets made of bull's horns which announce the upcoming *turupukllay*.[42] They cry when the *comuneros* are dispossessed of their land by the *mistis*.[43] They sing to support and encourage their men at critical moments of the narrative, during the bullfight, for example.[44] At no time, however, are they represented as agents of the novel's central conflict. In *Yawar Fiesta*, women are little more than spectators to the struggle over modernization, in which, moreover, they are actively prevented from participating. Before leaving to capture a wild bull for the *turupukllay*, for example, the *comuneros* from one of Puquio's *ayllus* assemble in the plaza to gather their courage and urge each other on, "ripping open their shirts and baring their chests."[45] Women and children are violently excluded from the ritual of masculine bravado: "Some of the *comuneros* nudged the little children with their feet and kicked the women to make them take the babies away. 'Damn *k'anra*! Take little kid away quick. Nothing but men in square!'."[46] Expelled from the public space of the plaza, women are directed to assume the domestic task of caring for children. In this respect, Arguedas's first novel is not significantly different from other *indigenista* works of the period.

Yawar Fiesta's narrative form, on the other hand, is a notable departure from the *indigenista* literary tradition. Arguedas, for example, does not use an intrusive narrator who speaks directly to, and guides the reader through, the novel. The narrator of *Yawar Fiesta*, rather, orchestrates the unfolding of the narrative from behind the scenes, without calling attention to himself or interpreting events or characters' thoughts and actions in the manner of the intrusive narrator of *Broad and Alien is the World*. Arguedas's narrator reveals himself to be a *serrano* from Puquio, for he refers to it as "our" town, and he makes no secret of his sympathy for the *ayllus*, but for the most part he narrates in a calm and neutral tone, leaving it up to the reader to draw his or her own conclusions about Puquio's social groups and their role in the conflict over the bullfight. Moreover, the story of the bullfight in *Yawar Fiesta* is presented from the multiple perspectives of Puquio's different social groups as the narrator moves back and forth "between the worlds of whites, *mestizos*, and *comuneros*, civilians or police, Quechua or Spanish speakers, Andeans or costeños, Christianity and animism, reason and magic."[47] At times the narrator speaks for himself, describing landscapes and recounting local history, while at other moments he speaks in the voices and varied accents of the novel's collective protagonists, reproducing dialogue between them or providing one group's view of the others in a narrative voice approaching indirect interior monologue. The novel's social groups, therefore, are linguistically differentiated. As Mario Vargas Llosa points out, the narrator of *Yawar Fiesta* has "has an extremely fine ear capable of registering the differences of tone, accent, and pronunciation between social groups, and a stylistic ease that permits him to make the reader aware of which social group is speaking at any given moment.[48]

While virtually absent from *Broad and Alien is the World*, such linguistic differentiation is not uncommon in the *indigenista* genre. Enrique López Albújar or Jorge Icaza's short stories and novels, for example, are peppered with isolated Quechua words and phrases, and their indigenous characters speak a truncated, fragmentary Spanish. Arguedas, however, took a qualitatively different approach, as most critics have not failed to note. In "La novela y el problema de la expresión literaria en el Perú", an essay published in 1950 that accompanies most subsequent editions of *Yawar Fiesta*, Arguedas drew attention to his invention of a special version of Spanish based on Quechua syntax and pronunciation to represent in Spanish conversations indigenous characters would have had in Quechua. After a long struggle to find "the subtle disorderings that would make of Spanish . . . an adequate instrument" for representing indigenous speech, he created a version of Spanish based on "the Spanish words incorporated into Quechua and the elementary Spanish that some Indians are able to acquire *in their own villages*."[49]

As Sylvia Spitta has noted, the subtle disordering of Spanish by Quechua to which Arguedas refers includes

> the use of Quechua words; the elimination of articles; the disregard of Spanish concordance; the use of sentences constructions favoring the gerund; the loss of the pronominal form of the personal pronoun; the prolif-

eration of diminutives and their extension to adverbs and gerunds that normally do not take them; the phonetic confusion between *e* and *i* and between *o* and *u* and the indiscriminate use of formal and informal forms of address.[50]

Arguedas's narrator, though capable of reproducing Quechua dialogue in this manner, does not himself use this new literary language, which he reserves for Quechua-speaking characters primarily, though not exclusively (for the *mistis*, too, speak Quechua), the *comuneros*.[51] Antonio Cornejo Polar argues that this invented literary language sets Arguedas's works apart from previous *indigenista* narrative, in that his fiction not only defends indigenous interests but also assimilates some of the literary or aesthetic forms of its indigenous referent. In Arguedas's novels and short stories, and in *Yawar Fiesta* in particular, the Quechua language, more than just the referent, is also a source of literary creation.[52]

There is another, more neglected dimension to the role of Andean culture in *Yawar Fiesta*. Just as the Spanish language used in Arguedas's first novel is "subtly disordered" by Quechua syntax and pronunciation, the otherwise conventionally realist narrative as a whole is similarly "disordered" by the incorporation of Andean oral tradition. The Andean cosmology implicit in a legend Arguedas inserts at a crucial moment of the narrative serves as an alternative interpretive code which cross-cuts that of the novel's apparent social realism. Readings of *Yawar Fiesta* that limit themselves to the interpretive code of social realism easily lead to the conclusion that the novel constitutes a defense of an essential and unchanging indigenous tradition against the encroachments of a modernity defined exclusively in Western terms.[53] A reading that relies on Andean oral tradition as an interpretive code, however, produces the very different, if not contrary, conclusion that indigenous Andean culture is one source of a possible alternative modernity for Peru. Since the two codes are derived from two cultures in conflict, Arguedas's novel expresses at the level of narrative form something of the social conflicts of modernization that are its theme. *Yawar Fiesta*'s complexity and the scholarly interest it still attracts are due to the tension between these two interpretive codes.

A brief overview of the novel's structure may help clarify the relationship between its contrasting cultural codes. Through chapter 6 and in its final three chapters, *Yawar Fiesta* is a linear realist narrative, though not without references to indigenous beliefs, which at first seem to have little more than a descriptive, rather than an interpretive function. The first two chapters, indeed, provide a virtually ethnographic description of Puquio and a summary of its history which set up the ensuing conflict.[54] These are followed by four chapters on the tradition of the bullfight and the eruption of conflict over it. The concluding three chapters of the novel, chapters nine through eleven, continue the linear recounting of the escalating conflict and bring it to a climax (though not exactly a resolution) in the bullfight itself. Between chapters six and nine, however, the story of the bullfight is suspended in favor of extended accounts of two historical events, which, though they are related to the struggle over the bullfight, hardly seem essential to it.

The first of these is the narrative in chapter 7 of the *comuneros'* construction of a road from Puquio to the coast and of the consequences of this link for both Puquio and, especially, Lima. The *ayllus'* construction of the road demonstrates a capacity for self-transformation and national modernization that seems at odds with their defense, in the rest of the novel, of the apparently static Andean tradition of the bullfight. The novel's other digression into the past occurs in chapter 8, which opens with a legend about the mythical origins of a wild bull called Misitu and recounts a powerful *misti's* attempt to capture it some years before the narrative present of the 1930s. The Andean cosmology embedded in the account of the bull's origins, based on the indigenous oral tradition of the mythological serpent figure known as the *amaru*, provides the key to understanding one *ayllu's* ultimately successful capture of Misitu and their confrontation with the state in the subsequent bullfight as a reinvention of a dynamic cultural practice rather than a retreat into unchanging tradition. It also illuminates the meaning of and resonates with earlier references to indigenous beliefs in the apparently more straightforward, realist chapters of the novel. The Andean oral tradition of the *amaru*, discussed more fully below, links the bullfight and the struggle over it to the road-building episode, not as the latter's traditionalist opposite, but as a complementary demonstration of indigenous intervention in, rather than a rejection of, processes of modernization.

Though perhaps not as deeply permeated by Andean belief systems as some of Arguedas's later novels, *Yawar Fiesta* nevertheless deploys Andean cosmology at a crucial moment of the narrative to inflect the superficial or literal meaning of the conflict over the bullfight.[55] Through such narrative transculturation, *Yawar Fiesta* models, at the level of narrative structure, what is implicit in the struggle over the bullfight and its outcome: an alternative project of social transformation driven by and rooted in the dynamism and creative capacity of indigenous Andean culture. That is, much as Arguedas draws on Andean (oral) literary traditions to renew *indigenista* narrative form, the *comuneros* represented in *Yawar Fiesta* respond to a project of modernization imposed from above, not by retreating into a supposedly static indigenous tradition, but rather by transforming that tradition from within and opening the possibility of an alternative, Andean modernity. The key here is the narrative function of the bull, which cannot be understood without some knowledge of Andean traditions.

Bulls, Condors, and Social Conflict

Before turning to a more detailed analysis of *Yawar Fiesta* and the role of Andean culture in it, an introduction to the *turupukllay*, or Andean bull-fight, is in order. Bulls and bullfights were brought to Peru by the Spanish, but over time were thoroughly Andeanized by the native population, who adapted both the animal and the ritual to their own needs. The Andean bullfight differs from the Spanish one in that several bullfighters confront the bull at once. In addition, in some versions of the *turupukllay*, a condor is tied to the back of the bull to peck at the animal and enrage it. Both the bull and the bullfighters may be injured or killed, but the condor usually survives and is released. The *turupukllay* was quite common in Andean communities when Arguedas wrote *Yawar Fiesta* and remained a wide-spread practice well into the 1990s. It played and continues to play an important symbolic role in community life. The symbolism of the *turupukllay*, however, is a contested matter.

In a study of Andean bullfights that include both bulls and condors, Fanni Muñoz notes that "the most frequent interpretation suggests that these symbols make manifest the opposition between Hispanic culture and Andean culture."[56] The bull, introduced to the Andes by the Spanish, is taken to represent the Western, Hispanic culture imposed on Andean peoples by the conquest, while the condor, an animal native to the Andes, is identified with indigenous Andean culture. Consequently, the *turupukllay* dramatizes the confrontation between the two cultures that began with the conquest. However, as Muñoz is quick to point out, such an explanation may be too simplistic, for "the bull has been incorporated into the Andean world and is not necessarily a symbol of confrontation and opposition."[57]

Indeed, the Andean bullfight is open to multiple interpretations, which vary according to the social group doing the interpreting. Muñoz observes that, on the whole, indigenous peasants tend to see the *turupukllay* as a propitiatory ritual directed at the *apus*, or mountain gods. By means of the bullfight, the community seeks to please the *apus* and avoid their wrath in order to ensure a good crop. According to this interpretation, "the bull is a symbol of fertility, the condor a symbol of justice. Both belong to the Apu. The blood spilled during the afternoon bullfight is intended to quench 'the thirst of *pachamama* [mother earth]': the shedding of blood indicates a good year for the town."[58] This view is not generally shared by *mestizos*, who increasingly have come to control the bullfight in many parts of the Andes and interpret it as symbolic of their own hybrid identity:

> in recent decades the festival has been resignified as the [indigenous] peas-
> ants lost control of it. Changes in the economy, in particular a decline in the
> importance of agriculture, and in Andean society have resulted in a larger
> role for *mestizos* in the organization of the festival. For them the bullfight
> is not a propitiatory ritual, but rather a performance of the encounter and
> confrontation between the Andes (the condor) and the West (the bull). This
> conflict is resolved through a *mestizaje* whose symbolism could not be more
> dramatic: the shedding of both Andean and Western blood.[59]

As Andean communities have been integrated into the national economy, the importance in those communities of traditional agriculture, practiced by the indigenous population, has declined relative to that of commerce, in which *mestizos* commonly serve as intermediaries. With the growth in their economic power, argues Muñoz, *mestizos* assumed a more prominent role in the *turupukllay* and began to interpret the festival as a validation of their new status in the community. In the Andes, the bull-ring is one of the arenas in which debates over cultural identity and struggles for economic and political power are played out.[60]

Given the contested nature of the *turupukllay*, it is not surprising that Arguedas should use it as a means of representing the social conflicts of modernization in the southern Andes. However, his fictional version of the Andean bullfight diverges from those described above in several respects. Puquio's *turupukllay*, for example, no longer features a condor, a lack lamented by the *mistis*, who nostalgically recall the bullfights of twenty years before:

> when they used to tie a condor to the back of the wildest bull, to make him
> even more furious. With the condor pecking him, the bull would roll the
> Indians around as if it were nothing at all. And then the townsmen [*vecinos*]
> would go in on horseback and kill the bull . . . At the end of the fiesta they
> would sew streamers onto the condor's wings and turn him loose, amid
> shouting and singing. . . . Months and months later, up in the high country,
> that condor would still be flying from snowy peak to snowy peak, trailing
> his streamers.[61]

The memory clearly marks the *turupukllay* as an evolving social prac-
tice rather than a static tradition. Unlike the changes described by Muñoz, however, this evolution is associated in the novel with an increase, not a decrease, of indigenous control over the bullfight. In the *turupukllay* of the narrative present, only the *comuneros* enter the bullring, while the *mistis* have been reduced to spectator status and no longer take an active part in Puquio's most important public ritual. In addition, the *comuneros*

in *Yawar Fiesta* use dynamite against the bull. This appears to be Arguedas's invention, for according to Rodrigo Montoya, an anthropologist raised in Puquio, "the killing of the bull by means of a stick of dynamite hurled by an Indian bullfighter is a fiction, pure and simple. Such a custom has never existed in any part of the Peruvian Andes."[62] The bullfight in the novel is clearly more than an ethnographic reproduction of actual practices, and its interpretation requires an analysis not only of how closely it corresponds to social reality, but also of its relationships to other elements of the text.

Urban Form as Social Structure and Colonial History

The story of the bullfight in *Yawar Fiesta* is developed in several stages, each one characterized by a new alignment of the social groups who are the novel's protagonists. Puquio is initially described as divided between a *misti* elite, the town's four indigenous *ayllus* (K'ayau, Pichk'achuri, Chaupi, and K'ollana), and an intermediate group of *mestizos*. In its opening pages, the novel maps this social hierarchy topographically. The *mistis*, colonizers who dispossessed the *ayllus* of much of their land to become the town's dominant social group, occupy the crest of the ridge on which Puquio is built. The colonized *ayllus* were left with the lower slopes of the ridge, while *mestizos* inhabit its middle elevations. However, because Puquio was colonized rather late (due to a lack of mines in the area), the *mistis* encountered strong resistance from an already established indigenous town, which they were unable to make fully theirs. They failed to impose the Spanish language and Western culture, and instead learned Quechua and adopted many elements of indigenous Andean culture. The traces of this history, and the limits to the *mistis'* dominance, are also reflected in Puquio's urban topography, for the center of *misti* power, the town plaza that houses the institutions of both church and state, is located away from the center, on the edge of town. The *mistis* succeeded in forcing their main street, the jirón Bolívar, through the center of Puquio, but were obliged to build their plaza on the outskirts of town. The *ayllus'* resistance allowed Puquio's original indigenous inhabitants to hold on to more of their land and a greater degree of autonomy and power than was the case in other parts of the southern Andes.

This rather complex relationship between *mistis* and *comuneros* is evident in the preparations for the annual *yawar fiesta* and its culmination, the *turupukllay*. In early July, K'ayau, one of the town's four indigenous *ayllus*, secures permission from don Julián Aranguena, one of Puquio's most powerful and abusive *misti* landowners, to capture a wild bull on his property for use in the upcoming *turupukllay*. The bull, known as Misitu, is a particularly savage beast of mythical proportions, and

51

K'ayau's announcement that they will capture it inspires both awe and excitement on the part of *comuneros* and *mistis* alike. Though their shared enthusiasm for the *turupukllay* does not dissolve the antagonism between the two groups, it does unite them in opposition to another set of protagonists in the conflict over the bullfight: government officials posted in Puquio. If at the beginning of the novel Puquio is split along the colonial divide between *comuneros* and *mistis*, in this second stage the regional culture of the *sierra*, rooted in indigenous traditions partially shared by the *mistis*, is opposed to the Westernized *costeño* culture promoted by the national government through its local representatives: the Subprefect, the judge, and the captain.

For the Subprefect and his colleagues, all of them *costeños*, the bullfight is "a savage custom", an expression of *serrano* barbarism that has no place in the official culture of the nation.[63] For both the *comuneros* and the *mistis*, on the other hand, it is a defining element of their identity, one which differentiates both groups from the *costeño* officials. As the *mistis* explain to the newly appointed and rather skeptical Subprefect, the bullfight is even more significant for them than the patriotic occasion it nominally commemorates: "Without the *turupukllay*, the twenty-eighth [national independence day] would be like any other day."[64] Their regional identity, rooted in cultural traditions controlled by the *comuneros*, takes precedence over their identification with the nation. The *mistis* may despise the *comuneros*, but they also have much in common with them: Andean music, dance, and cultural traditions like the *turupukllay*. Without negating the earlier colonial divide between *comuneros* and *mistis*, the narrative superimposes upon it a new opposition between the Andean traditions of the *sierra* and the official national culture of the *costa*.

The Bullfight and Modernization

Puquio's social divisions are complicated further when the Subprefect announces a government edict banning the *turupukllay*. Ostensibly motivated by the state's paternalistic concern for the welfare of indigenous bullfighters, who are often injured or even killed in the ring, this "civilizing" initiative is resisted by the *ayllus* and splits the *misti* elite. Some of the latter, like the Mayor, don Antenor, repress their enthusiasm for local tradition and support the edict in order to curry favor with the Subprefect. Others, like the *gamonal* don Julián Aranguena and the merchant don Pancho Jiménez, side with the *ayllus* because they see the *turupukllay* as crucial to their own identity. Their opposition to the state, however, ultimately leads to the arrest of both Aranguena and Jiménez, who are imprisoned "like Indians", the first *mistis* ever to see the inside of the local jail.[65] This alone gives some indication of the magnitude of the social change occurring in Puquio.

Yet another social group is drawn into the conflict when the Mayor and the town council resolve to substitute a more "civilized" Spanish version of the bullfight for the "barbaric" Andean one. In order to contract a professional bullfighter in the capital, the town council is obliged to call upon the members of the Centro Unión Lucanas, an organization of indigenous and *mestizo* migrants from Puquio and the surrounding province of Lucanas who now live in Lima. The urban migrants of the Centro Unión Lucanas see the *turupukllay* as just another form of oppression, a ritual of colonial power relations in which indigenous bullfighters get themselves killed for the entertainment of the *misti* elite. Inspired by Mariátegui's socialist *indigenismo*, the members of the Centro Unión Lucanas welcome the government edict as an opportunity for a tactical alliance with the state against Puquio's *mistis*. They contract a professional bullfighter in Lima, a Spaniard, and return to their home town hoping to assume leadership of the indigenous masses. At this stage of the conflict, Puquio is divided along political lines, between, on the one hand, the state, the "modernizing" faction of the *misti* elite, and the urban *indigenistas* of the Centro Unión Lucanas, and, on the other, the *ayllus* and "traditionalist" *mistis* like Arangüena and Jiménez.

Each of these alliances, however, is internally divided. The Subprefect seeks to enforce the edict only to advance his career and be transferred out of Puquio as soon as possible. He has nothing but contempt for his *misti* allies, who in turn support him only to preserve their power and not because they believe in the state's civilizing initiative. The *indigenista* migrants' immediate objective is to use the Subprefect to destroy the *misti* elite, a goal they partially attain by having Arangüena thrown in jail. Their ultimate aim, however, is to position themselves as the revolutionary vanguard of the indigenous masses in order to lead the latter in a struggle for state power. On the other side, the shopkeeper don Pancho Jiménez, who maintains cordial relations with the *ayllus*, and the *gamonal* don Julián Arangüena, who exploits his indigenous peons mercilessly, oppose the government edict because their own identity as *mistis* is largely dependent on Andean traditions controlled by the *ayllus*. As don Pancho explains to the Subprefect, "the Indians are the town, the real Puquio."[66]

The *ayllus*, for their part, resist the edict in order to defend their traditions, but also to maintain control of a festival from which they derive a degree of symbolic power because of the *mistis* dependence on it. The *mistis*' enjoyment of the music and dances performed by the *ayllus* during the *yawar fiesta*, for example, intensifies the *comuneros*' sense of their own power and agency and reinforces their hostility toward Puquio's elite: "Watching the [elite] citizens' faces, the *comuneros* from the four *ayllus* had a ball; the rejoicing was the same for all the Indians of Puquio. And inside themselves they taunted the *mistis*."[67] The struggle for power in Puquio is waged at least in part on the terrain of culture, one of the few areas of social life in which the *ayllus* are dominant. Because it would force them to relinquish control over Puquio's most important public ritual, the government edict implies for the *comuneros* increased subordination to both the state and the *mistis*.

Despite their resistance, the *comuneros* are ultimately talked into complying with the ban on the *turupukllay*. Though they capture the bull Misitu and bring it to Puquio, the Subprefect and his allies prevail as the *ayllus*' epic demonstration of collective agency serves only to deliver the mythological animal to the authorities for a Spanish-style bullfight. Things go awry for the state's civilizing project, however, when Misitu turns out to be too powerful for the professional bullfighter contracted in Lima. As the Spaniard flees the ring, the Mayor calls in the indigenous bullfighters, who rush at the bull with sticks of dynamite in hand. The novel ends here, at the height of the action, with one indigenous bull-fighter gored, but still standing, and the bull staggering from wounds inflicted by the dynamite. The narrative seems to revert to a cultural division between *sierra* and *costa* as the Mayor's alliance with the Subprefect breaks down in the excitement of the moment. The state's authority is undermined by the apparent lapse back into "barbaric" regional tradition, while the returned migrants of the Centro Unión Lucanas find themselves isolated from the masses they had hoped to lead. Puquio's indigenous *ayllus* seem to get their way, at least in part, but so does the *misti* elite, including its "modernizing" faction, whose support for the government edict was never more than cynical opportunism.

What is one to make of this rather enigmatic ending? Mario Vargas Llosa, for one, claims that it is difficult "to imagine a more *conservative* work of fiction than *Yawar Fiesta*, in spite of its denunciation of and indignation at the abuses inflicted by the *mistis* on the Indians."[68] The novel, he claims, is animated by a desire "to freeze time and detain the course of history" and amounts to "an argument against the modernization of the Andean people."[69] On this reading, the survival of indigenous culture in *Yawar Fiesta* is premised on the *comuneros*' continued subordination to the *misti* elite. *Misti* oppression, in other words, is preferable to state-directed modernization because the former is compatible with indigenous culture, which the *mistis* partially share, while the latter implies its destruction. However, Vargas Llosa's reading fails to capture the novel's complexity, for these are not the only options presented in it.

The state's modernizing project is clearly the loser in *Yawar Fiesta*, but the *ayllus*' subversion of the government edict does not necessarily imply an embrace of the *mistis*. Though it is the Mayor who calls the indigenous bullfighters into the ring, their eagerness to enter is not a form of submission to *misti* authority nor does it negate the underlying antagonism between *comuneros* and *mistis*. In rejecting the state's attempt to determine the form of the bullfight, the *ayllus* do not reject change itself, only change imposed from above. Indeed, even before the government edict is announced, the *ayllus* themselves begin to transform their own cultural traditions. Their capture of Misitu, for example, is not a repetition of local customs, but rather a departure from them, for this is no ordinary bull. The indigenous bullfighters' final confrontation with Misitu is likewise no simple return to tradition, but rather a symbolic engagement with the changes wrought by modernization, in which the *comuneros* seek an active role.

Andean Traditions of Change

The *turupukllay* in *Yawar Fiesta* is associated not only with tradition, but also with social change. The *comuneros'* capture of the bull Misitu, for example, is prefigured in a key episode that serves as the novel's clearest reference to modernization: the construction in the 1920s of a road linking Puquio to the coastal city of Nazca. The two events are compared explicitly when Puquio's *mistis* evoke the road construction as a precedent for the seemingly impossible capture of the mythological bull: "they're going to bring Misitu, Señor Subprefect! Our Indians are determined. . . . Now you know the road you came on was made by the Indians in twenty-eight days."[70] Though they are bitter enemies of the *mistis*, the urban migrants of the Centro Unión Lucanas explain K'ayau's ultimately successful capture of Misitu in virtually the same terms: "They've done it out of pride, to show the whole world how strong they are, how strong the *ayllu* can be when it wants to. That's how they built the road to Nazca."[71] In addition, it is no coincidence that the road construction of the 1920s starts in early July and culminates a few weeks later on July 28, national independence day, exactly the same time period over which the conflict over the bullfight occurs a decade later. The construction of the road and Misitu's capture are both identified as epic feats of communal labor that demonstrate the *ayllus'* power and collective agency.

However, although they are equated in this respect, the two events seem to bear contrary relationships to modernization. As Peter Elmore has observed, "the two undertakings share a similar rationality, that of communal labor, and belie the oligarchic stereotype of the melancholic and passive Indian. A divergence is notable, however, in the significance of these two achievements: the road to Nazca implies a modernizing intent that is lacking in the traditional bullfight."[72] And yet, as Elmore is quick to point out, "even this distinction turns out to be less clear than one might initially think."[73] The two epic feats turn out to have more in common than is at first apparent. In the construction of the road, the *ayllus* draw on their cultural traditions to initiate change of far-reaching consequences. In capturing the bull, they transform those cultural traditions themselves.

The construction of the road is narrated in chapter 7, the capture of Misitu in chapter 10. What allows one to identify both as examples of social change initiated by the *ayllus* is the intervention of Andean oral tradition in a brief account of Misitu's mythical origins, which appears at the beginning of chapter 8, immediately after the road construction episode. Chapters seven and eight seem to provide little more than background information that at first appears incidental to the main plot about the conflict over the bullfight, yet they interrupt the linear unfolding of that plot with the only temporal flashbacks in the novel.[74] Why call attention in this fashion to what appear to be detours from the main narrative? The placement of these successive chapters suggests that they are more central to the novel than their contents would seem to indicate, and that those contents bear close scrutiny. The ostensible purpose of the road construction episode in chapter 7, for example, is to introduce the urban migrants of the Centro Unión Lucanas and to explain their presence in Lima. However, the space devoted to the road construction and the resulting migration to Lima, and the detail in which both are narrated suggest that this is not the chapter's only or even principal function. Rather, Arguedas uses the road construction project to represent indigenous tradition as a source of social change. Similarly, the account of Misitu's mythical origins in chapter 8 would seem to be little more than a flourish of local color. However, it marks K'ayau's capture of the bull as a revision rather than a repetition of tradition. The symbolic importance of the bull from the perspective of the *ayllus* is crucial to understanding how Arguedas uses indigenous Andean culture to revise the established forms of realist narrative associated with the *indigenista* genre in the first decades of the twentieth century.

In *Yawar Fiesta*, the road from Puquio to Nazca is not a government project, nor is it an initiative of the Puquio elite. Indeed, "the town's [elite] citizens had never even dared to think about a highway from Nazca, in spite of the fact that they were the ones who would benefit most from it. It was impossible."[75] The *ayllus* themselves decide to build the road, not because they seek economic advantage from it, but rather as a competition with the rival town of Coracora, the capital of a neighboring province, to see who can complete a road to the coast first. Working collectively, the indigenous communities of Puquio and the surrounding province of Lucanas triumph over their rivals by constructing

150 km (or 300 km, the novel gives both figures) of road across rugged terrain in just 28 days.[76] Moreover, the *comuneros* of Lucanas province approach the road building not as an onerous task, but as a *minga*, a pre-Columbian Andean tradition of collective labor that still exists today:

> They worked from dawn until well into the night. And from the passes, from the valleys, from the little farms and villages that are in the mountains, people heard the songs of the Andamarkas, of the Aukaras, of the Chakrallas. At night they played the flute and sang by *ayllus*, 100, 200, 500 at a time, depending on the towns. They lit bonfires of brushwood and dry grass by the roadside near the places where the tools were kept; they sang holiday, carnival, and *k'adihua* melodies. . . . Little by little, as the moon was entering the sky, the *comuneros* would grow quiet, they'd lie down on the ground, by the bonfires, to sleep. When the *ayllus'* song had ended, the song of the *pukupuku* birds could be heard clearly, on all the mountains, and the sound of the river would rise up from the bottom of the valley.[77]

The language itself here appears infused with indigenous tradition. The presence of untranslated Quechua words (of which there are several more in the Spanish edition) and the rhythm of repeated series of places, peoples, plants, and types of music associated with community festivals give the passage an oral quality, while references to decimal-based Andean social organization ("they played the flute and sang by *ayllus*, 100, 200, 500 at a time") and the relationship of the social to the natural world, which appears unperturbed by the *comuneros'* construction project, draw indigenous culture into the Spanish text. Indeed, it is indigenous tradition which facilitates the new link to the coast, for only by treating the work as a kind of festival are the *comuneros* able to complete the road to Nazca in record time.

The *ayllus'* feat earns the admiration of the newspapers in Lima, not generally inclined to take note of happenings in the hinterland, and is soon imitated by other indigenous communities throughout the southern Andes. Inspired by the *comuneros'* example, the state and *misti* elites subsequently launch road-building projects it had never previously occurred to them to undertake. These, however, stand in sharp contrast to the *ayllus'* construction of the Puquio to Nazca road:

> Finally, the national government remembered some of the towns, sending engineers, money, and tools. Then the hacienda owners fought amongst themselves to have the roads pass through their farms. And the highways that the engineers planned would almost always curve around and go down into the valleys, breaking through the crags and rocky places for months on end, sometimes for years, so that the road might enter the important

people's haciendas. The people in the towns began to lose their confidence in, their enthusiasm for the highways. From then on, road building was a business. And the people from the towns worked as day laborers, or because they were forced to do so.[78]

Here again the language is adapted to its referent and underlines the contrast between the *comuneros'* initiative, rooted in indigenous traditions of collectivism, and the state's belated efforts, motivated by the potential for individual profit. Gone are the oral rhythm and the words in Quechua, the references to indigenous social organization and Andean culture's harmonious relationship to the natural world. In their place, the narrator deploys a more terse style to describe the state's authoritarian project of modernization.

The passage alludes to the government-sponsored road building boom facilitated by the Leguía regime's *Ley de Conscripción Vial* of 1920, which authorized the involuntary conscription of all adult males for unpaid work on road construction projects.[79] Leguía's initiative is rendered in *Yawar Fiesta* not as a public works project intended to benefit the nation as a whole, but rather as a business venture driven by narrow private interests. Road construction for profit, moreover, compares unfavorably in every respect with the collective, disinterested labor of the *comuneros*. The state-sponsored roads, for example, are drawn out and inefficient projects because they meander from one *misti* landowner's property to the next, while the work itself is depicted as a form of exploitation rather than a creative activity.

As Elmore notes, the contrast between the road built by the *comuneros* of Lucanas and those built by the government presents two competing projects of modernization in Peru: "the text opposes a modernization generated from below, by the active will of popular sectors, to a forced modernization imposed from above."[80] In *Yawar Fiesta*, unlike in the vast majority of *indigenista* novels, social change does not come only from the outside and its consequences for the indigenous population are not inevitably negative. Change is initiated here from within indigenous communities, and the modernization effected by the *comuneros* is more efficient and democratic than that promoted by the government. Moreover, indigenous communities are shown to be capable not only of self-transformation but also of transforming Lima and the nation, for the roads made possible by indigenous initiative and labor facilitate Andean migration to the coast.

As a result of this migration, Lima comes to more accurately reflect the ethnic composition and cultural traditions of the nation as a whole. *Yawar Fiesta* is perhaps the first Peruvian novel to register Andean migrants' arrival in and cultural transformation of the national capital:

Once again, after 600 years, perhaps after 1,000 years, Andean people were going down to the coast in multitudes. While various governments were building four-lane, asphalt avenues and having "American" buildings constructed, while the newspapers and magazines were publishing pretty European-style poems, and gentlemen in derby hats and frock-coats were responding to invitations from the national government, embassies, and clubs, the highlanders [*serranos*], Indians, half-*mistis*, and "*chalos*", were coming down from the uplands with their *charangos*, their *bandurrias*, their *kirkinchos*, and their Indian Spanish. They'd buy or appropriate some land near the city. There they'd remain, living in roofless enclosures, brush arbors, and mud brick houses, without façades or running water. . . . And in their houses, in their brush arbors protected with adobe walls, illuminated by little kerosene lanterns as in Puquio, Aukará, Chalhuanca, or in Masma and Huancavelica, the highlanders would hold their *fiestas*, with *huayno* and *bandurrias*, with harps and *quenas*.[81]

Arguedas here contrasts the dependent, imitative, and ultimately false modernity of the *criollo* elite, which José Guillermo Nugent terms a "counter-modernity", to the image of the urban Andean fiesta in order to indicate the *serrano* migrants' active engagement with their new environment.[82] Rather than mere victims of the *criollo* "counter-modernity" theorized by Nugent, the *serranos* in Lima are represented as producers of their own alternative modernity and public sphere.[83]

Lima had been a *criollo* stronghold until the 1920s road construction boom. Indeed, for most urban *criollos* it had been the nation itself, for few of them ventured beyond the capital unless it was to go to Paris or New York. Lima, and Peru, would never be the same again, and Arguedas, as a provincial migrant himself, was one of the first to understand the implications of Andean migration for national identity and power relations.[84] The vitality, creativity, and collective power demonstrated by the *comuneros* of Lucanas province in the road building episode and the transformation of Lima recounted in chapter 7 express Arguedas's belief that indigenous peoples could, by drawing on their own cultural traditions, play an active role in shaping a modern and more democratic nation. The *misti* elite, on the other hand, is represented as decidedly more passive and dependent on foreign cultural models.

A similar pattern is repeated in the capture of the bull. In chapter 8, the *misti* landowner Julián Arangüena and his *mestizo* ranch hands fail to capture Misitu. In chapter 10, which takes place some years later, the *comuneros* of K'ayau succeed where the *misti* had failed and bring Misitu to Puquio for the independence day bullfight. The significance of the *comuneros*' feat is alluded to by the description of Misitu's mythical origins at the beginning of chapter 8. The indigenous people of K'oñani, known as the *punarunas* because they live, like Misitu, on the high *puna* plateau above Puquio, recount how the bull emerged from a mountain lake after a violent storm:

> The K'oñanis said that he had come out of Torkok'ocha, that he had neither father nor mother. That one night, when all of the old people on the puna were still babies, a storm had fallen upon the lake; that all of the lightning bolts had struck the water . . . And that at daybreak, with the dawn light, when the storm was dying down . . . a whirlpool formed in the middle of the lake by the big island, and in the middle of the whirlpool Misitu appeared, bellowing and tossing his head.[85]

As Fanni Muñoz notes, the passage closely resembles Andean legends about the *amaru*, a mythological Andean serpent figure also said to live at the bottom of mountain lakes.[86] The description of Misitu's mythical origins draws on Arguedas's ethnographic research, in which he documented the displacement of the *amaru* by the bull in Andean culture.[87] Indeed, a collection of oral traditions he co-edited with Francisco Izquierdo Ríos in 1947 includes legends about the *amaru* that closely resemble the fictional account of Misitu's origins in *Yawar Fiesta*.[88] The incorporation of Andean oral tradition into the novel here is more than an ethnographic detail, for according to Ricardo González Vigil, in Andean mythology "the appearance of the *amaru* is associated with cataclysms, announcements of great cosmic changes."[89] The *amaru*, Martin Lienhard confirms, "always appears in moments of cosmic crisis, of *pachackutiy*."[90] As an *amaru*, Misitu serves as a portent of a twentieth-century *pachakutiy*, which, in the context of the novel (the construction of roads, the imposition of central state authority over outlying regions), may be identified with the transformation effected by modernization in the Andes.

The allusion to the *amaru* in the description of the bull's mythical origins echoes the earlier use of serpent imagery to describe Puquio's urban form. In chapter 1, for example, the most visible manifestations of the *mistis*' presence in and domination of Puquio, the plaza de armas and the jirón Bolívar, are compared to the head and body of a snake: "Girón Bolívar is like a snake that cuts the town in two; the Plaza de Armas is like the head of the snake; there are the teeth, the eyes, the head, the tongue, jail, livestock pound, Subprefecture, Court; the body of the snake is Girón Bolivar."[91] The *ayllus*, one might recall, were dispossessed by the *mistis*, whose plaza and main street are the material traces of their conquest of Puquio. The jirón Bolívar is perceived as the tail and body of an alien creature whose head houses the repressive institutions responsible for the *ayllus*' subordination. The passage associates the colonial history embedded in the town's urban form with the mythological Andean serpent figure, thereby identifying the *mistis*' colonization of Puquio as a cataclysmic change.

The *comuneros'* response to the sight of the jirón Bolívar suggests that, despite their current subordination to *misti* rule, they have not resigned themselves to the social hierarchy imposed by the conquest:

> That's how life is on Girón Bolívar and in the neighborhoods. That's how the *misti* strangers came to Puquio. But when the Puquio people look down from above . . . when they see Girón Bolívar gleaming like a snake's back among the tiled roofs of the *ayllus*, they exclaim disgustedly:
> "Atatauya Bolívar street!"
> When the Indians look down and speak that way, in their eyes another hope glows, their real soul shines forth. They laugh loudly; they may be furious, too.[92]

In the image of the old cataclysm of the conquest, represented by the *amaru* embedded in Puquio's urban topography, the *comuneros* see the possibility of a new transformation, of which they seek to be the principal protagonists. In *Yawar Fiesta*, the figure of the *amaru* serves to link two key moments in Andean history: the colonial subjugation of the indigenous population after the conquest and the period of rapid modernization in the first decades of the twentieth century. The juxtaposition of the two is no accident, for the changes wrought in the Andean world by early twentieth-century modernization were comparable in scope to those produced by the conquest.[93] By capturing Misitu, the *comuneros* of K'ayau symbolically intervene in the twentieth-century transformation of their community.

Not all of Puquio's indigenous population is prepared to participate in this venture. The *punarunas* of Koñani, for example, fear Misitu and regard the mythological animal as an *auki*, a mountain god. They spread the legend of Misitu as well as their fear to others, including the *comuneros* of Puquio: "They had always used Misitu to frighten the Indians from Puquio."[94] From the narrator's perspective, the punarunas' version of Misitu's origins is a legend, for "Misitu was not from Koñani . . . . He had come to the Koñani punas when he was already a grown bull, escaping from another ranch . . . . And all the while, year after year, in the solitude of the woods, he kept getting wilder."[95] Nonetheless, the legend instills fear in those who believe it, fear not just of Misitu's fierceness, but of the cosmic forces of cataclysmic change incarnated in the bull/*amaru*. The *comuneros* of K'ayau break with such fear, though not with indigenous traditions as such, when they seek permission from don Julián Arangüena to capture Misitu. In reply to the *gamonal's* doubts, based on his own previous failure to capture the bull, the *varayoks* of K'ayau insist that nothing is impossible for the *ayllu*. Misitu, they argue, is no more than an especially large and fierce *sall'ka*, or wild bull: "Magic, magic, Pichk'achuri's saying *taytay*! Isn't any magic Don Jolián. . . . That's

61

a lie about magic. Misitu's nothing but a big savage, mad right down to his heart."[96] Their disbelief aligns them with the narrator and identifies their capture of the wild bull as a transformation of tradition.

The narrative here adds another level to the conflict over the bullfight by underlining the division between two indigenous groups: the punarunas of K'oñani, who are peons on one of don Julián Aranguena's properties, and the *comuneros* of K'ayau, who have held on to their land and thus preserved a greater degree of autonomy. The contrast between the two groups' perceptions of Misitu anticipates an argument Arguedas would develop in his anthropological essays of the 1950s:

> Indigenous communities that were able to preserve a certain degree of economic independence . . . have evolved differently than those which were dispossessed of their lands or were impoverished to the extreme of having to supplement their economy through the unavoidable performance of personal service.[97]

Indigenous communities that, like K'oñani, had been totally subordinated by *misti* elites, found themselves ill-prepared to deal with the changes wrought by modernization. Their servitude had isolated them from the world and frozen them in a defensive posture that made them much more fragile and vulnerable to change than those communities, such as K'ayau, whose economic independence had permitted them an ongoing engagement with outside influences and better prepared them to confront the forces of modernization. As Sylvia Spitta explains, "Areas that had remained accessible since the Conquest to influences from the West developed what he [Arguedas] called 'antibodies' to modernization, whereas isolated regions where Andean and Spaniard had remained opposed over the centuries disintegrated with the advent of new technologies."[98]

The *punarunas* of K'oñani oppose all attempts to capture Misitu, whether by don Julián or by K'ayau, because they fear the consequences. For them, Misitu incarnates cosmic forces best not tampered with and in any case not subject to human control. Their fear and passivity in the face of the cataclysmic change represented for them by Misitu leaves the *punarunas* of K'oñani unable to respond effectively to the modernization occurring around them. The *comuneros* of K'ayau, by contrast, prove more capable of taking the initiative in a time of rapid change. By capturing Misitu, the *comuneros* of K'ayau break with the fear inspired by the *amaru* legend. They demonstrate that the cosmic forces incarnated in the bull/*amaru* are in fact subject to human control, that resignation is not the only possible response to cataclysmic change. By transforming one of their own cultural traditions, they dramatically assert their agency at precisely the moment in which the state would deny it to them.

The urban migrants of the Centro Unión Lucanas, however,

(mis)understand the capture of Misitu as a step toward a wholesale repudiation of indigenous tradition: "They've killed an *auki*! And the day they kill all the *aukis* who are tormenting their minds, the day they become what we are now—'renegade "*chalos*"', as Don Julián says—we shall lead this country to a glory no one can imagine."[99] This interpretation leads them to believe, mistakenly, that having "killed an auki" (rather than resignifying a traditional belief), the *comuneros* will also consent to the Spanish-style bullfight. What the members of the Centro Unión Lucanas fail to grasp is that while the *comuneros* gain greater control of their destiny by capturing Misitu, submitting to the authority of the state would be an abdication of such agency. The K'ayau transform their traditions but do not renounce them. To capture Misitu, they rely not only on the combined strength of *ayllu* members, but also on prayers and offerings to the *apu* K'arwarasu, a mountain deity. For the *comuneros* of K'ayau, as well as for the narrator, there is no contradiction between modernity and indigenous tradition. Rather, the latter is a means of intervening in and shaping the former.

In the bullfight itself, the fact that the *ayllus* again succeed where both the *mistis* and the state had failed only underlines their agency *vis-à-vis* dominant groups and institutions. While Misitu may not be an *amaru* from the narrator's perspective, and is not considered one by the professional bullfighter contracted in Lima, its powers are more than sufficient to drive the Spaniard from the ring. The *comuneros* in any case stood little to gain from the switch to the purportedly more "civilized" Spanish version of the bullfight, which would have deprived them of their central role in Puquio's social life and further subordinated them to state authority, while leaving the power of the *mistis* as a class (though not necessarily all individuals within it) essentially intact. The *comuneros* of K'ayau may no longer believe in Misitu's mythical origins, but through the capture of the bull and in the bullfight they demonstrate to those who still do, the *punarunas* of Koñani, Puquio's other three *ayllus*, and perhaps even its *mestizos* and *mistis*, the possibility of controlling the cosmic forces represented by the bull.

Arguedas's fictional addition of dynamite to the bullfight suggests, moreover, the explosive nature of indigenous agency while at the same time linking the *turupukllay* to the theme of modernization. Dynamite is a modern technology used in mining and road construction in the Andes, one which would be pressed into service to great effect against the Peruvian state a half century later by the guerrillas of the Shining Path. By using dynamite, the *comuneros* avail themselves of modern means to contain and channel the forces represented by Misitu. Modern technology, nonetheless, is combined with indigenous tradition, for the bullfighters also draw strength from the Andean music that accompanies the *turupukllay*, in particular the singing of the women. The indigenous women's singing not only encourages their own men, but also unnerves the Spanish bullfighter and contributes to his indecorous flight from the ring. Moreover, in one of the final paragraphs of the novel, their song seems to have the power to clear the dust raised by a dynamite blast: "A dynamite blast went off at that moment, near the bull. The dust that swirled up in a whirlwind in the ring darkened the arena. The *wak'ra-pukus* played an attack melody and the women stood up to sing, divining where the ground of the arena was. The dust cleared, as if dissipated by the song."[100] In its final lines, the novel appears to suggest that indigenous tradition can serve as a guide through the confusion of modernization.

The bullfight in *Yawar Fiesta*, like the more obvious example of the road construction episode, is a representation of an alternative project of modernization generated from within indigenous Andean culture. The road construction that abruptly interrupts the main plot about the bullfight near the middle of the novel alerts the reader that this ostensibly simple story about a local tradition may be more complex than it first appears. Close attention to the road construction episode and to the description of the bull Misitu, which immediately follows it, reveals the Andean cultural code that crosscuts the narrative's apparent realism. The intervention of Andean oral tradition symbolically links the road building and the bullfight as expressions of indigenous Andeans' capacity for both self and national transformation as participants in the definition and direction of Peru's modernization. In both form and content, *Yawar Fiesta* is resolutely oriented toward the future, not the past. It is no retreat into timeless indigenous tradition, as Vargas Llosa would have it, nor is it content with existing literary forms. Arguedas's first novel, rather, is a transcultural narrative about the dilemmas and conflicts of social change in a society built upon the colonial divide. Unlike other *indigenista* novels of the period, including *Broad and Alien is the World*, *Yawar Fiesta* does not rely exclusively on the narrative forms of the dominant culture of the colonizers to represent and defend the interests of the colonized. Rather, it incorporates elements of the colonized culture to reproduce, at the level of narrative structure, the agency of indigenous people in the social conflicts of modernization which are the novel's theme.

2

FROM DEVELOPMENT THEORY TO *PACHAKUTIY*

José María Arguedas's Anthropology and Fiction in the 1950s

The attempts at radical social change between 1915 and 1932 were followed by nearly three decades of renewed oligarchic rule in Peru, interrupted only by José Bustamante y Rivera's short-lived reformist government of 1945–8. According to Peter Kláren, Bustamante y Rivera attempted "to replace the oligarchical-military rule of the past two decades with a genuinely democratic government, based on social justice, and in this way to forestall what he saw as the possibility of a violent revolutionary upheaval."[1] However, he was not in office long enough to effect lasting change, for conservative forces soon regained power in a military coup led by General Manuel Odría, which "closed a cycle in which a reorientation of economic policy toward industrialization and income redistribution had been attempted."[2] Under Odría's eight-year dictatorship (1948–56), Peru accelerated the pace of modernization and intensified its traditional dependence on US capital. Modernization, however, went hand in hand with the defense of semi-feudal landowners' properties in the Andes and the repression of popular opposition in both the city and in the countryside.[3] The corrupting, demoralizing effect on Peruvian society of the Odría dictatorship would later be fictionalized by a distant relative of Bustamante y Rivera's, Mario Vargas Llosa, in the novel *Conversación en La Catedral / Conversation in The Cathedral* (1970).

Despite Odría's deference to the *gamonal* class, the proportion of the national economy controlled by *sierra* landowners declined during his rule. Export-led growth, industrialization, and urbanization benefitted more modern, capitalist sectors of the economy, whose power grew relative to that of the *gamonales*.[4] By the time Odría fell in 1956, *sierra* landowners were no longer in as strong a position as before to defend their properties from indigenous peasant mobilization.[5] This, along with the easing of repression that accompanied the return to civilian rule, led in the late 1950s to a resurgence of indigenous struggles for land throughout the Andes.[6] Known as land recuperations by the indigenous communities and hacienda peons who participated in them, and land invasions by *gamonales* and the state, there were more than 400 such confrontations between 1956 and 1964.[7] The rising wave of unrest in the Andes, combined with the triumph of the Cuban revolution in 1959, would spark a renewal of the Peruvian Left in the 1960s. I examine literary representations of these conflicts over land in chapter 3.

In this chapter I will analyze the works José María Arguedas produced during the 1950s. These include numerous anthropological articles and a limited number of literary works, through which may be traced his evolving views on the consequences of rapid modernization for indigenous Andean cultures. In these years, capitalist modernization in the Andes produced a complex confrontation between three social groups: capitalist interests, semi-feudal landowners, and the indigenous population. Capitalism promised to liberate the latter from feudal bondage, but at the price of their cultural assimilation. Arguedas, concerned with both the liberation of indigenous Andeans from oppression and with their cultural survival, struggled to find a way to reconcile what seemed to be mutually exclusive objectives. He welcomed the erosion of feudal power relations by capitalist modernization, but was apprehensive about the latter's effects on indigenous culture. In the first half of the 1950s, during the Odría dictatorship, Arguedas embraced capitalist modernization and on occasion even advocated the disappearance of indigenous culture. Toward the middle of the decade, he still considered capitalist modernization the only alternative to feudalism in the Andean countryside, but now saw it as a means of renewing indigenous culture. By contrast, his work from the final years of the 1950s in certain respects anticipates the 1960s radicalization of Latin American politics, which would facilitate Arguedas's reencounter with socialism and lead him to look for common ground between indigenous Andean cultural values and the revolutionary projects of a new era.

I trace this evolution in his anthropological articles and the only novel he published in the 1950s. For most of the decade, Arguedas was more anthropologist than novelist. In the twenty years after *Yawar Fiesta* (1941), he published only four short stories and just one novel, *Los ríos profundos / Deep Rivers* (1958). Instead of fiction, during the 1950s he dedicated himself to anthropological research, on the basis of which he wrote a series of articles on modernization and culture change in the central and southern Andes.[8] These articles reflect the limited possibilities for radical social change in this period, for they attempt to make the best of what seemed like the inevitability of capitalist modernization in the Andes. At no time do they contemplate the possibility of organized, collective action, focusing instead on the dynamics of capitalism and individual responses to them as the motors of social change. The slightly later *Deep Rivers*, on the other hand, presages Arguedas's subsequent radicalization in the 1960s by deploying Andean oral traditions to imagine a collective, non-capitalist challenge to feudal power relations.

Two factors account for the difference between the anthropological articles and *Deep Rivers*. The first and preponderant one is historical: the resurgence of indigenous mobilization in the second half of the decade, which made it possible to envision non-capitalist alternatives to feudalism. However, the contrasting narrative forms of the articles and the novel also play an important role. The transcultural narrative form of *Deep Rivers*, that is, allowed Arguedas to think beyond the ideological horizons of the 1950s in a way that the social science writing of the period, with its requirements of objectivity, did not. Indeed, one can at times see Arguedas straining against the limitations of the latter in his anthropological articles. Nonetheless, in the last instance it was historical events that enabled Arguedas to imagine addressing Peru's social problems through means more radical than capitalist modernization.

Arguedas and Development Theory

The 1950s were the golden era of development theory, which Arturo Escobar has defined as a North American and European discourse that "created an extremely efficient apparatus for producing knowledge about, and the exercise of power over, the Third World."[9] Produced in the wake of the Second World War, the discourse of development promised abundance for all through economic growth, but "produced its opposite: massive underdevelopment and impoverishment, untold exploitation and oppression."[10] In spite of this failure, development "achieved the status of a certainty in the social imaginary" such that "it seemed impossible to conceptualize social reality in other terms."[11] Escobar contends that development discourse was so dominant that it rendered alternatives unimaginable and "those who were dissatisfied with this state of affairs had to struggle for bits and pieces of freedom within it, in the hope that in the process a different reality could be constructed."[12] This last observation provides a key to understanding Arguedas's anthropological articles of the 1950s. Under the Odría dictatorship, Peru's increased dependence on the US was both economic and ideological. Odría's Peru was fertile ground for experiments in modernization designed in North American universities, and US development theory was a powerful influence on Peruvian anthropology during the 1950s. Arguedas, who began his doctoral studies in anthropology at this time, did not escape such ideological pressures. During the 1950s, both Peruvian and North American proponents of development were his professors and mentors at the Institute of Ethnology at San Marcos University in Lima. His anthropological articles from this period, particularly the earlier ones, frequently refer to North American authorities and the assumptions of the development discourse then in vogue: that modernization is synonymous with Westernization, and that it requires the assimilation of indigenous peoples, whose cultures are destined to disappear under its impact.

Arguedas's treatment of the prevailing notions of development, however, is inconsistent. At times he seems to embrace them uncritically, while on other occasions he describes the changes wrought by modernization as a form of transculturation directed by indigenous Andeans themselves and capable of keeping alive their core traditions and values, which at still other moments he mourns as doomed to destruction. In general, the postulates of development theory are treated less critically in the earlier articles, in which Arguedas appears more firmly under the influence of North American social science, than in the later ones, in which he cites US academic authorities less frequently and begins to develop his own, more independent ideas about modernization and culture change in the Andes. However, individual articles from either end of the decade often espouse contradictory positions with regard to development theory. I argue that the frequently incongruous form of his articles is the result of such inconsistencies, and that these in turn are the product of Arguedas's attempt to open within developmentalist anthropology a space for indigenous culture and agency at a time of extremely limited prospects for the kind of struggles that motivated his youthful political commitment.

The fall of the Odría dictatorship in 1956, the subsequent resurgence of indigenous land struggles, and the triumph of the Cuban revolution in 1959 broadened the horizons of the possible for Arguedas, and helped revive in him the more radical politics of his youth. *Deep Rivers* anticipates the radicalization evident in both his anthropological articles and novels from the 1960s. *Deep Rivers* is Arguedas's best-known work and the only one of his novels to receive immediate critical acclaim, perhaps because of its lyricism and the fact that it seemed to fit readily into a recognized genre, the coming of age novel, or *Bildungsroman*. However, among Arguedas's novels, *Deep Rivers* is rivaled only by *The Fox from up Above and the Fox from Down Below* (1971) in its reliance on and incorporation of Andean cosmology. Indeed, it served as Rama's paradigmatic example of a transcultural narrative. An Andean cultural code inflects the coming of age story in *Deep Rivers*, allowing Arguedas to envision alternatives to the semi-feudal status quo more radical than the limited options outlined in his anthropological articles of the 1950s.

The Novelist as Anthropologist

Alberto Flores Galindo has noted on more than one occasion a rather striking contrast between Arguedas's novels and his anthropological articles. In Arguedas, he points out,

> there are two visions of the encounter between the West and the Andean world. Arguedas the novelist envisioned a violent world that could only change in an equally violent and radical manner. Arguedas the anthropologist hoped that this world could be changed gradually, without violence, such that there would be no clash between Andean peasants and capitalism, and the peasants would incorporate themselves into the capitalist world.[13]

In the novels, the violence of Peru's colonial divide can only be overcome by more violence, in the form of rebellion or revolution. The anthropological articles, by contrast, emphasize the gradual erosion of this divide and the attenuation of its violence through the hybridization of indigenous Andean culture and Western capitalism. In the articles, social change is the product of individual responses to capitalist modernization, while in the novels it is the product of collective, purposive action.

Several factors help to explain the difference. The first is geographical. While virtually all of Arguedas's literary works are set in the semi-feudal southern Andes, many of his anthropological articles from the 1950s address modernization in the central Andean Mantaro River valley, where feudal power relations were never firmly established. As a result, the literary works deal with a severely divided society resistant to the kind of gradual, non-confrontational social change Arguedas describes in his anthropological articles on the Mantaro valley. However, this is only a partial explanation, for some of Arguedas's anthropological articles analyze the effects of modernization in the southern Andes, in Puquio, for example, while others generalize about the Andes as a whole. Though there are some differences between the articles devoted to the central and southern Andean regions, they are not as great as those between Arguedas's novels and his anthropological research.

A second factor has to do with the contrasting requirements and possibilities of social science and fiction writing. Flores Galindo, for example, attributes the difference between Arguedas's novels and anthropological articles to the more personal, subjective nature of the former and the aspirations to scientific objectivity of the latter. In the articles, he suggests, "the *mestizo* seems to be the harbinger of a country in which the Andean and Western worlds would, in steps, merge with one another. But returning to the fiction, where passion imposes itself once more, there is little room for *mestizos* in a world that does not allow for intermediate situations: only resignation or rebellion, lamentation or conflagration."[14] The Western, scientific narrative form of the articles produces a vision of harmonious cultural fusion, while a vision of cultural confrontation emerges from the transcultural narrative form of the novels. However, the formal qualities of the two different kinds of writing are only a partial explanation as well. As Flores Galindo himself recognizes, "the contrast between literary and anthropological texts grew less sharp toward the end of his life, in the 1960s."[15]

This convergence in the 1960s suggests yet a third, historical explanation for the contrasting visions of the encounter between the Western and Andean worlds in Arguedas's novels and his 1950s anthropological articles. The contrast, that is, may have as much to do with the historical moments in which he wrote his fiction and non-fiction as it does with a difference in genre. It happens that virtually all of Arguedas's literary works were published during or on the cusp of the periods of social upheaval at the beginning and end of his writing career, from the short story collection *Agua* (1935) to *Yawar Fiesta* (1941) and from *Deep Rivers* (1958) to the posthumous *The Fox from Up Above and the Fox from Down Below* (1971). During the years of relative political calm and conservative oligarchic regimes between his first and second novels, when radical social change seemed impossible, if not unthinkable, Arguedas published primarily anthropological articles in which he emphasized gradualist solutions to Peru's ethnic divisions.

The literary exceptions to this periodization, the short stories "Diamantes y pedernales" (1954), "Orovilca" (1954) and "La muerte de los Arango" (1955), generally lack the emphasis on violent confrontation that distinguishes most of Arguedas's fiction from his anthropological articles of the 1950s. This is true even of the early fragments of *Deep Rivers* that appeared in journals between 1948 and 1951.[16] Though these fragments are recognizable in the final version of the novel, they constitute its more lyrical passages and do not address the question of social conflict. It is not until 1957 that the theme reemerges in the short story "Hijo Solo", followed shortly by the publication of *Deep Rivers* in 1958. One might argue, of course, that Arguedas had written, but not published, more conflictive portions of *Deep Rivers* in the 1940s or early 1950s, but his correspondence with his brother Arístides indicates that although he began the novel in 1944 or 1945, he made little progress on it initially and composed the bulk of the work in mid-1956.[17]

The relationship between the gap in Arguedas's literary production and the change in his vision of the encounter between Western and indigenous Andean cultures was more than coincidental. It appears that the defeat of the social movements of the 1920s and 1930s may have contributed to the bout of chronic depression that prompted Arguedas's abandonment of literature and his retreat from radical politics in the early 1940s.[18] As Cornejo Polar observes, the young Arguedas had expected radical changes in Peruvian society during the turbulent 1920s and early 1930s, and when these failed to materialize,

> Arguedas experienced the frustration of his hopes. He recalled that back then "we thought that social justice was just around the corner . . ." but it did not happen that way. Quite the contrary, the ideals of renewal had to be deferred to a distant and highly uncertain future. This disillusionment must have hit Arguedas exceptionally hard. It may have been one of the components of his first major psychological crisis, which made him literarily unproductive between 1942 and 1954. At the ideological level, it unleashed a deep skepticism regarding the political alternatives of the moment, which had failed to interpret the Andean people's deeply held interests and capacity for historical transformation.[19]

Given such disillusionment with the available political alternatives, and here Cornejo Polar alludes to the Communist Party and the APRA, it is not hard to imagine the appeal for Arguedas of North American functionalist anthropology, which presented itself as a scientific, and purportedly non-ideological, approach to the problem of social change. While I do not discount the influence of geography and narrative form on the contrast between Arguedas's anthropological articles of the 1950s and his novels, the attenuation of that contrast in the 1960s suggests that historical factors are largely responsible for it.[20]

Mestizaje *and Transculturation*

In the work of eminent North American anthropologists Arguedas found support for his own growing interest in the figure of the *mestizo* as the medium for and expression of social change in the Andes. In his articles from the early 1950s, he cites influential anthropological manuals by Ralph Linton and Melville J. Herskovits in support of his analysis of culture change in the Andes.[21] Though Arguedas does not use the term acculturation, his articles are clearly informed by the concept, although not as it was defined by Redfield, Linton and Herskovits, but rather as it was used by applied anthropologists.

Instead of acculturation, Arguedas prefers *mestizaje* and transcultura-tion, but in his articles both terms, which he uses interchangeably, seem to mean different things at different times. They sometimes appear to designate mutual cultural influence, but just as often they function as synonyms of assimilation. In "El complejo cultural en el Perú"/ "The Cultural Complex in Peru" (1952), for example, he begins by describing the vitality of pre-Columbian Andean culture and its capacity to absorb outside influences without losing its identity.[22] Over the centuries since the conquest, Arguedas notes, indigenous culture in the Andes has changed in virtually every way, "but has remained, through so many important changes, *different* than Western culture, in spite of the fact that such significant changes have been produced in indigenous culture by the influence wielded upon it by the culture of the conquistadors."[23] However, Arguedas goes on to argue that "to consider only the indige-nous as Peruvian" is incorrect.[24] The process of mutual cultural influence between Peru's Spanish and indigenous Andean cultures over several centuries changed both without erasing the differences between them, but also produced "a character or human product whose forceful actions are proving themselves to be ever more important: the *mestizo*."[25] Given the history and slippery nature of the word *mestizo*, it is not entirely clear what Arguedas is getting at here.

According to Ángel Rama, the figure of the *mestizo* in Arguedas's anthropological articles does not represent the disappearance of indige-nous Andean culture, but rather its best, or even only, chance for survival. For Arguedas, writes Rama, the *mestizo*

> is the safeguard of national identity, of the ethical and philosophical values that he [Arguedas] considers superior (concepts of property, work, group solidarity, nature, humanism). For him *mestizo* culture is not superior to the defensively armor-clad culture of the indigenous population of the Department of Puno. Rather, *mestizo* culture is an effective opportunity for the partial preservation of those values. This is particularly so given the desperate situation of culturally conservative indigenous groups: incapable of resisting the assault promoted by the bourgeois, capitalist, Western culture emanating from Lima, they are condemned to social and spiritual disintegration within their Andean bastions.[26]

The *mestizo*, in other words, is a kind of carrier of the core values of Andean culture, which is doomed to disappear (presumably in spite of its adaptability) as indigenous communities unprepared for the impact of modernization disintegrate.

Rama's interpretation of the *mestizo*'s role in these articles is plausible, for as early as 1939 Arguedas had argued that indigenous culture was the dominant component of *mestizo* identity in the Andes:

the West was unable to dominate the *mestizo* because his indigenous core protected him. As the *mestizo* acquired the spiritual power of the Andean people, the struggle in his soul between indigenous and Spanish culture . . . was defined. Indigenous culture is now predominant in the psychology of the Peruvian mestizo; it has won the battle.[27]

In Arguedas's articles of the 1950s, however, the words *mestizo* and *mestizaje* undergo a slippage akin to that between the broader, formal definition of acculturation and the narrower, actual usage of the term in applied anthropology. At times *mestizaje* seems to designate a multidirectional process of cultural influence and *mestizo* the product of such a process: an indigenous person who has become modern without losing what were for Arguedas the fundamental values of indigenous Andean culture. At other moments, *mestizaje* appears to denote a unidirectional process of Westernization and *mestizo* a fully Westernized successor to the indigenous Andean.

The Peru–Cornell Project

In "The Cultural Complex in Peru", Arguedas endorses a Cornell University applied anthropology project directed by Allan Holmberg at the Vicos hacienda in northern Peru:

> The study of the *mestizo* is one of the most important projects that Anthropology must undertake in Peru. Perhaps the most interesting information that came out of the recent Conference of Peruvianists was that presented by Dr. Holmberg of Cornell University, who announced the beginning of a comprehensive cultural study in the Callejón de Huaylas. One of the fundamental contributions of the study of the population in this region is precisely the study of transculturation, of *mestizaje*.[28]

Though Arguedas uses the terms *mestizaje* and transculturation here, implying mutual cultural influence, in this context both refer to a unidirectional process of Westernization, for as Priscilla Archibald notes, "Vicos was the pilot project for an experiment in 'rapid modernization' whose ultimate goal was the integration of indigenous populations within national society."[29] The Vicos hacienda was a property of the Peruvian state, which leased it, complete with workforce, to private individuals. In 1952, Cornell University rented the property for a period of five years, during which Holmberg and his North American and Peruvian associates set about inducing change among its indigenous Andean residents. Motivated by the best of intentions, project anthropologists saw themselves as turning peons into citizens by rescuing the Vicosinos from feudalism, a goal evident in the title of one of Holmberg's articles on the work he supervised at Vicos, "Del paternalismo a la democracia: el Proyecto Perú–Cornell / From Paternalism to Democracy: The Peru–Cornell Project."[30]

Traditional relations between the renter-*patrón* and the hacienda peons of Vicos were typical of the period: the former, though not the owner of the property, had absolute power over the latter. The problem Holmberg and his colleagues posed for themselves upon becoming the representatives of the Vicos hacienda's new *patrón*, Cornell University, was "how to change this state of affairs without a great deal of economic investment or by means of a revolution."[31] This formulation of the problem suggests that in addition to helping the hacienda peons, the Peru–Cornell project's goals at Vicos included demonstrating the possibility of avoiding revolution by modernizing the Andean countryside at minimal cost to the Peruvian state. Judged in these terms and by its economic benefits for the Vicosinos, the project's achievements were undeniably significant. Feudal power relations were abolished and the hacienda was turned into a kind of cooperative run by the Vicosinos. Agricultural productivity soared, a school and a clinic were built, and the residents of Vicos were eventually able to buy the land on which they had worked for centuries as peons.[32] However, the Vicos project never amounted to a viable model for structural reform in the Andes.[33] Since the property was owned by the state, the project did not affect the interests of private landowners, nor did it cost the state anything, because the Vicosinos assumed the burden of funding the local social programs formerly supported by the rent from the hacienda. The model of change implemented at Vicos avoided addressing the conflicts a genuine agrarian reform would have entailed in the Peruvian Andes, but perhaps this was the point. It is quite telling in this respect that the collection of articles on Vicos edited by Holmberg, several of which date from the early 1960s, makes no reference to the indigenous land struggles of 1958–1964.

Despite its success, the methods used at Vicos might well cause one to wonder whether the Peru–Cornell project was as much of an alternative to paternalism as the title "From Paternalism to Democracy" suggests. Though Holmberg and his colleagues emphasize that "the Peru–Cornell project has not established any ideal type or a Western civilizational model as the goal toward which Vicos is to be directed", their description of the philosophy on which their methods were based seems to contradict this claim.[34] An article coauthored by several of the project's anthropologists, for example, notes that

> The most general binary model of analysis used in the Project to analyze change in Vicos consists of establishing a contrast between industrialized Western civilization and medieval Western colonialism. The Peru–Cornell

Project considers the changes occurring in the culture and society of Vicos a process of "modernization" or "Westernization."[35]

While the feudal society of Vicos was governed by the "fundamental postulate" of inequality among individuals, which the Vicosinos are said to have internalized, equality is hailed as the "fundamental postulate" of modern Western civilization.[36] Liberation from feudalism required Westernization, which Holmberg and his colleagues define as "the introduction of modern 'fundamental postulates' into cultures that lack them."[37]

The process of cultural influence described would appear to be entirely unidirectional, and directed at replacing most, if not all, of the Vicosinos' culture. Indeed, there is no sense in the collection of articles edited by Holmberg that the anthropologists have anything to learn from their research subjects, other than how fast the latter can shed their feudal customs. Remarkably, aside from the reference to their feudal notion of inequality, there is no mention of the Vicosinos' beliefs or cultural practices. It is as if the sum total of their culture were the medieval feudalism implanted in the Andes by Spanish colonialism, which must now be uprooted in their own and the nation's interest, a task made possible by the technical assistance generously provided by foreign anthropologists. Though Holmberg and his colleagues repeatedly mention the democratic decision-making process they instituted at Vicos, and though they maintain that the project's goals were shared by the community, there is no evidence of either democracy or indigenous voice in the narrative form the anthropologists chose for reporting their research. The Vicosinos are never quoted in these articles, and appear only in the accompanying photographs, nameless.

It would perhaps be wrong to draw too many conclusions about Arguedas's views on culture change from his early endorsement of the Peru–Cornell project at Vicos. However, the closing paragraphs of his article "The Cultural Complex in Peru" leave little doubt that *mestizaje* refers here to a unidirectional process of cultural influence: "the Indian is being diluted in Peru at a frighteningly slow rate. In México he is already a small figure and will soon have lost himself within the greater national identity. In Peru the case of the Indian has become an increasingly serious problem. As we have already mentioned, the process of *mestizaje* proceeds at a dreadfully slow pace."[38] Arguedas begins "The Cultural Complex in Peru" by praising the dynamism and adaptability of indigenous culture, only to end by lamenting the slow pace of its disappearance.

The Anomalous Case of the Mantaro River Valley

A similar ambiguity afflicts "La sierra en el proceso de la cultura peruana"/ "The Andean Highlands in the Process of Peruvian Culture" (1953).[39] Here Arguedas briefly summarizes his ongoing research in the central Andean valley of the upper Mantaro River, where, due to a variety of factors, the feudal institutions of Spanish colonialism never took root, and indigenous Andeans were never forced into servitude. The latter held on to more of their land than was the case in the southern Andes, and their greater independence provided them with the resources and flexibility to adapt more successfully to modernization. Arguedas believed he had found proof in the Mantaro Valley that modernization could occur through the "harmonious fusion" of Western and indigenous Andean cultures rather than the disappearance of the latter.[40] The Mantaro region was key to this phase of Arguedas's thinking about culture contact and change because he saw in it an exception to the destructive pattern of modernization he had witnessed elsewhere in the Andes, where indigenous communities had begun to disintegrate under its impact:

> The influence of these complex factors transformed the Indian of the [Mantaro] valley into the current Spanish-speaking *mestizo*, without uprooting him or destroying his personality. Powerful forces of change, which in this zone acted simultaneously, produced a process of mass transculturation. Without the case of the Upper Mantaro, our vision of Andean Peru would still be bitter.[41]

In this passage both *mestizo* and transculturation seem to refer to a multidirectional cultural exchange.

In the final pages of the same article, however, the meaning of the terms seems to shift as Arguedas discusses what he calls the "irreconcilable" difference between Spanish and indigenous Andean cultures: their contrasting economic systems and conceptions of property and labor. He argues that the Western conception is "mercantile and individualist" while the pre-Columbian Andean one is "collectivist and religious." Consequently, "ancient Peruvians did not conceive of landownership as a source of unlimited individual accumulation of wealth. This concept was directly linked to their religious conception of land and of work."[42] Arguedas goes on to note that in spite of five centuries of contact and interaction between the two cultures, "the Indian has not yet succeeded in completely comprehending and assimilating the Western concepts of property and of work."[43] Though the reader of *Yawar Fiesta* might assume that indigenous Andeans' failure to internalize capitalist economic rationality is to be understood as a good thing, this, surprisingly, is not

76

Arguedas's view here. Rather, he describes indigenous Andeans as an obstacle to economic development because they aspire to none of the characteristic forms of modern life, the only example of which he offers is their failure to be good consumers.[44]

Arguedas then argues that this lamentable situation may be remedied under special circumstances, such as those present in the Mantaro Valley:

> When under special circumstances the Indian manages to understand this aspect of Western culture, when he arms himself with it, he proceeds like we do. He becomes a *mestizo* and a positive factor in economic production. His entire cultural structure undergoes a complete readjustment upon its base, or "axis." Upon changing not just one "of the superficial elements of his culture" but its fundamental nature, the disorder we observe in his culture presents itself as orderly, clear, and logical. That is, *his conduct is identified with our own*. All because he has become an individual who really participates in our culture. A total conversion in which, naturally, some of the old [cultural] elements retain their influence as simple terms that distinguish his personality, which is essentially motivated by incentives, *by ideals*, similar to our own. Such is the case of the ex-Indians of the Mantaro Valley ... the first case of mass transculturation, alluded to briefly in the first pages of this article.[45]

The passage is lengthy, but is worth reproducing in whole so as not to risk misinterpreting Arguedas's statements by citing them out of context. If this is a "harmonious fusion of cultures", it is one dominated by Western culture, particularly the acquisitive individualism at the heart of capitalist economic rationality. It is hard to see what else could be meant by the "complete readjustment" of indigenous culture or the "total conversion" of indigenous individuals who, though they will retain a few elements of their cultural personality, will essentially be motivated by incentives and ideals "similar to our own", where the possessive clearly refers to Peru's official, Westernized culture. In "The Andean Highlands in the Process of Peruvian Culture", Arguedas starts out by referring to transculturation as a harmonious fusion of two cultures, but ends up espousing what can only be described as the assimilation of one by the other.

Arguedas seems to have moderated this view within a few years, as is evident in his more detailed and in-depth study of the Mantaro valley, "Evolución de las comunidades indígenas. El Valle del Mantaro y la ciudad de Huancayo"/ "The Evolution of Indigenous Communities: The Mantaro Valley and the City of Huancayo" (1957).[46] Indeed, in his articles from the second half of the decade, he relies much less on formulas from US anthropological manuals and appears more confident of his own interpretations. In "The Evolution of Indigenous Communities", he relies on historical sources and ethnographies as well as his own field observations to develop fully his argument about the unique regional culture of the Mantaro Valley and its urban center, the city of Huancayo. In the dynamism and adaptability of the region's indigenous communities and individuals, Arguedas thought he saw proof that a violent confrontation between Western and indigenous Andean cultures, with the likely disappearance of the latter, was not the only possible outcome of modernization in the Andes.

Arguedas attributes the Mantaro Valley's exceptional prosperity to the fact that, from colonial times through to the present, it had remained free of feudal institutions and landownership patterns:

> This peaceful integration of castes and cultures in the Mantaro Valley is, as already mentioned, an exceptional case in the history of Peru's indigenous communities. It may be explained by the absence of the factor that made such an integration impossible in other heavily indigenous provinces . . . That factor is the large landowner, the one traditionally known as a "gamonal."[47]

The uniquely successful modernization and cultural integration of this region indicated for Arguedas that the obstacle to duplicating such success elsewhere was the one factor the Mantaro Valley did not have in common with other regions of the Peruvian Andes: feudal power relations. Where these prevailed, they isolated indigenous communities from the nation and the world, preventing them from gradually acquiring the means to resist being overwhelmed by the dramatic changes twentieth century capitalism would wreak in the Andes. Ossified by their isolation, such communities were brittle and shattered under the impact of modernization.

In the Mantaro Valley, by contrast, even *mestizo* communities adapted more easily to modernization than did their counterparts elsewhere in Andean Peru: "valley communities with a high *mestizo* population as well as traditionally indigenous communities have demonstrated a greater aptitude for the integration of new methods and norms than communities in provinces where feudal servitude was imposed."[48] The existence of feudal power relations would appear to be the determining factor for the fate not only of indigenous communities, but of entire regional cultures. In the absence of *gamonalismo*, Arguedas implies, indigenous communities would encounter more opportunity than danger in capitalist modernization. Free from feudal bonds, indigenous Andeans would become agents of modernization and of capitalism, which they would use to maintain their cultural identity, as indeed Arguedas believed they had in the Mantaro Valley. However, as Flores Galindo points out, the subsequent evolution of the region has not confirmed such optimism regarding capitalist modernization as a means of perpetuating Andean cultural identity, for the Mantaro Valley has increasingly become a cultural satellite of nearby Lima.[49]

In light of the extreme oppression Arguedas had witnessed, and experienced personally as a child, in the semi-feudal regional society of the southern Andes, capitalist forms of exploitation would no doubt seem relatively benign. Unfortunately, his revulsion at feudal oppression leads him to a remarkably naive view of the boundless opportunities afforded by capitalism. Indeed, at times his enthusiasm in this article seems inspired less by the survival through reinvention of indigenous Andean culture than by the indigenous entrepreneurialism he credits for it. Particularly in the second half of "Evolución de las comunidades indígenas", Arguedas treats capitalism, as Nelson Manrique observes, "as the horizon for the redemption of the indigenous world."[50] What Arguedas seems to find most attractive about the Mantaro valley's urban center, Huancayo, for example, are the energies of capitalist enterprise unleashed in it:

> the *mestizo* and the Indian, or the man of provincial origins, who arrive in this city do not find themselves in conflict with it. This is because the indigenous masses who visit or live there are autochthonous at bottom and not in the exotic manner of outward appearances. They are, moreover, moved by the impulse of activity, of commerce, of the modern spirit which spreads and stimulates.[51]

The activity, commerce, and modern spirit said to move the indigenous population of Huancayo amount to nothing less than the entrepreneurial spirit of capitalism.

Moreover, Arguedas maintains that this new world of boundless possibility in Huancayo does not require recently arrived *mestizo* or indigenous migrants to sacrifice their Andean cultural traditions, nor does it deny them the rights of citizenship because of their cultural identity or the language they speak:

> And given the opportunity they will reenact in the city, publicly and without shame, the festivals of their village and be able to dance in the streets according to the customs of their own ayllu or to join in the indigenous festivals and dances of the city itself, for these will not be foreign to them. And they will be citizens, albeit in the minimal, but nonetheless real, manner of the municipal street sweepers who, stretched out on the sidewalks in the morning, chew coca leaves and converse in Quechua, but with the assurance that they will receive a salary that will permit them, should they so choose, to enter the "El Olímpico" restaurant and sit down at a table near or next to a high government official, a traveling salesman or the very Prefect of the Department, and be free at all times of the fear that someone will brandish a whip over their heads. And without a doubt they will be able to hope for an improvement in their condition, because the city offers possi-

bilities for all without requiring anyone to renounce their gods in order to be admitted into its realm.[52]

That this is a utopian vision and not a reality is given away by the passage's tentative language ("given the opportunity", "if they so choose") and use of the future tense, which tend to project such rights and opportunities into a hypothetical moment beyond the present. In his vision of Huancayo as a "world of opportunity for all" argues Nelson Manrique, Arguedas in effect echoes "the promise held out by the dominant developmentalist discourse of the early 1950s."[53]

For Manrique, such dependence on North American developmentalist social science makes Arguedas, at least in this phase of his career, "a culturally colonized intellectual."[54] However, this is perhaps too harsh a judgement, based on an overly selective reading of Arguedas's work from the 1950s. Even in the articles in which the influence of development theory is strongest, one can find moments where Arguedas's deeply felt affinity for indigenous Andean culture grates against the requirements of scientific objectivity and the assumption that modernization is synonymous with Westernization. Though buried under simple formulas about the obstacles to modernization presented by traditional cultures, his concern for indigenous Andean culture and admiration for its creativity and adaptability surface repeatedly to disturb the assumptions of North American development theory. Many of Arguedas's ideas, even in this period, are an awkward fit with the latter, and often overflow the limits of the objective, scientific genre in which he attempted to contain them.[55]

Return to Puquio

In "Puquio, una cultura en proceso de cambio"/ "Puquio, a Changing Culture" (1956),[56] based on research he conducted during 1952 and 1956, Arguedas examines the transformation wrought by modernization in Puquio, the setting for his first novel. Since 1930, he argues, Puquio "after having been the capital of antiquated agricultural zone of a predominantly colonial type, has become a commercial center with a vibrant economy" thanks in large part to the construction of the road described in *Yawar Fiesta*.[57] Though he attempts to present some aspects of such modernization as beneficial to Puquio's four indigenous ayllus, enthusiasm for *mestizaje* is decidedly lacking here. Even his most positive account of the growth in Puquio's *mestizo* population seems somehow halfhearted and unconvincing:

A leader of Pichqachuri told us, very seriously, that his community was not progressing much because it had few *mistis* and *mestizos* and because of this, they, the elders, were determined that their children should become *mestizos*. This statement is important because it demonstrates the possibility of *mestizos* arising in the communities of Pichqachuri and Qayao as a result of a conscious transformation promoted by the Indians and not as a result of the traditional, inverse process of the *mistis'* impoverishment.[58]

A transformation of cultural identity is underway, driven by the *comuneros* themselves, but to what end? Instead of celebrating *mestizaje* as a means of creatively reinventing and perpetuating indigenous culture, the next paragraph undermines any such claim by citing older *comuneros'* complaints about the younger generation's changing customs. These, Arguedas fears, are leading to the imminent loss of indigenous traditions.

After devoting just five pages to the analysis of Puquio's changing social structure, Arguedas turns to the description, transcription and interpretation, over the next forty pages, of the oral traditions, music, and festivals he fears will disappear within a generation. Among these is the Inkarrí myth, the existence of which Arguedas was among the first to document. Several variants of the myth have been recorded throughout the southern Andes, but like the three versions from Puquio that Arguedas reproduces in this article, they are all anti-colonial allegories that symbolically undo the conquest. Inkarrí is portrayed as a founder and leader of Andean civilization defeated and beheaded by the Spanish, who buried his head and body separately. This, of course, is based on the similar fate of the historical Incas Atahualpa and Túpac Amaru, in 1532 and 1570 respectively, as well as a descendant of the latter, Túpac Amaru II (José Gabriel Condorcanqui), leader of a massive rebellion against Spanish rule in 1780. In the myth, Inkarrí's body is said to be slowly rejoining his severed head underground, and when the process is complete, he will revive and expel the Spanish.

In the Puquio article, the Inkarrí myth serves not only as an object of analysis, but also as a means of speculating about the future of indigenous Andean culture. The effect is quite jarring, given the era's "scientific" conventions of anthropological writing. In the conclusion to "Puquio, a Changing Culture", Arguedas first summarizes his findings in a neutral, objective tone:

> As far as the natives are concerned, we observe that this process [of change] is tending to facilitate their independence from the traditional despotism wielded against them, historically and to this day, by the gamonal and *mestizo* classes. But at the same time, the process is tearing the natives from the foundation that sustained their traditional culture, and the elements that will replace it are not yet apparent.[59]

He credits modernization with partially liberating Puquio's indigenous ayllus from feudal despotism, but also emphasizes the cultural loss this has entailed. What follows expresses, through a citation of one of the

Inkarrí myths analyzed earlier in the article, a much more personal, subjective sense of despair over such loss, but also hope in Andean cultural resilience:

> Inkarrí is returning, and we can not but fear his possible inability to join together individualisms perhaps irremediably developed. Unless he can detain the Sun, tying it down again with iron bands to the summit of Osqonta, and modify humanity. But anything is possible in the case of such a wise and resistant being.[60]

In stark contrast to the Mantaro Valley article's enthusiasm for entrepreneurialism, Puquio article reveals Arguedas's allegiance to the collectivism he considered the core value of indigenous Andean culture, a collectivism threatened, in his view, by the individualism fostered by capitalist modernization. There is such a marked contrast between Arguedas's intense focus in this article on the indigenous culture he fears is about to disappear, and the utter lack of interest in the subject shown by the Vicos researchers, that one could hardly accuse him of uncritically echoing development theory in this instance.

In spite of his critique of the "colonized" aspects of Arguedas's work in this period, Manrique also acknowledges that the colonization was not complete. In speculating about the factors that in the 1960s allowed Arguedas to "recover the socialist horizon that guided his youthful enthusiasm," Manrique lists, in addition to Arguedas's growing alarm over the increasingly destructive effects of Westernization in indigenous communities, and the radicalizing effects of the Cuban revolution, his literary sensibility. What saved Arguedas from complete intellectual colonization, argues Manrique, was

> his vocation as a literary creator, which kept him from renouncing intuition, sensitivity, and affect, elements in conflict with a positivist conception of "scientific work" . . . but which, in a country as challenging as Peru . . . helped him to avoid completely submitting to the rigid schemes of North American functionalism in the 1950s, and from replacing them with those of an imitative, servile, and similarly colonial Marxism in the following decade.[61]

While his literary sensibility kept Arguedas open to alternatives to development theory, he was nonetheless unable to imagine them, even in the relatively free medium of fiction, until the resurgence of indigenous land movements in the late 1950s made it possible to do so. However, just as he had not fully submitted to developmentalist orthodoxy in the 1950s, Arguedas would not be bound by some of the more rigid views of the Left in the 1960s.

Never content with the easy formulas of either socialism, in both the

1930s and the 1960s, nor with those of 1950s development theory, Arguedas's work within both ideological frameworks was often heterodox. The fate of indigenous Andean culture was his principal concern throughout his career, and this concern conditioned his intellectual engagement with both socialism and development theory.[62] Much as he had sought to reconcile socialism with indigenous traditions in his early fiction, in his ethnographic articles he tried to make compatible independent indigenous initiative based on Andean traditions compatible with a theoretical paradigm that assumed the imitation of North American modernity to be the goal of development. The attempt was fraught with contradictions in both moments, as it would be again in the 1960s when, despite his support for the Cuban revolution and the radicalization it inspired in Peru, Arguedas's allegiance to indigenous culture would fit uneasily with the revolutionary programs of a new generation of the Peruvian Left.

As Manrique notes, Arguedas's radicalization can be traced in his articles of the 1960s through the disappearance of references to *mestizaje* as a means to national integration. In "La cultura: patrimonio difícil de colonizar" / "Culture: A Heritage Not Easily Colonized" (1966), for example, the influence of North American theories of acculturation and development has clearly faded:

> The powers that dominate weak countries economically and politically are trying to consolidate that domination through the application of a process of cultural colonization. Through film, television, radio, and millions of publications, they are attempting to condition the mentality of the Latin American people. This enterprise has influential and powerful allies among the Latin American partners of the great consortia, because those partners are already, we won't say "colonized", but rather identified with the interests, and therefore, with the lifestyle, preferences, and concepts of good and evil.[63]

The vigorous denunciation of cultural imperialism indicates a loss of the faith that had animated his early 1950s citations of Linton's and Herskovits's anthropological manuals as well as his endorsement of the Vicos project: faith in North American guidance of Peru's modernization. In place of a "harmonious fusion of cultures", Arguedas now celebrates a different kind of transculturation, one in which the colonized resist subordination by making use of the colonizer's technology (radio, music recordings, television) to reinforce and propagate their own cultural traditions: "the very instruments that strengthen economic and political domination inevitably open new channels for the broader diffusion of expressions of traditional culture."[64]

Similarly, in his acceptance speech upon being awarded the Inca

Garcilaso prize in 1967, Arguedas rejects acculturation as a means to overcoming Peru's colonial divide. The cultural heritage of the West and that of the Andes could and should be combined, but "the path need not be, nor is it possible that it could be that which was demanded with the imperiousness of pillaging conquerors, that is, that the defeated nation renounce its soul . . . and assume that of the conquerors, that it acculturate. I am not acculturated."[65]/ Finally, in "El indigenismo en el Perú"/ "Indigenismo in Peru" (1965) he argues that the acculturation or assimilation of indigenous peoples is not a prerequisite for national integration, which he describes as a process that does not preclude "the conservation or intervention of some of the characteristic features, not of a distant Inca tradition, but of the living Hispano-Quechua one, which retained many elements of the former."[66] Indeed, Arguedas sees national integration proceeding through the adoption by the country as a whole of cultural traditions formerly exclusive to indigenous communities: "We thus believe in the survival of communal forms of work and social organization that have been put into practice . . . not only among the masses of Andean origin but also among the very heterogeneous masses of the '*barriadas*' who have participated and continue to participate with enthusiasm in the communal practices that once were exclusive to indigenous Andean communities."[67] This is a long way from his advocacy of capitalist economic rationality twelve years earlier in "The Andean Highlands in the Process of Peruvian Culture" (1953).

The radicalization visible in his articles of the 1960s is anticipated by Arguedas's return, in *Deep Rivers*, to the literary genre of the novel. It is here that he begins to envision more radical alternatives to the unfulfilled promises of development theory. He does so in a manner analogous to that of "Puquio, a Changing Culture", where indigenous myth serves not only as the object of social analysis but also as the medium for alternative visions of social change. In *Deep Rivers*, a vision of radical social change is constructed from the undercurrent of indigenous Andean beliefs that runs beneath the Western surface of the novel. These "deep rivers" of the title provide the symbolic code for understanding Arguedas's return to the novel form in 1958 as a reencounter with the leftist politics of his youth.

Coming of Age in the Andes

Deep Rivers is a coming of age story set in the sharply divided world of the southern Andes. The novel's adolescent protagonist and narrator, Ernesto, struggles to find a place for himself in an unjust, violent society split by the colonial divide between the *misti* elite and the indigenous Andeans they have reduced to servitude. That divide is particulary extreme in *Deep Rivers*, for there are no independent indigenous communities in this novel, only *colonos* (hacienda peons) and *pongos* (domestic servants), while the few *mestizos* who appear in its pages are firmly in the *misti* camp. Like Arguedas himself, Ernesto does not fit easily into the divided society into which he was born. Indeed, there are many parallels between author and protagonist. Ernesto's family are *mistis*, but he is from a relatively destitute branch of it. His father is not a landowner but rather a lawyer compelled by circumstances to travel the southern Andes in search of work. When Ernesto was young, his father left him in the care of another, wealthier *misti* family, which abused the boy much as they abused their indigenous servants. This common fate led Ernesto to identify with the latter, who sheltered and protected him.

Partly raised by indigenous servants, the adolescent Ernesto not only speaks Quechua but also remains immersed in Andean traditions. However, his allegiance to indigenous culture and animosity to the *misti* landowning class make extremely difficult his coming of age in a society dominated by the *mistis* and their values. Indeed, by subordinating the indigenous population of Abancay to such an extent that they are denied even minimal control over their own lives, the *misti* elite infantilize them, freezing the *colonos* in a kind of perpetual childhood. By identifying with indigenous culture, Ernesto remains, in effect, a child, his path to adulthood blocked by his society's exclusion of indigenous Andeans from active participation in it. To make matters worse, he must find a way to adulthood on his own, for his father, no longer able to take Ernesto along on his travels, leaves him at a religious boarding school in Abancay, a southern Andean town completely surrounded by, and dependent on, an enormous hacienda. Having become accustomed to the company of his father, Ernesto suddenly finds himself alone in a divided and violent world. All the injustices and brutality of the larger society are intensified in Abancay, which Ernesto describes as "a world fraught with monsters and fire."[68] There, as Ariel Dorfman points out, the adolescent protagonist and narrator must negotiate his passage to adulthood "in solitude and helplessness, struggling with the infernal powers that govern the Andean people and the religious boarding school he is forced to attend."[69]

Moreover, Ernesto's coming of age in his divided society requires him to choose, for, according to Dorfman, "growth is, above all, a concrete act of being integrated into an already functioning social structure: it is to elect (for those fortunate enough to have such a margin of freedom) a position, and therefore to make an ethical choice, placing oneself on one side or the other of the fight for power, wealth, and conscience."[70] Given his refusal to incorporate himself into the *misti* elite, and the impossibility of becoming one of their peons or of joining an indigenous community, for there are none of the latter near Abancay, Ernesto's choice to enter adulthood without renouncing indigenous culture implies a rejection of the existing, *misti*-dominated social structure. To conceive of an adulthood ethically acceptable to him, Ernesto must imagine a different kind of society, one ruled by the values of solidarity and generosity he associates with indigenous culture. His means for imagining such an alternative are Andean oral traditions and the cosmology embedded in them, in which the required social change takes the form of a cosmic upheaval, not a gradual evolution.

However, imagination alone is not enough. Ernesto's integration into his society is made possible only by the beginnings of social transformation in Abancay, in the form of two rebellions he witnesses. The first occurs near the middle of the novel, in chapter 7, and is a rare example in *indigenista* narrative of women's agency. It is a rebellion of the *mestizas* who run the town's *chicherías* (small bars where both *chicha* and food are served). The *chicheras*, as they are known, rise up against the state authorities' monopoly on salt, a scarce and highly valued necessity. In order to prevent the state from selling all the salt to *misti* landowners for their livestock while others go without, the *chicheras* take over Abancay's salt storehouse and equitably distribute the precious commodity among the townspeople as well as the *colonos* of the surrounding hacienda. The *chicheras*' rebellion is eventually put down by government troops sent from the coast, but its leader doña Felipa is never captured and the prospect of her return haunts the *mistis* of Abancay. The second rebellion occurs in the last chapter, when the *colonos* themselves enter Abancay during a typhus epidemic to demand that the priest celebrate mass for them in order to ward off the disease. Because of the *colonos*' numbers, the government troops are powerless to stop them. Though the *colonos* leave peacefully after their demands are met, their unprecedented takeover of the town symbolizes the possibility of a social transformation led by the most oppressed sector of the indigenous population.

The *chicheras*' and the *colonos*' rebellions mark the initiation of a popular struggle which might itself be seen as a kind of passage to adulthood by an oppressed people long denied their autonomy. For Dorfman, Ernesto's coming of age is closely linked to the coming of age of a people.[71] Indeed, the latter facilitates the former, for only through a symbolic alliance with subordinated groups does Ernesto succeed "in reaching what is his maximum aspiration: to grow because other human beings have done it, to link his destiny to the collective destiny."[72] He is able to integrate himself into his society because the *chicheras*' and the *colonos*' rebellions have already begun to change it. By asserting their agency and taking control of their own destiny, the *chicheras* and the *colonos* open a new social space that Ernesto can enter as an adult without sacrificing his values. *Deep Rivers* links the boy's coming of age to that

of the people not only through Ernesto's support for and limited participation in the two rebellions, but also by the way the rebellions are
prefigured in his Andeanized perceptions of the society into which he was
born.

Because Ernesto, who is also the novel's principal narrator, sees his
society and imagines a place for himself within it largely through the lens
of traditional Andean beliefs, the uninformed reader is likely to find the
novel fragmentary or even incomprehensible. Read according to a
Western interpretive code, many episodes "follow one upon another as
independent units with little causal connection between them."[73] *Deep
Rivers* functions in great part according to an associative narrative logic
drawn from Andean cosmology rather than the linear logic of cause and
effect more typical of Western realism.[74] What connects one event to
another, and the novel's many lyrical descriptions to the events on which
they often seem to have little bearing, is an Andean symbolic code unfa-
miliar to most Western readers and critics who, as Ricardo González Vigíl
notes, have often accused *Deep Rivers* of a "supposed lack of organic
unity."[75]

It is not my aim here to give a comprehensive reading or full structural
analysis of *Deep Rivers*, for several fine studies of the novel already
exist.[76] Rather, I focus on selected examples of how indigenous Andean
beliefs function in the novel as a means of imagining the radical transformation of an unjust society while at the same time symbolically linking
apparently unrelated parts of the narrative. Of particular interest are two
episodes from the novel's densely symbolic first chapter, which not only
illuminate Ernesto's relationship to the rebellions already described, but
also resonate with similar uses of Andean oral tradition in *Yawar Fiesta*
(1941) and in *Todas las sangres / All the Worlds* (1964), Arguedas's first
and third novels, respectively. These examples suggest that *Deep Rivers*
recovers the vision of social change articulated in the former and anticipates, in tentative, preliminary form, that of the latter.

Rivers of Change

Very little seems to happen in the first chapter of *Deep Rivers*, entitled
"The Old Man." Ernesto and his father, Gabriel, arrive in Cusco, the
capital of the Inca empire and symbolic center of the Andean world. There
they are humiliated by a wealthy and powerful relative, the Old Man of
the title, whom Gabriel despises but whose assistance he requires in order
to carry out a "peculiar plan."[77] Having failed to extract from the Old
Man any support for the mysterious plan, which is never explained or
mentioned again after this chapter, Gabriel and his son leave Cusco for
Abancay. Indeed, the first chapter consists less of narrative than of

descriptions of a setting to which the novel never returns. What little does occur during the visit to Cusco appears to have only a tenuous relationship to the rest of the novel, which focuses on Ernesto's experiences at the boarding school in Abancay. However, this superficial reading ignores the fact that the first chapter introduces all of the novel's principal themes. As Rama notes, "the whole novel is already in this first chapter."[78]

In Cusco, which he visits for the first time in his life, Ernesto not only encounters an extreme example of Peru's colonial divide and the injustice and suffering that flow from it, but also begins to perceive the forces that might right such wrongs and remove the obstacles to his passage to adulthood. The colonial divide appears most clearly in the opposition between the Old Man and his indigenous domestic servant, or *pongo*. The latter, a peon from one of the Old Man's haciendas, has been so subjugated that he barely speaks in front of *mistis* and, as a horrified Ernesto observes, bows down before them "like a worm asking to be crushed."[79] The Old Man, by contrast, wields a power so absolute he is implicitly compared to the Inca whose empire he has usurped. Just as the Inca presided over the four *suyus* (quadrants) of his empire from its center, Cusco, so the Old Man owns four haciendas in addition to his colonial mansion in the former imperial city. The latter's power, however, is accompanied by an avarice and cruelty that lead Ernesto to consider him a kind of demonic anti-Inca. Having never before seen a *pongo* nor confronted *gamonales* as rapacious as the Old Man, Ernesto concludes that "nowhere else must human beings suffer so much" as in Cusco.[80] Moreover, the Old Man and *gamonales* like him have degraded not only the descendants of the Inca's subjects, such as the *pongo*, but Cusco itself and even the natural world. Ernesto speculates, for example, that no trees grow in the imperial city's main plaza because "all the miserly *señores* who had dwelt on those ancient sites since the Conquest had poisoned the earth of the city with their breath."[81]

Indeed, such degradation is Ernesto's initial impression of Cusco, which at first sight bears little resemblance to the city described for him by his father, a native of the former Inca capital. Arriving at night, Ernesto first sees the superficial trappings of a somewhat shabby modernity: streetlights more feeble than in much smaller towns, the railroad station, a wide avenue, modern houses. These are followed by the threadbare colonial splendor of the Old Man's mansion and the filth of the room he has reserved for his guests. Only later that evening is Ernesto able to contemplate one of the Inca walls that survived the conquest. Even these, however, were debased by Cusco's conquerors, who used the remnants of walls that once enclosed Inca palaces as a foundation for colonial residences. The physical position of the Inca walls in effect parallels the social position of the *pongo*, for both support a colonial edifice: just as *misti* houses rest on indigenous foundations, Cusco's hierarchical society is built on the exploitation of indigenous labor. The degradation continues into the present, for as Ernesto contemplates a wall that was once part of the palace of Inca Roca, a drunk urinates nearby in the narrow street.

Nevertheless, Ernesto perceives the Inca wall not as a degraded ruin but rather as a living source of the energies required for the transformation of Cusco's unjust society. Indeed, his nocturnal visit to the Inca wall is a kind of epiphany from which much of the rest of the novel flows, for it is here that Ernesto discovers the subterranean power of indigenous tradition:

> I walked along the wall, stone by stone. I stood back a few steps, contem-plating it, and then came closer again. I touched the stone with my hands, following the line, which was as undulating and unpredictable as a river, where the blocks of stone were joined. In the dark street, in the silence, the wall appeared to be alive, the lines I touched between the stones burned on the palm of my hands. . . . The stones of the Inca wall were larger and stranger than I had imagined them; they seemed to be bubbling up beneath the whitewashed second story, which had no windows on the side facing the narrow street. Then I remembered the Quechua songs which continu-ally repeat one pathetic phrase: *yawar mayu*, "blood river"; *yawar unu*, "blood water"; *puk'tik' yawar k'ocha*, "boiling blood lake"; *yawar wek'e*, "blood tears." Couldn't one say *yawar rumi*, "blood stone", o *puk'tik' yawar rumi*, "boiling blood stone"? The wall was stationary, but all its lines were seething and its surface was as changeable as that of the flooding summer rivers which have similar crests near the center, where the current flows the swiftest and is the most terrifying. The Indians call these muddy rivers *yawar mayu* because when the sun shines on them they seem to glisten like blood. They also call the violent moment of the war dances, when the dancers fight, *yawar mayu*.[82]

In this passage, Arguedas rewrites the *indigenista* cliché that associates indigenous people with the endurance, but also the immobility and passivity of stone. The stones of the Inca wall are indeed enduring, but they are anything but static in Ernesto's eyes.

Through a series of associations, he links the wall to the possibility of overturning Cusco's colonial hierarchy. Because of the stones' irregular shapes, the joints between them do not form perfectly straight lines and right angles but rather meander like a river. A characteristic feature of Inca construction, the wall's erratic lines produce the appearance of move-ment, which Ernesto describes as a bubbling or seething. The wall in apparent motion evokes the image, drawn from Andean songs, of a *yawar mayu*, a flood-swollen river seemingly formed of blood. The same term, as it happens, refers to the ritual combat that occurs during certain Andean dances. Indigenous Andean oral traditions here serve as a means of imagining a social transformation carried out by indigenous Andeans themselves. The Inca wall's bubbling and seething, for instance, imply an instability and unrest that threaten the colonial edifice built atop it. In a literal sense, the danger is to the physical structures that rest on Inca foundations: if the stones really were to move, they would bring down the houses of the *mistis* like an earthquake. This is clearly what Ernesto has in mind, for after claiming that "this wall can walk; it could rise up into the sky or travel to the end of the world and back" he asks his father "aren't the people who live in there afraid?"[83] There is also a metaphorical sense to the image of the seething wall: the destruction not simply of *misti* houses, but of the whole colonial social structure based on *misti* domination. Similarly, the comparison of the wall to Andean rivers in flood-time suggests that the currents of indigenous tradition have the power to sweep away the oppression on which that social structure rests.[84]

The final link in Ernesto's chain of associations, the ritual combat also known as *yawar mayu*, identifies indigenous Andeans themselves as the potential agents of this social transformation. Ernesto's Andeanized vision of the Inca wall integrates the apparently anomalous first chapter into the rest of the narrative by linking it to the rebellions that occur in later chapters. It also prefigures the depiction of indigenous land struggle as a *yawar mayu* in his subsequent novel, *All the Worlds*. The adolescent narrator's youth and immersion in indigenous culture make such connections possible, permitting him to see what others do not. Compare, for example, the perspective of the Old Man, who is completely oblivious to the power of indigenous tradition and declares that the Inca wall's irregular shapes show "the chaos of the heathens, of primitive minds."[85]

Visions of pachakutiy

Ernesto's epiphany at the Inca wall is only one example of the links, forged by way of Andean traditions, between chapter 1 and the remainder of the novel. Accompanied now by his father, Ernesto visits the nearby Amaru Cancha, the former palace of the Inca Huayna Capac. The walls of this Inca ruin are dead, as are the serpents, or *amarus*, carved above its doorway. As father and son contemplate the stones of Amaru Cancha, the bell of the cathedral tolls, echoing off the Inca walls and prompting in Ernesto a new chain of associations that link the sound to a vision of cosmic upheaval or *pachakutiy*.

The bell of the Cusco cathedral is known as the María Angola after a seventeenth-century woman who, according to local legend, donated one hundred pounds of gold for its manufacture. The gold, as Ernesto's father explains to him, "was from Inca times", perhaps from the Inca Temple of the Sun, Inti Cancha.[86] Because of the Inca gold it contains, the María

Angola bell has a particularly pure and intense sound that can be heard up to five leagues away. The bell's tolling turns the world to gold for Ernesto and recalls the image of the indigenous community leaders who protected him from his wealthy *misti* guardians' abuse when he was a child. Though the María Angola might be interpreted as a symbol of the Catholic Church and an instrument of Western domination over Andean society, and though the Inca gold it contains clearly associates it with the conquest, Ernesto identifies the syncretic cathedral bell with indigenous tradition. The María Angola's power to make everything appear golden in the dark of night derives from the gold inside it, which may once have formed part of the Sun or other idols from the Inti Cancha, and reveals the Inca past to be as immanent in all of Cusco as it is in the bell itself. That past is clearly linked to the indigenous present, for upon hearing the María Angola, Ernesto thinks not of conquerors or *mistis* or even Incas but of his indigenous Andean protectors and surrogate fathers. He suggests that the María Angola mourns the suffering of oppressed people everywhere, and associates the bell with the *pongo*, whom he later compares to the Christ in the Cusco cathedral, known as Our Lord of Earthquakes.[87] This is clearly a different sort of Christianity than that which accompanied the conquest, one which anticipates the commitment to the poor and oppressed of 1960s liberation theology.[88]

The sound of the cathedral bell also evokes for Ernesto an indigenous oral tradition that alludes to cosmic upheaval:

> In the large lakes, especially those that have islands and clumps of giant cattail reeds, there are bells that ring at midnight. At their mournful tolling, bulls of fire, or of gold, emerge from the water dragging chains; they climb to the mountain peaks and bellow in the frost, because in Peru lakes are in the highlands. I thought that those bells must be *illas*, reflections of the María Angola, which would change the *amarus* into bulls. From the center of the world the voice of the bell, sinking down into the lakes, must have transformed the ancient creatures.[89]

The passage recalls the legend of the bull Misitu's origins in *Yawar Fiesta*. Here the bulls that inhabit high mountain lakes are explicitly identified as *amarus*, the mythological Andean serpents associated with moments of cataclysmic change, or *pachakutiy*. The oral tradition explains the transformation of *amarus* into bulls as the work of the María Angola through its *illas* or reflections in the mountain lakes, but it would be a mistake to assume that this metamorphosis neutralizes the serpents' Andean symbolism. Rather, the fact that the bulls are made of gold suggests that they are incorporated into Andean tradition and imbued with the redemptive qualities Ernesto associates with it.

The María Angola, at any rate, animates both animals, infusing them with the same energy that turns the world to gold. As Cusco's cathedral bell peals at midnight, for example, the bulls emerge from their highland lakes and climb the peaks, many of which are regarded by indigenous Andeans as *apus*, or mountain deities. There the bulls bellow in the night, perhaps calling to the *apus*. Similarly, after the María Angola tolls, Ernesto observes the formerly inert serpents of the Amaru Cancha come to life: "The carved serpents over the door of Huayna Capac's palace were writhing in the darkness. They were the only things moving. . . . They followed us, slithering, to the house."[90] There, at the Old Man's house, Ernesto attempts to speak with the *pongo*, but the oppression the latter has internalized makes conversation impossible. Filled with sadness and anger, Ernesto has another vision that unites the *pongo*, the *amarus*, the bell, and the bulls: "My eyes filled with tears. I saw the hacienda Indian, his bewildered face, the little snakes of the Amaru Cancha, the lakes rippling to the sound of the bell. The bulls must be plodding off now, seeking the mountain peaks."[91] The English translation here fails to capture the ardent tone of the last sentence. Rather than mere conjecture, the original Spanish expresses a fervent hope: "¡Estarían marchando los toros a esa hora, buscando las cumbres!"[92] This hope is that the tolling of the bell, the reawakening of the petrified *amarus*, and the bulls' emergence from their lakes to bellow on Andean peaks announce a coming *pachakutiy* that will restore to the *pongo* and all those like him the freedom and dignity of which the *misti* elite has deprived them.

The Old Man and the River

The lack of action in the first chapter disguises the deep significance it carries in relation to the rest of the novel. Indeed, its structure symbolizes the passage from oppression (and a painful adolescence) to liberation (and an ethical adulthood). The chapter begins at night in a dark, degraded Cusco and ends in brilliant Andean sunlight on the high *pampa* above the imperial city. It opens with a portrait of the demonic Old Man, and closes with Ernesto's description of the Apurímac River, which he and his father approach on their way to Abancay. If the Old Man is a *misti* demon, the Apurímac is an Andean deity, for in Quechua its name means the "God-who-speaks."[93] The latter, it would appear, holds the promise of an alternative to the suffering Ernesto has witnessed in Cusco, for as one nears the Apurímac, "the voice of the river grows louder, but doesn't become deafening; instead it makes one feel excited. It charms children, giving them intimations of unknown worlds. . . . 'Apurímac mayu! Apurímac mayu!' the Quechua-speaking children repeat with tenderness and a touch of fear."[94] The irony, of course, is that Ernesto is headed for

Abancay and the religious boarding school, where he will encounter misery and cruelty even more extreme than in Cusco.

However, in Abancay he will also see his visions of social transformation begin to be realized by the two rebellions that break out during his stay there. These rebellions clearly resonate with those earlier visions from chapter 1. The *chicheras'* protest march, for example is said to be "like a flash flood."[95] The crowd's movements in the town plaza are characterized as "wavelike."[96] Both descriptions recall the undulation of the stones in the Inca wall in Cusco and the *yawar mayu* suggested by them. As the *chicheras* confront the authorities, the crowd is also subtly compared to an *amaru*: "'Onward, onward!' It was now a single cry that was repeated to the tail end of the mob. The cry ran like an undulation in the body of a snake."[97] In the rebellion at the very end of the novel, the *colonos*, too, surge up from the river valley into Abancay like a flood. Later, having overcome the typhus outbreak, or so Ernesto hopes, they retreat toward the river, which will carry the fever away: "If the *colonos*, with their curses and songs, had annihilated the fever, perhaps from the height of the bridge I would see it float by swept along by the current, in the shadow of the trees."[98] Read literally, the *colonos'* rebellion does not seem like much of a model for social transformation. Though they overcome government troops in order to enter Abancay, the *colonos* apparently do so only to submit to a religion complicit with their subordination. And yet, as is evident in the example of the María Angola in chapter 1, Catholicism in the Andes is a syncretic religion whose symbols are subject to interpretation according to Andean as well as Western codes. If the typhus epidemic in Abancay is not merely a natural phenomenon, but also a representation of the evils of an unjust, colonial society, then the *colonos'* possible exorcism of the disease with their Andean prayers, songs and curses may presage the beginning of that society's transformation.

This, at any rate, is how Ernesto sees things. When Abancay is evacuated, Ernesto's father instructs him by telegram to go to one of the Old Man's haciendas until it is safe to return to the boarding school. However, recalling from his visit to Cusco the image of the Old Man and the *pongo*, Ernesto decides to defy his father's instructions and the attempt of the priests from the boarding school to enforce them. Instead of heading in the direction of the Old Man's hacienda, he turns toward the river, following the path of the *colonos*, for their rebellion has given him a vision of an alternative to the evils of Abancay and creates for him an option he did not have before: that of choosing adulthood in a more just society. In *Deep Rivers*, personal and social transformation alike flow from a mythical Andean world-view that makes it possible to imagine, and struggle for, alternatives to existing power relations.[99]

The representation of social change in *Deep Rivers* is quite different than that in Arguedas's anthropological articles of the 1950s for all of the reasons already alluded to. In part, the more subjective, autobiographical nature of the novel allowed Arguedas to express more freely his revulsion at the oppression of the indigenous population. In addition, *Deep Rivers* is set in Cusco and Abancay, where the opposition between indigenous Andeans and their conquerors was much more stark and violent than in some of the regions Arguedas analyzed in his anthropological articles, such as the Mantaro Valley or even Puquio. The novel, unlike most of the articles, addresses the problem of feudalism, not indigenous communities' adaptation to capitalist modernization.

However, there is also a historical dimension to the differences between *Deep Rivers* and the articles of 1952–57. Though Arguedas worked on this novel for most of a decade, he finished and published it just as the indigenous land movements of the late 1950s were breaking out. Indeed, he would later claim that *Deep Rivers* had anticipated such movements:

> The thesis was this: these people rise up for purely magical reasons. Why would they not do the same, then, to struggle not for a magical belief, but for something much more direct, like their very lives? Four years later the uprising in the Convención Valley broke out. I was sure that these people [hacienda peons] would rebel before the free communities, because they were on the verge of death and much more severely affected than the free communities that have a little bit of land. The *colonos* faced this dilemma: either take over hacienda land or die of hunger and in such cases men instinctively defend their lives. So these were the people who rose up first, the ones who have shown the most courage. This was the thesis of the novel, and it drove me crazy when critics commented upon the book and did not see this.[100]

Arguedas refers here to the indigenous land movement in the Convención Valley in the Department of Cusco, led by the Trotskyist activist Hugo Blanco from 1960 until his arrest in 1963.[101] Blanco subsequently spent nearly eight years in prison, where he wrote *Tierra o muerte*, an account of his organizing experience in the Convención Valley that would achieve the status of a manual for revolution. Indeed, even before the publication of *Tierra o muerte*, the imprisoned Blanco had come to personify radical social change in the Andes. In the last year of his life, Arguedas corresponded (in Quechua) with the imprisoned Blanco, who praised the novelist's works as complementary to the revolutionary struggle.

Despite such familiarity with Blanco and the movement he helped to organize, Arguedas's comparison of the *colonos* in *Deep Rivers* to the indigenous peasants of the Convención Valley is not entirely accurate. The indigenous peasants with whom Blanco had worked were *comuneros* who migrated from their highland communities to an agricultural frontier where they became hacienda peons for the first time. They were *colonos* in 1960, but unlike the *colonos* of *Deep Rivers*, they had not always been hacienda peons.[102] At any rate, though the high point of the confrontation with Convención Valley landowners occurred in 1962, as Arguedas indicates, peasant union organizing had been going on in the region since the early 1950s and had accelerated after the fall of Odría in 1956. The beginnings of such activism paralleled the final years of Arguedas's work on *Deep Rivers*.

The opening up of new avenues for social change in these years liberated Arguedas from the developmental schemes of 1950s functionalist anthropology, based on the assumption that capitalist modernization imported from the US was not only inevitable, but also capable of resolving class and ethnic conflicts. Arguedas's liberation from such schemes is not evident in his anthropological articles until the 1960s leftward ideological shift in Peruvian social science. Nonetheless, *Deep Rivers* registers the beginnings of its author's radicalization thanks to the novel's transcultural narrative form, which permitted Arguedas to imagine the disappearance of feudal social structures not as a gift of capitalist development, but as the result of a struggle motivated by Andean beliefs and values.

3

BETWEEN FEUDALISM AND IMPERIALISM

Indigenous Culture and Class Struggle in *All the Worlds* and *Drums for Rancas*

The wave of indigenous land recuperation movements that swept the Peruvian Andes between 1958 and 1963 put agrarian reform high on the national agenda. The Peruvian state's response, however, was equivocal. While police and army units initially massacred dozens of *comuneros* who had taken over hacienda lands, government repression of the indigenous land movements gradually abated, perhaps because defending the interests of an anachronistic *gamonal* class, whose economic and political power was in any case declining relative to that of coastal elites, did not seem worth the risks of a potentially dangerous escalation of the conflict.[1] Whatever the case, a stalemate of sorts emerged, for though *serrano* landowners' ability to compel the state's armed defense of their interests was in ebb, and some indigenous communities were able to hold on to the hacienda lands they had occupied, the *gamonal* class retained enough political power to block even weak agrarian reform initiatives through the early 1960s. After several timid, and never fully enacted, proposals by civilian governments, the stalemate was broken in 1968 with the advent of the reformist military government of Juan Velasco Alvarado, which implemented a thorough, though flawed, agrarian reform in 1969. Velasco's initiative, aimed at defusing tensions in the countryside in order to avoid an outbreak of revolution, effectively broke the *sierra* landowning class and put an end to *gamonalismo*, without, however, opening the top-down agrarian reform process to participation by the indigenous communities and hacienda peons who had pushed for it for over a decade.

The indigenous land struggles of the late 1950s and early 1960s, combined with the triumph of the Cuban revolution in 1959, also contributed to the radicalization of Peruvian politics and the rise of a largely university-based New Left in the 1960s. As was the case elsewhere in Latin America during this period, the desire to replicate the Cuban experience produced several Guevarist guerrilla *focos* in Peru.[2] Formed mainly by middle-class university students, Peruvian guerrilla groups of the 1960s interpreted the indigenous land mobilizations as forerunners of a revolutionary upheaval in the Andes, or at any rate as fertile ground for initiating armed struggle. Indeed, it was partly for this reason that Che Guevara himself initially chose the Peruvian Andes as the base from which to launch a continent-wide revolution (he subsequently revised his plans and located his *foco* in Bolivia for logistical reasons having to do with the setbacks suffered by the Peruvian MIR and ELN guerrilla groups in 1965).[3] The Andes, of course, turned out not to be an especially propitious venue for armed revolution in the 1960s, but popular organizing flourished in Peru for the next two decades despite the defeat of guerrilla movements.

In this chapter, I examine contrasting representations of the 1958–63 land struggles in José María Arguedas's third novel, *Todas las sangres / All the Worlds* (1964) and Manuel Scorza's *Redoble por Rancas / Drums for Rancas* (1970), the first installment of a five-novel cycle called *La guerra silenciosa / The Silent War*, which also includes *Garabombo, el invisible / Garabombo, the Invisible* (1972), *El jinete insomne / The Sleepless Rider* (1977), *Cantar de Agapito Robles / The Ballad of Agapito Robles* (1977), and *La tumba del relámpago / Requiem for a Lightning Bolt* (1979). The two authors had rather different relationships to the indigenous movements they would seek to represent in their novels. Arguedas, though he spoke Quechua and had intimate personal and professional knowledge of indigenous culture, had no first-hand experience of such movements. Thanks to the critical success of *Deep Rivers*, Arguedas was by this point an internationally recognized novelist, though one without the luxury of being able to support himself by fiction writing alone. Even after gaining national and international renown, he continued to hold down several jobs. Indeed, the early 1960s were a period of particularly intense activity for Arguedas as he took a faculty position at the Universidad Agraria La Molina in Lima (1962), completed his doctorate in Anthropology at the Universidad Nacional Mayor de San Marcos (1963), directed the Casa de la Cultura (1963–4) then the Museo Nacional de Historia (1964–6), edited several popular and academic journals and traveled frequently outside of Peru.[4] He was, in short, a public intellectual employed by a variety of state educational and cultural institutions. As a result, he spent most of his time in Lima and had little direct contact with the indigenous land movements in the Andes. What radicalization he underwent during the period was largely mediated by contact with other intellectuals as well as his students.

Scorza, though he spoke no Quechua and lacked Arguedas's familiarity with indigenous culture, was more directly involved in indigenous struggles. Indeed, he had a long history of radical politics. Like Ciro Alegría, he had been an APRA militant whose activism led to arrest, prison and exile. Detained by the Odría dictatorship in 1948, he spent a year in prison before being expelled from Peru. He spent the remaining years of the dictatorship in Chile, Argentina, Brazil, and eventually Mexico, where from 1952 to 1956 he studied at the UNAM. Outraged by the APRA's abandonment of anti-imperialism and Haya de la Torre's rapprochement with the US, Scorza publicly quit the party in 1954 by publishing an open letter sardonically titled "Good-bye, Mister Haya." His disillusionment with the APRA did not, however, lead him to abandon his commitment to radical social change. In 1956, after the fall of Odría's dictatorship, Scorza returned to Peru, where he plunged back into politics by joining the Movimiento Comunal del Perú and participating in the 1958–63 struggle by indigenous communities in the central Andes to protect their land from the US-owned Cerro de Pasco Copper Corporation.[5]

Before writing narrative fiction, Scorza had been known as an accomplished and politically engaged poet. Though Odría's police destroyed his first collection of poems in 1949, Scorza's subsequent work won Peru's prestigious Premio Nacional de Poesía in 1956, the year of his return from exile. His poems, like his later narrative works, engage social reality directly. In his first major volume of poetry, *Las imprecaciones*, Scorza argued that poets had a social responsibility and that as long as there was injustice in the world it was irresponsible for poetry not to be political. For example, in "Epístola a los poetas que vendrán", the first poem of *Las imprecaciones*, he writes that

> perhaps tomorrow poets will ask / why our poems / were long avenues / along which advanced a burning anger. / I respond: / we heard the crying all around us . . . / There are higher things / than bemoaning lost loves: / the sound of a people awakening / is more beautiful than the morning dew![6]

In another poem from the same collection he claims to speak for the oppressed who have long been silenced: "I am the voice of those who have no voice."[7] Scorza's turn to narrative was motivated by the same desire to make known the unsung struggles of the poor. He wrote the five novels of the *The Silent War* between 1968 and 1978, during a self-imposed exile in France, in order to prevent the land recuperation movement in which he had participated from being forgotten.

Arguedas and Scorza shared the goal of constructing a just society in Peru, which for both meant an Andean version of socialism. In their novels, both authors sought to combine socialism with indigenous cultural values, but they approached this objective from different directions. Arguedas started from indigenous culture and attempted to adapt the Left's class politics to Andean values. Scorza, by contrast, started from the class politics of the Left and sought to adapt indigenous culture to the requirements of class struggle. Both Arguedas and Scorza made use of Andean cosmology and myth to represent the potential role of indigenous Andeans in the construction of an alternative modernity. However, they deployed these elements in contrasting ways, and to somewhat different ends, which make for very different narrative styles.

All the Worlds (1964), Arguedas's most self-consciously political but least highly regarded novel, describes the collapse of a semi-feudal social order in an Andean community undergoing rapid capitalist modernization. Written in a social realist style that looked dated alongside the modernist Boom narratives of the 1960s, it was not well received and has not been the object of much critical attention. I maintain, however, that *All the Worlds* merits closer attention than it has received, for even in this least appreciated of his works, Arguedas structures an apparently conventional Western realist narrative according to an Andean mythological world-view. Moreover, through its transcultural form *All the Worlds* attempts to demonstrate the compatibility of indigenous Andean culture and class struggle. Though the attempt is not entirely successful, it is nonetheless notable for a time when much of the Peruvian Left, including many of the novel's critics, perceived indigenous traditions as backward obstacles to social change. In the attention he gave to the intersection of ethnic and class struggle in *All the Worlds*, Arguedas was ahead of his time.

Scorza employs a very different narrative form in *Drums for Rancas*, which renews the *indigenista* genre by infusing it with humor, irony, and the new narrative techniques associated with the Boom (fragmented, non-linear narration and "magical realism"). He uses these techniques to construct a complex representation of the relationship between modernity and indigenous Andean myth, in which the latter functions as both a means and an obstacle to the attainment of the former. The other novels of *The Silent War* cycle represent a gradual stripping down of Scorza's complex representation of indigenous culture, such that by the end of the cycle, in *Requiem for a Lightning Bolt*, indigenous beliefs appear primarily as an obstacle to social change.

All the Worlds: Fiction and Social Analysis

All the Worlds is an ambitious work of epic proportions that explores in literary form the consequences of and alternatives to capitalist modernization in Peru. To chronicle the conflicts between multiple social groups represented by dozens of characters, the novel ranges from Andean villages and haciendas to migrant shantytowns and corporate boardrooms in Lima. As Arguedas would note shortly after its publication, the story he told in *All the Worlds* was not limited to the struggle of one indigenous community, but rather encompassed the entire nation and beyond: "all of Peru is involved this struggle, and not only Peru, but also a little of the great powers that manipulate Peru and all small countries in every part of the world."[8] Despite its scope and ambition, however, Arguedas's novelistic attempt at social analysis has gone largely unappreciated. At a roundtable discussion of *All the Worlds* held at Lima's Instituto de Estudios Peruanos in 1965, literary critics and social scientists alike found the novel's analysis of Peruvian society wanting, while offering only lukewarm praise for its literary qualities.[9]

This critical opinion has not improved with time. Indeed, as Sylvia Spitta notes, *All the Worlds* "has been bypassed by critics and readers alike" because it is "more than anything else, a thesis novel" that sacrifices literariness in order to develop an ideological argument.[10] Mario Vargas Llosa, one of the most acerbic critics of the ideological novel, argues that Arguedas's attempt in *All the Worlds* to defend a political position by literary means undermines the work's powers of persuasion, resulting in an unconvincing "frustrated novel."[11] If it were just an ideological novel, both critics imply, *All the Worlds* would deserve the relative obscurity into which it has fallen. What makes the novel worthy of continued attention, they suggest, is the presence in it of Andean beliefs, which give the narrative a creative tension and complexity it would otherwise lack.

For Spitta, *All the Worlds* is a predominantly Western work in both its form and ideology, but one which has its transcultural moments nonetheless, for "myths and magical events from the Andean world irrupt in the text and disrupt the flow of the Western rational structure."[12] However, Spitta seems unsure of whether this "subverts or affirms the novel's sociological explanatory system."[13] For Vargas Llosa, the indigenous Andean cosmology that periodically surfaces in *All the Worlds* unambiguously subverts the novel's dominant, Western world-view, which he equates with the "ideological" Marxist doctrine of history as class struggle. Vargas Llosa, who considers both Marxist and Andean conceptions of the world obsolete, is drawn to the opposition he sees between them precisely because, in his view, the novel's intertwined Andean and Marxist discourses are entirely incompatible and neutralize each other. The opposition between them, he maintains, undermines the coherence of the novel's ideological thesis or message, thereby partially salvaging it as literature: "at the same time that it succumbs to ideologism, the novel internally contests it with a magical-religious vision opposed to an ideological one. And this contradiction gives the novel a certain tension in spite of its defects."[14]

The tension between Western and Andean elements is indeed what makes *All the Worlds* more interesting than most ideological or thesis novels, but not for the reasons Vargas Llosa cites. Rather than subverting or negating the narrative's broadly Marxist social analysis, the Andean oral traditions incorporated into *All the Worlds* complement that analysis by giving it a cultural dimension. As early as 1950, Arguedas had argued that class is not the only basis of power relations in the Andes: "social classes also have a particularly important cultural foundation in Andean Peru. When they struggle . . . the conflict is motivated not only by economic interests, but also by deep and violent spiritual forces that inflame the contending groups and agitate them with implacable force."[15] Fourteen years later in *All the Worlds*, he explored how modernization in the Andes was transforming regional power structures in all of their dimensions and complexity. To do so, Arguedas drew on indigenous Andean beliefs to represent struggles between *gamonales* and indigenous Andeans, between feudalism and capitalism, between a national bourgeoisie and transnational capital, between transnational capital and indigenous Andeans, as simultaneously class and cultural conflicts. His attempt to analyze through narrative fiction the intersection of class and cultural identity in the social conflicts generated or exacerbated by modernization in the Andes is not entirely successful. However, it is notable in that it anticipates by two decades the renewed attention that would be devoted to the topic in the 1980s and 1990s.[16]

At the roundtable discussion of *All the Worlds* in 1965, Arguedas was accused of having produced an unrealistic representation of Andean Peru. Under the sway of the economic reductionism and unilinear conception of history in vogue at the time, his critics expected modernization to make a clean break with the traditions of the past by rapidly eliminating both feudalism and indigenous Andean culture. Arguedas, by contrast, registered in *All the Worlds* the persistence of Andean traditions and their power to influence the course of modernization in Peru. If he saw the ongoing transformation of Andean Peru differently than his contemporaries, literary critics and social scientists alike, it is because he was more sensitive to the role of culture in processes of social change. Though not as transcultural as Arguedas's earlier novels, *All the Worlds* nevertheless relies on Andean beliefs to develop its representation of capitalist modernization and resistance to it.

Allegories of the Future

The novel opens with the very public suicide of don Andrés Aragón de Peralta, the most powerful landowner or *gran señor* in the fictional southern Andean municipality of San Pedro de Lahuaymarca. Dispossessed by his own sons of his haciendas and indigenous serfs, or *colonos*, don Andrés climbs to the top of the church's bell tower after Mass one day in order to publicly declare his last will and testament before killing himself. With the entire town as witness, he repudiates his sons Fermín and Bruno by leaving his remaining property and possessions to San Pedro's *comuneros* and poor *señores*, then returns home and poisons himself. As Spitta notes, "His demise signals the end of a (feudal) way of life, since an appeal to Indians in such a matter (one's death and testimony as a *misti*) would have been unthinkable even ten years before."[17] In the hour of his self-inflicted death, don Andrés undergoes a conversion, transferring his loyalties from the masters of a semi-feudal society to its victims. The existence of impoverished *señores*, moreover, indicates that the feudalism represented by don Andrés has been in decline for some time and that his suicide is merely the latest, though perhaps fatal, blow to an already weakened social order. Indeed, the reader is soon informed that "gradually, over the course of more than a century, the citizens of the town, that is to say, the *señores*, had become impoverished."[18] Having dispatched don Andrés in the first few pages, *All the Worlds* dedicates itself to exploring the question of what comes after the collapse of the semi-feudal social order he represents.

Critics have commonly interpreted the novel's principal characters as representations of Peru's options for the future.[19] Don Andrés's eldest son, Fermín Aragón de Peralta, for example, personifies a nascent national bourgeoisie that regards both *gamonalismo* and indigenous collectivism as anachronistic obstacles to its capitalist program of modernization. His brother Bruno, by contrast, is a feudal relic and medieval Catholic who resists what he considers the corrupting influence of modernization. The Aragón de Peralta brothers' contrasting visions of the future are summed up succinctly at the end of the novel by Fermín, who explains that while he dreams of turning Peru into a country like England, "Bruno wants a republic of Indians, run by charitable *señores*."[20] Demetrio Rendón Willka, the novel's third principal character, represents the possibility of a modernity constructed on a foundation of indigenous traditions. An educated, Spanish-speaking *comunero* who spent several years in Lima and Huancayo, he exemplifies the modern indigenous Andean. Referred

102

to by the narrator as an "ex-Indian", Rendón Willka nonetheless emphasizes his continued allegiance to his indigenous roots by describing himself as "an educated *comunero*, but still a *comunero*."[21] *All the Worlds* develops its representation of modernization in Peru through these characters' conflicts and shifting alliances over Fermín's attempt to develop a mine on the property he seized from his father.

Initially, all three join forces to develop the mine, albeit for different reasons. Bruno sends *colonos* from his hacienda to work in the mine not because he approves of his brother's modernizing project, but because he considers Fermín's competitors, a mining consortium backed by US capital, an even worse alternative. Rendón Willka goes to work in the mine as the *colonos*' foreman in order to help Fermín destroy *gamonalismo* and develop the nation's resources, but his ultimate aim is to replace Fermín's capitalist project of modernization with one based on indigenous collectivism. Fermín, for his part, plans to eliminate both of his temporary allies as soon as he no longer needs their help to fend off the transnational consortium's hostile takeover bid. However, he is outmaneuvered by the consortium and obliged to sell the mine, a capitulation that registers in fictional form the Peruvian bourgeoisie's historical failure to construct a modern capitalist economy, a failure facilitated by its proclivity for subordinating itself to imperialism in order to advance its own interests at the expense of the nation. The transnational consortium's takeover of the mine, at any rate, prompts a realignment of the relationships among the three main characters. Rendón Willka becomes Bruno's hacienda administrator, while Fermín takes the millions he received from the consortium and retires to one of his remaining properties to pursue a new venture, the modernization of Andean agriculture. He subsequently plays only a minor role in the narrative, which focuses instead on the alliance between Rendón Willka and Bruno.

That alliance has long troubled critics, who have found it unrealistic, confusing, or even retrograde. Indeed, Arguedas's representation of Bruno, Rendón Willka, and the alliance between them was what most disturbed the participants in the 1965 roundtable discussion of *All the Worlds* at the *Instituto de Estudios Peruanos*. Writer Sebastián Sálazar Bondy, for example, identified with Fermín and was frustrated by the novel's apparent sympathy for Bruno, which he interpreted as a defense of feudalism.[22] Literary critic José Miguel Oviedo was similarly puzzled by Rendón Willka's willingness to ally himself with a *gamonal* like Bruno after having spent years in Lima.[23] French sociologist Henri Favre objected to what he perceived as Rendón Willka's re-indigenization in the second half of the novel. Favre, who argued that Andean peasants were an exploited class rather than a cultural group, did not consider Rendón Willka's apparent transformation from urban *cholo* to born again *comunero* "politically defensible or scientifically valid."[24] Sociologist Aníbal Quijano echoed his colleague Favre's objections to the representation of Rendón Willka, whom he considered an "extremely equivocal character."[25] Rendón Willka's dual allegiance to modernity and indigenous Andean culture, Quijano argued, demonstrates the incoherence of the novel's attempt to reconcile two mutually exclusive theories of social change. According to one, change occurs through the replacement of indigenous culture by what Quijano called modern culture. According to the other, which Quijano did not consider viable, indigenous culture is capable of transformation from within and can integrate itself into modern culture *without losing its content*."[26] For Quijano, the contradictory presence of both processes in one character reflects "the author's ideological vacillation regarding the peasant problem."[27]

Arguedas's 1960s critics saw indigenous and modern as mutually exclusive terms, and conceived of social change as proceeding inexorably from the former to the latter. In their view, modernization implied an irrecoverable loss of indigenous Andean cultural identity, making the notion of an Andean modernity oxymoronic. Because they could not conceive of what Arguedas in another context called "a modern Quechua individual" they interpreted Rendón Willka's reintegration into his indigenous community as a rejection of modernity and an impossible cultural regression.[28] Similarly, the critics' linear, unidirectional concept of social change left them bewildered by the proletarianized Rendón Willka's apparently illogical alliance with a feudal relic like Bruno. Because they saw the national capitalism represented by Fermín as a (or the only possible) progressive option for Peru, they could not understand Rendón Willka's break with Fermín in favor of Bruno as anything but a retrograde endorsement of feudalism.

The novel's sympathetic representation of Bruno is no doubt an example of what Rama identified as an underlying "patrician vision" in much of Arguedas's work, that is, a "subreptitious and unwanted attraction toward aristocratic remnants."[29] However, Arguedas's rather indulgent treatment of the "patrician" Bruno is not due to the youngest Aragón de Peralta's feudal ways, but rather to his defense of a regional culture rooted in indigenous Andean traditions against a modernization imposed from outside. Bruno, moreover, is so steeped in Andean traditions that he comes to defend not only the indigenous population's culture but also their material interests. Over the course of the narrative, he undergoes a conversion from a traditional *gamonalismo* legitimated by a medieval Catholicism to a benevolent authoritarianism informed by something akin to the "preferential option for the poor" of liberation theology, which was just emerging as Arguedas wrote *All the Worlds*.[30] Though he never completely relinquishes his belief in a divinely sanctioned feudal hierarchy, the paternalistic reforms he implements on his hacienda and his defense of indigenous communities against the depredations of other *gamonales* constitute a fundamental break with the latter, who come to consider him more dangerous than the communist and *aprista* agitators in the region.[31] Indeed, toward the end of the novel Bruno lives up to his new reputation when he kills a tyrannical *gamonal* in order, he explains, to redeem himself, and seriously wounds Fermín, whom he holds responsible for the mining consortium's destruction of San Pedro.

Bruno, in other words, is not a typical gamonal. He does not represent the existing feudal order. Rather, he aspires to return to an imagined golden age of a benevolent feudalism that never existed. This vision of the future as a return to an idealized past is, of course, still very much at odds with Rendón Willka's project of a modernity compatible with indigenous traditions. Nonetheless, Bruno's and Rendón Willka's disparate visions of the future are inspired by a shared set of Andean cultural values that the two characters recognize in each other, and this recognition facilitates their alliance in spite of their different objectives. The alliance, however, is temporary, for the contrasting means they use to pursue their objectives limit both its scope and duration.[32] Rendón Willka takes a collective approach to social change by using his position as hacienda administrator to organize an indigenous rebellion. Bruno, on the other hand, seeks his own personal redemption and vengeance by attacking the individuals who represent for him the forces that threaten to destroy his world: the abusive gamonal and the capitalist Fermín. Not only is his solitary approach to social change ineffective, it also lands him in jail for murder and puts an end to his alliance with Rendón Willka.[33] The rebellion the latter has organized breaks out soon afterward but is almost immediately put down by military force. Rendón Willka is executed, and the novel ends with a massacre, in what seems like typical *indigenista* fashion.

Read according to the allegorical function of its major characters, the novel's thesis remains elusive, for neither Fermín, nor Bruno, nor Rendón Willka realize their visions for the future. *All the Worlds* appears remarkably ambiguous for an ideological or thesis novel, and critics have consequently interpreted it as a failed example of the genre. Perhaps, however, the fault is not with the novel, but with the reading. As Alberto Escobar urged at the 1965 roundtable discussion of *All the Worlds*, the novel should be analyzed as a whole rather than reducing its meaning to the allegorical function of individual characters:

> we're trying to read the meaning of Bruno, along with the meaning of Fermín, along with the meaning of Rendón Willka, and I think that we'll never get to the symbolic meaning [of the novel] this way. . . . what I want to say is that the novel operates on two levels; and one is the socioeconomic conflict in the struggle between the vision of a decadent feudalism that tries

to renew itself, or tries to defend itself, or tries to regroup by means of a magical-paternalist vision; and another one, which is the conflict implicit in all of Arguedas's work: the conflict between a Western perspective and an aboriginal one. These two conflicts, then, do not appear in linear form, but rather mixed, confused, split.[34]

Escobar's emphasis on the presence and significance of an indigenous Andean perspective in *All the Worlds* is reminiscent of Rama's concept of narrative transculturation, which it anticipates by more than a decade. Escobar suggests, in effect, that the critics' perplexity at what they perceived as the novel's ideological incoherence was the product of their attempt to read a transcultural narrative from an exclusively Western perspective. By limiting their analysis to the socioeconomic significance of individual characters, an approach that might have been appropriate for a social realist novel like Vallejo's *El tungsteno*, they failed to capture the complexity of a transcultural narrative like *All the Worlds*, which develops its critique of modernization in part through the use of indigenous Andean traditions.

The Yawar Mayu

Such traditions are less evident in the qualities of individual characters than in the narrator's descriptions of the contexts in which those characters speak and act. The *yawar mayu*, or river of blood, whose literary possibilities Arguedas first explored in *Deep Rivers*, is perhaps the most frequently cited indigenous tradition incorporated into the narrative. However, critics generally refer to only one example of it: at the very end of *All the Worlds*, just as Rendón Willka is executed, characters from San Pedro to Lima hear the sound of "great torrents which made the ground shake, as if the mountains had begun to move . . . . as if the waters of an underground river were on the rise."[35] By virtue of its association with the *yawar mayu*, Rendón Willka's death acquires a significance it might not have had otherwise. Instead of defeat, his death signals an imminent resurgence of indigenous agency. Indeed, Arguedas would note that in *All the Worlds* "the Andean *yawar mayu* conquers, and conquers completely. It is my own victory."[36] As in *Deep Rivers*, the *yawar mayu* here symbolizes the power of indigenous culture to shape the future.

If this were the *yawar mayu*'s only appearance in *All the Worlds*, one might dismiss it as merely a concluding flourish of local color. However, the rumbling sound heard at the end of the novel is but the culmination of a series of allusions to the *yawar mayu*. Indeed, the subterranean *yawar mayu* surfaces at many of the novel's most crucial moments, linking them together according to an Andean cultural logic that provides an alternative key to their interpretation. The multiple references to the *yawar mayu* may be visualized as tributaries which flow together over the course of the narrative to form an unstoppable torrent of rebellion against both a feudal past and a capitalist, neocolonial future. The confluence of blood lines or currents of resistance in the *yawar mayu* evokes the novel's title, which alludes to Arguedas's vision of a modernity constructed by and for all of Peru's peoples rather than national and foreign elites, a modernity governed by the spirit of cooperation and solidarity he associated with indigenous Andean communities. By tracing the *yawar mayu* from its varied sources to the roaring flood with which *All the Worlds* concludes, it is possible to identify this vision and shed light on some of the novel's apparent contradictions.

It is surprising that critics have paid so little attention to the references to blood in a work that includes the Spanish word for blood in its original title, *Todas las sangres*. Indeed, blood and the mythological river formed of it appear repeatedly in the novel's most important scenes, including its first one. In the opening pages of *All the Worlds*, for example, don Andrés Aragón de Peralta's public announcement of his suicide is interspersed with references to an Andean peak that rises above San Pedro. Considered a mountain deity by the indigenous population, the peak Apukintu is described as covered in red flowers: "behind the church, the sacred peak that watched over the town appeared red, blanketed by k'antu flowers."[37] The k'antu flowers, moreover, are compared to blood and associated with indigenous beliefs that recall the *yawar mayu*:

> It is the only flower of winter. It opens its bell-like blossoms, which are not only the color of blood but have its sheen as well, precisely when the surface of the earth seems dead. . . . In this parched world, patches of k'antu flowers appear like the pool or lake of blood mentioned in the hymns sung during bullfights, the pool of blood into which disillusioned condors dive in order to drown themselves.[38]

The symbolism here is complex. On one hand, the k'antu flowers are described as the only sign of life during the dry Andean winter, as they are associated with the life-giving quality of blood; however, the fields of k'antu flowers simultaneously project an image of death: a lake of blood in which condors drown themselves. Condors are generally considered representatives of mountain deities, which would seem to suggest the death of Andean beliefs.[39] However, in this case the enormous birds more likely allude to don Andrés, who moments earlier is referred to as a "feeble condor."[40] The condors' fatal dive into the lake of blood evoked by the k'antu is symbolic of don Andrés's suicide and the death of the semi-feudal social order he represents.

As don Andrés prepares to kill himself, he turns almost completely away from the *misti* world represented by the Catholic Church, the

Spanish language, and his heirs, to embrace the Andean world of the mountain Apukintu, the Quechua language in which he declares his last will and the indigenous population to whom he leaves his possessions. From the church bell tower, for example, he directs his attention to the k'antu-covered peak and expresses his affinity for Andean traditions by exclaiming "I prefer you 'Apukintu!'."[41] The ex-*gamonal*'s Andeanization at the end of his life suggests the collapse of *misti* domination over the indigenous population and prefigures his son Bruno's subsequent transformation. Don Andrés's deathbed immersion in the Andean world, figured in the image of the condors' suicidal plunge, functions as a kind of self-immolation, an offering of himself and his possessions to the deity Apukintu. The blood represented by the k'antu flowers, then, is associated with both death, that of the old *gamonal* and the system of domination he represents; and life, that of the indigenous Andean resurgence made possible by his death. The lake of blood represented by the fields of k'antu flowers on the slopes of Apukintu, a reservoir of blood set in motion by don Andrés's suicide and the collapse of the social order he embodied, may be seen as one of the sources of the mythological *yawar mayu* that underlies the social realist surface of the narrative.

References to the *yawar mayu* crop up again when the transnational consortium destroys the impoverished *señores* of San Pedro by expropriating their best agricultural lands for its mining operations. The expropriation occurs at a time when the passing of the k'antu's blooming season has drained the sacred mountain Apukintu of its blood red color, symbolic, perhaps, of the *misti* town's fading fortunes. While the majority of San Pedro's ruined *señores* resign themselves to defeat and, in their grief and despair, burn down the church and other buildings before departing for Lima, one of them resists. As San Pedro burns, Asunta de la Torre, the mayor's spinster daughter, walks into the home of the consortium's manager at the mine and calmly kills him. Her courage inspires one of the witnesses to the murder, a reformist young engineer from an aristocratic *costeño* family, to quit his job with the consortium. As he accompanies Asunta to the provincial capital where she is to be tried for murder, a strange sound is heard in the distance. When asked what it is, Asunta explains that it is the river and that "the river's song travels first to the stars and from there into our hearts."[42] Though he initially finds the explanation absurd, the young engineer is soon won over to her Andean perspective. The narrative does not clarify whether the sound emanates from a real or a mythological river, but Asunta's magical description of it suggests the latter and permits one to identify it as a tributary of the *yawar mayu* heard at the end of the novel. The allusion to the *yawar mayu* serves to link Asunta's act of resistance and the engineer's rejection of the consortium to the Andean traditions symbolized by the mythological river.

More explicit still is the reaction of the *kurku* (hunchback) Gertrudis to the destruction of San Pedro. A long-suffering former servant of the Aragón de Peralta family, she is taken in by the indigenous community of Lahuaymarca after don Andrés's suicide and the subsequent death of his wife from the alcoholism to which he drove her. When the dispossessed *señores* of San Pedro stop in Lahuaymarca before continuing on to Lima, Gertrudis welcomes them with a hymn like an *harawi*, an ancient Andean musical form.[43] Singing the *harawi* moves her to tears, prompting the sexton of San Pedro's razed church to comment that "a river of blood surges from the heart of one of god's elect."[44] Her tears, he explains, will drown those in the mining consortium responsible for the dispossession and destruction of San Pedro. Indigenous Andean culture, in the form of the Quechua hymn, is associated with the *yawar mayu*, which in turn is linked to the struggle against imperialism. The scene suggests that while the town's semi-feudal landowners are defeated by the transnational consortium, the indigenous resistance symbolized by the *yawar mayu* will frustrate the imperialist project of modernization. Indeed, as the consortium's bulldozers begin to clear the expropriated agricultural fields, they encounter resistance not from San Pedro's *señores*, but from Anto, don Andrés's former servant, who had inherited a plot of land from his *patrón*. In defense of the land and of his home, Anto destroys the advancing bulldozers, and himself, with dynamite. His act of resistance is announced by another allusion to the *yawar mayu*: a sound "like a distant river" made by a giant eucalyptus tree swaying in the wind.[45]

The *yawar mayu* also plays a role in Bruno's evolution from traditional *gamonal* to paternalistic protector of indigenous interests. That transformation is first signaled by the *pisonay* tree in the patio of his hacienda, which has flowers the color of blood and is the first place where the *yawar mayu* at the end of the novel is heard.[46] Like the k'antu flowers, the *pisonay* is one of the sources from which the *yawar mayu* springs, and it seems to transmit some of the mythical force of the latter to Bruno. When he threatens the *colonos* on his hacienda near the beginning of the novel, for example, the *pisonay* flowers close up, expressing the disapproval of the Andean world. They open again only when he stops his haranguing and deigns to consider, and ultimately grant, a request from the *colonos*.[47] The opening of the *pisonay* flowers, that is, signals his own opening to the needs of indigenous Andeans and announces the beginning of his conversion.

Over the course of the novel, the force of the *yawar mayu* gradually builds within him and ultimately motivates his murder of the tyrannical *gamonal*, and his attempted murder of Fermín. As Bruno sets out from his hacienda in search of the two, his wife sees a river of blood in his eyes, as do both of his victims when he confronts them.[48] That river is explicitly referred to as a *yawar mayu*, and it washes over Bruno's enemies, which now include traditional *gamonales* as well as capitalists like Fermín. However, Bruno can not contain the force of the *yawar mayu*, for after having driven him to kill, "the river of blood, contained for so many hours in Bruno's chest, overflowed its banks. It had already destroyed those it needed to destroy; now it had to flow out of Bruno or kill him from inside."[49] As it spills out into the world, this branch of the *yawar mayu* flows from Bruno, who can no longer contain it, into its main channel: Rendón Willka and his indigenous movement.

This confluence, too, is mediated by the *pisonay* tree. After Bruno's arrest, the *pisonay* presides over Rendón Willka's organization of resistance to government troops. As Rendón Willka frees the *colonos* from servitude, and as they swear to stand firm and not to run from the troops, the *pisonay* swells with the force of their resolve: "It became taller and thicker, more reddish."[50] When the soldiers execute Rendón Willka under the same tree a few days later, the *colonos*' resolve is unleashed on their enemies in the form of the *yawar mayu* with which the novel concludes. As Rendón Willka explains to the officer who is about to execute him,

> rifles will not shut out the sun, nor dry up the rivers, nor least of all take the lives of all the Indians. Keep shooting. We do not have factory-made weapons, which are of no use. Our hearts are burning, here and everywhere. We have come to know our country at last. And you will not kill the nation, sir. Here it is, it seems dead. No! The pisonay tree cries; growing, it will shed its flowers for all eternity. Now out of sadness, tomorrow from joy. The factory-made rifle is deaf, it is like a stick; it does not understand. We are men who will live forever. If you want, if you feel like it, kill me, give me the little death, Captain.[51]

The soldiers' guns, produced in modern factories, are no match for indigenous culture, which Rendón Willka associates with natural forces: the sun (the principal Inca deity), the rivers, and the *pisonay* tree. Indigenous Andeans will live eternally, he insists, through traditions invulnerable to Western modernity's most dubious achievement: military technology. Rendón Willka's execution is but a "little" death, not the death of the movement in which he lives on. He can go calmly to his execution because he knows that his work is done, that the movement he organized has the force of a *yawar mayu* and will continue without him.

In each of these examples, allusions to the *yawar mayu* accompany acts of resistance against the semi-feudal order, capitalist modernization, or both. The agents of such resistance are diverse: Andeanized *gamonales* like don Andrés and his son Bruno, their former servants Gertrudis and Anto, children of impoverished *señores* like Asunta, aristocratic *costeños* like the young mining engineer, indigenous migrants like Rendón Willka, as well as the *comuneros* and *colonos* he leads. Despite their diversity, they are all motivated, albeit to varying degrees, by the value of solidarity, with one's community, with the poor and oppressed, with the natural world that Arguedas associated with indigenous Andean culture. Nonetheless, they act on those values in different ways. Bruno, for example, attempts to destroy the social systems he opposes by killing the individuals who represent them. The same might be said of Asunta and Anto. Their attempts are ultimately futile and serve as precursors of, or tributaries to, Rendón Willka's organization of a more effective, collective challenge to both the semi-feudal order and capitalist modernization. Though he dies and the outcome of the movement he organizes is not revealed, the narrative clearly privileges the collective force of *comuneros* and *colonos* by making it the ultimate expression of the *yawar mayu* and the trigger for a broader social movement, for the indigenous rebellion is soon seconded by a strike of the workers in the consortium's mine.

By means of the *yawar mayu*, *All the Worlds* proposes a new project of nationhood rooted in Andean popular culture. The novel's ending suggests that, given the historical failure of the Peruvian bourgeoisie to construct an independent national economy and cultural identity, only a popular movement led by the indigenous majority is capable of overcoming the principal obstacles to such a project: *gamonalismo* and imperialism. This does not mean that there is no place in this national project for individuals such as the young reformist engineer, Bruno, or even Fermín, and the social classes or fractions of classes they represent; only that their participation is contingent on the subordination of their interests to the national-popular interest. Indeed, as Spitta notes, the fact that the subterranean rumbling sound of the *yawar mayu* with which the novel concludes is heard by all characters except the president of the mining consortium suggests "that solidarity alone will save the Andean world."[52] The solidarity to which she refers, however, is clearly a solidarity expressed by non-indigenous characters and social groups for the indigenous Andean cultural values symbolized by the *yawar mayu*. The nascent national community represented in *All the Worlds* encompasses diverse cultural groups and social classes, but indigenous values are hegemonic within it.

As Alberto Escobar argued at the 1965 roundtable discussion of *All the Worlds*, the novel's message ultimately derives less from the allegorical function of its principal characters, than from the indigenous cultural values represented by the *yawar mayu*. To answer the question posed in its opening pages, the question of what comes after the semi-feudal order represented by don Andrés, *All the Worlds* uses the *yawar mayu* to articulate a moral or ethical vision which rejects both capitalist modernization and feudal restoration, posing instead the possibility of a modernity built on the indigenous cultural values of solidarity and cooperation. As Arguedas explained at the *Primer encuentro de narradores peruanos* in 1965,

> aggressive individualism will not serve humanity well but rather will destroy it. It is human fellowship that will make possible the greatness not only of Peru but of humanity. This is what the Indians practice, and they practice it with an order, a system, a tradition . . . more or less demonstrated in *All the Worlds*.[53]

In *All the Worlds*, Arguedas, like Mariátegui before him, looked to indigenous Andean culture as a means of constructing a socialist, Andean modernity directly on the ruins of feudalism in order to resist imperialism. *All the Worlds* uses the indigenous Andean tradition of the *yawar mayu* to articulate a simultaneously anti-feudal and anti-imperialist thesis. By means of its transcultural narrative form *All the Worlds* attempts to open up Marxism to the importance of indigenous Andean identity and culture for the struggle against both feudalism and imperialism. Though rejected at the time by leftist literary critics and social scientists alike, Arguedas's insistence in *All the Worlds* on the ethnic as well as the class dimensions of indigenous struggles, and the compatibility between the two, was groundbreaking.

Drums for Rancas: Andean Echoes of the Boom

For Tomás Escajadillo, Scorza's novelistic cycle *The Silent War* constitutes "one of the most important examples of Peruvian narrative in this century."[54] Escajadillo bases his judgement on both the political significance and the literary qualities of Scorza's narrative fiction. *Drums for Rancas* and the other four novels of *The Silent War*, for example, were directly inspired by social struggles in Peru and had a visibly greater political impact than is usually the case for literary works. At the same time, they represent a major formal innovation in the *indigenista* tradition and in Peruvian narrative in general.

Unlike the majority of *indigenista* authors, Escajadillo notes, Scorza wrote about real events in which he had participated.[55] Scorza himself has explained that the novels of *The Silent War* were based on his own experiences as an activist in an indigenous land movement in the central Andean department of Cerro de Pasco. Between 1960 and 1963, he notes, "I participated in one of the biggest peasant rebellions there has ever been in Peru. . . . First as a member, then as General Secretary of the Communal Movement. . . . I collected all the testimony I could."[56] Scorza has explained that he intended to use the documentary materials he had gathered to write a political report on the Cerro de Pasco indigenous land movement and the government's repression of it, but that he found the journalistic genre an inadequate medium for communicating what he had witnessed: "upon writing it [the report], I saw that it lacked the stunning dimension of the events, that there was no way of putting this into a rational report."[57]

The events themselves, he alleges, demanded a different and more literary form: "these events, which I had witnessed on the margins of Peruvian history, led me to conceive *Drums for Rancas*. One day I wrote it from the first to the last line."[58] While this may be a sincere account of the creative process through which Scorza transformed his lived experience into a work of narrative fiction, the claim to have written it in one sitting makes one wonder whether the statement might not be yet another example of the hyperbole that fills the pages of *Drums for Rancas* and the other novels of *La guerra silenciosa*. What is certain is that the form of Scorza's novels comes not from the events narrated in them but from a variety of literary sources that will be examined below.

Though he wrote fiction rather than political journalism, Scorza insisted that his novels faithfully chronicled real events and exposed actual abuses. As he explains in the Foreword to *Drums for Rancas*,

> This book is the exasperatingly true account of a lonely battle: the battle fought in the Central Andes, between 1950 and 1962, by the men from certain villages found only on the military maps of the army detachments that wiped them out. The protagonists, the crimes, the betrayal and the glory almost all are here called by their real names. . . . The author is not a novelist so much as a witness. The photographs (which will be published separately) and the tapes which attest to the atrocities will show that the excesses narrated in this book are but pale reflections of reality. Certain names, certain events, and the exact time of their occurrence have, in exceptional cases, been changed to protect the just from the prevailing system of justice.[59]

Historical sources corroborate many of the events narrated in *Drums for Rancas* and the other four novels of the cycle.[60] In addition, at least some of Scorza's characters are indeed based on real individuals, one of whom even sued the author for defamation (unsuccessfully, as it turned out).[61]

Moreover, despite what Escajadillo has referred to as a critical "'conspiracy of silence' regarding Scorza's works", *Drums for Rancas* had significant political repercussions in Peru.[62] As Scorza was proud of repeating, the attention the novel brought to the case of its real-life protagonist Héctor Chacón won his release from prison shortly after it was published: "The Word liberated Chacón. He languished, forgotten, in a

South American prison for eleven years until a novel rescued him from oblivion."[63] The success of this intervention in Peruvian politics, as well as the international popularity of Scorza's novels, are due as much to the works' literary qualities as to their overtly political content and connection to actual events.[64] Though they are relatively faithful representations of actual social conflicts, Scorza's novels are also imaginative works of fiction. As such, they require an analysis not only of their correspondence to social reality but also of the manner in which they represent that reality.

Combining the formal innovations of the boom with the social commitment of *indigenista* narrative, Scorza's novels straddle two rather disparate literary traditions. *The Silent War*, Antonio Cornejo Polar notes, "occupies a double literary space: on one hand it is obviously conditioned by the new Latin American narrative [of the Boom]; on the other hand, it refers to a previous tradition, such as that of the *indigenista* novel, largely contradicted and negated by the Boom."[65] As Escajadillo has observed, Scorza's works use the "basic scheme of *Broad and Alien is the World*; a struggle, first legal and later armed, between one or various communities and a powerful local gamonal, a battle that ends with the annihilation of the Indians."[66] However, like *All the Worlds*, *Drums for Rancas* and the other novels of *The Silent War* also update this basic *indigenista* plot by including indigenous communities' struggle against imperialism, represented by the US-owned Cerro de Pasco Corporation.[67]

Moreover, while the five novels of *The Silent War* follow in the tradition of earlier *indigenista* works like Alegría's *Broad and Alien is the World* and Arguedas's *All the Worlds*, they present familiar plots in new ways. Scorza's innovations are drawn from his early career as a poet, from popular speech, from the novels of the Boom and from other works of Western literature (notably *Don Quiote*, from which it borrows its humorous chapter headings). They include hyperbolic and highly (some have said excessively) metaphoric language, the use of humor and irony (rarely encountered in the somber *indigenista* genre), a fragmented, nonlinear narrative structure, and a version of magical realism. More than mere novelties, such innovations have a narrative function.

The mordantly ironic humor in *Drums for Rancas* reinforces the novel's denunciation of the multiple injustices of Peruvian society. Indeed, it is the most common form of such denunciation, for in *Drums for Rancas* Scorza's satire of established authority is virtually unrelenting. When a teacher requests the help of a government agency, for example, a colleague questions her sanity by wondering "who would ever think of appealing to a government office for help in a matter concerning the common good?"[68] After the Prefect of Cerro de Pasco hides from the *comuneros* who have come to his office to complain about the Cerro de Pasco

Corporation's illegal seizure of their land, the narrator observes that "The Prefect was not in. The authorities are never in. In Peru no one has been in for centuries."[69] When the *comuneros* turn to a judge for help, he demands a bribe, a request motivated by what the narrator delicately describes as the distinguished jurist's desire to "increase his private collection of circulating currency."[70] Finally, government authorities' unwillingness to confront the Cerro de Pasco Corporation is rendered as a disease that prevents them from seeing the fence with which the mining company has enclosed indigenous communities' lands, thereby appropriating them for its livestock division:

> an epidemic attacked Cerro de Pasco. An unknown virus infected the eyes of its citizens. Apparently the victims enjoyed perfect vision except for a mysterious partial blindness that made certain objects invisible to them. A patient affected by the disease, who was able to describe, for example, the spots on a sheep half a mile away, could not see a fence at a distance of one hundred yards. . . . Prefect Figuerola, Judge Parrales, Commandant Canchucaja, District Attorney Moreyna, and even the officers of the Guardia Civil barracks stopped seeing certain things.[71]

Scorza's use of humor contrasts markedly with the seriousness of both the *indigenista* tradition and much of the Boom.

The fragmentary, episodic and non-linear structure of Scorza's novels is another departure from *indigenista* tradition, but one clearly influenced by, though by no means identical to, the narrative structure of Boom novels such as Carlos Fuentes's *The Death of Artemio Cruz* (1962) and Mario Vargas Llosa's *The Green House* (1967). *Drums for Rancas*, for example, consists of two intertwined and alternating narratives.[72] The first of these, developed in the odd-numbered chapters of the novel, takes place in the indigenous community of Yanacocha and the provincial capital Yanahuanca. It tells the classic *indigenista* tale of an indigenous community's struggle against semi-feudal oppression, rendered in this case as a conflict between the *comunero* Héctor Chacón, of Yanacocha, and the judge and landowner Francisco Montenegro, of Yanahuanca. Within the Chacón/Montenegro narrative, chapters dedicated to Chacón alternate with those dedicated to Montenegro. The second narrative, developed in the even-numbered chapters of the novel, is set in the indigenous community of Rancas and the departmental capital Cerro de Pasco. It concerns an indigenous community's struggle against imperialism, represented as a land conflict between Rancas and the US-owned Cerro de Pasco Corporation, which expands its livestock division by illegally dispossessing communities like Rancas of their land.

Within each line of narrative, events are not recounted in chronological order, such that the story told in each one must be reconstructed by the reader. To read the Chacón/Montenegro narrative in chronological order, for instance, would require skipping back and forth among the odd-numbered chapters in the following sequence: 1–9–19–11–13–5–3–7–17–21–23–25–27–29–31–33. The corresponding sequence for the Rancas/Cerro de Pasco Corporation conflict is equally tangled: 4–16–6–10–14–8–18–20–22–24–26–28–12–30–2–32–34.

Moreover, the two narratives, though parallel and intertwined, do not overlap. That is, they occur in different locations, share just one character and make no reference to each other. In *Drums for Rancas*, unlike in *All the Worlds*, though indigenous communities struggle against both feudalism and imperialism, the two are represented as independent processes with no connection to each other. The presence and expansion of the Cerro de Pasco Corporation in the region appears to affect only indigenous communities, not *gamonales*, who seem to have no relationship to the foreign company.

The two lines of narrative are nonetheless structurally similar, for each describes *comuneros'* initially mystified perception of power and the consequent paralysis of indigenous resistance, followed by a gradual awakening of political consciousness and the rise of organized resistance, which leads to a violent confrontation with the state, acting on behalf of Montenegro and the Cerro de Pasco Corporation, and the *comuneros'* defeat. Indeed, all but one of the five novels in Scorza's narrative cycle follow this pattern and, despite their unorthodox structure, end in orthodox *indigenista* fashion with the massacre of an indigenous community, an event ironically referred to in *The Ballad of Agapito Robles* as virtually a part of the natural order: "In the Andes, massacres occur with the changing of the seasons. In the rest of the world there are four seasons; in the Andes five: Spring, Summer, Fall, Winter, and Massacre."[73]

While the structure of *Drums for Rancas* may seem mechanical and arbitrary (that of the other four novels of the cycle is similar, if not quite as symmetrical) it serves the function of aligning the reader's perspective with that of the novel's indigenous protagonists. The first several chapters dedicated to the struggle between Rancas and the Cerro de Pasco Corporation, for example, describe, but do not explain, the sudden appearance of a fence that devours indigenous communities' lands, leaving the reader just as mystified by the strange event as are the fence's indigenous victims. The limits on the reader's perception of the mysterious fence are reinforced by the switch from third to first person narration in chapters six, eight and ten, in which an indigenous character takes over from the narrator.

The reader, at least initially, is given no more information than the *comuneros* themselves. The fence is not identified as the work of the Cerro de Pasco Corporation until chapter 14, and the reader is not fully informed of the fence's origins until chapter 16, which offers a historical account of the US-owned mining company and the rapid expansion of its landholdings. The *comuneros* of Rancas, now lagging somewhat behind the reader in their comprehension of the threat they face, begin their resistance to the Cerro de Pasco Corporation's land grab only in chapter 18, and only after the local priest, Father Chasán, explains that "the Fence is not the work of God, my children. It is the work of the Americans. It is not enough to pray. You must fight."[74] The structure of *Drums for Rancas*, in effect, takes the reader through the same process of coming to consciousness about the real nature of the novel's conflict, as the work's indigenous protagonists themselves undergo, a process analogous to the political consciousness raising method of liberation theology, with which Father Chasán is here clearly associated.[75]

Some critics have even suggested that the structure of Scorza's novels is a representation of indigenous Andeans' mythological world-view.[76] This interpretation finds support in the author's claim that "my personal experience prevented me from showing the true world of the *comuneros*. I decided to eliminate myself from the story and write the book from the point of view of its protagonists. It was necessarily a mythological point of view because events offered themselves in mythical form. . . . Resorting to myth was in this case the only possible form of realism."[77] A mythological narrative, Scorza claimed, was the only realist means of representing a people who, in his view, still perceived the world in a predominantly ahistorical, mythical fashion. However, while Scorza may well have intended the narrative structure of *Drums for Rancas* and the other novels of the cycle to represent an indigenous world-view, that structure has less in common with Andean mythology than with the narrative techniques of the Boom, which themselves drew on European and North American modernism, particularly the works of Joyce, Flaubert, and Faulkner. Scorza's use of modern Western literary techniques in order to represent what he took to be indigenous Andean tradition widens the gap between indigenous referent and Western means of representation that characterizes *indigenista* narrative and makes his novels appear even more heterogeneous than earlier works of the genre. Unlike Arguedas, Scorza relied primarily on Western literary forms to represent an indigenous Andean perspective on the social conflicts of modernization in the central highlands of Peru.

This is particularly evident in Scorza's other means of representing the mythological world-view he attributed to indigenous culture: his version of magical realism.[78] While Arguedas drew the mythological elements in his works from existing Andean beliefs and oral traditions, the magical, fantastic events in Scorza's novels are largely his own invention.[79] The fence that encloses Rancas's lands, for example, is rather improbably perceived by the *comuneros* as a living creature (though one associated with death by virtue of its "birth" in the cemetery):

> One Thursday, behind one of the cemetery walls, the night gave birth to the Fence. . . . the Fence crawled around the cemetery and came down to the highway. It's the time when the trucks pant toward Huánuco, happy to descend below tree line. At the edge of the highway, the Fence stopped, pondered for an hour or so, and then split into two. The road to Huánuco began to run between two barbed-wire fences. The Fence crawled along for two miles and headed for the dark fields of Cafepampa.[80]

Scorza claims in an interview that his literary representation of the fence is based on actual *comuneros'* perception of it as an "inexplicable serpent."[81] While this might suggest a link to the Andean oral tradition of the *amaru*, *Drums for Rancas* never develops this possible connection. Rather than representing indigenous culture as a source of power and political agency, as the *amaru* does in Arguedas's novels, the image of the fence as a mythological being in *Drums for Rancas* has the contrary effect. That is, the fictional *comuneros'* initial inability to see the fence as the work of transnational capital suggests that the persistence of indigenous beliefs impedes historical consciousness and the development of indigenous political agency. It is only after an outsider to Rancas, Father Chasán, demystifies the fence, that the community is able to identify its real enemy and initiate resistance against it.

A similar process occurs in the other line of narrative about the conflict between Héctor Chacón and judge Montenegro. The judge, like the fence, is initially perceived as an unstoppable, supernatural force. In the opening lines of the novel, for example, he is described not as a living, much less human, being, but as a black suit "exhaled" by the twilight: "One damp September, from around the corner of the main square of Yanahuanca, the same corner from which the assault troops would one day emerge to open the second cemetery at Chinche, the late afternoon breathed forth a black suit."[82] Despite the association of both the judge and the fence with cemeteries and death, the representation of one is in a sense the inverse of the other, for while the fence is an object imbued with the qualities of a living being, Montenegro is a human being reduced metonymically to the status of an object, the black suit. Nonetheless, the effect is the same in both cases, for just as the *comuneros* of Rancas are helpless to resist the fence's invasion of their land, so the residents of Yanahuanca are paralyzed by the judge's mythical aura of omnipotence.

Nobody, for example, has ever dared to perturb Montenegro's daily stroll around the plaza of Yanahuanca:

> Just as on every afternoon for the past thirty years, the black suit came down to the square and began its unperturbable sixty-minute stroll. . . . At four

o'clock the square is teeming with life, at five it is still a public place, at six it is deserted. There is no law against walking at that hour, but whether it be that fatigue overtakes the strollers, or that their stomachs call for supper, at six o'clock the square is empty. . . . Even the dogs know that no barking is allowed between six and seven.[83]

The judge's authority is so absolute that it is capable of privatizing nominally public space. It also paralyzes the entire community, blocking any possibility of change in the social order. When a coin falls out of Montenegro's pocket during his stroll, for example, none of the towns-people dare to pick it up, or even to tell the judge: "At four o'clock an eight-year-old boy was bold enough to poke at it with a stick: that was as far as the province's courage went. No one touched it again for the next twelve months."[84]

As in the case of the fence, demystification of the judge's power falls, if not exactly to an outsider, to a *comunero* politicized in prison through his contact with communists and *apristas*. Hector Chacón, sentenced to a long prison term by Montenegro, returns to Yanahuanca upon his release and disrupts the judge's invariable routine by not vacating the plaza during the forbidden hour:

> At one of the corners he put down a green cardboard suitcase, squatted, and took out a small box. Dr. Montenegro appeared at the opposite corner. It was time for his stroll. . . . The stranger [Chacón] began to smoke. Dr. Montenegro, nearsighted when it came to field hands, continued walking. Héctor Chacón, Hawkeye, began to laugh: his laughter grew into a shout. . . . People came to their doors. In the barracks, the Civil Guards cocked their rifles. Children and dogs stopped chasing each other. The old women crossed themselves.[85]

With his laughter Chacón reappropriates the plaza as public space by demonstrating the possibility of challenging the judge's apparently absolute authority.

If the demystification of Montenegro's power may be said to begin with Chacón's defiant laughter, it is taken to its limit, if not exactly completed, by the *comuneros*' organization of a plot to kill the judge. Upon receiving a note from an informant alerting him to the danger he faces, Montenegro's mythical aura drains from him like the blood from his face as he reads the anonymous missive:

> That is when the Magistrate learned the power of literature. A few words scrawled by a writer who could not even boast of good handwriting or correct spelling (the word "Judge" was barely recognizable without its "d"), a few smudged lines hurriedly scribbled by an artist who would perhaps never leave the obscurity of his province – these moved him to paleness. . . . He was ashen. Was it verse? Was it prose? No matter: the fruit of the

unknown artist's inspiration had reduced the Magistrate to the color of the pale paper.[86]

Immediately afterward, the judge flees his hacienda and goes into hiding, revealing his fear and vulnerability.[87]

Such examples suggest that a mythological indigenous world-view is represented in *Drums for Rancas* exclusively as an obstacle to indigenous political agency. As Ada María Teja notes, the novel "shows how the Indian's mental disposition to live with myth may be used by the feudal bourgeoisie [sic] and by imperialism as an element that instills respect and paralyzes the liberatory function to the benefit of the status quo."[88] The demystification of both feudal and imperialist power that makes resistance possible, moreover, comes from outside the indigenous world, in the form of the priest Father Chasán and the returned convict Héctor Chacón, who, though a *comunero*, has undergone a transformation thanks to the political education he received in prison. It would seem then, that *Drums for Rancas* premises indigenous Andeans' liberation on the abandonment of their cultural identity.

This is a plausible reading given Scorza's comments on myth and magic, which he equates with indigenous cultural identity: "in the Andes, in these spatially and temporally remote heights, myth is natural. . . . The indigenous world has always been magical. Even today it expresses itself magically."[89] For Scorza, the mythological nature of indigenous culture was a result of the Conquest; myth was:

> the only possibility of existence left to conquered peoples. These peoples were offered an intolerable history *in which there was no place for them.* The Conquest forced the survivors among [indigenous] American cultures into a history that denied their very *being*, that questioned their status as humans, their possibilities for life. They were violently torn out of history in this manner.[90]

However, though it may have allowed indigenous cultures to survive, a mythological response to domination was not an adequate form of resistance to power according to Scorza, who claimed that "the purely mythical response is naive and dangerous . . . myth is also a form of power-lessness."[91] To become active historical agents, to make their own history, Scorza suggested, indigenous peoples need to emerge from their defensive mythological shell. Moreover, he saw his novels as a medium for this transition from myth to history: "in my five books I tried to make, and I think I succeeded, the passage from a mythological society to contemporary society."[92] Scorza imagined his own relationship to indigenous Andeans as corresponding to the role of Father Chasán: a sympathetic outsider who assists them in attaining political consciousness by abandoning their mythological world-view.

Nonetheless, this is not the whole story, for the invented myths that are substituted for indigenous culture in Scorza's novels also serve as a means of resistance. Héctor Chacón, for example, does not rely on rational methods alone in his struggle against Montenegro. In order to kill the judge and spark a more widespread revolt, he enlists the help of marginal characters with magical abilities such as the Horse Thief (who speaks with horses), the Rustler (who sees the future in his dreams), and Pisser (a feared master of poisons). Similarly, in subsequent novels of the cycle, Garabombo uses his invisibility, the product of official indifference to indigenous demands, to organize a new uprising, and Agapito Robles prevents a massacre by stopping the advance of government troops with a traditional Andean dance, the huayno, which sets the world, and presumably indigenous resistance, on fire.[93] One could cite many more examples, but clearly myth and magic have a dual function in *Drums for Rancas* and subsequent novels in Scorza's cycle as both an obstacle to and a means of indigenous agency. As Cornejo Polar argues, there is in Scorza's novels "a certain ambiguity regarding indigenous rationality, which is rejected as much as it is vindicated."[94]

However, such ambiguity gradually erodes over the course of the cycle. In the first four novels, the mobilization of myth as a means of resistance confronts myth as a form of paralysis and an obstacle to active political organization. In the fifth and final novel, *Requiem for a Lightning Bolt*, which Scorza considered his best, the tension between these opposed representations of myth disappears.[95] Here the *comuneros* are relegated to the background and serve as a "necessary but no longer fundamental pretext for the situation narrated."[96] Instead, "Scorza focuses all the final interest of this series on the fate of the intellectual leaders of the rebellion, among whom he presents himself as one of the principal protagonists."[97] The rational, Western perspective of such *mestizo* intellectuals dominates the novel, while the mythological perspective associated with indigenous culture is reduced to the status of an impediment to effective political agency. Indeed, in the novel, a regional indigenous rebellion led by the *mestizo* intellectual and erstwhile mayor of Cerro de Pasco, Genaro Ledesma, fails because of what is represented as indigenous superstition. Ledesma organizes the simultaneous occupation of multiple haciendas by a confederation of indigenous communities, but the community of Yarusyacán does not wait until the appointed day and acts alone. It does so because Santa Maca, a locally venerated popular saint, appears to one of its members in a dream and urges the community to recuperate its land immediately. Yarusyacán's premature, unilateral action spoils Ledesma's plan of a unified and simultaneous indigenous land recuperation throughout the Department of Pasco, making it easier for the army to suppress the uprising with another massacre.

Here Scorza has manipulated the historical record, for though the actual, as opposed to the fictional, *comuneros* of Yarusyacán did act prematurely, "they did not do so because of a dream or a supernatural sign, but rather as a spontaneous protest against a legal judgement that harmed the community."[98] In *Requiem for a Lightning Bolt*, Scorza strays from his repeatedly claimed fidelity to historical events in order to make a political statement about indigenous identity. By presenting the failure of the land invasion as the result of an irrational mythological world view, he rejects the mobilization of myth as a form of resistance. The passage from myth to history is completed in this final novel of the cycle, which proposes that myth and indigenous culture are not an effective basis for political organization. Scorza concludes *The Silent War* with a "painful negation of the mobilizing capacity of myth and the conviction that revolution requires a modern and pragmatic rationality."[99] Indigenous people, according to *Requiem for a Lightning Bolt*, must shed their culture, assume a class identity and follow the guidance of *mestizo* intellectuals if they are to achieve liberation from both feudal and imperialist oppression.

The pessimism of *Requiem for a Lightning Bolt* is difficult to understand, for the period in which Scorza wrote the novel was a time of significant successes for both the Left and indigenous Andean communities. The five main parties of the Left polled 33 percent of the vote in the 1978 Consituent Assembly elections, with the real-life Genaro Ledesma's *Frente Obrero, Campesino, Estudiantil y Popular* (FOCEP), co-founded by Scorza himself, garnering nearly half of that total. In addition, although the indigenous rebellions of the late 1950s and early 1960s often fell short of their objectives, the 1969 agrarian reform and a new wave of indigenous mobilization in the 1970s ultimately succeeded in breaking the power of the rural landowning class. According to Rodrigo Montoya, "landowners lost the battle in the wave of land takeovers between 1972 and 1980."[100] Nonetheless, for Scorza the indigenous rebellion fails definitively in *Requiem for a Lightning Bolt*. It is but a flash of heroic resistance in a long history of oppression: "no one will scribble even the humblest epitaph on the tombstone of this uprising. No hand will toss a flower on the grave of this bolt of lightning."[101] Scorza's five novels about the uprising, including the one that ends with these lines, of course belie this claim by their very existence. The final irony of Scorza's novelistic cycle points to his own work as the rather elaborate epitaph for an otherwise forgotten struggle.

Antonio Cornejo Polar has argued that despite their obvious differences, Arguedas's and Scorza's novels have much in common:

Scorza was primarily interested . . . in determining how mythological thought and modern historical thought could serve as the material for a complex process of transculturation that would make future [indigenous] peasant movements more effective, which is evidently associated . . . with the main theme of the best indigenismo: the unresolved contradiction between the duty to preserve indigenous peoples' identity and their right to modernity. In this sense, in spite of the obvious and essential differences between them, the works of José María Arguedas and those of Manuel Scorza coincide in their examination of the same problematic space. For Arguedas the ultimate value was [indigenous] identity, although he accepted and was even enthusiastic about a modernity that might develop from this base, while for Scorza, who was much more political, the proportions are just the inverse.[102]

Nonetheless, there is more to the contrast than this. Scorza's novels represent the transculturation of indigenous communities, but are not themselves transcultural works. Moreover, even the process of transculturation represented in them eventually breaks down and becomes something more like a one-way *mestizaje*, or Westernization of indigenous communities. Arguedas takes the opposite approach, transculturating the novel form itself in order to represent at the level of both form and content indigenous peoples' adaptation of leftist politics to their own needs. Though one might judge Arguedas's vision of the future as utopian and unrealistic, the attempt to radically change Peruvian society without making room in it for indigenous cultural traditions would be proved at least as unrealistic, even catastrophic, by the Shining Path guerrilla movement in subsequent decades.

Scorza died in an airline crash in 1983, at the beginning of the Shining Path's war against the Peruvian state, and one can only speculate how he might have responded to the Maoist guerrilla movement's attempt to incorporate indigenous communities, but not their cultural traditions, into its armed struggle and vision of Peru's future. According to Tomás Escajadillo, just before he died Scorza was planning on writing a novel on the subject, which he had tentatively titled *Retablo ayacuchano*.[103] Since Scorza's tragic death, indigenous peoples have become political actors, both in their respective nations and internationally, primarily through the deployment of their cultural identity, suggesting that Arguedas's *All the Worlds*, in its overall vision, if not in all of its details, may have been a less utopian representation of indigenous agency than has been previously acknowledged.

4

THE *CRIOLLO* CITY TRANSFORMED

Andean Migration in Urban Narrative

Between 1940 and 1960 Lima's population tripled, from just over half a million inhabitants to well over one and a half million.[1] By 1991 it had reached six and a half million, 44 percent of whom were immigrants from other parts of Peru, primarily the Andes. Similar growth rates due to Andean migration were registered in other coastal cities, such that the share of the national population living on the coast grew from 34 percent in 1940 to 52 percent in 1994 (28 percent in Lima alone), while the *sierra* population declined from 60 percent to 36 percent of the national total in the same period.[2] Andean and other rural migrants to Lima settled for the most part in the desert at the outskirts of the city, taking over vacant land and constructing communities known as *barriadas* or, more euphemistically, *pueblos jóvenes*.[3] Provincial clubs, such as the Centro Unión Lucanas portrayed in Arguedas's *Yawar Fiesta*, have played an important role in these squatter settlements, maintaining Andean migrants' links to their places of origin while at the same time helping them to forge new forms of community and solidarity.[4] Starting out as little more than shantytowns, *barriadas* gradually acquired a more permanent aspect and, through the organized efforts of their residents, successfully extracted from the state basic services (running water, electricity) and the right to political representation. By the early 1980s, the population of the largest *barriadas* numbered in the hundreds of thousands, and their residents' level of organization and demands upon the state seemed to announce the beginning of a profound and long-awaited democratization of Peruvian society.[5]

Lima's explosive population growth was driven more by the stagnation of the rural economy than by demand for labor in the city. Such "urbanization without industrialization" resulted in widespread poverty, for the urban economy was unable to provide employment for more than a fraction of the rapidly growing migrant population of the *barriadas*.[6] However, the poverty of these new arrivals is to be distinguished from the poverty found in the *tugurios*, or slums, of Lima's decaying older neighborhoods. Poverty in the *barriadas* is not a result of the deterioration of older parts of the city, but rather a product of modernization.[7] *Barriadas*, that is, are places to which migrants have been driven by the effects of modernization on rural society.

This does not mean that rural migrants are passive victims of modernization, for they have creatively sought to construct a better life in the *barriadas* than the one they left behind in their home communities. As José Guillermo Nugent observes, "the creation of the *barriadas* and the hope for progress are inseparable, it turns out."[8] In addition, Nugent notes that progress in the *barriadas* does not mean moving individually to more "desirable" parts of the city when one's resources permit, but rather using those hard-won resources collectively to improve life in the barriada itself.[9] Poverty, moreover, is not seen as a dead end, but rather as a starting point for a new life. According to Nugent's suggestive analysis, the growth of *barriadas* has produced a popular transformation of cities formerly monopolized by the *criollo* elite:

> The appearance that the *barriada* brings to urban space has been of such force that it has simply transformed *the face* of the city. . . . The territory of the *barriada* is not the product of urban decay. Rather, what has occurred is a renovation of urban space by poverty. . . . Strictly speaking, to characterize the *barriadas* as marginal populations makes no sense and not only for quantitative reasons. One is not dealing here with people "on the outskirts" or at the "margins" of the city. To the contrary, what is at issue is a sudden redefinition of urban space. The city renews itself, but this new skin is overwhelmingly marked by poverty.[10]

Nugent recognizes that there is nothing enviable or admirable about poverty itself, but argues nonetheless that its leveling effect in the *barriadas*, along with the solidarity required not only for survival, but for the kind of progress migrants seek, have facilitated the construction of new collective identities with which to combat the exclusion of poor majorities from political and economic power. Such developments have not been welcomed by Lima's traditional *criollo* elite, which has perceived itself as surrounded and under siege by masses of migrants who, in the elite's view, have "invaded" the capital. The *criollo* elite has responded to rural migrants' transformation or "takeover" of Lima by retreating from the city center towards the ocean and isolating itself in exclusive districts like Miraflores and San Isidro.[11]

Rural to urban migration and *criollo* responses to it would begin to be registered in Peruvian literature in the late 1950s and early 1960s.[12] As Efraín Kristal has argued, the shift from *indigenista* to urban narrative that occurred at this time may be explained, at least in part, by the reading public's increased firsthand familiarity with indigenous Andeans once masses of the latter arrived in urban areas:

> It is impossible to explain the transition from *indigenismo* to urban narra-
> tive in terms of a rejection of the local or the regional . . . the transition is
> the product of a moment in Peruvian history in which the arrival of masses
> of Indians to the cities eliminates one of *indigenismo*'s reasons for being:
> the curiosity that urban readers had had about a population that made up
> a majority of the country, but whose culture and way of life had been
> ignored because it lived in another geographical region. Once Indians
> arrived in the city, curiosity about them decreased considerably because for
> the first time in Peruvian history urban inhabitants found themselves
> obliged to coexist with Indians.[13]

Indigenista narrative had always provided, in Kristal's words, an image of "the Andes viewed from the city."[14] Concerned with explaining rural, indigenous society to an urban reading public, *indigenista* narrative declined when its rural referent and urban reader came into direct contact.[15] With indigenous Andeans' physical presence in urban readers' lives, there was less need for *indigenista* writers to mediate the relationship between the two groups through literature. Readers' interest in rural indigenous topics waned, and authors, including *indigenista* authors, began to produce narratives of urban life.

Initially, the new urban narratives addressed the arrival of Andean migrants to urban centers. As Kristal notes, "in some ways this literature, like that of *indigenismo*, provided the wealthy information about the lower classes. The descriptions of the *barriadas* and of the Indian's arrival were destined for urban readers already established in the city, who observed the arrival of the Indian and the formation of these marginal settlements."[16] However, once Andean migrants had become established in coastal cities and were familiar to urban readers, the emphasis of urban narratives changed:

> While in an initial moment one could read these narratives as *indigenista*
> works had been read, that is, as stories about populations probably
> unknown to readers, subsequently this becomes impossible since Indians by
> then had already been thoroughly integrated into a city profoundly trans-
> formed by their presence. It is at this point that narrative begins to explore
> characters and situations inherent to the new city.[17]

Indigenous Andeans would remain a presence in some later urban narratives, but they would not be the focus of such works, which tended to represent them as an urban lower class without emphasizing their distinct cultural identity.

That migrants were not the principal theme of urban narrative should not be surprising, for modernization of course did more than drive rural-to-urban migration. It also prompted a reconfiguration of the elite itself, as the traditional landowning class's economic and political power declined relative to that of an emergent industrial and commercial sector. To survive, landowners modernized and industrialized their operations and diversified their holdings by investing in urban industries and commerce. Those who failed to do so were often compelled to sell their rural properties and move to the cities, where they joined the urban middle class. The latter grew rapidly, not only as a consequence of the impoverishment of some landowners, mainly *gamonales* from the Andean interior, but also through the expansion of the state bureaucracy. As Kristal observes,

> Simplifying considerably, we can sum up the configuration of the new dominant sector in three groups: 1) a decaying oligarchy that controlled land but fell with the rise of industrialists and exporters; 2) a new middle class that benefits from the arrival of the Indian, made up of groups that for the first time can have servants, cooks, chauffeurs, and cheap labor for construction and other smaller-scale projects; and 3) a new dominant sector connected to international commerce, which directly participates in and benefits from extensive export-import projects and in some cases industrialization.[18]

The transformation of the urban class structure and the relations among its constituent social groups would increasingly attract the attention of writers, many of whom were the product of such changes and had personal experience of them.

The authors who initiated the transition from rural to urban narrative are generally referred to as the generation of 1950.[19] In addition to turning from rural to urban themes, they sought to "renew Peruvian narrative and bring it up to date by incorporating into it the advances in [literary] expression achieved by Western narrative."[20] Their project constituted a literary counterpart to the modernization, understood as Westernization, occurring at the same time in the socioeconomic sphere. As such, it prepared the ground for the formally more complex new urban narratives that would be produced in the 1960s by younger writers such as Mario Vargas Llosa and Alfredo Bryce Echenique, who also drew on Western models for their innovations in narrative form. Whatever their differences in form, the works of both the generation of 1950 and those of their successors tend to be highly critical of the *criollo* elite's response to the ongoing transformation of what had been its urban bastion.

In *No una sino muchas muertes / Not Just One but Rather Many Deaths* (1958), for example, Enrique Congrains Martin examines the bleak lives of youth in Lima's *barriadas*, a consequence of the exclusionary modernity promoted by the elite. Sebastián Salazar Bondy's essay *Lima la horrible / Lima the Horrible* (1964) analyzes the nature of that modernity by dissecting the Lima elite's *"pasatismo"*, or infatuation with the image of a colonial golden age that had never resembled the paradise *criollos* nostalgically "remembered." While assuming the superficial, technological trappings of modern life, Salazar Bondy argues, the *criollo* elite blocked the social changes normally associated with modernity by clinging to a false image of the past, which, despite its falsity, served to legitimize continued *criollo* domination of Peruvian society. Through the story of an aristocratic young man's descent into delincuency, Julio Ramón Ribeyro's *Los geniecillos dominicales / The Weekend Geniuses* (1965) chronicles the fate of a "fallen oligarchy that has held onto its name but lost its power and is obliged to coexist with low or marginal sectors of the urban area."[21] In *En octubre no hay Milagros / There Are No Miracles in October* (1965), Oswaldo Reynoso explores the class anxiety and frustrations of a lower middle class that finds its precarious social status endangered by a corrupt elite's monopolization of economic and political power. Alfredo Bryce Echenique's *Un mundo para Julius / A World for Julius* (1970) vividly portrays the *criollo* oligarchy and its relations with the less privileged majority. Mario Vargas Llosa's *Conversación en la cathedral / Conversation in The Cathedral* (1970) masterfully examines the opportunism and corruption of the Odría years, which in the novel lead some middle-class professionals to serve the dictatorship in exchange for a share of wealth and power. The protagonist's ethical rejection of this path, however, leads to a life of unremitting mediocrity and leaves him wondering "at what moment had Peru screwed up?"[22]

The urban narratives of the 1950s and 1960s generally hold the *criollo* elite responsible for the bleakness of modern life in Lima. With few exceptions, such works are narrated from the exclusively Western perspective of the privileged classes they critique. When indigenous Andeans appear in urban narratives at all, they tend to be represented as little more than the exploited and generally mute victims of the elite. Moreover, they often serve as the means for a self-interested middle-class challenge to the *criollo* elite's maintenance of colonial power structures in a nominally modern, purportedly democratic society. In this chapter, I examine how three significantly different works of urban narrative make use of the *barriada* and/or its Andean migrant residents to critique the *criollo* elite's continued domination of Peruvian society. I begin with Julio Ramón Ribeyro's short story "La piel de un indio no cuesta caro" / "An Indian's Hide is Cheap" (1961), in which, through a spare and precise realism, Ribeyro explores both the elite's mistreatment of Andean migrants and the middle class's ultimate unwillingness to jeopardize its own status to rectify such injustice.[23] I then turn to a key section of Alfredo Bryce Echenique's novel *A World for Julius* (1970), which makes use of an exuberantly oral style and an ever-shifting narrative perspective to represent the relationship between the *criollo* elite and Andean migrants. Both works, in different ways, focus on the upper and middle classes' perceptions of and reactions to the presence of Andean migrants in Lima and elicit readers' sympathy for the abuses suffered by the latter. Finally, I contrast to both of these José María Arguedas's transcultural use of Andean mythology and beliefs, both contemporary and pre-Columbian, to represent indigenous Andean migrants' experience of urban life in *The Fox from Up Above and the Fox from Down Below* (1971). Through his use of a transcultural narrative form, Arguedas does more than incite sympathy for Andean migrants' struggles for survival in a hostile urban environment; he challenges readers to imagine a heterogeneous nation made up of diverse cultures that nonetheless enjoy the same status, a nation in which all citizens participate as equals regardless of their ethnic background.

Julio Ramón Ribeyro: The Price of Modernity

Julio Ramón Ribeyro (1929–94) was from a once illustrious Lima family whose political influence and economic fortunes had declined markedly by the time of his birth.[24] In part as a result of his personal experience of the social changes that contributed to his family's decline, his work "shows an acute consciousness of historical change and the Peru portrayed in his narratives is a society in transition."[25] However, though Ribeyro's Peru is a rapidly changing society, it is one that nonetheless remains essentially the same in spite of its ongoing transformation.[26] As Julio Ortega aptly observes, many of Ribeyro's short stories, for which he is best known, "set up situations typical of the conflict of a middle class moving through the modest hell of a precapitalist society undergoing modernization without democratization."[27] The result, as Ismael Márquez and César Ferreira note, is "a vision of Peru's, and in particular Lima's, middle and popular classes, in which mediocrity, disillusionment, and impotence are the norms that govern the destiny of those 'excluded from life's banquet,' beings alienated by a society that traps and destroys them inexorably."[28]

Some of Ribeyro's best known short stories take place in Lima and chronicle the urban poor and rural (but not necessarily Andean) migrants'

struggles for survival in a city that offers them few prospects. The protagonists of "Los gallinazos sin plumas" / "The Featherless Vultures"
(1954) for example, pick through wealthy families' trash to support themselves, while those of "Al pie del acantilado" / "At the Foot of the Cliff"
(1958) build their home on vacant land by the ocean, but are evicted by
the government and forced to start over again. However, both of these
works focus on characters of unspecified ethnicity.[29] For a more explicit
reference to the theme of Andean migration, one must turn to the lesser
known "La piel de un indio no cuesta caro" / "An Indian's Hide is Cheap"
(1961), which examines the multiple relationships between Andean
migrants, the middle class, and a superficially modernized *criollo* elite.
Though Cornejo Polar considers Ribeyro's work an example of literary
homogeneity, this story displays clear evidence of heterogeneity, in that
not every element of the narrative is from the same (middle class)cultural
universe. "An Indian's Hide is Cheap" includes an indigenous referent and
thereby recognizes the existence of an Andean world outside of Lima.[30]
Nonetheless, the story is a less heterogeneous work than most *indigenista*
narratives. Though it revolves around the tragic fate of an indigenous boy,
the reader is given no access to the subjectivity of the young Andean
migrant, who is described only in passing and serves as a mere pretext for
a critique of the *criollo* elite and urban middle class by one of their own,
directed at readers from the same social groups. Ribeyro's short story,
though not completely homogeneous, is not particularly heterogeneous
either.

"An Indian's Hide is Cheap" has to do with the tragic, accidental death
of a fourteen-year-old indigenous boy. More precisely, it deals with the
middle and upper classes' reaction to his death. The boy, Pancho, originally from Cuzco, works for a young couple, Miguel and Dora, at their
country home in the hills, an hour's drive from Lima. Miguel, an architect, has taken a liking to Pancho, whom he plans to educate and employ
at his architectural firm in Lima. The relationship between the architect
and the indigenous Andean migrant, however, is only part of the story's
representation of class and race in urban Peru, for Miguel, a middle-class
professional, is nearly as dependent on the *criollo* elite as Pancho is on
him. Dora, Miguel's wife, is a member of that elite, and it is only through
her uncle that the young couple are able to build their weekend vacation
home at the private club of which the uncle is president. Miguel, moreover, depends on his influential in-law not only for vacation property, but
also for work. As Dora's uncle announces on a visit to the couple's home:
"I have good news for your husband . . . Just now, during lunch, we
decided to build a new bar next to the swimming pool. The members want
something modern, you know? We agreed to have Miguel design it."[31]

Miguel of necessity draws his clientele from his wife's social class, for they are the only ones in a position to pay for his services. His potential new clients at the club, apparently members of the emergent commercial and industrial elite, want a "modern" design, but their vision of modernity has nothing to do with productive infrastructure like roads, factories, or schools, much less housing for the urban poor. Rather, the club members seek a "modern" space for private leisure made possible, of course, by the labor of migrants like Pancho. The exclusive and restricted modernity represented by the club not only reinforces Peru's traditional social hierarchy, but also proves fatal to Pancho, creating for Miguel an ethical dilemma around which the story revolves.

While playing with the club president's children, Pancho is electrocuted by an improperly installed power line that supplies the club with electricity and is located on its property. His death, therefore, is the result of a defective form of modernization. Without worrying about the club's liability for the accident, Miguel immediately takes the severely injured boy to a doctor, then reports the accident to the police after Pancho is pronounced dead. However, in order to cover up the club's negligence and avoid taking responsibility for the accident, the club president undoes Miguel's efforts by bribing the doctor and the police to declare Pancho's death the result of a congenital heart condition. Disgusted by such corruption, Miguel resolves to leave for Lima that very night in order to personally inform Pancho's parents of the circumstances of the boy's death so that they may take whatever legal action they see fit.

However, Miguel does not follow through on his decision, in part because Dora cajoles him into resigning himself to her uncle's coverup of the incident. She does so by subtly reminding Miguel of his inferior class status: "Don't be like that . . . Come on, put on a respectable face [No te hagas mala sangre . . . A ver, pon cara de gente decente]."[32] By not behaving like "respectable people", she implies that Miguel is putting in jeopardy the class status he has acquired only through his marriage to her, and if he wants to preserve that status he should put the appropriate mask back on. Given the intertwined nature of class and race in Peru, the references (in the original Spanish) to blood and facial appearance also suggest Miguel's perceived racial inferiority vis-à-vis the elite into which he has married. It would be a mistake, however, to attribute his ethical capitulation entirely to Dora, for though she is of the elite, she is allowed only a very limited and largely ornamental role within it because of her gender. Miguel never consults with her about what to do, and this is the only occasion on which she intervenes in the discussions between her husband and her uncle, from which she is otherwise excluded. Indeed, Dora spends most of the story in a kind of idle daze, wandering in the garden, napping, reading, and changing into and out of different outfits at her husband's request.

Miguel ultimately gives up his opposition to the coverup less because of Dora than because he comes to realize the futility of his efforts after discovering that in addition to bribing the doctor and the police, the club president has also erased all evidence of the accident by having the faulty power line repaired that same night. To persist in the effort to secure some justice for Pancho's family, Miguel concludes, would not only be costly, because he would lose the business his powerful in-law has promised to arrange for him, but also ineffectual, for now he has no evidence at all to back up his account of the boy's tragic death and the club's liability for it: "There remained not a single trace of the accident, not a wire out of place, not even the echo of a scream."[33] Though revolted by the club's attempt to buy its way out of responsibility for the accident with a check made out to the boy's parents, for a sum much smaller than they might have gotten in court, Miguel ultimately resigns himself to the overwhelming power of the elite. He accepts the price of an indigenous life alluded to in the title, refrains from tearing up the check, and abandons his plan to leave for Lima that night, choosing instead to go to a party at the club, where he is to be introduced to potential clients.[34] The price of what the story represents as a defective modernity is quite low for the elite, relatively high for Miguel, who sacrifices morality for self-interest, but incomparably higher still for Pancho and his family.

"An Indian's Hide is Cheap", like many of Ribeyro's stories, focuses on the middle class's impotence in the face of its subordination to a seemingly omnipotent *criollo* elite. The latter's dominance, moreover, is exercised in part through the written record, as the club president makes clear to Miguel upon showing him the fraudulent medical and police reports: "Written proof is all that matters in these cases."[35] In this statement the narrative seems to affirm writing's historical complicity with established power and the impossibility of effecting social change through the written word. Writing, that is, would seem to be as impotent as the Peruvian middle class to resist serving the interests of the elite. However, the story is itself a version of the written record, one which reveals both the truth that the club president's false documents are meant to obscure and the plot to cover up that truth. While the fictional character Miguel fails to make public the elite's responsibility for Pancho's death, the writer Julio Ramón Ribeyro succeeds in exposing the elite's responsibility for Peru's defective modernity and its consequences.

Nevertheless, as in early *indigenista* works, the story's critique of the Peruvian upper and middle classes and the version of modernity to which they aspire is carried out by reducing its lone indigenous character to the status of a virtually mute victim. Indeed, Pancho serves as little more than a device for exposing the attitudes of the elite and of the professional middle class toward indigenous Andeans. He is given only five words to speak, all of them on the first page and all in response to his employer's questions. With understated irony, the scene presents Miguel's good intentions in a most unflattering light, without, however, granting Pancho even a modicum of subjectivity. When Dora asks her husband "Do you intend to keep him?", as if Pancho were a kind of pet, Miguel responds by calling the boy over and having him perform a few tricks, in the form of addition and multiplication problems the architect has recently taught his young servant to solve.[36] Pancho correctly answers each of the three question he is asked, replying to each only with a number, and these three numbers, along with a "Yes, sir" at the end of the quiz, are his only lines in the story. Before the boy returns to his duties, Miguel, quite satisfied with himself, declares that "we can do something for this boy. I like him."[37] The irony of the statement, of course, is that Miguel's self-satisfaction quickly evaporates as he proves utterly incapable of doing anything for Pancho or the boy's family.

Though it deals with the presence of Andean migrants in the city, "An Indian's Hide is Cheap" does not attempt to represent the perspective of those migrants, leaving out a good part of the story of the class and ethnic conflicts of modernization in 1950s and 1960s Peru. It reduces those conflicts, in effect, to the internal moral choice faced by a middle class ultimately unwilling to risk its own precarious social position in a confrontation with the elite over the democratization of a rapidly modernizing society. Instead of demanding modernization with democracy, the middle class settles for a "modern" veneer laid over an anachronistically colonial social structure. Though "An Indian's Hide is Cheap" displays a limited degree of cultural heterogeneity, the story nonetheless does not delve into Andean migrants' subjectivity, much less draw on Andean cultural traditions, to disturb the middle and upper classes' contemplation of themselves.

Alfredo Bryce Echenique: A World for Julius, But What Kind?

Alfredo Bryce Echenique's *A World for Julius* is about coming of age in a deeply divided society.[38] The novel takes place in the urban setting of 1950s Lima and registers "the profound sociological changes of the Peruvian capital during the years 1945–70" through the eyes of its eponymous and at least partly autobiographical child protagonist.[39] As the scion of an old oligarchic family, Julius, much like Bryce Echenique himself, grows up in a world of privilege insulated from the misery on which it feeds.[40] *A World for Julius* chronicles its protagonist's life from age five to eleven, a period in which the young boy becomes painfully aware of his society's injustice and his family's responsibility for it. As Abelardo Oquendo has succinctly observed, the household in which Julius is raised functions as a microcosm of Peruvian society, the inequity of which is revealed to the reader through the young boy's growing consciousness of it:

> A World for Julius reproduces, with uncommon impartiality, the privileged life of masters and the precarious one of slaves; it condenses social injustice within one family home, a simplifying mirror of an economic system in whose center it places, like an accusation, the perplexed innocence of Julius, a sensitive and solitary child who discovers a cruel reality he does not understand but gradually learns about with sorrow and regret.[41]

At the beginning of the novel, the reader finds Julius living in an opulent mansion complete with a nineteenth-century, horse-drawn carriage in which his great-grandfather rode when he was President. The mansion, in other words, is an anachronism, much like the social class into which Julius was born. His father personifies the old landowning oligarchy, while his equally aristocratic mother, Susan, was educated according to the nineteenth-century elite tradition of sending children to study in Europe rather than the more modern, twentieth-century one of sending them to the US. Educated in England, where she anglicized her name, Susan unconsciously flaunts her social status by habitually peppering her conversation with English words and phrases. Julius's parents, in other words, embody both colonial tradition and the Peruvian elite's mimicry of European models of modernity.

The mansion in which Julius grows up serves as a microcosm of Peruvian society in another sense as well, for it is divided between a *criollo* elite and servants drawn from all over Peru. Julius's nanny, Vilma, for example, is described as a *chola* from Puquio. The family's butlers, Celso and Daniel, are also Andean migrants, the former from an indigenous community in the Department of Cuzco. Carlos, the chauffeur, is Afro-Peruvian, while Nilda, the cook, is from the Amazon region. However, while their various regional origins are duly noted, these do not seem to imply any great cultural differences, which the novel scarcely mentions. Vilma and Nilda tell Julius stories from the Andes and the jungle, respectively. Celso is said to be the treasurer of the Club de Amigos de Huarocondo, the Andean migrant association of his home community. Carlos is attributed a sarcastic wit the novel associates with Afro-Peruvians. For the most part, though, the servants are represented as simply poor and subordinate to their *criollo* employers.

The static initial image of Julius's family soon undergoes an upheaval that parallels the historical transformation of the oligarchy initiated in the 1950s by the shift in the Peruvian economy from agriculture to commerce and industry. When Julius is just a year and a half old, his father dies of cancer, an allusion to the traditional, landowning oligarchy's fatal decline in these years.[42] When the boy is five, his widowed mother marries not another aristocrat, but rather the modern entrepreneur Juan Lucas, who personifies the rise of the new commercial and industrial sectors of the oligarchy. However, though Susan's second husband cuts a more modern figure than her first, the changes he implements in the household are largely cosmetic and lead to no significant transformation of social relations. Juan Lucas, for example, moves the family out of the old mansion to a suite at the Country Club while he constructs a modern new mansion, but the latter will still require servants, whom he treats with disdain. To Susan's anglophilia he adds his own infatuation with all things North American: business practices and partners, fast cars, Country Clubs, and golf courses. The modernization represented by Juan Lucas, that is, leaves intact Peru's colonial social hierarchy while merely substituting North American capitalism and consumer society for English gentility as the model of modernity to be imitated. Like Ribeyro, Bryce Echenique depicts a dependent modernization without democratization.

It is in this rapidly changing, but still rigidly stratified society that the young Julius must find a place for himself. A sensitive and solitary boy with a mother who pays only sporadic attention to him and a stepfather and older brothers who take no interest in him at all, Julius spends much of his time with the servants. Still too young to have internalized the class divide that separates him from them, he treats the servants like human beings.[43] However, Julius's subsequent socialization and experiences "end up developing in him a contradiction between the values he holds and those which predominate in his society."[44] As he grows up, the values learned from the servants complicate Julius's identification with his own social class, while at the same time his growing awareness of the injustice of his society makes it increasingly difficult for him to maintain the innocence of his relationship with the servants. Julius, in other words, "is an outsider . . . he is out of place in his own familial world, and he cannot really fit into the world of the servants."[45] Through its protagonist's conflicted coming of age and his ultimate inability to resolve the contradictions of his provisional, precariously intermediate position in Peru's divided society, the novel implicitly critiques the *criollo* elite and the modernity to which that elite aspires.

Published in 1970, *A World for Julius* was initially interpreted as a merciless satire of the class Velasco Alvarado's populist military dictatorship was then busy expropriating. Though Bryce Echenique has always resolutely denied that his writing has any political purpose or message, at the time of its publication *A World for Julius* was hailed as a contribution to Velasco's populist "revolution."[46] Indeed, during the ceremony at which the novel was awarded the National Prize for Literature in 1972, the military regime's Minister of Education bombastically claimed that "General Velasco, the President of the Republic, and Alfredo Bryce had destroyed the Peruvian oligarchy."[47] Over the years critics have tempered this interpretation with a recognition of Bryce Echenique's ambivalent treatment of the *criollo* oligarchy. Tomás Escajadillo, for example, observed as early as 1977 that "there is in Bryce, along with a sometimes biting satire, a kind of sympathy . . . for the world of the bourgeoisie. *A World for Julius* is a parody of the oligarchy, but one with a note of ambiguous fascination with that oligarchy; up to a point it constitutes an elegy . . . for a disappearing world."[48] Bryce Echenique's novel does not lack a certain affection for the object of its satire.

The critique of the elite in *A World for Julius*, at any rate, is not overt. The novel exposes the injustice of Peruvian society not through explicit denunciation but rather through the subtly ironic manner in which it is narrated. Contributing to this irony are an oral, conversational style and the constantly shifting narrative perspective Bryce Echenique achieves through the use of free indirect discourse.[49] The text's orality is dominated by the narrator, who uses it to great ironic effect, representing the elite's euphemistic use (or abuse) of diminutives and its pretentious flaunting of Anglicisms as comical, if not ridiculous. In addition, the narrator mocks elite values by consistently associating certain characters with ironic adjectives.[50] For example, the repetition of the phrase "Susan, linda / Susan, lovely", even in contexts where the modifier is utterly irrelevant, subtly critiques the ornamental role to which Susan's class and society have condemned her as well as the frivolity and obliviousness to the world around her that are its result.

The use of free indirect discourse also "permits the narrative to be diffused with irony."[51] As Wolfgang Luchting noted in an early study of *A World for Julius*, Bryce Echenique's novel has "a lively narrator, disposed at any moment . . . to imitate the *manner* of speech of others, to assume the *words* of another person, in brief, to appropriate, fleetingly or over long passages, the *point of view* of another character in the novel."[52] This constant shifting of narrative voice and point of view produces a complex representation of Peru's social hierarchy as seen from the multiple and often contradictory perspectives of its constituent classes as well as that of the narrator himself.

Bryce Echenique's use of such techniques and the resulting representation of the relationship between Lima's *criollo* elite and Andean migrants is particularly notable in a crucial twenty-page section midway through the novel in which Julius first becomes aware of the existence of *barriadas* and of the gulf that separates him from the servants to whom he feels so close. The section opens with a brief flashback in which Susan informs the servants that, rather than staying at the old mansion during the construction of the modern, new one, the family will be moving to a suite at the Country Club and will not need the household staff, who will be given several months of paid vacation. After this background, the episode unfolds in three parts. In the first, the family's aged washerwoman, Arminda, travels to the Country Club from her temporary quarters at a friend's shack in a *barriada*, crossing from one end of Lima to the other in order to deliver a bundle of clean laundry and birthday presents for Julius, who turns nine on what turns out to be a pivotal day in his life. The second part narrates Arminda's arrival at the Country Club and Susan and Juan Lucas's awkward attempt to deal with her unwanted presence in their suite while they wait for Julius to appear and accept his birthday presents so they can be rid of the old woman. In the third part, Julius accompanies Arminda back to her interim residence in the *barriada*, traversing Lima again, this time in the family limousine. The section has a certain symmetry that facilitates the comparison not only of Lima's rich and poor districts but also of the two classes' perceptions of each other and their respective parts of the city. First a poor woman travels from *barriada* to Country Club and enters the home of the rich; then a wealthy boy travels from Country Club to a shack in a *barriada* and witnesses, for the first time, the lives of the poor.

Though Arminda is not explicitly identified as an Andean migrant, the repeated references to her long black hair seem to suggest that is the case. Even if not from the Andes herself, Arminda is crucial to the novel's representation of the elite's relationship to urban Andeans, for she serves as the principal link between Julius and the *barriadas* in which so many Andean migrants, like the butlers Celso and Daniel, strive to make a new life for themselves. Indeed, the episode is less about Arminda herself than about the contrast between life at the Country Club and in the *barriadas*, a theme introduced in the section's opening paragraph:

The Señora [Susan] informed everyone that they would get several months of paid vacation. Celso and Daniel were extremely happy because now they could begin to erect their house. Erect. That was the word they used and why bother with builders or architects? We'll do it ourselves. The dictionary must include a lot about the word erect: it's etymology and, of course, its Latin roots and all, but what the hell, they were actually going to erect on their own and they grinned showing all their teeth and you finally picked up on the associations with the word erect. For instance, there were big buildings, apartments, hotels, suites and they continued to smile with pieces of bread stuck between their enormous teeth. And now a long paid vacation; so they were going to erect. As they dipped their bread into their coffee and milk at the table in the pantry, the association of words continued to grow and the color of the coffee and milk slammed you directly against the brown wall of the mud hut and all that about building lost its edifying quality and, as they dipped their bread, their faces made you realize that the dictionary gave no idea of the sadness, the caricature of the word, the insignificance of the word . . . If you could have seen them building in the sense of bits of bread stuck between their smiling teeth, with their coffee cups in front of them, just a few moments before leaving the old mansion in order to begin to . . . on their lot in the *barriada*.[53]

Presented in free indirect discourse and alternating between Julius's understanding of the verb "to erect" and Celso's and Daniel's usage of it, the passage vividly evokes the kitchen table conversation in which the wealthy young boy first encounters a concept he finds virtually incomprehensible: that of the *barriada* and its do-it-yourself ethic.

Julius initially becomes aware of the difference between the butlers' lives and his own through the linguistic contrast between the official meaning of the word erect, as defined in the dictionary, and its vernacular usage by Andean migrants. The boy's vision of architects and engineers is countered by a "we'll do it ourselves" from Celso and Daniel, who are building their homes in the *barriada* with their own hands. The chain of images the word evokes for Julius – large buildings, apartments, hotels, suites (the only kinds of structures with which he is familiar) – is immediately contradicted by the sight, described in subtly racial terms, of Celso and Daniel eating their bread dipped in coffee made with milk. The "enormous" teeth revealed by their smiles identify them as indigenous Andeans; their table manners suggest their lower-class status; while the muddy color of the coffee itself leads Julius to comprehend the insignificance, from his perspective, of their meaning of the verb "to erect." Celso and Daniel, he suddenly realizes, are not building luxury apartments but rather mud huts, dwellings he can barely comprehend. This linguistic exposure to *barriadas* and mud huts prefigures his subsequent personal encounter with them, which will leave him even more perturbed.

Arminda, for her part, experiences Julius's Lima of large buildings, luxury hotels, and apartments as unremittingly hostile. Halfway through her exhausting trek to the Country Club, as she waits for a bus across the street from an imposing government office building, she reflects on the official, *criollo* city's indifference toward the poor:

So, dressed in black with her coal-black hair hanging down loosely, she just stood there and looked at the city around her; she felt something was really wrong because there were no benches anywhere and she was desperate to sit down. Huh! What a city, eh? Full of enormous buildings, really high ones from which people jump and commit suicide, yellow ones, dirty ones, lower ones, more modern ones, old houses, and then pure cement and no benches and she so needed to sit down. Such a big government building and not one

138

bench in front and oh how her feet hurt. The dirt floor at my friend's house is so damp that now my kidneys hurt too. Pure cement and no benches, what a city, eh? How can it be, then? Everyone walks and they never take rests? They need benches, and it won't be long before she plops down on the ground. Maybe I could set the package down on the hood of that parked car and lean a little bit against the fender.[54]

Here the narrator's third-person descriptions of Arminda alternate with her own first-person impressions of Lima, rendered in free indirect discourse, to produce a subtle critique of an exclusionary form of urban public space—symbolized most clearly by the inhospitable government building with no benches nearby—hostile to Andean migrants and the poor in general.

At the end of Arminda's tiring traverse of the city, the narrative switches from her perspective to that of her employers, for whom her arrival at the Country Club is anything but welcome. In the old family mansion, Arminda rarely ventured outside the laundry room in the servants' quarters and was largely invisible to those whose clothing she washed and ironed. In the family's suite at the Country Club, however, she is uncomfortably out of place, an unpleasant reminder to Susan and Juan Lucas of the poverty on which their privilege depends. Both are momentarily paralyzed by a situation that puts them into unprecedented and uncomfortably personal contact with their washerwoman:

Arminda took three timid steps and she was inside the suite, absurd. Susan observed that it was starting to get sorrowfully dark, which could depress her, and she went over to close the drapes, trying to make the night come sooner and with it the cocktail party. . . . Arminda remained standing there, three steps inside, and suddenly looked dirty and then murmured something. But Juan Lucas wasn't around anymore and Susan wasn't quite tuned in, because for her everything functioned somewhere in the subconscious, just a little behind everything else until, that is, she took a sip of sherry, returned the goblet to the table and now, finally, she could see Arminda and begin to deal with her. There must be some money somewhere, someone has to get it, give it to her, pay her and then take the shirts. Yes, let's do it right now, Arminda, just a second. Darling, *can you give me some money please*? [spoken in English] Juan Lucas, who was sitting down again and pretending to be engrossed in a *Time* magazine, pulled out his wallet and, without taking his eyes off the magazine because the article had suddenly become even more interesting, extended his arm and gave it to Susan.[55]

Juan Lucas, unable or unwilling in this context even to look at the woman who washes and irons his shirts, pretends to read *Time*. Susan, somewhat less insultingly, must fortify herself with sherry before she can face the challenge of paying Arminda.

When after receiving her pay Arminda nonetheless insists on waiting for Julius to give him his birthday presents in person, the situation reaches crisis proportions for Susan:

> She immediately went over to the glass of sherry and took a sip to see if that would resolve anything because the old woman remained in the suite and what were they going to do with her, particularly since Julius might not return for hours? To talk or not to talk, poor Susan must have been thinking, because Arminda's presence grew ever larger: she stepped neither forward nor backward, nor did she start to leave, nor anything, and soon the sherry would be all gone. Susan, too, neither sat down nor went to get changed, and Juan Lucas was quite capable of asking her to fetch his glasses that he's never had, now that he's so interested in the *Time* article. All that was lacking was for him to have been reading the magazine upside down in order for the suite to explode.[56]

Upon Julius's arrival a few minutes later, he breaks the tension with a friendly hello to Arminda, who immediately becomes more animated when treated like a human being rather than an object to be ejected from the room as quickly as possible. Indeed, the relationship between the two seems a closer one than Julius has with his mother and stepfather, who, unlike Arminda, had forgotten his birthday until that morning, and were planning on celebrating it only after going to a cocktail party.

And yet Arminda's visit turns into one of the most painful moments of Julius's short life, because the inappropriateness of her presents – a cheap, garish pair of socks and aftershave lotion – drives home for him, as his mother looks on, the enormous class distance that separates him from the washerwoman in spite of their close personal relationship:

> Susan . . . very interested in it all . . . watched the package being opened with energetic yet false enthusiasm. What she wasn't sure about was whether she could maintain that enthusiasm because the truth was the tiny package was losing the status of I've-brought-you-a-gift and was becoming what it really was – a gift from a poor woman to a rich kid – and turning into sorrow . . . a sorrow that you'll never forget, Julius.[57]

The renewed tension is broken when Susan, in one of her occasional outbursts of charity, or perhaps simply to alleviate the discomfort the servant causes her, suggests that the family chauffeur, Carlos, give Arminda a ride home and that Julius accompany them. The boy enthusiastically agrees, hoping that the ride and a conversation with the two servants will help erase the sadness produced by the painful scene of the birthday presents.

The limousine ride offers Julius his first view of a true cross-section of Lima, from the elegance of the Country Club to the poverty of the *barriada*:

The contrasts were less noticeable at night, but it was still possible to see the different areas of Lima that the Mercedes was traveling through: today's Lima, yesterday's Lima, the Lima that had disappeared, the Lima that should have disappeared, the one for which it was high time it disappeared, in sum: Lima. Whether by day or by night, the fact is that the houses were no longer mansions or castles and began to lose their large yards, and everything started to get smaller. Now there were fewer trees and the houses became less attractive, they were even ugly, because they had just left the we-have-the-prettiest-neighborhoods-in-the-world-neighborhood, just ask any foreigner who has been in Lima, and those ugly square buildings that always seem to be lacking a coat of paint began to appear.[58]

The view becomes even more shocking for the boy as they enter the *barriada*, and Julius suddenly recognizes the huts Celso and Daniel had spoken of:

> at first Julius is bewildered, he can't believe it, he can't imagine what they are. Of course! Huts! Of course! And the area became replete with do-it-yourselfers . . . and then, pam! a hut, so that you'll see one Julius, look, it seems like it's on fire but they're cooking inside. . . . The Mercedes pushes on, lost, enabling Julius to see more of this strange area, which seems as remote as the moon from the Country Club.[59]

Once inside the humble, dirt-floored home of Arminda's friend, Guadalupe, Julius is disoriented by the structure's lack of resemblance to the houses with which he is familiar. While trying to fit what he sees into the only categories he knows, he begins to feel that his very presence among such poverty is an insult to his hosts:

> this was the first time he had been in a house where, in the middle of the dining room with no living room in sight, a chicken was looking at him distrustfully, nervous, under a dim light bulb that hung from a humid ceiling. Frankly the whole place was on the verge of a short circuit that would start a fire and then the family would be out on the street. He didn't know what to look at, so he looked this way so as not to look that way and he felt like he was insulting Guadalupe, Arminda, and even Carlos.[60]

None of the three actually feel insulted, of course, nor do they give the boy any reason to think so. Julius's assumption that he has insulted them is merely a projection of the guilt he suddenly feels. Confronted for the first time with the gulf between the wealth he takes for granted and the poverty in which his family's servants live, he assumes that they must hate him for mentally comparing Guadalupe's home to his own, for having what they do not, for existing at all at their expense. He becomes so distraught that he throws up as Arminda serves him a cup of tea and a roll.

In a literal sense, Julius's vomiting is triggered by the sight of Arminda's gnarled hand pushing a roll towards him, suggesting a physical reaction to sanitary conditions in the *barriada*. However, there is clearly more to it than that. Just before he throws up, Julius mentally contrasts Arminda's bare hand to the white gloves Celso and Daniel wear to serve food at the mansion. The gloves, that is, come off here to reveal what they are meant to obscure: the reality of physical labor inscribed in the hands of the poor. The butlers' white gloves once allowed Julius to maintain the illusion that there were no insurmountable differences between him and them. The sight of Arminda's bare hand amidst the squalor of the *barriada* destroys that illusion and forces him to confront for the first time the inequality that divides a society he had once thought whole. It is revulsion at social, in addition to sanitary, conditions that causes him to vomit. If at the beginning of this episode Julius finds the *concept* of the *barriada* difficult to comprehend linguistically, here at the end he experiences the *reality* of the *barriada* as physically unbearable because it reveals for him the true nature of the world in which he must find a place for himself.

However, Julius's painful epiphany has few consequences. The trip to the *barriada* is followed by a series of banal scenes featuring Susan, Juan Lucas, and their friends, and when Julius reappears, he does not seem much changed by his experience in the *barriada*. Near the end of the novel, when Arminda dies in the ironing room of the new mansion, Julius does engage in a sort of posthumous solidarity with the poor by surreptitiously ensuring that her body leaves the house through the front door, rather than out the back door as if it were trash. However, he fails to confront his family after learning that his former nanny Vilma was raped by his oldest brother, then fired by Juan Lucas, only to end up years later as a prostitute compelled to have sex with Julius's other brother. The young protagonist's discovery of his nanny's fate and of his family's responsibility for it leads him to tears.

A World for Julius stands in sharp contrast to the other coming-of-age novel analyzed in chapter 2, Arguedas's *Deep Rivers*. In that work, Ernesto, barely older than Julius at the end of Bryce Echenique's novel, rejects the landowning elite of Abancay and defies his father's orders to travel from the plague-ridden town to the Old Man's hacienda. Instead of doing what he is told, he risks death from the plague by following the retreating *colonos*. Ernesto draws the strength to break with his social class and ethnic group from the cultural traditions of the indigenous Andeans with whom he expresses his solidarity. Julius, by contrast, has no such alternative image of the world on which to base his resistance to the values of his family and class.

Like Miguel in Ribeyro's "An Indian's Hide is Cheap", Julius is ultimately unable to reject an elite whose values he does not share. It is true that the novel leaves open the possibility of a break with his family, for it ends when Julius is only eleven, but it hardly seems likely. Nonetheless, and unlike Ribeyro's short story, *A World for Julius* does attempt to provide the reader some access to the perspective of Andean migrants in Lima through the use of free indirect discourse. However, because it represents all of the servants through the common denominator of poverty, the novel gives no indication that migrants' experience of the city and of poverty might be culturally inflected, and that their cultural traditions might provide a means not only for survival, but also for challenging *criollo* domination of Peruvian society. By contrast, José María Arguedas's final, posthumously published novel, *The Fox from Up Above and the Fox from Down Below*, not only treats such themes but also relies on Andean cultural traditions to do so.

José María Arguedas: Migration, Myth, and Modernity

Unlike most urban narratives of the period, *The Fox from Up Above and the Fox from Down Below* takes place not in Lima but in the northern coastal city of Chimbote, which until the mid-1950s had been a quiet fishing town of some 12,000 inhabitants. A decade later, by the time Arguedas began writing his last novel, the explosive growth of the anchovy fishing industry had transformed Chimbote into a boomtown that drew migrants not only from the Andes but also, in smaller numbers, from other parts of Peru and even from abroad. The population quickly swelled to over 100,000, most of it concentrated in the *barriadas* that sprang up seemingly overnight in the desert around the original town's small urban core. Chimbote soon became the largest fishing port in the world and a major producer of fish-meal for export, primarily to the US, where it was used in livestock feed.[61] Demand from abroad drove the astonishing expansion of Chimbote's fishing and fish-meal processing industry. The depletion of anchovy stocks through over-fishing would eventually cause the boom to go bust, but it was still in full swing as Arguedas worked on his last novel.

The Fox from Up Above and the Fox from Down Below was inspired by Arguedas's ethnographic research in Chimbote. He initially traveled to the fish-meal boomtown to gather folklore, but ended up studying the effects of rapid modernization.[62] As part of his fieldwork, Arguedas interviewed Andean and other migrants turned fishermen, industrial workers, market vendors, and *barriada* dwellers, some of whom would serve as models for characters in *The Fox from Up Above and the Fox from Down Below*.[63] Even more important for the conception of the novel, however, were the differences his field research revealed between the effects of Andean migration on Chimbote and on Lima. Because Chimbote had been a small town, Andean migration had an even greater impact there than in Lima. Arguedas estimated in 1967 that 70 percent of Chimbote's population was of Andean origin, a considerably higher percentage than in Lima at the time.[64] Moreover, having never been the seat of state power, Chimbote lacked Lima's entrenched *criollo* oligarchy and aristocratic colonial traditions. Indigenous Andeans consequently encountered a somewhat less hostile urban environment in Chimbote than they did in Lima.[65] However, though Andean migrants might not have had to contend with semi-feudal landowners and *criollo* oligarchs in Chimbote, they did face a formidable foe in transnational capital, which controlled a good part of the fishing industry.

Though Arguedas found the social and cultural ferment of Chimbote exhilarating, he was unsure of its outcome. In this city of migrants he saw the possibility of an alternative modernity in which indigenous Andeans, free of colonial forms of domination, could participate fully without renouncing their cultural traditions. At the same time, he feared that those traditions would disappear in the maelstrom of capitalist modernization he had witnessed in Chimbote. Though inspired by the hope of an alternative, Andean modernity, *The Fox from Up Above and the Fox from Down Below* is haunted by Arguedas's despair at the possible destruction of indigenous culture. Indeed, hope and despair are virtually inseparable throughout the narrative.

Andean migrants' struggle to survive with dignity is the novel's principal source of hope, while the destruction wrought by the unbridled capitalism of the anchovy boom produces only despair. Indeed, *The Fox from Up Above and the Fox from Down Below* shows little of the enthusiasm for the liberating effects of capitalism seen in some of Arguedas's anthropological articles of the 1950s. Rather, capitalism is represented here as a dark and malevolent force that degrades both the natural and social environment of Chimbote. The fishing industry's waste, for example, pollutes both the air and the sea: "the dense odor of the waste matter, of blood, of the tiny entrails trampled in the trawlers and hosed out over the sea, and the smell of the water that gushed out of the factories onto the beach made gelatinous worms emerge out of the sand; that stench kept drifting along at ground level and rising."[66]

In a similar fashion, the fishing companies contaminate the social environment by setting up bars and brothels in which workers give part of their wages back to their employers. As a fish-meal plant manager explains: "We'll pay them hundreds and even thousands of *soles* and by God, since they don't know what to do with so much money, we'll also have them spend it on drunken binges and afterward on whores."[67] In the bars and brothels, moreover, workers turn against each other in drunken brawls that erode class solidarity and distract them from organizing. To encourage such conflicts, the manager recalls, plant owners organized a "mafia" of thugs: "we trained a certain number of *criollos* and Highlanders, even some Indians, to be. . . . What's the word, what do ya call'em? To be 'provocateurs'! They'd create disturbances; they'd draw a knife and teach people how to draw a knife and how to kick the whores; they'd applaud when somebody lit a cigar with a ten-or five-hundred *sol* bill, or watered the floors of the bars and brothels with beer and even with whiskey."[68]

The degrading effects of transnational capitalism are not limited to Chimbote's bars and brothels, for the *barriadas*, too, are plagued by crime and corruption. *The Fox from Up Above and the Fox from Down Below* nonetheless focuses on the emergence of solidarity amidst the degradation. As the Andean migrant character Cecilio Encarnación observes near the end of the novel, poverty in the *barriadas* produces not only crime and corruption, but also cooperation:

> Here in Chimbote the most of us shanty town people has all come out more or less equal these last years; we've all come out equal at bein' the poorest of the poor . . . here you have gathered together the people forsaken by God and the ones forsaken by the earth, because by now nobodies in the slums of Chimbote is from any parts or any town. . . . here the people with important names, bigger or littler, don't treat the so-called homble *cholos* with contempt. There might not be much helpin' between neighbors and instead they might even rob one another, misfortunately they'll fight each other a little; but outright contempt there's none and when a big opportunity comes along, we lift one another up the way I lift me *compadre* and me nephews up. That's the way it is. The poverty in the shantytowns is what we might call the itch that makes the forsaken person lift himself up.[69]

The migrants in Chimbote's *barriadas* join together to resist, not modernization itself, but rather the degradation to which the capitalist form of it has subjected them.

Mario Vargas Llosa has claimed that "the Evil . . . that contaminates the world of the novel is rooted in the essence of the industrial system . . . the very notion of development, of modernization, of technological progress, is exorcised in the book."[70] *The Fox from Up Above and the Fox from Down Below*, he asserts, is animated by a vision "hostile to industrial development, anti-urban, backward-looking. With all the injustices and cruelties they may suffer in their Andean highland communities, Indians are better off there than in Chimbote. This is the moral of the book."[71] However, this fails to describe a work in which Andean migrant characters embrace modern machinery, ideas, and urban life alike without renouncing their cultural traditions.[72] For Arguedas, what stands in the way of an alternative modernity compatible with indigenous Andean cultural traditions is not industrial production or urbanization as such, but the capitalist version of both. Far from urging a retreat into what Vargas Llosa calls the "archaic utopia" of rural indigenous life, *The Fox from Up Above and the Fox from Down Below* seeks to articulate an urban Andean vision of modernity.

In Chimbote, Arguedas confronted a new historical reality unlike those he had written about in his earlier novels, a reality of which he had only limited direct experience. Though he was fascinated by the migrant boomtown, he never felt that he fully understood it. Chimbote, he confessed, was "the city I understand the least and the one I'm most enthusiastic about."[73] Nonetheless, his limited comprehension of this city of Andean migrants did not prevent him from recognizing that what he had witnessed there required new forms of literary expression.[74] As Jean Franco has noted, the social realism that Arguedas had combined with Andean cultural traditions throughout his literary career proved inadequate to the task of representing the historically unprecedented social and cultural transformation of Chimbote.[75] The search for a new literary language and form would become for Arguedas a matter of life or death.[76]

Because writing was his means of participating in the social struggles of his time, and because such participation gave meaning to his life, Arguedas found the inability to write intolerable. The already challenging task of finding an adequate literary means of representing the changes occurring in Chimbote was made almost impossibly difficult by a recurrence of the severe depression that had afflicted him intermittently since the early 1940s. Indeed, Arguedas would not finish *The Fox from Up Above and the Fox from Down Below*, for depression made it nearly as difficult for him to write fiction in the late 1960s as it had in the 1940s and early 1950s. Feeling that he was no longer able to fulfill the creative role that made his life worth living, he shot himself on 28 November 1969 and died a few days later. Ironically, the novel he left behind, one he considered a "maimed and uneven narrative", is remarkable despite its incompleteness.[77] As Mario Vargas Llosa admits, "in a novel in which he said that he was going to kill himself because he felt he lacked the energy to keep creating, Arguedas gave the most convincing proof that he was a creator."[78]

Indeed, *The Fox from Up Above and the Fox from Down Below* is Arguedas's most strikingly original and innovative work. Mythological narrative, testimonial fiction, ethnography, diary, suicide note, and novel all at once, *The Fox from Up Above and the Fox from Down Below* defies easy classification. Advised by his psychologists to write about the difficulty of writing the novel as a means of working through creatively unproductive periods, Arguedas ultimately incorporated his diaries into the narrative, alternating them with the fictional chapters he was able to complete. In the diaries, he reflects on his deepening depression, his first, failed suicide attempt of 1966 and his plans to try again, his struggle to write the novel and the difficulty of doing so, his relationships to other Latin American novelists, particularly those of the Boom, as well as the place and value of his work alongside theirs. In the final diary and an epilogue consisting of letters to his publisher and the rector and students of the university where he worked, he outlines how the novel might have concluded, explains his inability to finish it and his reasons for killing himself.

The polished language of the diaries, particularly in several highly lyrical passages informed by an Andean perspective on the natural world, indicates that Arguedas's reflections were more than random jottings. Indeed, they are an integral part of the book. The inclusion of the diaries, for example, foregrounds Arguedas's struggle to give literary form to the vision of an alternative modernity he had glimpsed in Chimbote, adding a reflexive dimension to *The Fox from Up Above and the Fox from Down Below* that his earlier novels had lacked. Constantly reminded not only that the chapters which alternate with the diaries are creative works of fiction, but also of the challenge of representing new realities for which adequate literary forms had yet to be imagined, the reader is made aware of the problematic relationship of language to social reality and of the lag between historical change and the availability of the means for comprehending it.

The form Arguedas ultimately gave the fictional chapters of the narrative is particularly complex. As in his earlier novels, in *The Fox from Up Above and the Fox from Down Below* he transculturates the Western novel by incorporating into it elements of indigenous Andean culture, which are themselves transformed in the process. Here, however, what gets transculturated is not social realism but rather a modernism akin to that of early twentieth-century European and North American urban narratives such as James Joyce's *Ulysses* (1922) or John dos Passos's *Manhattan Transfer* (1925). Martin Lienhard suggests that, confronted with "the painful novelty of modern urban life", such authors developed "a narrative aesthetic that renders the uprootedness, the frustration, individuals' lack of personal and historical options."[79] Half a century later, Arguedas would rely in part on similar narrative techniques in order to represent a dependent, neo-colonial version of modern urban life. Lienhard does not attribute the narrative complexities of *The Fox from Up Above and the Fox from Down Below* to any direct Euro-North American modernist influence, for there is no evidence that Arguedas had read Joyce or Dos Passos. Rather, he suggests that, confronted with an analogous (though not identical) historical situation, Arguedas developed comparable narrative techniques.[80]

The events related in the fictional chapters of *The Fox from Up Above and the Fox from Down Below*, for example, do not unfold in a linear, cause-and-effect fashion, nor do they progress, as in *Deep Rivers* or *All the Worlds*, toward anything resembling the climactic resolution of an initial conflict. In place of a plot, Arguedas's last novel offers only a series of loosely interconnected episodes, often cutting abruptly from one to another in cinematic fashion.[81] In addition, *The Fox from Up Above and the Fox from Down Below* lacks a central protagonist or hero and dispenses with an omniscient narrator in favor of one whose perspective is as limited as that of the novel's many characters, who are developed primarily through their own words. The fictional chapters in effect consist of extended dialogues between characters from the Andes and the coast, from Peru and the United States, who engage each other across the cultural differences that divide them. As a result, the narrative represents Chimbote from multiple perspectives, shifting continually from one to another. However, the novel's modernist narrative techniques do not exhaust its complexity, for Arguedas also draws on Andean cultural traditions. As Lienhard has observed, "Quechua culture may be considered a 'text' or group of 'texts' that, within *The Fox*, has the same function that texts from the past generally have in literary works: raw material that is destroyed and reelaborated. In this case the text is not a predominantly verbal product, but rather a complex system made up of verbal, musical, gestural, and other kinds of signs."[82] In addition to Western literary works, the novel's intertexts include several forms of indigenous culture, such as the Quechua language, pre-Columbian mythology, and contemporary Andean music and dance. Moreover, these play a structural role in the novel.

Quechua pronunciation and syntax, for example, "subtly disorder" the Spanish language of Andean migrant characters in *The Fox from Up Above and the Fox from Down Below*. As already discussed in chapter 1, Arguedas had used a similar technique in *Yawar Fiesta* to represent dialogue in Quechua. The difference here is that the "subtly disordered" Spanish is not meant to represent spoken Quechua, but rather the Andeanized Spanish used by indigenous migrants to the coast. Moreover, in order to suggest the mutual cultural influence between characters from the coast and the Andes, Arguedas varies the degree to which their Spanish is "disordered" by Quechua linguistic patterns. This is true not only of Andean migrant characters, but also of certain characters from the coast and even the US, whose Spanish at times undergoes a sudden, temporary quechuanization that serves to indicate their susceptibility to Andean cultural influence.

In addition, *The Fox from Up Above and the Fox from Down Below* rests on a substratum of Andean mythology. The novel's title, for example, alludes to an Andean conceptual division of the universe that dates to pre-Columbian times but is still extant in many indigenous communities today. In Andean mythology, the world consists of complementary upper (*hanan*) and lower (*hurin*) halves, viewed, moreover, as masculine and feminine, respectively.[83] In order to represent the modern version of the encounter and relationship between the Andes and the coast, Arguedas draws on pre-Columbian oral traditions collected at the beginning of the seventeenth century by the priest and "extirpator of idolatry", Francisco de Ávila. De Ávila's purpose in gathering such material from native informants in his parish in the central Andean region of Huarochirí was to better eradicate pre-Columbian beliefs that the colonial church considered idolatrous. In the process, however, he left a valuable record of Andean mythology.[84] Arguedas translated de Ávila's manuscript from Quechua to Spanish in 1966 and considered it "a kind of *Popol Vuh* of Andean antiquity."[85]

In the Huarochirí manuscript, Arguedas thought he had found the key to the problem of representing the changes he had witnessed in Chimbote. As Ana María Gazzolo notes, "the allusion to the pre-Hispanic past is not intended as a melancholy evocation of something that no longer exists, something irremediably lost. Rather, the allusion posits the thought that created these myths as valid, as having a future, and as having transcended the limits of the Andean."[86] Andean myth would provide the means for turning the modern Western novel into an adequate instrument for representing the transformation of Chimbote and of Peru. What appear as chapters five and twelve in the Huarochirí manuscript are of particular importance for *The Fox from Up Above and the Fox from Down Below*.

In chapter 5, from which the novel draws its title, a conversation between two foxes, one from the Andes up above, the other from the coast down below, helps a poor man, Huatyacuri, son of the god Pariacaca, triumph over the wealthy. As he naps one day on a mountainside, Huatyacuri overhears the foxes' conversation, from which he learns the cause of a rich man's illness. Armed with this information, Pariacaca's impoverished son finds the rich man and cures him in exchange for permission to marry the man's youngest daughter. The marriage, however, provokes the jealousy of one of the rich man's other, wealthy sons-in-law, who challenges Huatyacuri to a series of contests in which song and dance figure prominently. With the help of Pariacaca and various animals, Huatyacuri easily triumphs over his rival in every contest. Indeed, so powerful is Huatyacuri's singing that it causes the world to move and turns his adversary into a deer. Much like they help the poor man Huatyacuri triumph over the wealthy in the Huarochirí manuscript, in *The Fox from Up Above and the Fox from Down Below* the mythological foxes embody the role of Andean tradition in the struggle of the poor, from above and from below, against the rich.

Arguedas apparently intended the foxes to be the narrators of the novel's fictional chapters.[87] Through their dialogues, they were to relate the transformation of Chimbote. However, the foxes turned out to be more difficult to handle than Arguedas had expected. In the novel's second diary, for example, he asks himself "why on earth did I put such difficult foxes into the novel?", while in the third he complains that "These Foxes have gotten out of my reach; either they run a lot or else they're far away. Maybe I aimed at a target that was too far away or perhaps I'll suddenly catch up with the *Foxes* and never let go of them again."[88] Indeed, Arguedas completed only two fragments of the dialogues through which the foxes were to narrate the fictional chapters of *The Fox from Up Above and the Fox from Down Below.*[89] By some accounts, the mythological animals merely serve as "names attributed to a function, that of narrating events from up above and from down below."[90] Nonetheless, this is not their only role in the novel, for they also appear as characters on several occasions.

Chapter 12 of the Huarochirí manuscript relates a story about another of Pariacaca's sons, Tutaykire, a mythological Andean leader who sets out to conquer the coast. After some early success, he is himself conquered by a coastal woman who seduces him with drink and sex. The woman

> waited for him in her field thinking to beguile him by showing off her . . . private parts and her breasts. "Rest a while, sir; have a little sip of this maize beer and a taste of this *ticti*", she said. At that moment, in that way, he fell behind. When they saw him do that, his other brothers likewise stayed behind, carrying the conquest only as far as the place called Pacha Marca in Lower Allauca. If this woman hadn't beguiled them, the Huaro Cheri and Quinti fields would now reach as far as Lower Caranco and Chilca.[91]

The masculine Tutaykire, from up above in the Andes, fails to conquer the coast down below, represented as feminine, because he succumbs to the temptations offered by what is, for him, an alien culture. The mythological tale of Tutaykire anticipates by several centuries the main theme of *The Fox from Up Above and the Fox from Down Below*: the twentieth-century Andean "reconquest" of the coast through migration. Arguedas uses the Tutaykire story from the Huarochirí manuscript as a means of representing the dangers Andean migrants face in their modern attempt to secure survival and citizenship in Chimbote and the rest of coastal, *criollo* Peru. As will be discussed below, chapter 12 of the

Huarochirí manuscript underlies and serves as an interpretive code for understanding chapter 1 of *The Fox from Up Above and the Fox from Down Below*.

Finally, just as pre-Columbian music and dance from the Andes play a key role in the Huatyacuri tale from the Huarochirí manuscript, contemporary Andean music and dance, performed by foxes, no less, are integral to *The Fox from Up Above and the Fox from Down Below*. In chapter 3, for example, during an extended dialogue between a semi-mythological fox-like character from the Andes and the manager of a Chimbote fish-meal processing plant, the Andean character performs a dance so captivating and infectious that the plant manager finds himself possessed by indigenous tradition and begins to sing and dance. Much like the *mistis'* admiration for Andean dance in *Yawar Fiesta*, the exchange between the two characters in chapter 3 of *The Fox from Up Above and the Fox from Down Below* illustrates the powerful influence of indigenous Andean culture even on Westernized elites. However, the importance of music and dance is not limited to their inclusion in the novel as mere content, for as Martin Lienhard has demonstrated, the extended dialogue in chapter 3 reproduces as printed text the form of Andean ceremonial dance competitions from the province of Lucanas, the setting of *Yawar Fiesta*.[92] Andean dance, that is, gives the narrative its very form in this chapter, a form evident only to a reader intimately familiar with the indigenous cultural traditions of the Andes.[93]

Though the transcultural complexity of *The Fox from Up Above and the Fox from Down Below* delayed critical comprehension and appreciation of the novel, the bibliography on Arguedas's last work has grown steadily in recent years, particularly since the publication of Martin Lienhard's ground breaking study, *Cultura popular andina y forma novelesca: zorros y danzantes en la última novela de Arguedas / Andean Popular Culture and Novelistic Form: Foxes and Dancers in Arguedas's Last Novel* (1981).[94] Rather than analyze the entire novel, in the remainder of this chapter I examines Arguedas's use of the Tutaykire myth, of the foxes from the Huatyacuri myth, of Andean music and dance, and of Quechua-inflected Spanish in three examples from the fictional chapters of the narrative.

The first example, or cluster of examples, comes from chapter 1, which takes place largely in and around one of Chimbote's brothels. Prostitution and the degradation that results from it are the organizing themes of the chapter, which draws a parallel between the exploitation of women in the brothels set up by the fishing industry and the exploitation of Peru's natural resources by foreign capital. A male character visiting the brothel, for example, at one point describes the bay on which Chimbote is located as both a female sexual organ and a prostitute: "That's the big 'pussy' nowadays, the sea of Chimbote. It used to be a mirror, now it's the most generous, foul-smelling whore 'pussy' there is."[95] Shortly thereafter, he compares the orders a prostitute takes from men to the orders Chimbote receives from abroad. The prostitute, he says, is "like the great 'pussy' of Chimbote when they send the orders down from New York to Lima and from Lima to Chimbote."[96] Associating the female body with the nation, and using the violation of female characters by foreign ones to represent the violation of national territory by foreign interests, are of course old, and tired, nationalist tropes. Within the *indigenista* narrative tradition one can trace them back at least to Vallejo's *El tungsteno* (1932), and its use by Arguedas in the late 1960s is no innovation.

What is new is the way Arguedas combines these old nationalist and *indigenista* tropes with Andean mythology. The narrator's description of the lowest class of prostitutes at the brothel, for example, clearly alludes to the Tutaykire myth from the Huarochirí manuscript: "Wearing cotton dresses, the prostitutes appeared seated in the back of the rooms, on low boxes. Almost all of them sat with their legs apart, showing their sex, their 'pussy,' shaved or not."[97] The allusion is made quite explicit at the end of chapter 1 when, in the foxes' second conversation, the fox from up above recalls that Tutaykire "was detained by a harlot virgin who awaited him with bare legs widespread, her breasts uncovered, and with a large jug of corn beer [chicha]."[98] By evoking the Tutaykire myth in the description of the prostitutes, the narrative identifies contemporary Andean migrants with the mythological hero and the brothels created by the anchovy boom with the woman who frustrated Tutaykire's conquest of the coast. The parallel suggests that the brothels, and, more generally, the capitalist form of modernization responsible for their existence, threaten Andean migrants' modern conquest of coastal Peru.

However, the threat may be overcome, as the account of Asto's visit to the brothel indicates. An Andean migrant turned fisherman, Asto earns more money than he has ever seen before in his life. Arriving at the brothel flush with cash, he attempts to prove that he has acculturated, that he is no longer a despised *serrano*, by paying for sex with and verbally abusing "La Argentina", the whitest, most expensive prostitute in the brothel: "You, lazy white whore. Here it is, damnit. Two hundred *soles* nothin' to me. Whoring whore."[99] By sexually dominating the white Argentine prostitute and addressing her in exaggeratedly *machista* language, Asto whitens himself by symbolically reversing the conquest (in which Spanish men raped indigenous women) and inverting the colonial hierarchy between dominant *criollos* and subordinate Andeans, or so he seems to think. As he comes out of the brothel, for example, he triumphantly exclaims, "Me *criollo* . . . from the coast, goddamnit; me from Argentina, goddamnit. Who highlander now?"[100]

However, his self-alienated attempt to pass as a *criollo* fails when he boards a taxi to go home and the driver, hearing Asto's heavily Andeanized Spanish, easily identifies him as a "dumb *serrano*."[101] When Asto tries to assert his newly acquired "*criollo*" identity by force, the driver throws him out of the cab, calling him a "highland *cholo* son of a bitch."[102] Returning to the brothel on foot, Asto realizes that imitating *criollos* and degrading women will not get him the respect he seeks. Rather than continuing on a course of alienated acculturation, he stops denying his indigenous identity and abandons his effort to define himself as a *criollo* through the subordination and exploitation of others. He marks the change by removing his sister from the brothel, where he had been prostituting her. Their taxi ride home, moreover, contrasts sharply with Asto's initial departure: "Soon after the car pulled out the driver heard the passenger speaking Quechua loudly, then almost shouting. The woman answered him the same way. Then they both spoke at the same time. They seemed a happy, but desperate pair."[103] Now unashamed of speaking Quechua, Asto no longer pretends to be a *criollo*. That this is not a definitive liberation from the degradation of Chimbote, for either Asto or his sister, is underscored by the narrator's contradictory description of the two as simultaneously happy and desperate, an incongruous pairing of adjectives that suggests the uncertain outcome of Chimbote's, and Peru's, ongoing transformation.[104]

Jean Franco has rightly criticized women's limited and passive role in Arguedas's and other male novelists' representations of modernization in the 1960s.[105] To be sure, in Arguedas's fiction, female characters tend to be either nurturing, asexual, maternal figures, or exploited, sexually debased women, and in *The Fox from Up Above and the Fox from Down Below*, the options are narrowed even further as the former representation gives way almost completely to the latter.[106] Nonetheless, just as there are exceptions to this pattern in Arguedas's earlier works (the chicheras in *Deep Rivers*, perhaps also Asunta in *All the Worlds*) there is at least one powerful moment in *The Fox from Up Above and the Fox from Down Below* in which a female character, albeit still a prostitute, takes on a more active role, drawing on Andean cultural tradition to condemn and reject the degradation to which she has been subjected.

As three prostitutes, all of them from the Andes, ascend a sand dune to their homes in the *barriada* after working most of the night at the brothel, one of them turns to look back at Chimbote and exclaims "Down there's hell" as she points to the port.[107] The concentrated image of that hell, moreover, appears reflected in her eyes. This nameless prostitute and Andean migrant, the most exploited among the exploited, is one of the few characters in the novel who takes in all of Chimbote and clearly perceives it for what it is. She does not, however, passively resign herself to her subordination. Turning toward the fish meal factories along the bay, she begins to dance and sing, denouncing the fishing port and those who run it: "removing her hat, she arched her arm as in a dance and flourished her hat, making its band shine; dancing to an ancient *carnaval* tune she sang: Serpent Tinoco / serpent Chimbote / serpent asphalt / serpent Zavala / serpent Braschi /sand dune serpent / fish meal factory serpent."[108] Moreover, her dance and song soon expand to take in all of Peru: "serpent, serpent / up mountain, serpent / down mountain serpent / Peruvian flag serpent."[109]

The carnival melody to which she dances here is no accident, for carnival in the Andes is a festival that resembles ancient war rituals and includes "slow, mono-rhythmic singing . . . frequently characterized by the evocation of a dark and violent universe."[110] The traditional Andean carnival song and dance serve as a means not only of denouncing the violence and degradation of Chimbote, but also of symbolically attacking it. The snake imagery in her lyrics, moreover, recalls Arguedas's use of the mythological *amaru* figure in *Yawar Fiesta* and *Deep Rivers*. The word "serpent" repeatedly paired with all aspects of Chimbote identifies the changes underway in the fishing port as a *pachakutiy*, or cataclysmic transformation of the world. The prostitute clearly perceives this transformation as negative, and though there is no explicit reference here to a new *pachakutiy* that would right the wrongs of Chimbote, the symbolic inversion associated with carnival celebrations does suggest such a possibility. Likewise, the prostitute's song and dance evokes the mythological Andean hero Huatyacuri. Just as the poor son of Pariacaca defeated a rich rival in a contest of song and dance, the prostitute here symbolically subdues the forces that oppress her. Though William Rowe may be right when he states that the episode fails to articulate a broader vision that would hold the narrative together, it does nonetheless concentrate the work's most important themes in an intense and dramatic fashion.[111]

In the second example, from chapter 4, Arguedas uses somewhat different elements of indigenous culture to represent Andean migrants' resistance to oppression. Chapter 4 of *The Fox from Up Above and the Fox from Down Below* concerns the friendship between the Afro-Peruvian costeño Moncada and the Andean migrant Esteban de la Cruz, which in William Rowe's opinion "is one of the novel's most moving motifs."[112] The lunatic yet uncannily lucid Moncada speaks the truth ignored by, or invisible to, the sane. Dressed in a variety of extravagant costumes and pouring forth an equally extravagant torrent of words, he "preaches" the truth of Chimbote in the port's markets and on its street corners.[113] His neighbor and compadre, Esteban de la Cruz, left his indigenous community in the Andes in search of a better life, working in a wealthy family's home in Lima and in a coal mine and before arriving in Chimbote, where he initially made his living selling popsicles and repairing shoes. He no longer works much, however, for he is dying of black lung disease contracted in the coal mine.

Esteban de la Cruz and his wife occasionally feed their Afro-Peruvian neighbor, while Moncada often cares for his friend during the latter's increasingly frequent coughing fits. The two grow very close in spite of their cultural and linguistic differences. As Esteban de la Cruz notes in his Andeanized Spanish, Moncada is "a witness to me life; I to his, too."[114] Indeed, the Andean migrant regularly recounts his life to Moncada, who listens with great interest, later incorporating the information into his "sermons." Though he does not share all of Esteban de la Cruz's Andean beliefs, Moncada is respectful of them. As Rowe observes, Moncada, "though from the coast, is receptive to the highland sensibility and capable of incorporating it into his own vision of things."[115] Moncada, for example, supports his friend's recourse to an unconventional Andean folk cure for black lung disease recommended by an *aukillu*, or Andean shaman. After hearing of another miner who, following the *aukillu*'s instructions, survived black lung disease by coughing up the coal dust in his lungs bit by bit, Esteban de la Cruz resolves to do the same. Believing that he will be cured when he expels five ounces of coal dust from his lungs, he regularly coughs up black phlegm onto old newspapers and carefully keeps track of the total. Moncada, though not fully convinced, supports his friend's decision nonetheless.

Arguedas was apparently planning to have Esteban de la Cruz die of black lung disease at the end of the novel, but whether Andean folk cures are capable of restoring the former coal miner's health is not the main point here. More important is the symbolic significance of Esteban de la Cruz's struggle against death. By coughing up the black contents of his lungs onto old newspapers, he uses the evidence of his exploitation in the coal mine to overwrite the print-based, official public sphere of those responsible for literally working him to death. As if in retaliation against an elite public sphere that excludes him and those like him, Esteban de la Cruz blacks out the news that blacks him out.[116]

His friend Moncada takes the symbolic protest even further. Inspired by a conversation with Esteban de la Cruz, Moncada sets out to preach in the city center, where he lets loose a chaotic flood of words. Despite its turbulent opacity, his sermon projects his friend's suffering into the official public sphere. Pacing back and forth along Chimbote's main street, for example, he denounces the elite as vampires who suck the blood out of the poor: "Some people get drunk to devour innocent-warm human blood – I swear it!"[117] Bursting into an elite gala at the exclusive Hotel Chimú, he threatens to cover the dance floor with the evidence of Esteban de la Cruz's exploitation: "Gentlemen, ladies, terrestrial authorities . . .

I'm going to piss coal on the waxed surface of this floor. Don't be afraid! The coal-water will spring from 'me eye,' from 'me chest'."[118] Reproducing in part his dying friend's Andeanized Spanish, Moncada brings into the exclusive center of the official public sphere that which is normally ignored within it: the suffering of the poor and the elite's responsibility for it. Together, Esteban de la Cruz and Moncada draw on an emergent, Andeanized, urban popular culture to forge an alternative, oral public sphere through which they challenge the official version of Chimbote's modernization articulated in the exclusive, print-based public sphere of the elite.

My final example is from the second part of the novel, which is divided not into chapters but into shorter units of dialogue that Arguedas called *hervores* or "boilings." The last of these relates the cultural conversion of the former Peace Corps volunteer Maxwell and his attempt to explain that conversion to the US Catholic priest and missionary Michael Cardozo. The priest, concerned about his young compatriot's recent resignation from the Peace Corps and permanent move to a *barriada* of Andean migrants, has called Maxwell in to his office to justify these actions, which strike Cardozo as imprudent. For Maxwell, however, they are the logical outcome of his conversion to Andean culture.

That conversion, he explains, occurred through music and dance. As he watched a group of Andean dancers perform in a Lima theatre, he was so overcome that he decided "That's what I will be; that's a part of me and to be it wholly, I must go thousands and thousands of kilometers and stars forward in time and perhaps even farther – maybe I didn't know it and I don't know it – maybe I have to go backward in time with them."[119] He accompanied the dancers to their indigenous community near Lake Titicaca, where he stayed for six months. There Maxwell immersed himself in Andean culture. He learned to play the charango and, encouraged by an individual of fox-like aspect, joined in indigenous dances. No longer completely North American after six months in the Andes, Maxwell nonetheless realized that he would never be fully indigenous, so he left the community in search of what he calls "my true place", which he eventually found among the Andean migrants of Chimbote's *barriadas*.[120] As a result of his transformation through a process of *mestizaje* in reverse, that is, of cultural influence in a direction opposite the one usually designated by the term, he quit the Peace Corps and decided to remain in Peru permanently. In addition to representing Andean migrants' resistance to oppression, here indigenous music and dance suggest the global relevance of Andean culture and its power to transform individuals from any part of the world.

Despite Maxwell's passionate account of his cultural conversion, Cardozo remains troubled. Though a believer in liberation theology (a portrait of Che Guevara hangs alongside a crucifix in his office) Cardozo is no radical. Rather than organize Andean migrants in the *barriadas*, he oversees reformist aid programs funded by the US and seeks to mediate between the rich and the poor. In Cardozo's eyes, to openly side with the poor, as Maxwell has done, would jeopardize the church's mission in Chimbote and the aid programs the priests administer. Maxwell, however, dismisses these as paternalistic and chastises the priest for remaining "in the outer layers of this country . . . the shell that defends and oppresses."[121] True solidarity with the poor, Maxwell insists, requires full participation in their culture and their struggles. However, it will not be Maxwell, but rather the direct intervention of indigenous Andean culture that ultimately shakes Cardozo's confidence in his paternalistic reformism.

That intervention takes the form of a fox-like messenger whose unexpected arrival with Maxwell's charango in hand interrupts the conversation in Cardozo's office. The messenger, an incarnation of one of the foxes from the Huatyacuri myth, immediately exerts a strange influence on the priest, registered in the "muddy torrent of unexpectedly intricate . . . language in which the priest spoke, or else in which that messenger was inducing him to speak."[122] In suddenly Andeanized Spanish, the priest delivers a radical impromptu sermon at odds with his reformism: "The Lord made Che and Che has repercussions on the Lord for the Catholic's redemption, and through that redemption, for the liberation of humanity; pretty soon it's going to be stronger than those big bosses of the millionaire community who keep people's strength of thought in darkness . . . people's arms chained."[123] To the intervention of the pre-Columbian mythological figure of the fox, the narrative soon adds contemporary Andean music and dance.

As Maxwell begins to strum the charango, the mysterious fox-like visitor initiates a dance and, through his movements, the Andean world invades Cardozo's office: "he did a somersault in the air and made the lamp swing, making a sound like water, like the voices of the highland ducks, of the *totora* reed plumes, which, wailing, resist the force of the wind."[124] Soon afterward, overcome by the dance, Cardozo exclaims "Motherfuckin' gringos!" and asks himself "Are we learning?", suggesting that he has recognized the superficiality of his own knowledge of Peru and the need to break through the nation's oppressive shell to arrive at its popular, Andean core.[125]

In these examples indigenous Andean culture is represented not only as a source of resistance to exploitation and degradation, but also as a force capable of transforming coastal Peru. However, while its sympathy for indigenous migrants and their culture is never in doubt, the novel comes to no conclusions about the outcome of the twentieth-century Andean conquest of Chimbote, and by extension of Peru. There is no heroic ending here, as in *All the Worlds*, not even a provisional triumph over oppression, as in *Deep Rivers*. *The Fox from Up Above and the Fox from Down Below* offers no thesis, only uncertainty. In dialogue with his counterpart from up above, the mythological fox from down below, for example, describes Chimbote as "a mishmash of dying and dawning", but the novel ultimately gives little indication of which will prevail. The old Peru is dying, and a new nation is being born in Chimbote, the fox's words suggest, but *The Fox from Up Above and the Fox from Down Below* is never able to clearly articulate its vision of the new, modern and Andean Peru.[126] It says even less about how such an ideal is to be achieved.

Nonetheless, while the plot of the novel is not explicit on this point, its narrative form offers some clues. In each of the examples above, elements of indigenous Andean culture serve as more than mere content. Rather, they structure the fictional chapters in such a way that ignorance of Andean cultural traditions makes much of the narrative incomprehensible. *The Fox from Up Above and the Fox from Down Below*, in effect, requires of readers the kind of bi-cultural competence displayed by many of the novel's characters. Since few such readers existed at the time, *The Fox from Up Above and the Fox from Down Below* evokes, as Martin Lienhard has observed, the image of a future reader.[127] In such an ideal reader, equally versed in Andean and Western cultures, modern without having to choose between the two, one can glimpse the utopian future that Arguedas imagined might be one of the outcomes of the changes he witnessed in Chimbote: an inclusive, modern nation in which all citizens and their cultures enjoyed equal status.

The transcultural form of *The Fox from Up Above and the Fox from Down Below* is what most distinguishes it from other urban narratives of the period. Ribeyro and Bryce Echenique's works, for example, criticize Lima's *criollo* elite and are sympathetic to the plight of Andean migrants, yet ultimately represent the latter as a foreign and disconcerting presence in a city thereby implicitly assumed to be white and Western. *The Fox from Up Above and the Fox from Down Below*, by contrast, challenges readers to imagine a city, and a nation, in which no citizen is perceived or treated as foreign, while also demanding from them the kind of engagement with multiple cultures that would make such a nation possible.

Migrant Utopias

Long before most other Peruvian intellectuals, Arguedas realized that rural to urban migration was producing something other than the inevitable assimilation of indigenous Andeans into the *criollo* elite's

Westernized, purportedly national culture.[128] Indeed, he was among the first to perceive indigenous Andean migrants to coastal cities, particularly Lima, as the potential architects of a more modern, democratic, inclusive, and independent nation than the one dominated by the *criollo* elite. Where others saw a disturbing, disruptive presence that threatened the self-satisfied and largely imaginary civility of *criollo* urban life, Arguedas glimpsed the outline of an alternative, Andean modernity.

Fifteen years after his death, in the midst of the nation's worst economic and political crisis in a century, Arguedas's lead would be followed by Peruvian social scientists of both the Left and the Right. Like Arguedas, they looked to the creative energies of urban Andeans as a means of constructing a democratic alternative to an unacceptably authoritarian present. In the early 1980s, authoritarianism manifested itself mainly in two opposed and equally extremist forms: the state and the Shining Path guerrilla movement. Despite a return to formal democracy in 1980 after more than a decade of military rule, the state failed to break with its authoritarian habits and proved unable or unwilling to respond to popular demands. The Shining Path, for its part, arrogated to itself the authority to determine what "the people" wanted and to eliminate anyone who disagreed. In practice, the enemies of "the people" included not only the state but also many rural and urban indigenous Andeans, whom the Shining Path ostensibly represented, but whose popular organizations it did not hesitate to destroy if they refused to submit to its authority.

Confronted with an escalating and increasingly brutal civil war, intellectuals across the political spectrum searched for other options. On the democratic Left, José Matos Mar proposed in his influential *Desborde popular y crisis del estado: El nuevo rostro del Perú en la década de 1980 / The Rise of the Popular and the Crisis of the State: The New Face of Peru in the 1980s* (1984) that Andean migration had overflowed the channels in which an authoritarian state had attempted to contain popular agency, and that the resulting transformation of Lima heralded the possibility of building a new, more democratic and socialist society. On the then emergent neoliberal Right, Hernando de Soto suggested in *The Other Path: The Invisible Revolution in the Third World* (1986) that the entrepreneurial activity of the urban underclass in the informal or underground economy represented the beginnings of a truly free market capable of democratizing Peruvian society if only the state could be reduced to its minimal role of enforcing property rights and contracts. This, he argued, was a more promising route to freedom and equality than that of the Shining Path's armed revolution.

Matos Mar and de Soto agreed that rural migrants to Lima encountered only hostility or, at best, indifference from the state and responded by establishing their own parallel economy and civil society. However, they offered diametrically opposed interpretations of this response. According to Matos Mar,

> Two economic circuits have been forming: an official one made up of the registered universe of individuals engaged in commerce, production, transport, and services under the protection of civil law; and another, contestatory and popular one that operates in a universe of unregistered enterprises and activities, which occur outside the law or on its margins, frequently adapting the strategies, norms, and immemorial customs of Andean society to a new environment.[129]

For Matos Mar, the principal actors in the informal economy and migrant civil society are not entrepreneurial individuals, but rather extended families and migrant associations that function according to Andean traditions of reciprocity and mutual aid: "particularly important among the new forms of urban social organization that arise from highland contributions, are the migrant associations that combine trade-union forms of organization with Andean communal systems of reciprocity and affiliation."[130] Emphasizing migrants' Andean cultural identity, Matos Mar characterizes rural-to-urban migration as a process that "finds its modes in Andean traditions of ecological adaptability and mutual aid and ends up breaking through the formal crust of traditional *criollo* society."[131] Much like Mariátegui and Arguedas, he sees indigenous traditions of collectivism as a foundation on which to construct a new, more democratic nation.

After the massive popular mobilizations of the late 1970s and early 1980s, in which indigenous Andeans and urban migrants played an important role, this seemed a plausible vision of the future. However, the deepening economic crisis of the second half of the 1980s and the escalating violence of the civil war soon took a heavy toll on popular organizations and the parties of the parliamentary Left, which were targeted by both the Shining Path and the state. Grassroots organizations, which had seemed on the verge of radically transforming Peruvian society in the early 1980s, found themselves simply struggling to survive just a few years later. The parliamentary Left, which had drawn on the late 1970s and early 1980s wave of popular activism to attain unprecedented success in municipal and national elections, disintegrated by 1990.

Like the democratic Left, the neoliberal Right represented by de Soto opposed Peru's traditional power structure. Unlike scholars on the Left, however, neoliberal intellectuals opposed not only the existing state, but the very concept of the state. De Soto shares Matos Mar's desire for democratization as well as his faith in the agency of the urban poor, but equates democratization not with the collective, organized efforts of poor migrants, but rather with the entrepreneurial activity of individuals in the free market. For de Soto, the urban poor are popular entrepreneurs struggling against what he calls "mercantilism", an economic system characterized by an insider relationship between an entrenched merchant or business class and a powerful state. Peru has never had a true market economy, de Soto maintains, because the state has used arcane laws and regulations to exclude all but a privileged elite from participation in the legal, formal economy: "although the protagonists of our economic life – the state, private enterprise, and consumers – are the same as in a market economy, the state's tremendous power and its ties with certain private individuals make the relationship among them essentially mercantilist."[132] The result is economic stagnation due to the absence of the competitive spirit fostered by a truly free market. Positing the market as akin to a force of nature, de Soto attributes Peru's and Latin America's economic and social problems to the fact that the region's economies are "governed by politics rather than markets."[133]

The solution, according to de Soto, is to free the economy from "unnatural" political control so that "natural" market forces may produce greater efficiency, wealth and equality of opportunity (though not necessarily of result) for all. De Soto gives the familiar liberal doctrine a twist, however, by identifying the free market not with the traditional business class, tainted in Peru by its close relationship to the state, but with the popular entrepreneurialism of urban migrants. Excluded by the state and its cronies from participation in the legal, formal economy, urban migrants and the poor in general have produced a parallel, informal economy that de Soto sees as a nascent free market and a model for the nation as a whole:

> They have demonstrated their initiative by migrating, breaking with the past without any prospect of a secure future, they have learned how to identify and satisfy others' needs, and their confidence in their abilities is greater than their fear of competition. . . . This ability to take risks and calculate is important because it means that a broad entrepreneurial base is already being created.[134]

Though based on extensive field research, de Soto's book nonetheless overlooks the role of urban migrants' cultural identity in the constitution of the informal economy. Aside from a brief reference to the importance of the extended family, there is no mention of Andean cultural traditions. For de Soto, Andean migrants are the stripped-down, profit-maximizing, abstract individuals of liberal theory. If they have culture at all, it is irrelevant to his argument, for the market, as a natural phenomenon, is assumed to be compatible with all cultures. If cultural values were to conflict with market forces, they would undoubtedly constitute for de

Soto an "unnatural" distortion of the latter, much like politics. Such ideas fit nicely with the neoliberal doctrine emanating, then and still, from the US and Britain, and de Soto's book received a warm reception in Ronald Reagan's America. It was almost immediately published in an English translation with a glowing recommendation from then Vice-President George H. W. Bush on the back cover.

However, as Cornejo Polar notes regarding de Soto's interpretation of Andean migration to Lima:

> it is imprecise to imagine that migration operates as an invincible and all-powerful force that reconstructs peasant migrants' identity from the roots, converting them, for example, into the protagonists of the 'long march'—supposedly almost always successful—toward private property and capitalism (de Soto, 1986). This is so because, among many other reasons, migrants tend to repeat in the city modes of production and social relations— like reciprocity, the economic role of the extended family, or the compadre system—that modern capitalism finds it difficult to incorporate into its own norms.[135]

This failure to address the cultural dimension of Andean migrants' transformation of Lima and of Peru would prove fatal to the most concerted attempt to put de Soto's utopian neoliberal vision into practice: Mario Vargas Llosa's presidential campaign of 1990. Vargas Llosa had written the introduction to *The Other Path*, which served as a kind of blueprint for his political platform. However, his blindness to the Andean cultural identity of the urban poor was even more extreme than de Soto's and would contribute to his defeat in the 1990 presidential elections, which I examine in the following chapter.[136]

5

MARIO VARGAS LLOSA WRITES OF(F) THE NATIVE

Cultural Heterogeneity and Neoliberal Modernity

By the 1980s, the rise of the social movements Andean migrants organized to make their way in a hostile environment and the resulting transformation of coastal cities had come to be interpreted by many analysts as the beginning of a thoroughgoing democratization of Peruvian society.[1] Such an interpretation seemed quite justified in the early eighties, when urban grassroots movements affiliated themselves with the Left and helped elect a Marxist mayor of Lima. However, the war that the Shining Path initiated against the Peruvian state in 1980 would soon trump democratization as the country descended into its deepest political and economic crisis in a century. Social movements and the parties of the parliamentary Left found themselves under attack from opposite ends of the ideological spectrum, by both the Shining Path insurgency and government security forces, each of which accused those who were not with them of being against them.[2]

The *Partido Comunista del Perú "Sendero Luminoso"* (PCP-SL), as it is formally known, emerged out of the splintering of the Peruvian Communist Party in the wake of the Sino-Soviet split of the early 1960s. The Maoist faction that would become the Shining Path got its start during this period in Ayacucho, one of the poorest and most indigenous regions of Peru. Though remote, Ayacucho was nonetheless home to the Universidad Nacional San Cristóbal de Huamanga, originally founded in 1677, but closed in 1886 and reopened only in 1959.[3] According to Carlos Iván Degregori, in Ayacucho in the 1960s "the modernizing element was

163

not economic (mines, industry, commercial agriculture), but rather fundamentally ideological: a university . . . one could say that in Ayacucho the [modernization] process is inverted and it is not economic change that leads to social and cultural transformations. Rather, the *idea* arrives first."[4] The presence of a modern university with high-caliber faculty in an economically stagnant area like Ayacucho made for a rather jarring dissonance between the idea of modernity and the reality of regional society, generating a "contrast, which over the years would become explosive, between the expansion of intellectual horizons and economic backwardness."[5]

Though the Shining Path was initially perceived by some as a millenarian indigenous uprising, its ideology subsequently proved to have nothing to do with indigenous cultural traditions, which, to the contrary, party documents consistently disparage.[6] The Shining Path's emergence and growth is now widely understood as a perverse and unforeseen consequence not of indigenous traditions but rather of modernization. Specifically, the group's organization of a social base from which to wage armed struggle was facilitated by contradictions in two of the most important modernizing initiatives of the 1960s and 1970s: the rapid expansion of the Peruvian public education system, particularly of higher education, and the military government's agrarian reform of 1969. While the opening of new universities in the provinces provided opportunities for higher education to formerly excluded social sectors with a virtually religious faith in education as a means of social mobility, provincial Andean students soon discovered that their university degrees granted them only very limited mobility in a caste-like society still dominated by the *criollo* elite.

Degregori suggests that at the University of Huamanga in Ayacucho, the Shining Path "arose as a result of the encounter . . . between a provincial, *mestizo*, intellectual elite and similarly provincial, Andean and *mestizo* youth."[7] The former, university professors like Shining Path founder and ideologue Abimael Guzmán, propounded a particularly rigid and dogmatic version of Marxism-Leninism-Maoism, considered extreme even at a time when Marxism was hegemonic in Peruvian universities. The University of Huamanga student body, for its part, was made up of

> young people who found themselves in a no-man's land between two worlds: the traditional Andean one of their parents, whose myths, rituals and customs they no longer fully shared; and the Western or, more precisely, urban-*criollo* world that rejected them because they were provincial, Quechua-speakers, and *mestizos*. These young people demanded *coherence*, a vision of the world to replace the traditional Andean one that was no longer theirs. . . . And they believed they had found what they were looking for in a rigid ideology that presented itself as the sole truth and gave them the illusion of absolute coherence: Marxism-Leninism-Maoism.[8]

For these uprooted provincial university students who would make up the initial core and eventual mid-level cadre of the Shining Path, Abimael Guzmán's simplified version of Marxism proved enormously seductive, providing them with material for the construction of a new identity with which to confront an increasingly modern, yet still hierarchical and racist, society that rejected them.[9] Paradoxically, this new identity was simultaneously modern, or at least was perceived as such by its adherents, and fundamentalist.[10]

The contradictions of the Velasco regime's 1969 agrarian reform also stimulated the growth of the Shining Path. Because the generals mistrusted any autonomous form of popular mobilization, they implemented the reform from above, without consulting its intended beneficiaries or involving them in the process.[11] The populist military government gave hacienda peons and indigenous communities land but not the autonomy and power to decide for themselves how to use it. Instead, the Velasco regime attempted to replace *gamonales* with state managers and technicians. While the old landowning class disappeared, real power in the Andean countryside never devolved to the indigenous peasantry. As Flores Galindo notes, "the new agrarian reform did not empower the peasantry. Carried out by the state in a manner that prevented autonomous mobilization, it attempted to replace the deteriorated power of landowners with that of state functionaries."[12]

However, the government's managers and technicians failed to fill the power vacuum produced by the *gamonales'* demise. The Shining Path was able to expand from its initial base at the University of Huamanga in part by stepping into the gap the agrarian reform of 1969 opened in the rural Andean social structure by expropriating, and thereby destroying, the traditional *misti* landowning class. The guerrillas in effect assumed the structural role formerly played by *gamonal* landowners.[13] As Degregori observes, the Shining Path's authoritarian relationship to indigenous communities was a "new way of being *misti*."[14] The Shining Path, that is, sought to monopolize power in the same fashion as the old *gamonal* landowning elite had done: through intimidation, violence, and terror, directed not only at the state, but also at what it regarded as an even more dangerous enemy: autonomous social movements and leftist political parties that refused to submit themselves to its authority. The Shining Path's violence and terror would be more than matched by government security forces, which were at least as responsible as the guerrillas for the scale and brutality of the conflict. Between 1980 and 1992, the war would claim "30,000 dead, 600,000 displaced, 40,000 orphans, 20,000 widows, 4,000 disappeared, 500,000 children under 18 years of age with post-traumatic stress, and 435 destroyed communities."[15] These human costs, moreover, would be borne disproportionately by indigenous civilians.

Though the Shining Path's victims were primarily indigenous, and though there was nothing indigenous about the organization's leadership or ideology, many *criollos* would perceive the violence of the 1980s in racist terms, as a product of indigenous barbarism. This was to be expected, of course, for the *criollo* elite had traditionally perceived the indigenous population as the source of Peru's problems and backwardness. In this chapter, I trace the late twentieth-century resurgence of this view by examining the recent work of Peru's most famous living novelist, Mario Vargas Llosa. Though he had denounced the effects of modernization on indigenous peoples in early novels such as *La casa verde / The Green House* (1966), by the late 1980s Vargas Llosa saw indigenous cultures as an obstacle to social progress and modernity. This change is the product of his broader ideological evolution.

Over the course of his prolific career, Vargas Llosa has traversed the ideological spectrum from Left to Right.[16] Once a fellow-traveler of the Cuban Revolution, he is now a champion of neoliberal, free market orthodoxy whose model for a just society is Thatcherite Britain.[17] An enthusiastic admirer of Jean Paul Sartre in the 1960s, Vargas Llosa repudiated the leftist Sartre in the 1970s in favor of the liberal reformism of Albert Camus, and now considers Isaiah Berlin, Karl Popper, and Frederich von Hayek his intellectual mentors.[18] While he once advocated collective projects for achieving social and economic equality, he now sees these as dangerous utopias that inevitably lead to tyranny, and subscribes instead to an abstract notion of liberty, incarnated in the free market, from which both generalized prosperity (though not exactly equality) and democracy are assumed to follow "naturally." The nuanced, flexible approach to social reality of his youth, during which he attempted to balance collective needs with individual rights, has hardened into a rigid, intolerant advocacy of individual freedom over all other values.[19] In 1990, in what was perhaps the culmination of his political trajectory, Vargas Llosa ran for President of Peru as the candidate of a rejuvenated Right. After losing the elections, the defeated novelist withdrew from national politics and left Peru.

Vargas Llosa had begun to distance himself from the Left in the early 1970s, but it was not until the 1980s that he made the break definitive by openly embracing the Right and becoming a champion of neoliberalism. The Peruvian political context—the escalating violence of the Shining Path's war against the state *and* civil society as well as the spectacular failure of Alan García's populist APRA government (1985–90) to stave off economic collapse and neutralize the guerrillas—played a role in this ideological about-face by helping to convince Vargas Llosa that all Marxisms and populisms "inevitably" devolve into terror and totalitarianism. Perhaps the most obvious literary expression of this influence is his novel *Historia de Mayta / The Real Life of Alejandro Mayta* (1984), in which a narrator who closely resembles the author researches the failure, in the 1950s, of Peru's first leftist guerilla movement, led by the fictional Trotskyist Alejandro Mayta, who may or may not have been a childhood friend of the narrator. The story of the stillborn 1950s insurgency is narrated against the apocalyptic backdrop of a fictional 1980s Peru plunged into civil war and facing imminent invasion by both the US Marines and Cuban troops.[20]

What interests me here, however, is the more specific question of how developments in Peru also led Vargas Llosa to revise his earlier position on the relationship of indigenous cultures to the Peruvian nation state and its projects of modernization. While he once believed in the compatibility of indigenous cultures with modernity and shared, to some degree, Arguedas's dream of combining the best features of both, by the mid-1980s he had concluded that indigenous cultures were an obstacle to the achievement of a modernity modeled on that of Europe (in particular Switzerland and Thatcherite Britain), leading him eventually to dismiss Arguedas's project as a backward-looking "archaic utopia."[21]

This chapter traces Vargas Llosa's ideological conversion as it is manifested in his engagement with Peruvian realities, in particular his position on the role of indigenous peoples in Peruvian society. Through readings of several novels and essays published during a decade marked by war and Peru's worst political and economic crisis of the century (1983–93), his view of the relationship of indigenous cultures to modernity is examined. Three of these works were published before the 1990 elections, during Vargas Llosa's gradual entry into Peruvian politics, while the remaining two were published afterward and reflect, both directly and obliquely, on the author's frustrating experience as a politician.

The first work to be considered is the report of a Peruvian government commission charged with investigating the murder of eight journalists and their guide near the indigenous community of Uchuraccay in 1983, at a time in which the two-year-old war between government security forces and the Shining Path insurgency was undergoing rapid escalation. Vargas Llosa chaired the commission at the request of President Belaúnde Terry and drafted its report.[22] The report largely absolved a beleaguered Belaúnde administration of responsibility for the killings by attributing them instead to the "backwardness" and isolation from national life of the *comuneros* of Uchuraccay, who maintained that they had attacked the journalists because they mistook them for guerrillas. Vargas Llosa's high-profile role in the Uchuraccay investigation and the controversy that surrounded it marks the beginning of his entry into Peruvian politics. Indeed, perhaps as a result of his service on the Uchuraccay Commission, the following year he was offered, but declined, the post of prime minister by Belaúnde, who would later back Vargas Llosa's bid for the presidency in 1990 (though not without first vying with the novelist for leadership of a resurgent Right).[23]

Vargas Llosa returns to some of the issues broached in the Uchuraccay report (the marginalization of indigenous peoples and their relations with a Westernized "official" Peru) in a subsequent essay on the conquest of Peru (1986). This essay has appeared in several versions and multiple venues, including *Harper's*, which published it in 1990 as "Questions of Conquest: What Columbus Wrought and What He Did Not."[24] In it Vargas Llosa argues that Peru's underdevelopment and extreme social inequality are due largely to the incomplete assimilation of indigenous peoples to the modern Westernized culture of the Peruvian elite.

In the novel *El hablador / The Storyteller* (1987), his first explicitly dedicated to an indigenous topic, Vargas Llosa takes up some of the same questions in a literary key through a fictionalized reflection on the fate of the Machiguenga, an indigenous group of the Peruvian Amazon whose cultural survival is threatened by modernization. *The Storyteller* was written simultaneously with the early versions of the *Harper's* essay, between 1985 and 1987, and finished just as Vargas Llosa once again entered the political arena, this time as spokesman for the right-wing opposition to President Alan García's attempt to nationalize the banking system. This new plunge into Peruvian politics would lead to Vargas Llosa's candidacy for president.[25]

These three texts, I contend, rehearse what would be the core themes of his 1990 presidential campaign: individual initiative (read: the free market) as the only path to modernity, and the incompatibility of Peru's cultural heterogeneity (read: indigenous cultures) with modernity. They also suggest that Vargas Llosa's fundamental misreading of class and ethnic conflict in contemporary Peru was at least partly responsible for his unexpected electoral defeat, to which I return after tracing the roots of that misreading in the Uchuraccay report, "Questions of Conquest" and *The Storyteller*. I examine the 1990 elections themselves through Vargas Llosa's memoir, *El pez en el agua / A Fish in the Water* (1993/1994), aided by Carlos Iván Degregori's illuminating essay on the role of culture in the elections.[26] Finally, I turn to the former presidential candidate's only sustained literary engagement with the Andes and indigenous Andean peoples, the first novel he published after losing the elections, *Lituma en los Andes / Death in the Andes* (1993), in which he returns to the theme of the Shining Path war. Both the memoir and the novel express Vargas Llosa's disillusionment with politics, with Peru, and with the indigenous Andean and *mestizo* popular classes who failed to elect him president.

Outside of Modernity in Uchuraccay

In January 1983, eight Peruvian journalists set out from the city of Ayacucho, capital of the department of Ayacucho and epicenter of the Shining Path insurgency, to investigate the lynching of alleged guerrillas in the remote indigenous community of Huaychao. None returned. All eight, six of them from Lima and two from Ayacucho, were found badly mutilated and buried in shallow graves near Uchuraccay, an indigenous community on the way to Huaychao. The killings occurred during escalating violence between the Shining Path and the Peruvian armed forces. In December of 1982, President Belaúnde had reluctantly declared a state of emergency in the department of Ayacucho, suspending civil liberties and transferring control of the department from civil authorities and the police, who had failed to stem the spread of Shining Path violence, to the military. Even before Ayacucho was turned over to the military, the police had committed serious human rights abuses, and at the time the journalists were killed the army was embarking on a campaign of severe and often indiscriminate repression, especially in the countryside, against the Shining Path and those it suspected of being Shining Path sympathizers. Under these circumstances, the military commanders of Ayacucho were understandably anxious to avoid press scrutiny of their counterinsurgency methods and discouraged journalists from venturing outside the city of Ayacucho to gather information independently, preferring that they obtain it from the army instead. In any case, the Shining Path made travel through rural areas of Ayacucho a risky proposition, and few journalists were disposed to abandon the relative safety of the departmental capital. Even fewer would do so after the chilling effect of the killings, which many on the Left attributed to the military, especially since some (though by no means all) of the eight journalists represented newspapers which had, at least initially, treated the Shining Path with a degree of sympathy.

Facing a storm of protest, President Belaúnde appointed a special Uchuraccay Commission headed by Vargas Llosa to investigate the killings, perhaps with the hope that the world-renowned novelist could lend the government some much needed legitimacy in the international human rights arena.[27] Indeed, Vargas Llosa's reputation and narrative skills at least gained the Commission's report, which he wrote, wide international circulation.[28] Within Peru, however, the Commission was criticized for its rather shoddy investigative procedures and accused of covering up military involvement in the killings. Commission members spent only a few hours in the indigenous community of Uchuraccay, where they arrived by helicopter accompanied by military officers. Members of the community were interviewed in the presence of the military, which had occupied the village.[29] Such limited on-site investigation did not prevent Vargas Llosa from drafting a thorough and detailed report on the killings, which nonetheless allowed for a degree of uncertainty by indicating the degree of confidence (absolute, relative, doubtful) the Commission had in each of its conclusions.

In spite of this acknowledgment of uncertainty, the report retains a tone of self-assured authority, and Vargas Llosa does not shy away from accusing the indigenous community of Uchuraccay of responsibility for the journalists' deaths, though he does acknowledge that there were mitigating circumstances. The report takes note of the atmosphere of violence and tension in which the killings occurred, and offers a list of contributing causes: Shining Path attacks; inadequate government response to indigenous communities' recent lynchings of guerrillas (though Vargas Llosa diplomatically refrains from naming names, both President Belaúnde and the military commander of the Ayacucho emergency zone had in fact publicly, the former on national television, celebrated the lynchings and encouraged such independent initiative); what are delicately, and briefly, referred to as the "excesses" of government security forces in their war against the Shining Path; the structural violence of poor living conditions in the Andean countryside; the extreme isolation of the indigenous communities in the region, the long-standing conflicts between them and their tradition of belligerence when threatened. The report nonetheless holds the residents of Uchuraccay ultimately responsible for the deaths and takes great pains to downplay possible government security forces involvement in or instigation of the killings.

According to Vargas Llosa, residents of Uchuraccay killed the eight journalists and their guide after mistaking them for a Shining Path guerrilla column, which the *comuneros* of Uchuraccay feared was coming to take reprisals for indigenous communities' recent lynchings of presumed guerrillas: "The Commission has arrived at the *absolute conviction* that the *comuneros* . . . confused the nine approaching strangers with a *senderista* detachment."[30] This was in fact the *comuneros*' own version, which they unanimously and steadfastly maintained throughout the investigation. The report's theory of mistaken identity requires that the journalists, three of whom spoke Quechua, had not had a chance to speak with their attackers and identify themselves: "The Commission holds with *relative conviction* that the journalists must have been attacked unexpectedly and en masse, without the mediation of any previous dialogue."[31] The subsequent discovery (or leak) of photographs taken by the journalists just before they were killed provided evidence which indicated that a group of *comuneros* from Uchuraccay had indeed attacked them.[32] However, the photographs also cast doubt on the report's mistaken identity theory by showing that the journalists had in fact had an opportunity to identify themselves before being attacked. In a later article, Vargas Llosa acknowledges the photographic evidence of a dialogue between the victims and their attackers, but does not address the problem this creates for the report's theory.[33] If the *comuneros* knew they were killing journalists and not guerrillas, why did they do it? Despite such inconsistencies and the lack of a serious field investigation, the report largely succeeded in absolving the government and its security forces of any direct responsibility for the murders.

Whether or not there actually was government involvement in the killings, the report makes use of various rhetorical ploys to downplay that possibility. Most relevant to the question of indigenous cultures' compatibility with modernity is the report's attempt to establish the independence of the *comuneros*' actions by interpreting them as an application of customary law and emphasizing the atavistic, ritual aspects of the killings. Vargas Llosa suggests that in killing the journalists whom they mistook for guerrillas, the *comuneros* of Uchuraccay were following local traditions. In isolated areas where the state has very little presence, indigenous communities often punish violations of customary law themselves without waiting for the arrival of government authorities. Cattle rustlers, for example, are often captured, judged, and punished by the community, and the punishment has sometimes been known to include execution. However, there is absolutely no evidence that customary law was applied in the case of the journalists. There was no accusation, no legal proceeding, no judgement, only an apparently unprovoked attack.

Vargas Llosa also notes that the Commission discovered "certain indications, judging by the characteristics of the wounds suffered by the victims and by the manner in which they were buried, of a socio-political crime that may also have had magico-religious aspects."[34] The indications were that the victims were stripped naked and buried face down as one would do with a devil or demon, and their eyes, mouth, and ankles appeared to have been mutilated, consistent with traditional Andean beliefs that doing so prevents victims from recognizing, denouncing, or returning to harass their killers. The report's language is highly speculative, however: "The wounds displayed by the cadavers, as described in the autopsy, point to *a certain coincidence* with these beliefs."[35] The emphasis on the ritual aspects of the killings effectively marks them as atavistic indigenous murder rather than state-sponsored violence. The killings are attributed neither to the government's encouragement nor to the *comuneros*' inherent savagery (the version preferred by some conservative commentators in Lima), but rather to the indigenous community's ignorance of and isolation from the modern world and the consequent persistence of traditional customs and beliefs. This allows Vargas Llosa to subtly shift responsibility for the killings from the state to the indigenous community, without, however, condemning the members of the community, for, it is implied, they were not fully aware of what they were doing.

The report at one point asks whether official Peru has the right to hold indigenous peoples, whom it has maintained in a state of stagnation and backwardness, to the same standards of behavior it expects from those Peruvians who "really participate in modernity" and adhere to laws, rites, and customs of which indigenous peoples are unaware and could in any case scarcely be expected to understand.[36] The question is rhetorical and Vargas Llosa provides no answer, but the paternalism implicit in it effectively silences the protagonists and only surviving witnesses to the events at Uchuraccay, closing off other lines of inquiry that might have explored the difficult choices faced by indigenous communities and individuals caught up in the war between the Shining Path and the state, the ways in which such choices were perceived, and the basis on which they were made. Anthropologist Enrique Mayer points out that such paternalism is reflected in the very narrative form of Vargas Llosa's report:

> Although the testimony given during the one meeting at Uchuraccay that the Commission had was carefully transcribed, not one single complete sentence has been reproduced in the printed final report. There are only three words from the *comuneros* that Vargas Llosa directly quotes . . . There is only one partial quote . . . The quotes are not attributed to anyone. The authenticity of their testimony is vouched for by Vargas Llosa alone. There is no way to evaluate whether there were dissenting voices, no variant forms of saying the same things, no opportunities to look beyond the mediated message conveyed by the Commission's report. People in Uchuraccay come through to us in the third person and in indirect speech.[37]

Vargas Llosa assumes the authority to speak for all the *comuneros* of Uchuraccay, who appear in his narrative as an undifferentiated and mostly mute mass. *He* explains what *must* have happened, leaving few loose ends from which a narrative ultimately favorable to the government might be unraveled.

The paternalism of the Uchuraccay report is the result, at least in part, of Vargas Llosa's reliance on a dubious theory of the existence of "two Perus" virtually incapable of communication with each other.[38] "Official" Peru is Western and modern, or at least modernizing, while "deep" Peru is indigenous, Andean, traditional. And although official Peru stands accused of abusing, exploiting and marginalizing deep Peru and is held responsible for the latter's "backwardness", official Peru is nonetheless the valorized term of this binary opposition. For Vargas Llosa, deep Peru is in effect a kind of anti-modernity defined by its lack of the positive characteristics associated with official Peru (e.g. education, civilization, the rule of law). Deep Peru evokes compassion, not the respect that is a precondition of any real dialogue and understanding. While the history of racism, abuse, exploitation and marginalization upon which the "two Peru" theory rests is real enough, the idea that deep Peru is so deeply isolated from official Peru that there is virtually no contact or communication between the two is untenable, given the long and continuing history of indigenous peoples' participation in national life.[39]

As Mayer points out, Vargas Llosa vastly exaggerates contemporary indigenous communities' isolation from the modern world and its conflicts:

> to suppose *comunero* ignorance of the world's current ideological debates is simplistic . . . At the time of these events, evangelical pastors were spreading the Protestant gospel and preaching against the evils of Catholicism and communism, and active recruitment by peasant federations and left-wing parties was also taking place throughout the department of Ayacucho.[40]

Moreover, Uchuraccay had received land as a result of the military government's 1969 land reform, which would have required some degree of ongoing engagement and negotiation with representatives of the state.[41] However, for Vargas Llosa the *comuneros* of Uchuraccay are not political actors in national life; they are merely acted upon. When threatened, they may *react*, but when they do, it is according to traditional beliefs and rituals and not as the result of a political consciousness. Given their alleged lack of communication with official Peru, he finds this quite understandable, if not completely excusable (three members of the community of Uchuraccay were ultimately tried and imprisoned for the killing of the journalists).

The Uchuraccay Commission was charged only with collecting information in order to clarify what happened to the eight journalists. It did not make any proposals regarding legal or other action in the case. Nonetheless, by attributing the killings at Uchuraccay, at least in part, to the backwardness and isolation of indigenous communities, for which it blames official Peru, the Commission's report implies that the remedy for such outbreaks of violence is an integration of the two Perus. Given the report's silencing of indigenous voices, however, it would seem that Vargas Llosa conceives this as a one-way process, a problem of economic development and education (in a word, modernization) to be resolved by the elite. Indigenous peoples are to be brought into modernity and integrated into national life, without, however, having a voice or role in the definition and construction of that modernity. This view, only implicit in the Uchuraccay report, is made quite explicit in Vargas Llosa's essay on the Conquest.

Questions of Conquest and Modernity

The 1990 *Harper's* version of Vargas Llosa's essay on the Conquest of Peru was clearly intended as an intervention in the then raging debates around the Quincentennial of the Conquest. Of interest here, however, are the conclusions Vargas Llosa draws from the chronicles of the Conquest about the incompatibility of indigenous cultures and modernity. "Questions of Conquest" argues that two hundred Spaniards led by Francisco Pizarro were able to conquer the Inca empire with relative ease because they possessed something unknown in the totalitarian, theocratic society of the Incas: a concept of the individual. In Vargas Llosa's selective version of history, the Conquest is over almost before it begins: when Pizarro ambushes and captures the Inca Atahualpa at Cajamarca, the Inca emperor's armies "give up the fight as if manacled by a magic force" and let themselves be slaughtered by the Spanish.[42] The Inca's subjects became paralyzed once their leader was captured because they "lacked the ability to make their own decisions" and "were incapable of taking individual initiative."[43] Vargas Llosa reduces the Conquest to this initial encounter, while virtually ignoring the subsequent 40 years (1532–72) of armed resistance against the Spanish. This resistance, even though it was ultimately unsuccessful, at least suggests that the Incas were more capable of taking initiative than is convenient for Vargas Llosa's argument.

Dismissing such resistance as isolated and irrelevant allows him to claim that Pizarro and his men prevailed because they could think for themselves and the Incas could not. The Conquest, however, was a cruel and bloody affair, and is a poor example of what individual initiative has contributed to human history. Acknowledging this, Vargas Llosa is quick to point out that individualism and the capacity for independent thought also enabled a critique of the Conquest from within the conquering culture, something he claims was unthinkable in any other civilization. Individualism produced not only a Pizarro, but also a Bartolomé de las Casas. The wider lesson of the Conquest of Peru, Vargas Llosa maintains, is that Europe came to dominate the world because it, and only it, had invented the sovereign individual and the concept of freedom: "The first culture to interrogate and question itself, the first to break up the masses into individual beings who with time gradually gained the right to think and act for themselves, was to become, thanks to that unknown exercise, freedom, the most powerful civilization in our world."[44] However, this projects back onto the Conquest a concept of the individual that would not emerge in Spain until well after Pizarro's 1532 ambush of Atahualpa in Cajamarca. As George Mariscal has shown, even in seventeenth-century Spain, "the interiorization of the subject, the formulation of the idea of the 'individual' as we understand it, was only just beginning to take place through the changing material conditions of everyday life."[45] Moreover, the conquest itself and the new colonial subjectivities it spawned (indigenous, *mestizo*, and *criollo*) exercised a profound influence on changing conditions, material and otherwise, in the imperial center, such that "the effects of the American experience on social relations and discursive formations at home cannot be overestimated."[46] The Conquest and its consequences played a bigger role in the emergence of individualism on the Iberian Peninsula than a hypothetical early sixteenth-century individualism did in the Spanish defeat of the Inca empire.

Nonetheless, for Vargas Llosa the conclusion is clear: if Europe achieved its modernity thanks to individual initiative, then becoming modern like Europe requires a concept of the autonomous individual. In contemporary Latin America, however, "this notion of individual sovereignty is still an unfinished business."[47] It is unfinished, Vargas Llosa claims, at least in part because of the cultural heterogeneity of many Latin American societies, which are split between a "modern, Western" culture and an "archaic, aboriginal" one. The conquistadores and their descendants created and maintain this cultural divide by discriminating against and exploiting Latin America's indigenous peoples, and this has prevented those Latin American nations with large indigenous populations from becoming fully modern. What this has to do with the unfinished business of individual sovereignty is not immediately apparent and must be teased out of Vargas Llosa's diagnosis of the "problem" of cultural heterogeneity and his proposed solution:

> Only in countries where the native population was small or nonexistent, or where the aboriginals were practically liquidated, can we talk of integrated societies. In the others, discreet, sometimes unconscious, but very effective apartheid prevails. Important as integration is, the obstacle to achieving it lies in the huge economic gap between the two communities. Indian peasants live in such a primitive way that communication is practically impossible. It is only when they move to the cities that they have the opportunity to mingle with the other Peru. The price they must pay for integration is high – renunciation of their culture, their language, their beliefs, their traditions, their customs, and the adoption of the culture of their ancient masters. . . . Perhaps there is no realistic way to integrate our societies other than by asking Indians to pay that price. Perhaps the ideal – that is, the preservation of the primitive cultures of America – is a utopia incompatible with this other and more urgent goal – the establishment of societies in which social and economic inequalities among citizens be reduced to human, reasonable limits and where everybody can enjoy at least a decent and free life. . . . If forced to choose between the preservation of Indian cultures and their complete assimilation, with great sadness I would choose the modernization of the Indian population because there

are priorities; and the first priority is, of course, to fight hunger and misery.[48]

Where there are no indigenous people, observes Vargas Llosa, there is no apartheid. In countries where the indigenous population survived the conquest and centuries of colonialism, apartheid prevails. His solution to this problem is integration, which he understands as a one-way process: indigenous peoples must be assimilated by Western culture. When there is no more cultural difference, there will be no more apartheid. In other words, ending apartheid requires the "liquidation", not of indigenous peoples themselves, as in the past, but of their cultural identity. Vargas Llosa never considers the possibility of modifying *criollo* attitudes and behavior toward the indigenous population. This is implicitly dismissed as unrealistic. Instead, he calls upon the conquered, not the conquerors, to bear the costs of remedying the injustices produced by the Conquest.

Vargas Llosa suggests that the "preservation" of "primitive" indigenous cultures is incompatible with the reduction of social and economic inequalities in Latin America, that somehow "primitive" indigenous cultures stand in the way of fighting (their own) hunger and misery and must therefore be modernized. This conclusion is based on dubious assumptions. The first is that modernization of the type Vargas Llosa has in mind will inevitably reduce inequality. To believe this, however, one must ignore Peru's last century and a half of *criollo*-led modernization, which has done little more than reproduce the inequality inaugurated by the conquest. One must also ignore the more recent consequences of the neoliberal model of modernization promoted by Vargas Llosa. Under this model, tariffs are lowered while state enterprises and social services are privatized in order to unleash the forces of the free market, which, it is assumed, will stimulate economic growth and guarantee prosperity for all. In Latin America, such measures *have* sometimes produced economic growth, but the benefits of that growth have been concentrated in the hands of a very few. As Carlos Vilas points out, neoliberal economic restructuring has widened the gap between rich and poor through "a movement of perverse causal reciprocity . . . in which inequality increases poverty and poverty expands inequalities, and in which economic growth and growing poverty become entirely compatible." As a result, "during the past decade, Latin America has produced poor people at twice the pace of its total population. The entire Latin American population grew by 22 percent while the poor increased by 44 percent."[49]

Vargas Llosa's second assumption is that indigenous peoples live primitive lives in isolation from the modern world. By portraying indigenous cultures as primitive and archaic, he implies that they (still) lack the capacity for individual initiative required by his free market model of modernization. In Peru, where massive rural-to-urban migration since the 1940s has transformed the country, where Andean migrants to urban areas maintain close links with their communities of origin, where indigenous peoples have for decades participated in peasant federations, leftist political parties, and other social movements to defend their land and demand education and citizenship from the state, the claim that "Indian peasants live in such a primitive way that communication is practically impossible" is simply not true. As anthropologist Carlos Iván Degregori notes, "contrary to what Mario Vargas Llosa thinks, the Andean world is not isolated, and that of Andean migrants to the cities even less so. Not only roads and the mass media connect it to the rest of the world. Today there is most likely not a single province and virtually no district of the country that does not have one of its natives living abroad."[50] The claim that communication with indigenous peoples is impossible may be influenced by Vargas Llosa's brief visit to Uchuraccay. Given the circumstances of that encounter, which occurred under a military occupation of the community, the alleged "primitiveness" of the *comuneros* hardly seems necessary to explain the communication difficulties he experienced on this occasion. For Vargas Llosa, nonetheless, indigenous cultures are a "primitive" obstacle to the full realization of his Western model of modernity. To become modern, he suggests, Latin America must emulate Europe and break up its indigenous masses into individual beings. Indigenous peoples must give up their collective identities in order to become the abstract individuals of liberal theory.

The very terms in which the dilemma is posed predetermine its resolution. Vargas Llosa sets up a false dichotomy by opposing Western modernization to the straw man of cultural "preservation", by which he means literally freezing "primitive" indigenous cultures in time. Having thus limited the options, he skips "from choices that Indians face to choosing for them", to use Doris Sommer's felicitous phrase.[51] If "forced to choose", Vargas Llosa informs us, *he* would choose modernization, though with great sadness. Yet who or what is forcing such a choice? Is preservation the only alternative to modernization? Is there only one form of modernization, the one that leads to a Western, neoliberal modernity? Are contemporary indigenous cultures not already the product of centuries of interaction with their European conquerors? In Vargas Llosa's binary vision, "archaic" cultures are to be replaced wholesale by another, modern one, as if culture were a repository of discrete, substitutable, and mutually exclusive collections of traits rather than a historical, creative social process. Unlike Arguedas, Vargas Llosa denies transculturation as both accomplished fact and possibility. Arguedas's ideal—a modern, but not acculturated or Westernized, Quechua individual—would seem to be an impossibility in Vargas Llosa's world, but not in that of most of his compatriots. According to Carlos Iván Degregori, most Peruvians are still "closer, after all, to the Arguedian ideal, both in its positive expression (modern Quechua individual) and in its definition by negation: I am not acculturated."[52]

At the end of "Questions of Conquest", Vargas Llosa refers to his novel *The Storyteller* to illustrate the dilemma of modernization vs preservation. *The Storyteller* is his first novel featuring an indigenous theme, and deals, ostensibly, with the Machiguenga, an indigenous people of the Peruvian Amazon threatened with the loss of their culture.[53] Although the novel initially appears to strike a balance between two autonomous lines of narrative – one Western, one indigenous – a close examination reveals that it is in fact structured by a hierarchical relationship in which the indigenous narrative is both subordinate to and a product of the Western one. Despite the differences in genre, the novel and the essay frame and resolve the "problem" of indigenous cultures in much the same way. In both cases, indigenous culture is represented as incompatible with modernity and must be sacrificed.

A Tale of Two Cultures?

The Storyteller combines the structures of two earlier Vargas Llosa novels, *La tía Julia y el escribidor / Aunt Julia and the Scriptwriter* (1977) and *Historia de Mayta / The Real Life of Alejandro Mayta* (1984). As in *Mayta*, a narrator resembling Vargas Llosa searches for information in order to reconstruct the life of a childhood friend. Like *Aunt Julia*, *The Storyteller* consists of two apparently unrelated parallel narratives. In one, which I will refer to as the Western narrative, an autobiographical male narrator on vacation in Florence tells the story of his fascination with the Machiguenga and of his college friend Saúl Zuratas, a student of anthropology who apparently "goes native" and becomes a Machiguenga. In the other, which I will refer to as the Machiguenga narrative, a *hablador*, or Machiguenga storyteller (literally "speaker"), tells tales of Machiguenga mythology. The *hablador* is eventually revealed to be Saúl Zuratas when his stories begin to mix in biblical tales, Zuratas's favorite Kafka story, and references to the large facial birthmark that earned Zuratas his college nickname in Lima: *Mascarita*, or mask. The first, Western narrative is told in chapters 1, 2, 4, 6, and 8, and frames the Machiguenga narrative, which alternates with it in chapters 3, 5, and 7.

The novel's division into alternating Western and Machiguenga narratives is mirrored within the Western narrative by the relationship between the narrator, who represents the West, and his friend Zuratas, who speaks for the Machiguenga. The narrator and Zuratas are described as opposites through a set of contrasts that identify the former with Vargas Llosa himself. Like Vargas Llosa, the narrator occupies the *criollo* center of Peruvian society. Zuratas, on the other hand, is doubly marginal: he is Jewish in a Catholic country, and the large birthmark covering half his face provokes revulsion among most of his fellow Peruvians, who see in him "a walking incitement to mockery and disgust."[54] Peru's ethnic division, in effect, is inscribed on Zuratas's face, causing *criollo* Peruvians confronted with it more than a little discomfort. Both protagonists start out studying Law, and both switch subjects. One chooses Literature and Western civilization, as did Vargas Llosa, the other Anthropology and indigenous culture. One studies with the historian Raúl Porras Barrenechea, an hispanist, the other with the anthropologist José Matos Mar, described as an *indigenista*. Porras Barrenechea and Matos Mar are real historical figures who taught at San Marcos University in Lima, and Vargas Llosa, like the narrator, studied with Porras Barrenechea.[55] The narrator, like Vargas Llosa in his youth, accepts a scholarship to study in Europe and moves toward the metropolitan center, while Zuratas rejects a similar offer and moves toward the margins, apparently disappearing into the Amazon jungle (though the official story is that he moved to Israel following his father's death). Both the narrator and Zuratas become storytellers: one a successful novelist, the other a Machiguenga *hablador*, or so it seems.

In chapter 2, the narrator and Zuratas engage in a debate in which the latter echoes one side of the false dichotomy of Vargas Llosa's *Harper's* essay. Zuratas takes the "cultural preservationist" position: the Machiguenga should be left alone and isolated from contact with the rest of Peru. The youthful narrator of 1956 argues the *indigenista* position that the Machiguenga could become Peruvians without giving up their culture and traditions. However, 29 years later in Florence, the narrator is quick to dismiss this vision as a youthful delusion and instead echoes the other side of Vargas Llosa's *Harper's* essay dichotomy: national development and modernization require the sacrifice of indigenous cultures.[56] A narrator's views of course do not necessarily reflect the politics of a novel as a whole, for the meaning of a narrator's statements is dependent on their relationship to other voices and discourses. In this case, however, the narrative structure of *The Storyteller* privileges the narrator's position by making him the ultimate authority in the text, suggesting that his statements are indeed to be taken as authoritative. This structure is perhaps best illustrated by the relationship between the alternating Western and Machiguenga narratives. The Machiguenga chapters, rather than constituting an autonomous narrative in an indigenous voice, are revealed to be the product of the Western narrator and therefore structurally subordinate to the Western narrative.

The Machiguenga narrative begins without introduction in chapter 3, immediately after the debate over the fate of the Machiguenga in chapter 2. The reader is plunged directly into it and must rely on internal markers to determine what sort of text she or he is now reading. This task is complicated further by the fact that there has been no explanation of the term *hablador* yet. The first definition of the word is offered only in chapter 4, in the Western narrative, and the narrator of the Machiguenga stories is not identified as an *hablador* until the beginning of chapter 5. The immediate plunge into a clearly mythic time, the bewildering variety and order of stories told, frequently repeated markers of orality, and the use of non-Spanish words and names soon indicate that the reader is dealing with some sort of oral, most likely indigenous, and presumably Machiguenga narrative.

The *hablador*'s stories can be grouped into four categories based on their content: (1) mythological accounts of the origin of the world and of human beings (for which Vargas Llosa draws heavily on ethnographies by the Dominican missionaries Vicente de Cenitagoya and Joaquín Barriales, sources cited in the text of the novel);[57] (2) historical accounts of uniformly negative contact with Westerners; (3) stories told to the speaker by the people he visits; and (4) stories told by the speaker of his own adventures and experiences. In these stories, all Machiguenga men share the same generic name, Tasurinchi, suggesting a lack of individual identity and the subordination of individuals to the collective. Even the *hablador* is more a social function than an individual: by circulating among dispersed Machiguenga communities and telling stories, he links these communities together and sustains a very mobile people's culture and collective identity.

The *hablador*'s stories do, however, ultimately identify him as an individual. He is revealed to be Zuratas in chapter 7, where the *hablador* explains how he discovered his calling, and how he acquired the little parrot that accompanies him on his travels. Zuratas, the attentive reader will recall, also had a parrot, which screeches his nickname, *Mascarita*, in chapter 1. The parrot is the *hablador*'s symbol, not only because it speaks, but because it was born "imperfect" like him (it has a deformed foot). The *hablador*'s "imperfection", it turns out, is a facial birthmark just like Zuratas's. The connection is clarified further when the *hablador* gives a Machiguenga rendition of Zuratas's favorite literary work: Kafka's *Metamorphosis*, followed by biblical stories of the persecution of the Jewish people, and the birth, life, and crucifiction of Jesus Christ. Finally, at the very end of the chapter, the *hablador* calls the parrot's name, which is identical to Zuratas's old college nickname: *Mascarita*. Zuratas's introduction of elements of the Western literary tradition into Machiguenga culture underlines the impossibility of the latter's "preservation" as well as of Zuratas's attempt to become a Machiguenga. Even the preservationist can not help but change Machiguenga culture in the very attempt to preserve it, and, as William Rowe observes, "the obvious impossibility of integrating with the Machiguenga is used to lend weight to the idea that they can only integrate with us, the central and stable implicit *nosotros* of the text."[58]

However, a close examination reveals that the attribution of the *hablador* narrative to Zuratas or to any actual *hablador* is the product of a sleight of hand. The Machiguenga narrative is, rather, the product of the principal narrator's long-standing desire and repeatedly frustrated effort to write about the *hablador*.[59] Though many years of effort have led nowhere, the principal narrator is finally able to write his Machiguenga story, presumably inspired by the photo exhibit about the Machiguenga he chances upon in Florence.[60] Since he has no way of knowing for sure that the figure in the photograph is an *hablador*, much less that it is Zuratas (he has not seen Zuratas in nearly 30 years and has never seen a *hablador*) the Western narrator is obliged to *invent* Zuratas's transformation into a *hablador*: "I have decided that it is he [Zuratas] who is the storyteller in Malfatti's photograph. A personal decision, since objectively I have no way of knowing."[61] The Machiguenga chapters are the outcome of this "personal decision" and do not have the same level of narrative authority as the Western chapters. The former are the product of the latter, and *The Storyteller* is based on ventriloquism, not dialogue. It does not maintain a tension between two genuine cultural alternatives. As Jorge Fornet points out, the Machiguenga narrative is "subordinate to the voice of the narrator" and "the voice of the Machiguenga *hablador* is no more than an illusion, a fiction constructed by the narrator."[62]

The novel's autobiographical narrator writes his long-planned Machiguenga story in Zuratas's voice, based on his own reading of the ethnographic sources cited in the text, many of which are real. Zuratas is thus the solution to the problem of how to represent an indigenous reality. The narrator uses his friend as an intermediary, a stand-in for himself, to represent a reality he feels unqualified to write about. Vargas Llosa, in turn, uses Zuratas to deflect attention from his appropriation of indigenous culture.[63] Where the Western novelist is unable to represent the indigenous Amazonian world directly, Saúl Zuratas as Machiguenga *hablador* will do it for him. Saúl Zuratas, the presumed *hablador*, is the mask worn by the modern novelist, both the narrator and Vargas Llosa, to represent the indigenous. It is no accident that Zuratas's nickname is *Mascarita*, and that the *hablador* repeats it three times at the end of chapter 7. Indeed, *Mascarita* is the last word of the Machiguenga narrative.

Despite its indigenous trappings, *The Storyteller* is not about

Machiguenga reality. It is about the contemporary Western problematic of representation. As M. Keith Booker puts it:

> A close examination shows that, rather than employing the Machiguenga hablador as an alternative to Western metanarrative structures, the modern novelist of *The Storyteller* simply appropriates the hablador for use in his own preexisting metanarrative of the Romantic artist. For him the Machiguengas consistently function not so much as a genuine Other to Western culture as an image of a prelapsarian Western past.[64]

Booker argues that this appropriation serves a critical function as a negative example, for "Vargas Llosa employs this novelist not as a figure of what artists should be, but what they should not."[65] This ironic reading of *The Storyteller* as a critique of intellectual authority hinges on the difference between the narrator's novelistic practice and that employed by Vargas Llosa himself. However, although Vargas Llosa the author may be distinguished from his narrator despite their many similarities, he engages in the same sort of appropriation by inventing the figure of the *hablador*. For while the Machiguenga are real, the *hablador* is not.[66] The autobiographical narrator of *The Storyteller* claims that "In the reports that the Dominican missionaries . . . wrote about [the Machiguenga] in the thirties and forties, there were frequent allusions to *habladores*."[67] The Dominicans cited are also real, but there are no such references in their published works, nor in other ethnographies on the Machiguenga.[68] Indeed, Vargas Llosa has invented not only the *hablador*, but also the Machiguenga's wandering nature and the use of the generic name Tasurinchi as a form of address for all Machiguenga men.[69] The author of *The Storyteller* does not live up to what Booker reads as his own model of intellectual responsibility. Vargas Llosa behaves in exactly the way in which *The Storyteller*, according to Booker, argues that artists should not.

For Vargas Llosa, the Machiguenga are just a vehicle for a story about the importance of stories, and of storytelling. Hence the fascination the *hablador* figure holds for the narrator, for whom "they're a tangible proof that storytelling can be something more than mere entertainment . . . Something primordial, something that the very existence of a people may depend on."[70] It is striking how much this description of the *hablador*'s role in Machiguenga society resembles the traditional role, or at least the self-image, of the writer/intellectual in Latin America.[71] The resemblance suggests that the narrator's interest in the *hablador* stems from a concern with his own social relevance and importance, for modernization affects not only the Machiguenga, but also the writer/intellectual. Latin American writer/intellectuals, the *letrados* or "universal intellectuals" who shaped and spoke for the nation and served as the respected custodians of its culture, have seen their authority eroded in the late twentieth century by the rise of the aural and visual culture of the mass media, which do not require literacy and therefore bypass the *letrados'* monopoly on print culture, undermining the writer/intellectual's position of privilege.[72] It is no surprise then to see the narrator of *The Storyteller* attempting to retain some authority by, so to speak, going to work for the competition: a television program. Seen in this light, the narrator's nostalgia for the *hablador*'s role comes as no surprise either. Moreover, it prefigures Vargas Llosa's revival of the nineteenth-century model of the *letrado* politician in a presidential campaign based, ironically, on a late twentieth-century technocratic neoliberalism that strives to sever the link between culture and politics by commodifying the former and restricting access to the latter. The rather contradictory and anachronistic nature of this project perhaps offers some clues to the premature truncation of Vargas Llosa's career as a politician. In *The Storyteller*, at any rate, despite the narrator's reflexive agonizing over how to represent another culture, Vargas Llosa does not attempt to represent the Machiguenga. Rather, he represents, and responds to, a crisis of his own intellectual authority by inventing the *hablador*, who serves as a projection of the writer's desired role and status in late twentieth-century Western society.

It should be noted, however, that whatever decline Vargas Llosa's intellectual authority and prestige have suffered is much more apparent in Peru than elsewhere. On the international literary circuit, he is a star who has adapted well to the changing cultural landscape by using his fame as a novelist to project his authority into other media: journalism, highbrow television, even the internet (he has participated in virtual chats in *El País digital*). Indeed, one might argue that, at least in the international arena, Vargas Llosa has successfully remade himself as a new kind of universal intellectual who has met the challenge of potentially democratizing new media with his authority intact, if not enhanced. Moreover, in his capacity as international cultural celebrity, he uses that authority to represent Peru to the rest of the world. Much of what large segments of the Western reading public know about Peruvian society is mediated by its most famous novelist, lending all the more weight to his essays and novels, both of which enjoy wide international circulation.

As one such representation of Peru, *The Storyteller* appears to give a voice to the Machiguenga in an international arena to which they have limited access. Far from being a truly dialogic or polyphonic text which lets the Machiguenga speak, however, *The Storyteller* is dominated by a single voice – that of the narrator, who closely resembles the author himself – which imposes its authority on other discourses.[73] Though the narrator laments the inevitable extinction of Machiguenga culture and of a primordial and fundamental form of narrative authority he feels the Western novelist has lost, it is hard to take the lament seriously in light of the absolute authority he wields over the novel's putatively "indigenous" voice, and of Vargas Llosa's still considerable, if not growing, international status and influence. The latter is due in no small part to novels such as *The Storyteller*, consumed in a globalized cultural marketplace as examples of a "universal" literature that rises above the mundane particularities of local contexts. In the end, *The Storyteller* is a metafiction more preoccupied with the process of writing and representation than with the fate of the Machiguenga. Its use of the Machiguenga to respond to a crisis of Western intellectual authority by, in effect, reinforcing that authority, is a calculated appropriation of indigenous culture.

A President Like Whom?

"Questions of Conquest" and *The Storyteller* were written between 1985 and 1987, during the prelude to Vargas Llosa's short-lived career as a politician.[74] He re-entered Peruvian politics in 1987 (just as *The Storyteller* was going to press and shortly after publishing an early version of "Questions of Conquest") by assuming the leadership of the mostly upper-and middle-class opposition to the Peruvian government's attempt to nationalize the banking system.[75] The success of this foray into national politics catalyzed the unification of the parties of the Peruvian Right, which rallied around the figure of the world famous novelist and made him their presidential candidate in the 1990 elections. Vargas Llosa ran on a platform that called for a neoliberal economic "shock" program and restructuring to create a free market economy in Peru. Such programs, though they have in some cases succeeded in reducing inflation and stimulating economic growth, have only increased the gap between the rich and the poor wherever they have been applied in Latin America.[76] Perhaps aware of this, Peru's poor majority voted against the cosmopolitan novelist despite his claims, reflected in the campaign slogan "you, too, can be an entrepreneur" ("tú también puedes ser empresario"), that the free market would reward the entrepreneurial efforts of the urban poor in the "informal" economy.[77]

However, his economic program was not the only reason Vargas Llosa lost the 1990 election. His views on culture and ethnicity also played a role in the presidential race. Vargas Llosa allied himself with the traditional parties of the *criollo* elite and promised to keep Peru from becoming a barbaric, "africanized" society. Instead, he would make it a civilized, modern European country like Switzerland, of which he spoke with a reverence bordering on naivete. It is perplexing that the author of complex early novels such as *La casa verde / The Green House* (1967), which display a nuanced understanding of Peru's multiethnic society and the (mostly negative) impact of modernization upon it, should espouse such a simplistic view of both Peru and Europe. As Carlos Iván Degregori points out,

> In *The Green House* . . . the "civilizing agents" (nuns, policemen, local authorities, businessmen) could turn out to be profoundly irrational, sometimes ridiculous, frequently archaic, almost without exception unjust and authoritarian if not outright cruel. . . . How could the same person who in *The Green House* painted a richly textured world, full of nuances, arrive at this naive and paradoxically premodern (almost magical) vision of modernity and of European countries?[78]

This vision of a Swiss future for Peru had little in common with the aspirations of most Peruvians. Vargas Llosa's poor understanding of and lack of identification with the indigenous and *mestizo* majority whose votes he was soliciting is perhaps best illustrated by a pair of anecdotes from the campaign. His description of a campaign stop that went awry, for example, speaks eloquently to the gulf that separated the writer-candidate from much of the electorate. As the Vargas Llosa campaign caravan pulls into a small town in the northern Department of Piura, it is attacked by a crowd of poor people:

> Armed with sticks and stones and all sorts of weapons to bruise and batter, an infuriated horde of men and women came to meet me, their faces distorted by hatred, who appeared to have emerged from the depths of time, a prehistory in which human beings and animals were indistinguishable, since for both life was a blind struggle for survival. Half naked, with very long hair and fingernails never touched by a pair of scissors, surrounded by emaciated children with huge swollen bellies, bellowing and shouting to keep their courage up, they hurled themselves on the caravan of vehicles as though fighting to save their lives or seeking to immolate themselves, with a rashness and savagery that said everything about the almost inconceivable levels of deterioration to which life for millions of Peruvians had sunk. What were they attacking? What were they defending themselves from? What phantoms were behind those threatening clubs and knives?[79]

Vargas Llosa presents this passage as his most vivid memory of a campaign swing through Piura, where heated political confrontations often occurred at his rallies, yet there is no hint here that the poor and unkempt might possess a political consciousness, or indeed, any consciousness at all. Instead, they appear to act out of a savage, prehistoric instinct, a remnant of a time "in which human beings and animals were indistinguishable." Reason, it seems, is reserved for the well groomed.

It does not occur to Vargas Llosa that the poor's hostility toward him could be interpreted as a quite rational response to his economic and political program. As Robert Richmond Ellis notes of this same passage, "from his perspective there is nothing about him that these people could logically reject, so in the end he attributes their rage to irrational, even mythic causes. Yet what they attack is not a phantom of some ancient crime, but Vargas Llosa himself as the bearer of a plan for economic and national recovery that in the final analysis would benefit not them but the minority white-elite to which he belongs."[80] Perhaps as a result of such unfortunate contacts between the voters and the candidate, on other occasions his campaign staff took greater care to insulate him from potentially unpleasant encounters with the masses, as is evident from the next anecdote, recounted by Beatriz Sarlo:

> Mario Vargas Llosa, who wanted to appear as an intellectual whose moral principles drove him into politics, posed for a photo in the backyard of his home. Those in charge of taking the picture had blocked off the swimming pool with a little wall of cardboard and tin, against which were arranged a group of poor people, made to look Indian and shabbily dressed, a boy with a dirty face, and some other props. The theme of the photo, which was included in a campaign video, was the visit of the candidate to a slum. But everything (the visit, the slum, the candidate himself) was reconstructed as if in a studio.[81]

Vargas Llosa could represent himself as sympathetic to the needs of Lima's overwhelmingly Andean urban poor without subjecting himself to the discomforts and risks of a real visit to one of Lima's *barriadas*.

By contrast, his opponent Alberto Fujimori, an obscure agronomist and political outsider, rode tractors and wore ponchos to campaign rallies, where he was unafraid to mix with the masses. Fujimori promised to revive the nation's economy gradually through a program of "honesty, technology and work" ("*honradez, tecnología y trabajo*") and used the audacious and improbable campaign slogan "a president like you" ("*un presidente como tú*").[82] His slogan, and the image of Fujimori in Andean attire, resonated with indigenous and *mestizo* voters, who felt they were able to identify the son of Japanese immigrants as someone "like them". This unlikely bond between the traditionally excluded and the self-styled "outsider" candidate testifies to the depth of feeling against the *criollo* ruling class that Vargas Llosa represented. Fujimori's campaign may have been pure demagoguery, but he displayed a deeper understanding of contemporary Peru than did Vargas Llosa. For the indigenous and *mestizo* majority who had struggled for decades to be recognized as Peruvians with full rights of citizenship and who had little interest in becoming Europeans, Fujimori held out the promise of a modernity they could call their own. As it turned out, the voters who elected Fujimori were to be disappointed: within a few weeks of taking office, he implemented an economic shock program even more severe than the one proposed by Vargas Llosa and went on to wield near-dictatorial power until a growing corruption scandal and mass popular protests forced him to step down and flee the country in 2001.

Nonetheless, while a vote for Fujimori was admittedly a gamble with unknown odds, it at least left open the possibility of a future different from the past. In the eyes of most indigenous and *mestizo* voters, Vargas Llosa's vision, on the other hand, meant the almost certain continuation of a century and a half of *criollo* minority rule. One can hardly blame them for this conclusion. In spite of its heavy reliance on the latest polling and marketing techniques recommended by North American public relations consultants (including Mark Malloch Brown, who went on to do public relations for the World Bank), Vargas Llosa's presidential campaign *was* strikingly reminiscent of nineteenth-century Latin American liberalism, not only in its revival of the *letrado* tradition of the writer-politician and its promotion of *laissez faire* economics, but also in its insistence on cultural homogeneity – achieved through the Westernization of native populations – as a prerequisite for modernization and national development. In this the Vargas Llosa campaign simply echoed ideas he had developed earlier in his essays and novels.

That Vargas Llosa expressed "great sadness" at the loss of indigenous cultures while promoting assimilation was of little comfort to the potential victims of his economic and political program. Such "sadness", too, is a familiar trope in the Western discourse of expansionist modernization, one which has done more to relieve the guilt of conquerors than the suffering of the conquered. Renato Rosaldo has coined the term "imperialist nostalgia" to describe the yearning felt by moderns for the vanished (and vanquished) cultures whose destruction was deemed a necessary and inevitable consequence of modernization.[83] In *The Storyteller* as in "Questions of Conquest", the imperialist nostalgia comes, paradoxically, before the fact: it is a nostalgia for the indigenous cultures one is about to destroy. And in an odd way, the nostalgia serves to justify the sacrifice of indigenous culture on the altar of national development and the common good, even though common people are unlikely to derive much good from it.

Vargas Llosa in the Andes

Vargas Llosa's first novel since losing the 1990 elections, *Lituma en los Andes / Death in the Andes* (1993), is also his first sustained literary engagement with the Andes and indigenous Andean peoples. Indeed, it could be argued that his entire literary career up until this novel has been based on an avoidance of the Andes, and *The Storyteller* is a good example of such avoidance. Cynthia Steele notes that the displacement of Peru's indigenous "problem" onto a small and "primitive" Amazonian group in *The Storyteller* downplays the challenge to the legitimacy of the Peruvian state represented by indigenous Andean peoples generally and by the Shining Path in particular.[84] To argue that cultural identity must be sacrificed to the cause of national development is, after all, an easier case to make about a few thousand Machiguenga than it is about several million Andean Quechua and Aymara speakers.

Such displacement is typical of Vargas Llosa's avoidance of the Andes. Though it may be a matter of personal taste, or distaste, such avoidance clearly also has a political dimension:

> I have never felt any sympathy for the Incas . . . I have always thought that Peruvians' sadness – an outstanding trait of our character – perhaps was born with the Inca Empire: a regimented and bureaucratic society of antlike men, in whom an omnipotent steam roller nullified all individual personality.[85]

This attitude toward the Andes and indigenous Andeans is expressed only indirectly in *The Storyteller*, but is clear in *Death in the Andes*, where the persistence of indigenous cultures is not simply an obstacle to the solution of pressing social problems, it *is* the problem, in the form of the Shining Path guerrilla insurgency. Although the guerrilla movement's hostility to indigenous culture is well-documented, and its fervent faith in modernization imposed from above even has something in common with Vargas Llosa's, in *Death in the Andes* the Maoist insurgency is portrayed as little more than the product of atavistic indigenous barbarism.[86]

Vargas Llosa's first Andean novel is set in the fictional highland mining community of Naccos at the height of the Shining Path's war against the Peruvian state. Two Civil Guards are stationed in Naccos to guard a government road construction project from guerrilla attack. The road here, as in Arguedas's *Yawar Fiesta*, is clearly a symbol of modernity. But unlike in *Yawar Fiesta*, the road construction is stalled, as is Peru's modernization, by bureaucratic inefficiency and the hostility of the Andean environment, which implicitly includes its inhabitants. Whereas in *Yawar Fiesta* the road to the coast (and therefore modernity) is constructed in record time by and on the initiative of the indigenous *ayllus* of Puquio, here the atmosphere of violence seemingly inherent to the Andes and indigenous Andeans undermines and effectively neutralizes the project of modernization represented by the road. Indeed, the road construction is ultimately abandoned after a *huayco*, or Andean landslide, destroys the construction camp and machinery.

One of the two Civil Guards stationed at Naccos is Lituma, a character familiar to readers of *The Green House*. Originally from the northern, lowland, and *criollo* city of Piura, Lituma does not speak Quechua and finds Andeans incomprehensible. He is completely out of his element in the Andes. The other Civil Guard is Lituma's Quechua-speaking subordinate Tomás Carreño, born in the Andean town of Sicuani, near Cuzco, but raised primarily in Lima. The two are friends despite Tomás's Andean origins, and Lituma even designates him an honorary *costeño*: "'You're the kind of man who should have been born on the coast.'"[87] They confront the ever-present threat of Shining Path attack as well as the distrust of the road construction workers and other locals. The narrative is set in motion by the mysterious disappearance of three of the construction workers, which it is Lituma's task to investigate. His investigation is in fact the guiding thread around which the other strands of the narrative are wrapped, and *Death in the Andes* may thus be read as a detective novel of sorts, a genre in which Vargas Llosa has dabbled before.[88] However, the fate of the three missing workers is not the only mystery in this novel, for Lituma's attempt to find out what happened to the disappeared men is simultaneously an investigation into the causes of the violence that has stopped Peru's modernity in its tracks. If *Death in the Andes* may be considered a detective novel, this is the larger mystery it attempts to solve.

It does so by weaving together four lines of narrative, of which Lituma's investigation is the first. The second narrative describes five Shining Path attacks, emphasizing the primitive brutality of the guerrillas and the innocence of their victims. The disappeared men it turns out, were survivors of three of these attacks. The next line of narrative concerns Dionisio and Adriana, owners of Naccos' only bar and social center as well as Lituma's prime suspects in the disappearances. The fourth and final narrative is the story Tomás recounts to Lituma about his unrequited love for and romance with a prostitute named Mercedes, who turns out to be the same Mercedes Lituma once knew in Piura. These stories are told in fragments, arranged, as in earlier Vargas Llosa novels such as *The Green House*, in a remarkably regular pattern. *Death in the Andes* is divided into two parts and an epilogue. Part One consists of five chapters, each of which has three sections. The first section of each chapter is always the story of Lituma's investigation, the second describes a Shining Path attack, and in the third Tomás recounts his romantic misadventures with Mercedes. There are four chapters in Part Two, each of which also has three sections. These are arranged in the same order as in Part One, except that the second section of each chapter is dedicated to Adriana and Dionisio instead of to the Shining Path. The epilogue has just two sections. In the first, Tomás and Mercedes are reunited in a happy conclusion to their frustrated romance, while the second recounts the frustrating and inconclusive results of Lituma's investigation.

The narrative form of *Death in the Andes* establishes a kind of structural equivalence between the Shining Path on the one hand and Adriana and Dionisio on the other. This structural equivalence is reinforced by Lituma's investigation, which links the two and identifies both as expressions of an atavistic indigenous barbarism. The alleged survival of pre-Columbian Andean beliefs and practices, such as ritual human sacrifice, is ultimately revealed to be the principal source of the violence that plagues late twentieth-century Peru. The only alternative to such violence offered by *Death in the Andes* is the love between the Piuran prostitute Mercedes and the Andean-born Civil Guard Tomás, a love that redeems the former and furthers the assimilation of the latter to the dominant, Westernized culture of coastal Peru. A full understanding of the novel's treatment of the problem of violence in Peru requires a closer examination of each of its four lines of narrative, beginning with the Shining Path attacks, following Lituma's investigation to Adriana and Dionisio, and ending with the romance between Tomás and Mercedes.

The Shining Path narrative consists of five self-contained sections told in the third person. The first describes the guerrilla's brutal murder of a French tourist couple for no apparent reason. In the second, guerrillas massacre a herd of vicuñas on what they consider a "reserve devised by imperialists", to the horror of the preserve's deaf-mute guardian, Pedrito Tinoco, whom they spare.[89] A Shining Path column occupies the town of Andamarca in the third section. They execute local government officials and set the residents against each other in a blood-letting frenzy of mutual denunciation for real and imagined offenses. A group of ecologists led by the aristocratic Hortensia d'Harcourt, a wealthy European-born environmentalist from Lima, are the Shining Path's victims in the fourth section. They are executed for collaborating with the government by working with Andean communities on reforestation projects. The fifth section tells the story of Casimiro Huarcaya, an albino itinerant merchant, who on one of his trips gets a young woman pregnant and then abandons her. When he encounters her again she is the leader of a Shining Path unit that condemns him to death. She is his executioner, but her shot misses, apparently on purpose, and he survives.

In real life, The Shining Path has in fact committed similar atrocities, and worse. However, *Death in the Andes* makes no attempt to examine the social context that gave rise to such apparently senseless violence, and as a result it presents both the guerrillas and their victims as little more than caricatures. The indigenous guerrillas are portrayed in such a one-dimensional fashion that one otherwise admiring review has to concede that "the members of the guerrilla group are mere outlines of characters, cardboard figures who coldly recite revolutionary slogans and justifications as they condemn their victims, all the while remaining impenetrable and immune to dialogue."[90] Their monologic, totalitarian mentality is reminiscent of Vargas Llosa's comments about the Incas.

While the Shining Path is the epitome of evil, its victims personify innocence, albeit to varying degrees. Casimiro Huarcaya and the residents of Andamarca, though not completely innocent, receive a punishment far out of proportion to their crimes. Despite their ties to the government, Hortensia d'Harcourt and her group of ecologists are certainly more innocent, and their work is even shown to benefit their indigenous executioners. The French couple Albert and Michèle are guilty of nothing more than a profound interest in Peru's indigenous cultures, an innocence which is underscored by the narrator's incessant, cloying references (25 of them in 8 pages) to "la *petite* Michèle." Moreover, the guerillas' human victims are racially coded on a scale of innocence and injustice. The whiter the victims, the more innocent, and the greater the outrage of the injustice committed against them by the Shining Path's undifferentiated indigenous masses.

As Lituma discovers in his investigation of the Naccos disappearances, however, the Shining Path is not the only source of violence in the Andes. All three of the disappeared men were survivors of guerrilla violence. Medardo Llantac, now a road construction foreman, escaped the fate of his government colleagues in Andamarca, where he had been mayor. The deaf-mute Pedrito Tinoco, now the Civil Guards' domestic servant, had been the massacred vicuñas' caretaker at the preserve. And Casimiro Huarcaya survived an execution attempt by the Shining Path. While all three are survivors of Shining Path violence, they eventually fall victim to an even more atavistic form of indigenous barbarism, killed by their fellow road construction workers at the urging of the bar owners Dionisio and Adriana. The indigenous workers murder the three men in order to protect themselves and the road construction project from both the Shining Path and the *apus*, or mountain deities.

By eliminating the three men who, because of their past history, are most likely to draw the guerrillas to the construction site, the workers guarantee their own safety. And, following ancient Andean tradition, they sacrifice their victims to the *apus* in exchange for the *apus*' acquiescence to the road construction through the mountains. Lituma does not uncover the true fate of the disappeared men on his own, however. He must rely on the Danish professor Paul Stirmsson, whose vast knowledge of Peru's indigenous cultures and languages is matched only by Lituma's ignorance of them. It is Stirmsson who explains for Lituma the ancient Chanca and Huanca customs: "It was their way of showing respect for the spirits of the mountains, of the earth, whom they were going to disturb. They did it to avoid reprisals and to assure their own survival. So there would be no landslides, no *huaycos*."[91] Lituma later

discovers that at least one of the human sacrifices involved ritual canni-
balism.

The third principal line of narrative concerns Dionisio and Adriana, the
sinister couple who incite the indigenous workers to engage in barbaric
rituals. Adriana entertains bar patrons with her story in two sections
narrated in the first person where Vargas Llosa deploys an "indigenous"
rendition of Greek myth.[92] Like Ariadne, who helped Theseus kill the
Minotaur in its labyrinth, Adriana helps her first lover Timoteo kill a *pishtaco*, a cannibalistic Andean mythical figure, in its labyrinthine mountain
cave. And as with Ariadne, who was abandoned by Theseus on the island
of Naxos where she later married Dionysius, Adriana is abandoned by
Timoteo in Naccos where she later marries Dionisio who, like his Greek
namesake, is a master of drink and dance who participates in the sacrifice
of ritual scapegoats.

However, the *pishtaco* is not an Andean Minotaur. It is, rather, an
indigenous Andean folk symbol of Spanish, and later *criollo*, colonialist
oppression. *Pishtacos* are represented as white foreigners, and in colonial
times they were said to render the fat from their victims' bodies for use in
the manufacture of church bells. In more contemporary versions of the
pishtaco myth, the body fat is exported to pay off Peru's staggering foreign
debt or used as a lubricant for all manner of motorized vehicles, as jet fuel
for commercial aircraft, and as propellant for US moon rockets.[93] Vargas
Llosa is aware of these versions of the *pishtaco* myth and of their critical
function.[94] However, by retelling Greek myth through the figure of the
pishtaco, he neutralizes an anti-colonialist indigenous tradition. Indeed,
he effectively inverts the *pishtaco* myth so that what was once an indigenous Andean critique of Spanish and *criollo* colonialism becomes, in
Death in the Andes, a *criollo* critique of Andean barbarism. The *pishtaco*
is no longer a foreign exploiter. He is now an indigenous monster, an
Andean Minotaur.

All three of these lines of narrative (the senseless Shining Path violence,
Lituma's investigation, and Dionisio and Adriana) clearly identify indigenous Andean barbarism as the principal, if not the only source of violence
in Peru. "I wonder . . . if what's going on in Peru isn't a resurrection of
all that buried violence. As if it had been hidden somewhere, and
suddenly, for some reason, it all surfaced again", mutters the blond engineer at the ironically named La Esperanza mine where Lituma meets Paul
Stirmsson.[95] Lituma himself later wonders,

> How was it possible that the laborers, many of whom had adopted modern
> ways and at least completed primary school, who had seen the cities,
> listened to the radio, went to the movies, dressed like civilized men – how
> could they behave liked naked, savage cannibals? You could understand if

they were Indians from the barrens who had never set foot in a school and still lived like their great-great-grandfathers, but with guys like these who played cards, who had been baptized, how could it be?[96]

The civilizing mission appears to have failed irremediably in Peru, and these three lines of narrative offer no solution to the resulting wave of violence. Lituma receives a transfer out of the Andes without arresting Dionisio and Adriana or anyone else, and the Shining Path continues to terrorize the country.

The story of Tomás and Mercedes' romance identifies official corruption as another source of violence in Peru. State-sponsored violence, however, does not seem to be as insuperable an obstacle to human happiness as is indigenous barbarism. Tomás begins his Civil Guard career as an official bodyguard for an important drug trafficker. He falls in love with Mercedes, the drug lord's mistress, and rescues her from the abusive criminal by murdering him. This puts them on the run from both the Peruvian Civil Guard and the drug mafia. Mercedes, who never really wanted to be rescued, abandons Tomás at the first opportunity, in Lima, and takes all his money with her. However, their love overcomes the corruption and violence in which it was born when she turns up in Naccos, and they are reunited at the end of the novel. This improbable story is the only part of *Death in the Andes* in which Vargas Llosa employs his trademark literary techniques. Tomás tells Lituma about his frustrated romance with Mercedes in nightly installments in order to ward off the boredom and tension of their remote Civil Guard post. The love story and the dialogues through which it is narrated are spliced into the conversations between Tomás and Lituma, but the interwoven dialogues or *"vasos comunicantes"* that Vargas Llosa used to such remarkable effect in *The Green House* and *Conversation in The Cathedral* are largely wasted here on a vapid melodrama.

The story is nonetheless crucial to the novel's project, for the romantic happy ending is the only one there is in *Death in the Andes*, and it is the only solution offered to Peru's problems. In the tradition of the nineteenth-century Latin American national romances Doris Sommer calls foundational fictions, Vargas Llosa refounds a divided and collapsing Peru through the romantic union of representatives from its conflicting parts.[97] Mercedes, from Piura, and Tomás, from the southern Andes and raised in Lima, are the future of Peru. The relationship and probable marriage between the white *piurana* and the "good", acculturated Indian is the only alternative to the barbaric violence of the Shining Path and the atavistic human sacrifices promoted by Dionisio and Adriana. Given the magnitude of Peru's contemporary problems, however, Vargas Llosa's solution seems even more woefully inadequate at the end of the twentieth century than it was in the nineteenth. Indeed, it is more of an escape than a solution, for it writes off the Andes as hopelessly barbaric and unfit for inclusion in the nation: Tomás receives a transfer to Mercedes' hometown Piura and, like Lituma, turns his back on the Andes.

In place of a social analysis of the bloody Peruvian conflict, Vargas Llosa offers the atavistic savagery of indigenous Andeans as the cause of the bloodshed. By doing so, he erases centuries of post-Conquest history and largely absolves official, *criollo* Peru of responsibility for the conditions which have given rise to dozens of indigenous rebellions over the past five centuries, as well as the Shining Path's war in the 1980s.[98] Lacking a substantive social analysis, *Death in the Andes* rules out a collective solution to the problem and proposes instead an escape into "love and intimacy" as an alternative to "the violence and tragedy of the highlands."[99]

Various critics have traced Vargas Llosa's focus on the indigenous roots of Peruvian violence in *Death in the Andes* back to his report on the murder of eight journalists near the Andean community of Uchuraccay in January 1983.[100] The attribution of the nation's problems to indigenous "backwardness", tentatively formulated in the Uchuraccay report of 1983, finds its culmination ten years later in *Death in the Andes*, which dispenses with all reference to the structural violence of poverty or the exclusion of indigenous peoples from national life. Instead, the novel burdens atavistic indigenous Andean barbarism with the full weight of everything that is wrong with Peru. While Vargas Llosa's earlier works, such as *The Green House* and *Conversation in The Cathedral*, explored complex reasons for Peru's social problems, *Death in the Andes* does not. Here the answer to the question posed in *Conversation in The Cathedral* – "At what point had Peru screwed up?" – seems to be: before the Conquest.[101]

EPILOGUE

More than Skin Deep? Social Change in Contemporary Peru

In spite of the hopes raised by the election in 2001 of Peru's first *cholo* President, Alejandro Toledo, the indigenous and the poor of Peru are not much better off today than they were thirty years ago when Vargas Llosa posed his famous question. Born to an impoverished indigenous family in the northern Andean department of Ancash, Toledo overcame the limitations such origins would ordinarily imply in Peru. Though as a youth he worked in several occupations virtually synonymous with the informal economy—among them shoe shine boy and soda and popsicle vendor— he went on to earn a graduate degree in business at Stanford University in California and worked for the World Bank and other international financial and development institutions. Returning to Peru in pursuit of a political career, he helped lead the opposition to the increasingly corrupt Fujimori regime and ran for President on three occasions between 1995 and 2001. His personal story seemed to make Toledo uniquely qualified to lead the nation in a new direction. Adding to his appeal was his Belgian wife, Eliane Karp, a Quechua-speaking anthropologist knowledgeable about indigenous Andean culture who, like her husband, had studied at Stanford and had worked for development agencies such as the World Bank and USAID.

During his successful presidential campaign of 2001, Toledo promised to fight the corruption of the Fujimori years, and to promote a free market economy with a human face. While reassuring domestic and international financial interests that he would not deviate from neoliberal policies, he also pledged to create jobs and attend to the needs of the poor. Both Toledo and Karp emphasized their commitment to the largely indigenous

195

and *cholo* poor by invoking Andean symbolism throughout the campaign, Toledo by stressing his indigenous origins and donning Andean and even "Inca" garb, Karp by addressing crowds in Quechua and at one rally even assuring voters that the *apus* or mountain deities had spoken to her and told her that her husband was good and sacred and would win the presidential election.[1] The symbolism carried through to Toledo's inauguration, a dual event that included not only the official ceremony in Lima on 28 July 2001, but also an Andean one at Machu Picchu the following day, "replete with two 'Inca priests,' traditional sacrificial offerings, replicated Inca insignia of power, repeated references to Toledo as the returning Pachacutec, and a materialized 'Incaic' discourse of geocultural unity based on reference to the four quarters of the Inca empire, 'Tahuantinsuyu'."[2]

The combination of Toledo's humble origins, educational as well as professional success, and use of Andean symbolism resonated with what de la Cadena has identified as the "indigenous *mestizo*" identity of many working-class residents of Cuzco and, presumably, other provincial cities as well.[3] These individuals identify themselves as *mestizo* rather than Indian, rejecting the stigma and inferiority signified by the latter term. However, rather than thinking of themselves as Westernized, they proudly embrace indigenous culture and see no contradiction between it and their formal education and urban way of life.[4] With his educational achievements, worldliness, and apparent loyalty to his Andean origins and culture, Toledo seemed to embody such an identity and the aspirations of indigenous *mestizos* for economic success without the sacrifice of cultural identity. As de la Cadena points out, Toledo's pose also appealed to elite versions of *mestizaje* as whitening: "notwithstanding the candidate's reverberant claims to a working class *cholo* identity, . . . his university degree, his 'studies abroad,' (and of course his marriage to a foreign white woman) loom large, and thus 'Alejandro'—as his elite peers familiarly call him—represents an 'ironed' choloness, one that has been tamed by education and is a useful political strategy."[5] Precisely because Toledo's combination of Andean and Western qualities made him so appealing to so many Peruvians, he was seen as useful by some in the less overtly racist, more neoliberal part of the *criollo* elite. Perhaps eager to avoid a repeat of Vargas Llosa's electoral débâcle of 1990, in 2001 this portion of the elite was willing to let a *cholo* face represent neoliberal interests.

According to de la Cadena, Toledo's image as a young *cholo* "microentrepreneur" educated abroad who returns to Peru as a successful, self-made man was "highly compatible with the persona that neoliberalism requires: a solitary achiever, able to succeed without the intervention of the state."[6] He seemed to personify the promise of a free market accessible to all regardless of cultural identity, a market that erodes old racial hierarchies and measures individuals' status according to other criteria.[7] However, the hopes inspired by Toledo's assumption of the presidency did not last long. When he entered office opinion polls registered an approval rating of some 60 percent, but this dropped to barely over 20 percent within a year and at present struggles to remain in double digits.[8] Indeed, Toledo's approval rating is currently even lower than that of his reviled predecessor Fujimori, a negative popular sentiment from which Eliane Karp is not immune.[9]

Several factors account for Toledo's unpopularity, among which the constant attacks upon him by his political opponents and those sectors of the mass media still affiliated with the previous regime can not be discounted. Nonetheless, popular opinion of Toledo has not been helped by his failure to deliver on his electoral promises of jobs and greater economic equality, particularly in light of the outrageous presidential salary of $18,000 per month he initially granted himself (public outcry has since forced him to reduce it to $3,600 per month).[10] Indeed, Toledo has done little to address the growing gap between rich and poor, terms that remain virtually synonymous with *criollo* and indigenous Andean (or *cholo*), respectively. While his neoliberal policies have produced one of the higher rates of economic growth in Latin America, they have done so at a cost shouldered disproportionately by the poor, who have benefited little from the reactivation of the economy.[11] Their discontent has expressed itself not only in consistently low opinion poll ratings for Toledo but also in recurring mass protests against his initiatives.[12]

Charges of corruption have also dogged Toledo's inner circle, leading to several resignations of government officials, the arrest of a close adviser, and countless reshufflings of the cabinet.[13] Eliane Karp has not escaped such charges, having been accused of misappropriating funds in her capacity as the director of the *Comisión Nacional de Pueblos Indígenas, Amazónicos y Afroperuanos* / National Commission of Indigenous, Amazonian, and Afroperuvian Peoples (CONAPA) and the *Fundación Pacha para el Cambio* / Pacha Foundation for Change, organizations supposedly dedicated to development projects benefiting the poor and indigenous communities, but which apparently have little to show for the substantial sums raised or appropriated for them.[14] She has also been accused of influence peddling for receiving $10,000 per month in consulting fees from a bank that had helped to spirit money out of the country for the Fujimori regime.[15] Whether or not such allegations are ultimately substantiated, they have severely damaged Toledo's image and eroded support for his government. Indeed, he is now the most unpopular president in modern Peruvian history, and some of the country's most respected newspapers and journals have begun to speculate publicly whether he will be able to finish his term, or even if he should.[16]

Toledo's swift disgrace suggests that a real democratization of Peruvian society is more likely to occur through the persistent, collective efforts of indigenous and other social movements than through the election of an indigenous president with closer ties to national and global elites than to Peru's poor majority. However, a nationwide indigenous movement such as those in neighboring Bolivia and Ecuador has yet to emerge in Peru. This does not mean that there has been no indigenous activism in Peru, only that it has not, (at least not yet), taken the same form as in neighboring Andean countries. [17] Nelson Manrique has offered at least three possible explanations for Peru's lack of such a movement. He suggests, first, that indigenous society in Peru never recovered from the Spanish colonial administration's destruction of the indigenous Andean elite after the defeat of Túpac Amaru II in 1782. This deprived Peru's indigenous population of intellectual and political leadership, a problem which, according to Manrique, persists to this day. Second, he points out that the concept of an urban Indian does not exist in Peru, while in Bolivia and Ecuador this social category "has been central . . . for the emergence of intellectuals capable of theorizing indigenism as a political alternative." [18] In Peru, indigenous Andeans who migrate to cities undergo a change in identity from Indian to *cholo*. While *cholo* identity includes many indigenous elements, it is nonetheless perceived as something other than indigenous and does not facilitate the representation of indigenous interests as readily as the Bolivian and Ecuadorian urban Indian. [19] Finally, Manrique argues that the political violence and civil war of the 1980s "did not allow for the emergence of new political alternatives." [20] Even after the war, the *criollo* elite's association of Shining Path violence with Andean tradition, exemplified by Vargas Llosa's *Death in the Andes*, has hampered the expression of indigenous demands, which runs the risk of being perceived as a threat of renewed violence. [21]

Others have suggested that Peru's particularly sharp cultural and geographic divide between the indigenous Andes and the *criollo* coast, as well as Lima's coastal location, in contrast to the Andean capitals of Ecuador and Bolivia, have impeded the emergence of a nationwide indigenous movement in Peru by isolating indigenous Andeans from the center of state power and national culture, at least until very recently. [22] The persistent effects of the de-indigenizing policies of Velasco Alvarado's populist dictatorship (1969–75), which redefined Indians as peasants, substituting a class identity for an ethnic one, are also frequently mentioned as a factor inhibiting the emergence of a self-identified indigenous movement in Peru. [23] Rodrigo Montoya adds that a generalized disillusionment with politics as such, a consequence in part of the Peruvian Left's failure to deliver on its promises from the 1960s through the 1980s, has produced a retreat from activism perceived as political. [24]

These explanations are not mutually exclusive, and it is likely that most or all of the factors alluded to have played a role in inhibiting the emergence of a nationwide indigenous movement in Peru. Whether such a movement arises in Peru remains to be seen, of course. What does seem clear is that a real democratization of Peruvian society is impossible without a collective, organized form of indigenous self-representation.

In arguing for the necessity of an indigenous movement, I do not mean to suggest that this alone would eliminate Peru's many divisions and inequalities. Such an outcome would depend on this hypothetical indigenous movement's program and alliances. Indigenous leaders and movements are no more immune to demagoguery, opportunism, and corruption than their *criollo* counterparts, nor are they free of internal conflicts. One does not need to believe that indigenous peoples and their cultural traditions are superior to those of the West—as some *indigenista* writers, including Arguedas, seemed to think, at least on occasion—in order to recognize that no solution to Peru's divisions and inequalities is possible without the active participation of its indigenous citizens in full exercise of their right to represent their own interests and visions of the nation's future. Whatever the risks of cooptation or corruption inherent to any social movement, Peru's divisions and inequalities require a collective response. They are unlikely to be ameliorated by the currently much-touted "magic" of the free market. As Rodrigo Montoya has observed, "there can be excellent projects of indigenous cultural revalorization and self-affirmation, but if power is not questioned, if an alternative is not offered to today's politics of capitalist restructuring, the fundamental problems will not be resolved."[25]

The relevance of literature for Peru's current predicament is not at all clear. In and of themselves, transcultural narratives such as those of Arguedas probably have little chance of directly affecting social conditions. However, this was always an unrealistic expectation, and neither Rama nor Arguedas ever claimed that narrative transculturation alone was capable of resolving Peru's deep class and ethnic divisions and the injustices generated by them. As Rama notes:

> Obviously Arguedas was not in a position to put transculturation into practice in Peru; . . . literature was for him a *reduced model of transculturation*, through which the eventual realization of transculturation could be demonstrated and proven. If it was possible in literature, that is, it could also be possible in the rest of culture. Because he was neither the government, nor a political power, nor a revolution, Arguedas could not adequately guide the process of transculturation. Instead, he did what he was able, or thought he was able, to do, applying all his energies to it: demonstrate transculturation in narrative fiction.[26]

Through his literary and anthropological works, Arguedas sought to make his readers aware not only of indigenous Andeans' existence and of the abuse they suffered, but also of the vigor and value of their culture. By demonstrating through his literary works the subordinated culture's compatibility with and contributions to modernity, he attempted to put indigenous Andean traditions on an equal footing with the dominant, Westernized culture of Peru's *criollo* elite.

Even this limited form of literary agency seems ambitious today. In the 1960s, when literature and literary intellectuals still played a central role in official national culture, it was possible to imagine that literary works could catalyze cultural and social change. This is no longer so, at least not to the same extent. Today, as Jean Franco notes, "new technologies of communication have created a class of technocrats and new audiences for whom print culture has lost its luster and now competes with – and is often superseded by – visual and aural culture."[27] The result is that "everywhere in contemporary Latin America, there is a sense of the literary intelligentsia's diminishing importance and displacement from public discourse."[28] In the face of these changes, the project of narrative transculturation would seem to have even less chance of democratizing official culture now than it did in Arguedas's day. Nonetheless, despite literature's diminished status, according to Franco, "literary representation is still thought indispensable among those formerly excluded from citizenship in what Ángel Rama called 'the lettered city' – the indigenous, the black and mulatto populations, women, and gays. Literature still confronts official versions of history."[29] Indeed, a modern indigenous literature and an indigenous socio-political movement could complement each other in Peru as they have begun to do elsewhere in Latin America, most notably Guatemala.[30]

Perhaps its very displacement from the center of official culture may yet permit literature, despite its limited circulation compared to the audiovisual mass media, to play a role, alongside other oppositional forms of cultural expression, in the democratization of Latin American societies. In a world of media conglomerates, literature may well be able to function as a space for independent critique and the articulation of alternatives to the present precisely because of its marginalization and relatively artesanal form of production (though distribution and circulation of literary works remains largely under highly centralized corporate control). While Arguedas's hope for a truly democratic, multicultural, and egalitarian Peru has yet to be realized, there is still something to be learned from his strategy of narrative transculturation as a powerful means of challenging readers to imagine a future free of the injustices of the present. As Rama observed, writers are not obliged to solve social problems in their literary works, only to represent them clearly. Arguedas represented Peru's divisions as clearly as anyone before or since, but he also went considerably beyond this, modeling in the transcultural form of his narratives an opening from within the purportedly "national" culture toward indigenous peoples and culture. That this opening has not yet produced the results Arguedas had hoped it would makes his vision no less attractive or necessary than it was a generation ago.

NOTES

Introduction   Social Conflict and Narrative Form

1   See, for example, Contreras and Cueto, who conclude their recent *Historia del Perú contemporáneo* by noting that "Peru is among those countries that new historiographic currents have called 'postcolonial'; that is, countries that emerged from a dense colonial past, which left a deep and enduring mark on their social structure and economic development. . . . Among the key elements of this *colonial heritage* . . . figures above all a fragmented social structure—what many specialists in recent years recognized as the *dualism* of Peruvian society—expressed in a difficult and conflictive coexistence between the inheritors of the colonizing culture and those of the colonized culture / el Perú forma parte de aquellos países que nuevas corrientes histo-riográficas han llamado 'postcoloniales'; es decir, países que emergieron de un denso pasado colonial, que marcó profunda y largamente su estructura social y su desarrollo económico. . . . Entre los elementos claves de esa *herencia colonial* . . . figura sobre todo la fragmentación de la estructura social—lo que muchos especialistas reconocieron hace unos años como el *dualismo* de la sociedad peruana—expresado en una convivencia difícil y conflictiva entre los herederos de la cultura colonizadora y los de la colo-nizada" (310–311). Translations are the author's unless otherwise noted. On the binary and racialized nature of this divide in the Andean region, see Weismantel, *Cholas and Pishtacos*, xxxii–xxxiii. Though the indigenous–*criollo* divide is Peru's primary social fault line, it is of course not the only one. Smaller populations of African and Asian descent further complicate Peru's fragmented ethnic or racial landscape. However, these groups appear much less frequently in Peruvian literature. Because of this and my limited knowledge of both Afro-Peruvian and Asian-Peruvian cultures, this book discusses them only in passing.

2   Flores Galindo has observed that the confrontation between Andean and European worlds in twentieth-century Peru in many respects echoed that of the sixteenth-century Conquest, though without the demographic collapse of the initial encounter. The twentieth century, he argues, was characterized by a renewed "Western cultural offensive against Andean culture / ofensiva de la cultura occidental sobre la cultura andina" (*Dos ensayos sobre José*

María Arguedas 16). Larson locates the beginning of this offensive in the latter half of the nineteenth century, a moment in which a liberalism recently imported from Europe reinvented and widened the colonial divide opened up by the conquest in the Andean region. She suggests, for example, that "the rise of emphatically binary discourses of race and space was, in reality, one of the important legacies of nineteenth century Andean liberalism . . . . The myths of *mestizaje* rarely inspired the *criollo* imaginary, which preferred the language of race, region, culture, and later class, to position its indigenous peoples at the margin of this fractured modernity. Indeed, it can be plausibly argued that the *criollo* elites of the Andean region deliberately availed themselves of the language and policy of internal colonialism (recently dressed up in a fashionably racialized discourse), precisely in order to control indigenous labor and avoid any sort of commotion . . . among their rural masses / el surgimiento de unos discursos rotundamente binarios de la raza y el espacio fue, en realidad, uno de los legados importantes del liberalismo andino decimonónico . . . . Los mitos del mestizaje rara vez encendieron el imaginario criollo, que prefirió lenguajes de raza, región, cultura y, posteriormente clase, para posicionar sus pueblos indígenas al margen de esta modernidad fracturada. De hecho, es plausible sostener que las élites criollas andinas se aferraron deliberadamante al lenguaje y la política del colonialismo interno (recién revestido del lenguaje racializado de moda), precisamente para controlar el trabajo indígena e impedir cualquier tipo de conmoción . . . entre sus masas rurales" (*Indígenas, élites y estado en la formación de las repúblicas andinas* 22–23).

3 "El fenómeno más importante en la cultura peruana del siglo XX es el aumento de la toma de conciencia acerca del indio entre escritores, artistas, hombres de ciencia y políticos" (Basadre, *Perú: problema y posibilidad* 326).

4 On the phenomenon of the *cholo*, see Quijano, *Dominación y cultura: lo cholo y el conflicto cultural en el Perú* and Nugent's brilliantly titled *El laberinto de la choledad*. According to Quijano, the social group called *cholo*, "emerges from the mass of the indigenous peasantry and begins to differentiate itself from that mass by adopting or elaborating certain elements that make up a new way of life consisting of materials from both Western-urban and contemporary indigenous cultures. The contemporary phenomenon of 'cholification' is a process in which certain layers of the indigenous peasant population abandon some elements of indigenous culture x while adopting those typical of Western criollo culture, and use both to elaborate a way of life distinct from the two fundamental cultures in our society, without losing its original connection to them. / se desprende de la masa del campesinado indígena y comienza a diferenciarse de ella adoptando o elaborando ciertos elementos que conforman un nuevo estilo de vida, integrado por elementos de procedencia urbano-occidental, como por los que provienen de la cultura indígena contemporánea. El fenómeno contemporáneo de 'cholificación' es un proceso en el cual determinadas capas de la población indígena campesina, van abandonando algunos de los elementos de la cultura indígena x, adoptando algunos de los que tipifican la cultura occidental criolla, y van elaborando con ellos un estilo de vida que se diferencia al mismo

tiempo de las dos culturas fundamentales de nuestra sociedad, sin perder por eso su vinculación original con ellas" (*Dominación y cultura* 63).

5 Nugent, *El laberinto de la choledad*, 80–82.

6 According to Flores Galindo, the term *gamonal* derives, appropriately enough (given the nature of the semi-feudal type of landowner it designates) from the name of a parasitic plant (*Buscando un Inca* 240).

7 These concepts are developed in Cornejo Polar, "El indigenismo y las literaturas heterogéneas: su doble estatuto socio-cultural" and Rama, *Tranculturación narrativa en América Latina*, a work which gathers together a series of essays written in the 1970s.

8 For notable exceptions, see Pratt, *Imperial Eyes: Travel Writing and Transculturation* and Spitta, *Between Two Waters: Narratives of Transculturation in Latin America*.

9 The 1970s, for example, witnessed the US-sponsored 1973 coup in Chile and the subsequent rise of military dictatorships throughout the Southern Cone, as well as the intensification of both revolutionary struggles and US counterrevolutionary intervention in Central America.

10 D'Allemand, *Latin American Cultural Criticism*, 9–13. For more on dependency theory, see Gunder Frank, *Capitalism and Underdevelopment*, Cardoso and Faletto, *Dependency and Development in Latin America*, and Kay, *Latin American Theories of Development and Underdevelopment*.

11 "Adecuar los principios y métodos de nuestro ejercicio crítico a las peculiaridades de la literatura latinoamericana" (Cornejo Polar, "El indigenismo y las literaturas heterogéneas" 7).

12 Cornejo Polar initially cites the following as examples of the trend: Rincón, "Para un plano de batalla por una nueva crítica en Latinoamérica" *Casa de las Américas* 67 (1971) and "Sobre crítica e historia de la literatura hoy en Latinoamérica" *Casa de las Américas* 80 (1973); Fernández Retamar, "Para una teoría de la literatura hispanoamericana" *Casa de las Américas* 80 (1973) and "Algunos problemas teóricos de la literatura hispanoamericana" *Revista de Crítica Literaria Latinoamericana* 1 (1975); Jitrik, *Producción literaria y producción social* (Buenos Aires: Sudamericana, 1975); Rama, "Sistema literario y sistema social en Hispanoamérica" *Literatura y praxis social en América Latina* (Caracas: Monte Avila, 1974); Losada, "Los sistemas literarios como instituciones sociales en América Latina" *Revista de Crítica Literaria Latinoamericana* 1 (1975); Osorio, "Las ideologías y los estudios de la literatura hispanoamericana" *Casa de las Américas* 94 (1976). He later also refers to Cueva, "Para una interpretación sociológica de *Cien años de soledad*" *Revista Mexicana de Sociología* 26.1 (1974) and Candido "Literatura e subdesenvolvimento" *Argumento* 1 (1973).

13 Quoted in Cornejo Polar, "El indigenismo y las literaturas heterogéneas", 8. Original in Mariátegui, *Seven Interpretive Essays*, 188.

14 "La producción, el texto resultante, su referente y el sistema de distribución y consumo" (Cornejo Polar, "El indigenismo y las literaturas heterogéneas" 11).

15 "Ponen en juego perspectivas propias de ciertos sectores de las capas medias urbanas . . . aluden referencialmente a la problemática del mismo estrato y

son leídos por un público de igual signo social. La producción literaria circula entonces dentro de un solo espacio social y cobra un grado muy alto de homogeneidad: es, podría decirse, una sociedad que se habla a sí misma" (Cornejo Polar, "El indigenismo y las literaturas heterogéneas" 11).

16 "La producción, el texto y su consumo corresponden a un universo y el referente a otro distinto y hasta opuesto" (Cornejo Polar, "El indigenismo y las literaturas heterogéneas" 13).

17 "Se detectan desviaciones formales que sólo se pueden explicar por la acción del referente sobre su enunciación cronística" (Cornejo Polar, "El indigenismo y las literaturas heterogéneas" 15).

18 "El proceso de producción sofocaba el referente, en éste, al contrario, el referente puede imponer ciertas condiciones y generar una modificación en la estructura formal de las crónicas" (Cornejo Polar, "El indigenismo y las literaturas heterogéneas" 15).

19 For more on this aspect of Guaman Poma's chronicle, see Rolena Adorno, *Guaman Poma: Wrting and Resistance in Colonial Peru*, Mercedes López-Baralt, *Guaman Poma: autor y artista*, and Mary Louise Pratt, "Transculturation and Autoethnography: Peru, 1615/1980".

20 "Las requisitorias contra España o las alabanzas a la independencia y a la libertad se procesan literariamente con acatamiento de los valores que rigen la literatura de la época" (Cornejo Polar, "El indigenismo y las literaturas heterogéneas" 15).

21 "El yaraví melgariano representa un acto de liberación más consistente que los poemas neoclásicos relativos a la independencia de nuestros países: si estos textos corresponden externamente al proceso histórico de la independencia, proceso al que de alguna manera traicionan por su apego a los modelos metropolitanos, el yaraví, en cambio, pese a no tematizar ninguna instancia política, realiza en la dimensión que le es propia, en el nivel literario, ese ideal de libertad e independencia que los otros poemas, desde su propia dependencia, sólo pueden anunciar" (Cornejo Polar, "El indigenismo y las literaturas heterogéneas" 16).

22 José Carlos Mariátegui once noted that the Peruvian republic came into being "without and against the Indian / sin el indio y contra el indio" (*Peruanicemos al Perú* 89). As Manrique observes, "an exclusive and segregationist type of state was generated in this fashion, one which inherited and embraced a racist, anti-indigenous, colonial discourse that saw Peruvian society as divided into castes or estates and considered whites intrinsically superior and Indians inferior for biological reasons. A social split was produced this way, one which persists to this day and makes social conflicts in Peru more than a clash of classes, a confrontation between workers and bourgeoisie, landowners and peasants. This split crosses such conflicts with ethnic and racial clashes between whites, *mestizos*, Indians, balcks, Asians and their descendants. . . . A state belonging to a minority that governs for the benefit of that minority and excludes the vast majority from the exercise of political power; a state that considers it normal that minorities simply have no means of political expression and, even worse, *minoritizes majorities.* . . . at issue is the exercise of power by a minority in defense of its own inter-

ests and behind the back of the majority of the nation. / Se generó así un tipo de Estado excluyente y segregacionista, que heredó e hizo suyo un discurso colonial racista antiindígena, que veía a la sociedad peruana como dividida en castas o estamentos y que consideraba que los blancos eran intrínsecamente superiores y los indios inferiores por razones biológicas. Se generó así una fractura social que aún permanece vigente hoy en día, y que hace que los conflictos sociales en el Perú asuman no sólo un carácter clasista, enfrentando a obreros con burgueses y a terratenientes con campesinos, sino que cruza estos conflictos con enfrentamientos de tipo étnico y racial entre blancos, mestizos, indios, negros, asiáticos y sus descendencias. . . . Un Estado de una minoría que gobierna para la minoría, excluyendo del ejercicio del poder político a las grandes mayorías; que encuentra normal que las minorías simplemente no tengan expresión política y, peor aún, *que minoriza a las mayorias.* . . . se trata del ejercicio del poder por una minoría en defensa de sus intereses y a espaldas de las mayorías nacionales" (*El tiempo del miedo* 57–58).

23 According to Mariátegui, "*indigenista* literature can not give us a rigorously realistic version of the Indian. It must idealize and stylize him. Neither can it give us his soul. It is still a *mestizo* literature. This is why it is called *indigenista* and not indigenous. / La literatura *indigenista* no puede darnos una versión rigurosamente verista del indio. Tiene que idealizarlo y estilizarlo. Tampoco puede darnos su propia ánima. Es todavía una literatura de mestizos. Por eso se llama *indigenista* y no indígena" (*7 ensayos* 242).

24 "Un lector distante, ajeno al universo que se le propone en el texto" (Cornejo Polar, "El indigenismo y las literaturas heterogéneas" 19).

25 "No sólo asume los intereses del campesinado indígena; asimila también, en grado diverso, tímida o audazmente, ciertas formas literarias que pertenecen orgánicamente al referente" (Cornejo Polar, "El indigenismo y las literaturas heterogéneas" 21).

26 Fernando Ortiz, *Contrapunteo cubano del tabaco y el azúcar*, 92–97.

27 Redfield, Herskovits, and Linton, "Memorandum for the Study of Acculturation", 149.

28 *Ibid.*, 149.

29 Melville J. Herskovits, *Acculturation*, 31.

30 *Ibid.*, 32.

31 Martin Lienhard, *La voz y su huella*, 97.

32 For more on Ortiz, Rama, and transculturation, see Coronil, "Transculturation and the Politics of Theory: Countering the Center, Cuban Counterpoint", in Ortiz, *Cuban Counterpoint: Tobacco and Sugar*, ix–lvi. This introduction by Coronil to Ortiz's *Cuban Counterpoint* (1940) situates the work in its original historical and political context while making an effective case for its relevance to contemprary debates. See also Spitta, *Between Two Waters: Narratives of Transculturation in Latin America*, 1–28.

33 On Arguedas's relationship to the Boom, for example, see Zapata, *Guamán Poma, indigenismo y estética de la dependencia en la cultura peruana*, 162–174.

34 See Rama, "El *boom* en perspectiva."

35 According to Bueno, "because the world is heterogeneous there is discursive heterogeneity (as Cornejo Polar says) . . . it should be clear that discursive (or literary, or, as Rama would say, narrative) transculturation exists because of the heterogeneity of the world; and that there is discursive heterogeneity because of the processes of transculturation generated by the heterogeneity of the world. / hay heterogeneidad discursiva (como dice Cornejo Polar) porque hay heterogeneidad de mundo . . . queda claro que hay transculturación discursiva (o literaria, o narrativa, como diría Rama) porque hay heterogeneidad de mundo; y que hay heterogeneidad discursiva porque hay dinámicas de transculturación generadas por la heterogeneidad de mundo" ("Sobre la heterogeneidad literaria y cultural de América Latina" 33)

36 "Los procesos de transculturación descritos por Rama implican exclusivamente cambios de las culturas dominadas. . . . la transculturación no afecta en ningún momento a la cultura dominante" (Schmidt, "¿Literaturas heterogéneas o literatura de la transculturación?" 194).

37 "La ideología del mestizaje es en antropología lo que sería la ideología de la conciliación de clases en la sociología. . . . el mestizaje como síntesis no conflictiva . . . es una forma de imaginar la conciliación por encima de los conflictos reales" (Cornejo Polar, *La cultura nacional* 14).

38 "La cobertura más sofisticada de la categoría de mestizaje" (Cornejo Polar, "Mestizaje e hibridez" 341).

39 Patricia D'Allemand, *Latin American Cultural Criticism*, 66.

40 John Beverley, *Subalternity and Representation*, 10.

41 *Ibid.*, 43.

42 *Ibid.*, 45.

43 *Ibid.*, 47.

44 Rama, *Transculturación narrativa*, 76–94.

45 For Beverley, Rama's *La ciudad letrada* constitutes "a kind of *self-criticism* of his own theory of transculturation" (*Subalternity and Representation* 48). For a similar view, see Carlos Alonso, "*Rama y sus retoños*: Figuring the Nineteenth Century in Spanish America."

46 Beverley and Zimmerman, *Literature and Politics in the Central American Revolutions*, 177.

47 Beverley, *Against Literature*, ix. See also Beverley, *Subalternity and Representation*, 48.

48 Beverley, *Subalternity and Representation*, 31.

49 Franco, *The Decline and Fall of the Lettered City*, 10.

50 "Expresamente concebida por su autor como contraparte de la concepción que animaba a *La ciudad letrada*" (Perus, "A propósito de las propuestas historiográficas de Ángel Rama" 67).

51 "[La] heterogeneidad de espacios, tiempos y movimientos, que reproduce las discontinuidades, las rupturas internas y los entreveros de procesos de modernización periférica en el ámbito específico de la literatura de acuerdo con las modalidades que le son propias, es la que Ángel Rama intenta aprehender mediante la traslación y adaptación de [sic] la narrativa de la noción antropológica de 'transculturación'" (Perus, "El dialogismo y la poética histórica" 43).

52 "Centra la problemática en torno a las respuestas y soluciones artísticas ...
encontradas por la literatura a las dificultades planteadas por esta misma
heterogeneidad cultural" (Perus, "El dialogismo y la poética histórica" 44).

53 "La estructura de poder entre centro y periferia está en abierta contradicción
con el proyecto emancipatorio de la modernidad. En la misma imposición de
sus ideas, en otras palabras, la modernidad está en contradicción consigo
misma, aunque esto sea sistemáticamente invisible en el centro" (Pratt, "La
modernidad desde las Américas" 833).

54 "Efectos emancipatorios para las mayorías subordinadas que tematizan",
"encuentros con la realidad y la historia no-metropolitanas en términos no
sentados por la metrópoli .... Su poder emancipatorio, como han señalado
a menudo los críticos, reside en su rechazo de la posición autoalienada de
receptividad impuesta" (Pratt, "La modernidad desde las Américas" 838).

55 John Beverley, *Subalternity and Representation*, 30.

56 *Ibid.*, 40.

57 "Lograron, al simular la existencia de voces radicalmente alternativas,
sugerir la riqueza de los universos discursivos que se desarrollan fuera de la
jurisdicción de la esfera letrada" (Lienhard, "Voces marginadas y poder
discursivo" 795).

58 Franco, *The Decline and Fall of the Lettered City*, 172.

59 "Arguedas es uno de esos personajes excepcionales que en su derrotero
lingüístico y en su tarea como escritor condensó las tensiones y las preocu-
paciones de una sociedad" (Flores Galindo, *Dos ensayos sobre José María
Arguedas* 10).

60 On this internalization of social conflict and the personal responsibility
Arguedas felt to help overcome Peru's division see "I Am Not
Acculturated", his acceptance speech upon being awarded the Inca
Garcilaso prize in 1969: "I attempted to transform into written language
what I was as an individual: a strong living link, capable of being universalized, between the great, walled-in nation and the generous, humane side
of the oppressors. The link could be universalized and extended; there was
a real live, functioning example of it. The encircling wall could and should
be destroyed; the copious streams [of wisdom and art] from the two nations
could and should be united" (*The Fox from Up Above and the Fox from
Down Below* 269). I have modified the translation slightly. The original
reads: "intenté convertir en lenguaje escrito lo que era como individuo: un
vínculo vivo, fuerte, capaz de universalizarse, de la gran nación cercada y
la parte generosa, humana, de los opresores. El vínculo podía universalizarse, extenderse; se mostraba un ejemplo concreto, actuante. El cerco
podía y debía ser destruido; el caudal de las dos naciones se podía y debía
unir" (*El zorro de arriba y el zorro de abajo* 257). See also Arguedas's letter to his publisher, Gonzalo Losada, in which he explains the reasons for
his suicide, namely, that he no longer feels capable of fulfilling his social
role: "Since I am sure that my faculties and weapons as a creator, professor, scholar, and as someone who rouses people to action have become so
debilitated as to be practically useless and since the only faculties I have left
would relegate me to the condition of being a passive, impotent spectator

of the formidable struggle humanity is waging in Peru and everywhere else, it would be impossible for me to tolerate such a fate. Either a doer, as I have been since I entered high school forty-three years ago, or nothing at all" (*The Fox from Up Above and the Fox from Down Below* 262–263). It is true that there were other, perhaps more significant factors in Arguedas's decision to kill himself: he had been psychologically traumatized as a child and had struggled for years against what appears to have been severe and recurrent depression. He had attempted suicide once before, in 1966, and in the months prior his second and successful suicide attempt on 28 November 1969, his condition had become particularly acute. Nonetheless, Arguedas's published reasons for killing himself are not incompatible with any of the above and can not be dismissed.

61 Franco, *The Decline and Fall of the Lettered City*, 170.
62 *Ibid.*, 172–173.
63 *Ibid.*, 173.
64 "La clase dominante del Perú de 1900 compartía ideales y orígenes sociales más bien burgueses que aristocráticos" (Contreras and Cueto, *Historia del Perú contemporáneo* 164).
65 On the República Aristocrática, see Flores Galindo and Burga, *Apogeo y crisis de la República Aristocrática*, and Cotler, *Clases, estado y nación en el Perú*, 119–184.
66 As Manrique notes, "for the Peruvian bourgeoisie, resigned to or comfortably installed in its role as the junior partner of imperialism, the highland landowners were only a problem if they attempted to hegemonize the state. But if they accepted their incorporation into the prevailing power bloc as a subordinate force, they were perfectly functional for the existing model of domination. Their role as the guarantors of social order in the interior areas under gamonal rule beautifully complemented a weak state that maintained only a precarious presence in the Andean interior. . . . However great the social contradictions between the mercantile bourgeoisie and the highland landowners seemed in the immediate postwar period, these were clearly secondary to those which opposed both groups to the indigenous peasantry. / para la burguesía peruana, resignada o cómodamente instalada en su papel de socia menor del imperialismo, los terratenientes serranos sólo eran una traba si pretendían hegemonizar el Estado. Pero si aceptaban incorporarse al bloque de poder como fuerza subordinada eran perfectamente funcionales al modelo de dominación establecido: su papel de garantes del orden social en los espacios del interior sometidos al imperio del gamonalismo empalmaba a las mil maravillas con la existencia de un débil Estado, cuya presencia en el interior serrano era precaria. . . . Por grandes que pudieran parecer las contradicciones sociales que enfrentaron a la burguesía mercantil y los terratenientes serranos en la inmediata postguerra, éstas eran evidentemente secundarias si se las compara con aquellas que oponían a ambas fuerzas al campesinado indígena" (*Yawar mayu* 182–183).
67 "Se sustentaba en el respaldo que podía recibir del imperialismo y en la violencia que los gamonales imponían en el interior del país" (Flores Galindo and Burga, *Apogeo y crisis de la República Aristocrática* 18).

68 Flores Galindo, *Buscando un Inca*, 248–281. See also Flores Galindo and Burga, *Apogeo y crisis de la República Aristocrática*. Flores Galindo and Burga interpret the indigenous rebellions between 1915 and 1924 as spontaneous, uncoordinated movements motivated by a nativist, millenarian ideology of a return to or resurrection of the Inca empire (185). Other scholars have recently challenged this interpretation, arguing that the rebellions were not millenarian in any simple sense and that in at least some cases they were not rebellions at all, but rather peaceful attempts by the *Comité Pro-Derecho Indígena Tawantinsuyo* to organize indigenous communities in defense of their land and rights. Such attempts were labeled rebellions by local authorities anxious to prod the central government into intervening on behalf of large landowners. See de la Cadena, *Indigenous Mestizos: The Politics of Race and Culture in Cuzco, Peru, 1919–1991* (89–106), and Jacobsen, *Mirages of Transition: The Peruvian Altiplano, 1780–1930* (348). Whatever the case, the upsurge in indigenous resistance profoundly influenced Lima-based intellectuals.

69 Contreras and Cueto, *Historia del Perú contemporáneo*, 187.

70 *Ibid.*, 190–192.

71 Cotler notes that "Simultaneously with the political dismantling of civilismo and of the social sector it represented, Leguía promulgated diverse measures that partially responded to popular demands and those of middle sectors. He did so with the express objective of attracting the support of these classes while at the same time neutralizing their independent political activity. / Simultáneamente al desmantelamiento político del civilismo y del sector social que ese partido representaba, Leguía dictó diversas medidas que parcialmente respondían a las exigencias populares y de los sectores medios, con la expresa finalidad de atraerse el respaldo de dichas clases y, al mismo tiempo, neutralizar su actividad política independiente" (*Clases, estado y nación en el Perú* 187).

72 Contreras and Cueto, *Historia del Perú contemporáneo*, 189; Klarén, *Peru: Society and Nationhood in the Andes*, 247–248.

73 Cotler, *Clases, estado y nación en el Peru*, 189–190; Contreras and Cueto, *Historia del Perú contemporáneo*, 189.

74 "La mecánica de la dominación tradicional, resultante de la articulación política entre el sector burgués y señorial que conformó la República Aristocrática, se restableció con Leguía pero sobre nuevas bases, sin afectar la condición precapitalista de las áreas rurales" (Cotler, *Clases, estado y nación en el Perú* 189).

75 "Las políticas populistas de Leguía alentaron la formación de varios movimientos sociales que acabaron desbordando las expectativas de control que el régimen quería señalarles" (Contreras and Cueto, *Historia del Perú contemporáneo*, 194).

76 "No forman el verdadero Perú las agrupaciones de criollos y extranjeros que habitan la faja de tierra situada entre el Pacífico y los Andes; la nación está formada por las muchedumbres de indios diseminadas en la banda oriental de la cordillera" (González Prada, *Páginas libres / Horas de lucha* 45–46).

77 Klarén, *Peru: Society and Nationhood in the Andes*, 246. For more on the

Asociación Pro Indígena, see Kapsoli, *El pensamiento de la Asociación Pro Indígena.*
78 Wise, "A Peruvian *Indigenista* Forum of the 1920s: José Carlos Mariátegui's *Amauta*", 76.
79 "Un grupo social nuevo, promovido por los imperativos del desarrollo económico modernizado . . . el cual plantea nítidas reivindicaciones a la sociedad que integra. Como todo grupo que ha adquirido movilidad – según lo apuntara Marx – extiende la reclamación que formula a todos los demás sectores sociales oprimidos y se hace intérprete de sus reclamaciones que entiende como propias" (Rama, *Transculturación narrativa* 142).
80 Contreras and Cueto, *Historia del Perú contemporáneo*, 195–199.
81 Klarén, *Peru: Society and Nationhood in the Andes*, 247; Wise, "A Peruvian *Indigenista* Forum of the 1920s: José Carlos Mariátegui's *Amauta*", 75. Castro Pozo held the post for just 2 years, after which he broke with Leguía.
82 De la Cadena, *Indigenous Mestizos: The Politics of Race and Culture in Cuzco, Peru, 1919–1991*, 89–90.
83 For a useful discussion of the politics of *indigenismo*, see Zapata, *Guamán Poma, indigenismo y estética de la dependencia en la cultura peruana*, 152–162.
84 "Durante los años veinte habría que hablar del 'indigenismo' de los mismos sectores terratenientes, del del pensamiento ilustrado de derecha, del de la pequeña burguesía radicalizada, sea de Lima o de provincias, y, finalmente, del indigenismo marxista de José Carlos Mariátegui y de los jóvenes comunistas del Cuzco" (Wise, "Indigenismo de izquierda y de derecha: dos planteamientos de los años 1920" 160).
85 For more on this phenomenon, see de la Cadena, *Indigenous Mestizos: The Politics of Race and Culture in Cuzco, Peru, 1919–1991*, 86–130.
86 Escobar, *Arguedas, o la utopía de la lengua*, 39–40.
87 Mariátegui's successors, led by Party Secretary Eudocio Ravines, changed the name to Peruvian Communist Party to demonstrate their allegiance to the Third, or Communist International, with which Mariátegui had had his differences. On Mariátegui's polemic with the Komintern, see Flores Galindo, *La agonía de Mariátegui* in his *Obras Completas II*, 385–511.
88 Mariátegui, for example, was a one of a group of young intellectuals gathered around the eccentric figure of Abraham Valdelomar, and published in the latter's short-lived journal *Colónida*.
89 Melis argues that "the encounter with the working class of northern Italy, during the crucial period of the factory occupations, was a decisive factor in Mariátegui's political and ideological education. / para Mariátegui el encuentro con la clase obrera del norte de Italia, en el período crucial de la ocupación de las fábricas, fue un factor decisivo en su formación política e ideológica" (*Leyendo Mariátegui* 272).
90 "El Perú era para Mariátegui una sociedad semicolonial y esta condición se iría agravando a medida que se fuera expandiendo el capital imperialista. No había forma de alcanzar la independencia nacional dentro del sistema capitalista" (Flores Galindo and Burga, *Apogeo y crisis de la República Aristocrática* 281).

91 Flores Galindo attributes this insight to the outbreak of indigenous rebellion in the Southern Andes in 1915, which, he argues, created for Mariátegui "the possibility of a reflection: that the old could be the new. Without having premeditated the matter, the event permitted him to discover a different meaning of tradition. / la posibilidad de una reflexión: lo antiguo puede ser lo nuevo. Sin haberlo premeditado, el acontecimiento le permite descubrir un sentido diferente de la tradición" (*Buscando un Inca* 251).

92 Melis notes that Mariátegui "takes from Lenin the definition of imperialism as the inevitable consequence of monopoly capitalism. This is precisely one of the fundamental motivations for his opposition to the APRA, which tended toward separating anti-imperialism from anti-capitalism and affirmed, through Haya de la Torre himself, that in Latin America imperialism was not the last but rather the first stage of capitalism. / retoma de Lenin la definición del imperialismo como consecuencia inevitable del capitalismo monopolista. Es precisamente éste uno de los motivos de fondo de la oposición al Apra, la cual apunta a escindir el antiimperialismo del anticapitalismo y afirma, con el mismo Haya de la Torre, que en América latina el imperialismo no es el último estadio de capitalismo, sino el primero" (*Leyendo Mariátegui* 271).

93 See for example Haya de la Torre, "Nuestro frente intelectual", *Amauta* 4 (December 1926): 3–4, 7–8, and "Sentido de la lucha anti-imperialista", *Amauta* 9 (May 1927): 37–39.

94 Manrique, *Yawar mayu*, 183.

95 Alegría and Scorza started out as *apristas*, but eventually broke with the APRA. Regardless of their party affiliations, their literary works show the strong influence of Mariátegui.

96 Mariátegui, *Seven Interpretive Essays*, 204.

97 On the movements of the late 1950s and early 1960s, see Handelman, *Struggle in the Andes: Peasant Political Mobilization in Peru*, Kapsoli, *Los movimientos campesinos en el Perú*, 101–124, and Flores Galindo, *Buscando un Inca*, 295–307. Flores Galindo counts 413 such movements between 1956 and 1964 (298).

Chapter 1   Modernity from the Margins

1 "Porque registra la aparición de veinte obras narrativas, varias capitales, que permiten hacer un corte horizontal en el continente, revisando las distintas orientaciones narrativas, las diversas generaciones, y las plurales áreas literarias de América" (Rama, "Medio siglo de narrativa latinoamericana" 141).

2 "Se bifurcan los senderos de la narrativa, pero no para oponer lo viejo a lo nuevo, sino para separar dentro de lo nuevo, que es mucho más amplio y rico de lo que se pretende, una pluralidad de líneas creativas" (Rama, "Medio siglo de narrativa latinoamericana" 143).

3 Escajadillo, *La narrativa indigenista peruana*, 62–63. For Escajadillo, orthodox *indigenista* works like *Broad and Alien is the World* and *Yawar Fiesta* share the following features: "a 'sense of social vindication' of the Indian, a rupture with past forms (especially the romantic treatment of the 'Indian theme,' the romantic idealization of the Indian), and a 'sufficient

proximity' to the world represented (the Andes and their inhabitants) / el 'sentimiento de reivindicación social' del indio, la ruptura con formas del pasado (especialmente el tratamiento romántico del 'tema indio', la idealización romántica del indígena), y la 'suficiente proximidad' en relación con el mundo recreado (el Ande y su habitante)" (49–50). He further argues that the period of orthodox indigenismo runs from Enrique López Albújar's *Cuentos andinos* (1920) through José María Arguedas's *Diamantes y pedernales* (1954), and that Arguedas's *Los ríos profundos* (1958) inaugurates a new period of what he calls "neoindigenismo." He distinguishes neo*indigenista* works from orthodox ones by their use of magical realism, by their more lyrical quality, and by an expansion of narrative horizons such that the indigenous question is seen as "an integral part of the problematic of the entire nation / parte integral de la problemática de toda una nación" (64).

4 Rama, "Medio siglo de narrativa latinoamericana", 178–194.

5 "Aceptación pasiva de modelos instaurados para otras circunstancias y medios" (Rama, "Medio siglo de narrativa latinoamericana" 180).

6 Indeed, as Arguedas himself has noted, his first works were inspired directly by Vallejo's *El tungsteno*: "I read it straight through, standing, in one of the patios of San Marcos [University]. I turned its pages feverishly, for they were a revelation for me. By the time I finished, I had already firmly decided to write about the tragedy of my country / Lo leí de un tirón, de pie, en un patio de San Marcos. Afiebradamente, recorrí sus páginas, que eran para mí una revelación. Cuando concluí, tenía ya la decisión firme de escribir sobre la tragedia de mi tierra" (quoted in Lévano, *Arguedas: un sentimiento trágico de la vida* 49).

7 Varona, *Ciro Alegría: trayectoria y mensaje*, 32–46. *Broad and Alien is the World* would eventually be translated into English, French, German, Italian, Portuguese, Russian, Hebrew, Dutch, Swedish, Norwegian, Danish, Chinese, Serbo-Croatian, Polish, Romanian, Arabic, and Czech (52). See also Varona, *La sombra del cóndor: biografía ilustrada de Ciro Alegría*, 190–191.

8 Rama, "Medio siglo de narrativa latinoamericana", 178.

9 For notable exceptions to this trend, see Cornejo Polar's introduction to the Biblioteca Ayacucho edition of *El mundo es ancho y ajeno* and Tomás Escajadillo's fine study, *Alegría y El mundo es ancho y ajeno*.

10 Book length author studies include Castro Klarén, *El mundo mágico de José María Arguedas* (1973); Cornejo Polar, *Los universos narrativos de José María Arguedas* (1973); Rowe, *Mito e ideología en la obra de José María Arguedas* (1979); Forgues, *José María Arguedas: del pensamiento dialéctico al pensamiento trágico* (1989); and Vargas Llosa, *La utopía arcaica: José María Arguedas y las ficciones del indigenismo* (1996). Collections of essays on Arguedas and his work include Juan Larco, *Recopilación de textos sobre José María Arguedas* (1976); Pérez and Garayar, *José María Arguedas: vida y obra* (1991), Manrique, *José María Arguedas: 20 años después* (1990); Martínez and Manrique, *José María Arguedas: 25 años después* (1995); and Sandoval and Boschetto-Sandoval, *José María Arguedas: Reconsiderations for Latin American Cultural Studies* (1998). Chapter 10 of Flores Galindo's *Buscando un Inca: Identidad y utopía en los Andes* (1986) and his *Dos*

ensayos sobre José María Arguedas (1992) offer a good overview of Arguedas's relevance to questions of modernization and cultural identity in Peru.

11 In addition to Rama's analysis of *Deep Rivers* in his *Transculturación narrativa en América Latina*, see Lienhard's study of *El zorro de arriba y el zorro de abajo* in his *Cultura andina y forma novelesca: zorros y danzantes en la última novela de Arguedas*, and Spitta's interpretation of *All the Worlds* in chapter 5 of her *Between Two Waters: Narratives of Transculturation in Latin America*.

12 "Ha sido un error frecuente cometido incluso por estudiosos muy importantes considerar mis relatos como interpretaciones más auténticas del indio que las de Ciro. No. Ambas son igualmente auténticas. Lo que ocurre es que Ciro interpretó la vida del pueblo peruano de la sierra norte donde los indios no hablan quechua, lo que significa que fueron culturalmente mucho más avasallados que el campesino de la región central y sur. Esos indios de Ciro son, en realidad, menos indios" (Arguedas, "Conversando con Arguedas" 23).

13 "Mi indio es el norteño: un indio que no habla quechua . . . El indio de Arguedas es el indio sureño y, más específicamente, el apurimeño: más silencioso y más lírico" (*Mucha suerte con harto palo*, 415).

14 See his discussion of the problem in Arguedas, "La novela y el problema de la expresión literaria en el Perú."

15 See Arguedas's account of his childhood in *Primer encuentro de narradores peruanos*, 36–38. See also the description of life in the indigenous community in Arguedas, *Canto Kechwa*, 5–6.

16 In various autobiographical statements, Arguedas described the contempt with which the *criollos* of coastal cities treated *mestizo* and indigenous *serranos* alike. As a migrant from the Andes to the coast, Arguedas experienced such contempt personally. However, he was also careful to note the warm welcome he received from writers and artists in Lima, particularly those involved in the movement for the defense of the indigenous population (*Canto kechwa* 8–9; *Primer encuentro de narradores peruanos* 39–40).

17 As Arguedas would explain near the end of his life, "I never claimed to be a politician nor did I believe I had the aptitude to follow party discipline, but it was socialist ideology that gave direction and permanence . . . to the energy I felt unleashed within me during my youth / no pretendí jamás ser un político ni me creí con aptitudes para practicar la disciplina de un partido, pero fue la ideología socialista lo que dió dirección y permanencia . . . a la energía que sentí desencadenarse durante la juventud" (Arguedas, "No soy un aculturado" 258).

18 Varona, *Ciro Alegría: trayectoria y mensaje*, 14–18.

19 Lévano, *Arguedas: un sentimiento trágico de la vida*, 21, Forgues, *José María Arguedas: la letra inmortal*, 85, 87.

20 Lévano, *Arguedas: un sentimiento trágico de la vida*, 33, Moreno Jimeno in Forgues, *José María Arguedas: la letra inmortal*, 29, Vargas Llosa, *La utopía arcaica*, 109. The students, many of whom belonged to the *Comité de Defensa de la República Española*, attempted to throw the fascist officer into

a fountain to protest the Italian Air Force's participation in the bombardment of the Spanish Republic. Lévano says that the General did in fact end up in the water, while Moreno Jimeno, a participant in the attempted dunking, and Vargas Llosa indicate that Arguedas and his comrades did not succeed in soaking the fascist.

21 Varona, *La sombra del cóndor: biografía ilustrada de Ciro Alegría*, 186.

22 Lévano, *Arguedas: un sentimiento trágico de la vida*, 22. Lévano refers to the defections of Eudocio Ravines, Communist Party Secretary for much of the 1930s, and Julio Portocarrero.

23 Vargas Llosa, "Ciro Alegría" in Varona, *Ciro Alegría: Trayectoria y mensaje*, 201.

24 Elmore, *Los muros invisibles*, 127.

25 Vargas Llosa, *La utopía arcaica*, 119.

26 "Hemos intervenido en instantes de apremio para aclarar algunos pensamientos y sentimientos confusos, ciertas reminiscencias truncas" (Alegría, *El mundo es ancho y ajeno* 40). This paragraph, in which the narrator reflects on his telling of the story, is omitted from the English translation of Alegría's novel.

27 Martin, *Journeys Through the Labyrinth*, 87.

28 That Alegría ends his novel in 1928, two years before the APRA arrived in Peru (it was founded by Haya de la Torre in 1924 during his exile in Mexico), suggests a thematic avoidance of the APRA, from which Alegría may already have been marking his distance.

29 On the writing of *Broad and Alien is the World*, see Alegría, *Mucha suerte con harto palo: memorias*, 188–189; and Varona, *La sombra del cóndor: Biografía illustrada de Ciro Alegría*, 141–147.

30 Escajadillo, *Alegría y El mundo es ancho y ajeno*, 1–18.

31 "La comunidad es el único lugar habitable (para el hombre andino)" (Escajadillo, *Alegría y El mundo es ancho y ajeno* 2).

32 Alegría, *Broad and Alien is the World*, 7.

33 *Ibid.*, 10.

34 *Ibid.*, 14.

35 Escajadillo, *Alegría y El mundo es ancho y ajeno*, 147–158.

36 Kapsoli, *El pensamiento de la Asociación Pro Indígena*, 14.

37 Alegría, *Broad and Alien is the World*, 149.

38 *Ibid.*, 157.

39 "Santiago se interesaba por el movimiento sindical y había leído mucho sobre eso, pero Benito, apenas le avanzaba algo respondía: '(Ah sí, se parece a mi comunidá, pero mi comunidá es mejor!' Todo lo arreglaba con la comunidad" (Alegría, *El mundo es ancho y ajeno* 319–320). The chapter in which this quote appears is omitted in the English edition.

40 "Resulta anómala cuando se la coteja con la imagen cristalizada de lo que, supuestamente, define a la escritura indigenista" (Elmore, *Los muros invisibles* 99–100).

41 "La novela *indigenista* tradicional reitera un esquema basado en la adición de despojos, usurpaciones y vejámenes hasta un punto tal que producen el aniquilamiento de la capacidad de respuesta del indio o, por reacción instin-

tiva, una respuesta violenta, heroica, pero siempre fracasada" (Cornejo Polar, *Los universos narrativos de José María Arguedas* 59).

42 Arguedas, *Yawar fiesta*, 20–21.

43 *Ibid.*, 14.

44 *Ibid.*, 143–144, 147.

45 *Ibid.*, 101–102.

46 *Ibid.*, 102.

47 "Entre los mundos de los blancos, mestizos y comuneros, paisanos o policías, quechua o hispanohablantes, andinos o costeños, el cristianismo y el animismo, la razón y la magia" (Vargas Llosa, *La utopía arcaica* 129).

48 "Un oído finísimo, capaz de registrar todas las diferencias de tono, acento y pronunciación entre los grupos sociales, y una desenvoltura estilística que le permite hacer saber al lector" (Vargas Llosa, *La utopía arcaica* 130).

49 "Los sutiles desordenamientos que harían del castellano . . . el instrumento adecuado" (Arguedas, "La novela y el problema de la expresión literaria en el Perú" 14). "las palabras castellanas incorporadas al quechua y el elemental castellano que alcanzan a saber algunos indios en *sus propias aldeas*" (Arguedas, "La novela y el problema de la expresión literaria en el Perú" 16).

50 Spitta, *Between Two Waters*, 166–67. For this useful summary of the features of Arguedas's new literary language, Spitta draws on Alberto Escobar, *Arguedas o la utopía de la lengua*, 65–92.

51 It is likely that Arguedas's teaching experience in Sicuani influenced his invention of this hybrid literary language. In "Entre el kechwa y el castellano: la angustia del mestizo", an article published in 1939, while he was writing *Yawar Fiesta*, Arguedas argued that "we are witnessing the agony of Spanish as spirit and as a pure, untouched language. I observe and feel it in my Spanish class in the 'Mateo Pumacahua' secondary school in Canchis. My *mestizo* students, in whose soul the indigenous is dominant, force the Spanish language. In the intimate morphology of the Spanish they speak and write, in their shattered syntax, I recognize the genius of Quechua. / Estamos asistiendo aquí a la agonía del castellano como espíritu y como idioma puro e intocado. Lo observo y lo siento en mi clase de castellano del Colegio 'Mateo Pumacahua' de Canchis. Mis alumnos mestizos en cuya alma lo indio es dominio, fuerzan el castellano, y en la morfología íntima de ese castellano que hablan y escriben, en su sintaxis destrozada, reconozco el genio del kechwa" (*Indios, mestizos y señores* 27).

52 See Cornejo Polar, "El indigenismo y las literaturas heterogéneas: su doble estatuto socio-cultural", 21.

53 See for example Vargas Llosa, *La utopía arcaica* 127–148, and S. Muñoz, *José María Arguedas y el mito de la salvación por la cultura*, 163–164.

54 As Cornejo Polar points out, *Yawar Fiesta*'s initial two chapters rehearse a conventional *indigenista* plot about the dispossession of indigenous communities as a prelude to the rather different and unorthodox story about the bullfight (*Los universos narrativos de José María Arguedas* 59).

55 On the later novels, see the final two chapters of Rama's *Transculturación narrativa en América Latina*, 229–305, dedicated to Arguedas's second

novel, *Deep Rivers*, and Lienhard, *Cultura andina y forma novelesca: Zorros y danzantes en la última novela de Arguedas.*

56 "La interpretación más frecuente sugiere que estos símbolos ponen de manifiesto la oposición entre la cultura hispánica y la cultura andina" (F. Muñoz, "La fiesta del turupukllay en el mundo andino" 213–214).

57 "El toro ha sido incorporado en el mundo andino y no es necesariamente símbolo de confrontación y oposición" (F. Muñoz, "La fiesta del turupukllay en el mundo andino" 214).

58 "El toro es símbolo de fecundidad, el cóndor símbolo de justicia. Ambos pertenecen al Apu. La sangre derramada en la tarde de corridas es para calmar 'la sed de la pachamama': el derramamiento de sangre es síntoma de un buen año para el pueblo" (F. Muñoz, "La fiesta del turupukllay en el mundo andino" 222–223).

59 "Lo que ha sucedido es que en las últimas décadas la fiesta ha sido resignificada en la medida que los campesinos perdían control de la organización de la misma. Los cambios en la economía – particularmente la pérdida de importancia de la actividad agropecuaria – y en la sociedad andina han derivado en un mayor protagonismo de los mestizos en la organización de la fiesta. Para ellos la fiesta más que ritual propiciatorio es la escenificación del encuentro y enfrentamiento entre lo andino (cóndor) y lo occidental (toro). Conflicto que se resuelve en un mestizaje cuyo simbolismo no puede ser más dramático: el derramamiento de ambas sangres" (F. Muñoz, "La fiesta del turupukllay en el mundo andino" 223).

60 Weismantel offers an amusing example from the indigenous community of Zumbagua, Ecuador: "The fiesta of that year [1985] featured new elements added by the people of the *centro* [*mestizos*] to make it more like the fiestas of the Inter-Andean Valley towns. There was a Saturday night dance and a beauty contest; as the main event, an important official from the provincial government of Cotopaxi put in an appearance. He and his wife watched some of the bullfighting and the costumed dancers, and then, during a lull in the performance, the couple descended to the ring and began to promenade around it, waving and smiling in the time-honored way of politicians. At this point it became apparent that not everyone in the parish shared the enthusiasm over these new, more "civic" aspects of the fiesta. Those who had been complaining that neither white customs nor white politicians should play a part in a Zumbagua fiesta saw their chance to protest. By a mysterious "accident", all of the bulls penned outside the ring were stampeded into it, and the politician and his high-heeled wife had to flee for their lives, scrambling over the barricades in a quite undignified fashion" (*Food, Gender, and Poverty in the Ecuadorian Andes* 81).

61 Arguedas, *Yawar Fiesta*, 34.

62 "La muerte del toro por el estallido de un cartucho de dinamita lanzado por un torero indio, es una pura y simple ficción. Nunca, en ninguna parte de los Andes peruanos, existió esa costumbre" (Montoya, "*Yawar fiesta*: una lectura antropológica" 59).

63 Arguedas, *Yawar Fiesta*, 35.

64 *Ibid.*, 33.

65 *Ibid.*, 134.
66 *Ibid.*, 53.
67 *Ibid.*, 30–31. I have modified the translation slightly. The original reads: "Mirando la cara de los vecinos, los comuneros de los cuatro *ayllus* tenían fiesta; el regocijo era igual para todos los indios de Puquio. Y desafiaban en su adentro a los mistis" (Arguedas, *Yawar fiesta* 55).
68 "¿Cabe imaginar una ficción que, a pesar de sus denuncias y su indignación frente a las iniquidades que infligen los *mistis* a los indios, sea más *conservadora* que *Yawar fiesta*?" (Vargas Llosa, *La utopía arcaica* 148).
69 "Congelar el tiempo, detener la historia" and "un alegato contra la modernización del pueblo andino" (Vargas Llosa, *La utopía arcaica* 148).
70 Arguedas, *Yawar Fiesta*, 33.
71 *Ibid.*, 121.
72 "Las dos empresas participan de una racionalidad semejante – es decir, la del trabajo comunitario – y desmienten el estereotipo oligárquico del indio melancólico y pasivo. Donde la divergencia se marca, sin embargo, es en las proyecciones de estos dos logros: el camino a Nazca supone una voluntad modernizadora que está ausente de la corrida tradicional" (Elmore, *Los muros invisibles* 118–119).
73 "Incluso ese deslinde resulta menos claro en el texto de lo que inicialmente se podría creer" (Elmore, *Los muros invisibles* 119).
74 Indeed, some critics have seen these chapters as superfluous. Castro Klarén, for example, argues that "the chapter that deals with the migration of Andeans to the coast adds nothing to the plot, since the plot could easily develop without this information. The chapter that deals with the mythical origins of Misitu . . . likewise is unnecessary to the plot / el capítulo que trata sobre la migración de los serranos a la costa no añade nada al argumento, puesto que el argumento bien podría pasar sin esa información. El capítulo que trata sobre el origen legendario del Misitu . . . tampoco es necesario respecto al argumento" (*El mundo mágico de José María Arguedas* 75).
75 Arguedas, *Yawar Fiesta*, 60.
76 The fictional account of the road construction in *Yawar Fiesta* is for the most part historically accurate: in the 1920s, 10,000 *comuneros* from the province of Lucanas really did build 159 km of road from Puquio to the coastal city of Nazca in just 20 days (Montoya, "*Yawar fiesta*: una lectura antropológica" 67).
77 Arguedas, *Yawar Fiesta*, 63.
78 *Ibid.*, 66–67.
79 Cotler, *Clases, estado y nación en el Perú*, 189–190.
80 "A una modernización forzosa, impuesta desde arriba, opone el texto la imagen de una modernización generada desde abajo, a partir de la voluntad activa de los sectores populares" (Elmore, *Los muros invisibles* 120).
81 Arguedas, *Yawar Fiesta*, 67–68.
82 Nugent, *El laberinto de la choledad*, 70.
83 For Arguedas's non-fictional account of the cultural effects of this migration, originally published in 1941, see "La canción popular mestiza en el Perú: su valor documental y poético" (Arguedas, *Indios, mestizos y señores* 71–74).

84 See Arguedas's account of his own arrival in Lima from the Andes in José María Arguedas, *Kanto Kechwa*, 8–9.

85 Arguedas, *Yawar Fiesta*, 75.

86 See F. Muñoz, "La fiesta del turupukllay en el mundo andino", 217.

87 See Arguedas, "Incorporación del toro a la cultura indígena. El interesante caso de la conversión del amaru" and the untitled introduction to the first issue of *Cultura y pueblo*.

88 See Arguedas and Izquierdo Ríos, *Mitos, leyendas y cuentos peruanos*, particularly the stories "El toro encantado", "Yanacocha", and "Amaru", 82–90.

89 "Se vincula la aparición del amaru con cataclismos, anuncios de grandes cambios cósmicos" (González Vigil, "Introducción" 156n).

90 "Aparece siempre en los momentos de crisis cósmica, de *pachakutiy*" (Lienhard, *La voz y su huella* 288). For more on the Andean concept of *pachakutiy*, see Flores Galindo, *Buscando un inca*, 33–34.

91 Arguedas, *Yawar Fiesta*, 5.

92 *Ibid.*, 9.

93 Flores Galindo, *Dos ensayos sobre José María Arguedas*, 16–17.

94 Arguedas, *Yawar Fiesta*, 83.

95 *Ibid.*, 81.

96 *Ibid.*, 24.

97 "Las comunidades indígenas que pudieron conservar cierto grado de independencia económica . . . han evolucionado de manera distinta que aquellas que fueron despojadas de sus propiedades o fueron empobrecidas al extremo de tener que compensar su economía con la prestación ineludible de trabajo personal" (Arguedas, "Cambio de cultura en las comunidades indígenas económicamente fuertes" 28).

98 Spitta, *Between Two Waters*, 7.

99 Arguedas, *Yawar Fiesta*, 121.

100 *Ibid.*, 147.

Chapter 2 From Development Theory to *Pachakutiy*

1 Klarén, *Peru: Society and Nationhood in the Andes*, 289.

2 "Clausuró un ciclo en el que se quiso apostar por una reorientación de la política económica hacia la industrialización y la redistribución del ingreso" (Contreras and Cueto, *Historia del Perú contemporáneo*, 239).

3 Cotler, *Clases, estado y nación en el Perú*, 272–287.

4 *Ibid.*, 286–87.

5 Flores Galindo, *Buscando un Inca*, 304.

6 Handelman, *Struggle in the Andes*, 63–64.

7 Flores Galindo, *Buscando un Inca*, 298. See also Kapsoli, *Los movimientos campesinos en el Perú*, 101–124.

8 The most important of these articles, as well as some from the 1960s, are collected in Arguedas, *Formación de una cultura nacional indoamericana*, edited by Rama.

9 Escobar, *Encountering Development*, 9.

10 *Ibid.*, 4.

11 *Ibid.*, 5. For an account of how development or modernization theory came to influence US foreign policy and counterinsurgency strategy in the 1960s, see Latham, *Modernization as Ideology: American Social Science and "Nation Building" in the Kennedy Era*. Latham argues that "modernization . . . was also an ideology, a conceptual framework that articulated a common collection of assumptions about the nature of American Society and its ability to transform a world perceived as both materially and culturally deficient" (5).

12 Escobar, *Encountering Development*, 5.

13 "Hay dos visiones sobre el encuentro entre occidente y el mundo andino. La visión del Arguedas novelista, de un mundo violento que sólo puede cambiarse de una manera igualmente violenta y radical, y la visión del antropólogo, donde hay una esperanza en cuanto a poder cambiar este mundo sin violencia, paulatinamente, en la medida en la cual no se produzca un choque entre los campesinos y el capitalismo, y los campesinos vayan incorporando el mundo capitalista" (Flores Galindo, *Dos ensayos sobre José María Arguedas* 22).

14 "El mestizo parece ser el anuncio de un país en el que por sucesivas aproximaciones se irían fusionando el mundo andino y el mundo occidental. Pero cuando se regresa a las ficciones y la pasión vuelve a imponerse, los mestizos no tienen mucho espacio en un mundo que no permite las situaciones intermedias: la resignación o la rebeldía, el llanto o el incendio" (Flores Galindo, *Buscando un Inca* 292).

15 "Las contraposiciones entre textos literarios y textos antropológicos fueron aproximándose cada vez más hacia el final de su vida, en los años 60" (Flores Galindo, *Dos ensayos sobre José María Arguedas* 22).

16 See Arguedas, "Los ríos profundos. Novela inédita", "El zumbayllu", and "Los ríos profundos."

17 In a letter from 7 February 1948, Arguedas notes that "after a great deal of time I was able to continue writing a novel that I began more than three years ago, but one which has advanced very little / después de mucho tiempo pude continuar escribiendo una novela que empecé, hace ya más de tres años y de la cual he adelantado muy poco" (Pinilla, *Arguedas en familia*, 208). A subsequent letter from 21 May 1956, indicates that much of the novel was written that year: "in this month and a half I have written four chapters of *Deep Rivers*, the novel that seemed condemned to death; just one chapter remains, and I will start it tomorrow / este mes y medio he escrito cuatro capítulos de *Los ríos profundos*, esa novela al parecer condenada ya a la muerte; y sólo me falta un capítulo que empezaré mañana mismo" (232).

18 In a last will and testament he wrote a month before his suicide in 1969, Arguedas identified the psychological ailment that had afflicted him for much of his adult life: "I expressly state for the record that since 1944 I have suffered from a process of chronic depression / Dejo expresa constancia de que padezco desde el año 1944 un proceso depresivo crónico" (Rescaniere, *José María Arguedas, recuerdos de una amistad* 295). Arguedas's frustration and disillusionment with the state educational and cultural bureaucracy in

which he worked also seems to have contributed to his first severe case of depression in the mid-1940s. In particular, the rejection of his proposals for educational reform in 1943 by conservative advisors to the Ministry of Education seems to have plunged him into a chronic depression that lasted several years (Pinilla, *Arguedas en familia* 32–55). Arguedas would struggle with depression the rest of his life. Despite the best efforts of a series of psychiatrists and psychologists, he lost that struggle and committed suicide in late 1969.

19 "Lo que quedó en el ánimo de Arguedas fue la experiencia de la frustración de una esperanza. El recuerda que por entonces "creíamos que la justicia social estaba a la vuelta de la esquina, teníamos una fe formidable en que la justicia social la iba a conquistar el hombre en muy poco tiempo"; y por cierto no fue así. Al revés, los ideales de renovación tuvieron que ser aplazados y remitidos a un futuro lejano y muy incierto. El impacto de la desilusión debió ser excepcionalmente fuerte en Arguedas. Tal vez fue uno de los componentes de su primera gran crisis psicológica, que lo mantuvo literariamente improductivo entre 1942 y 1954; en el nivel de las posiciones ideológicas, desencadena un agudo escepticismo frente a las alternativas políticas del momento que no logran interpretar los intereses profundos y la capacidad de transformación histórica del pueblo andino" (Cornejo Polar, *José María Arguedas, Antología comentada* 23).

20 Manrique, *La piel y la pluma*, 87.

21 In "La sierra en el proceso de la cultura peruana" an early article from 1953, Arguedas cites extensively from Linton, *The Study of Man* (1936) and Herskovits, *Man and His Works* (1947), influential anthropology manuals of the period (Arguedas, *Formación de una cultura nacional indoamericana*, 9–27).

22 Arguedas, *Formación de una cultura nacional indoamericana*, 1–8.

23 "Pero ha permanecido, a través de tantos cambios importantes, *distinta* de la occidental, a pesar de que tales y tan sustanciales cambios se han producido en la cultura autóctona peruana por la influencia que sobre ella ha ejercido la de los conquistadores" (Arguedas, *Formación de una cultura nacional indoamericana* 2).

24 "Considerar como peruano únicamente lo indio" (Arguedas, *Formación de una cultura nacional indoamericana* 2).

25 "Un producto humano que está desplegando una actividad poderosísima, cada vez más importante: el mestizo" (Arguedas, *Formación de una cultura nacional indoamericana* 2).

26 "Es el resguardo de la identidad nacional, de los valores éticos y filosóficos de la tradición indígena que entiende superiores (concepto de la propiedad, del trabajo, de la solidaridad del grupo, de la naturaleza, del humanismo). No es que para él la cultura mestiza sea superior a la abroquelada cultura de las poblaciones indias de departamento de Puno, sino que ella es una coyuntura eficaz de preservación parcial de aquellos valores, en tanto que los agrupamientos indígenas conservadores se encuentran en situación más desamparada: incapaces de resistir el asalto que promueve la cultura occidental burguesa y capitalista que viene de Lima, dentro de los bastiones

serranos, son condenados a la desintegración social y espiritual" (Rama, *Formación de una cultura nacional indoamericana* xx-xxi).

27 "No pudo dominar Occidente a este mestizo porque su profunda entraña india lo defendió. . . . Al mismo tiempo que el mestizo conquistaba el dominio espiritual del pueblo andino, se definía en su alma la lucha entre lo indio y lo español . . . Lo indio es ya dominio en la psicología del mestizo peruano; ha ganado la contienda . . ." (Arguedas, *Indios, mestizos y señores* 27).

28 "El estudio del mestizo es uno de los más importantes de los que la antropología está obligada a emprender en el Perú. . . . Quizá la noticia de mayor interés hecha pública en el reciente Congreso de Peruanistas fue la que dio el Dr. Holmberg, de la Universidad de Cornell, anunciando que se había iniciado el estudio de la cultura total en el Callejón de Huaylas. Uno de los aspectos fundamentales que ofrece el estudio del hombre de esa región es precisamente el de la transculturación, el del mestizaje" (Arguedas, *Formación de una cultura nacional indoamericana* 2).

29 Archibald, "Andean Anthropology in the Era of Development Theory", 5.

30 "Del paternalismo a la democracia: el Proyecto Perú–Cornell", in Holmberg, *Vicos: Método y práctica de antropología aplicada*, 25–33.

31 "Como [sic] cambiar este estado de cosas – sin gran inversión económica o amen de una revolución" (Holmberg, *Vicos: Método y práctica de antropología aplicada* 27).

32 Holmberg, *Vicos: Método y práctica de antropología aplicada*, 38–39.

33 Archibald, "Andean Anthropology in the Era of Development Theory", 7.

34 "El proyecto Perú–Cornell, no ha establecido un tipo ideal o un modelo de civilización Occidental como un blanco hacia el cual se dirige Vicos" (Holmberg and Dobyns, "El proceso de acelerar cambio cultural", *Vicos: Método y práctica de antropología aplicada* 69).

35 "El método de análisis dicotómico más general empleado en el Proyecto para analizar los cambios en Vicos consiste en establecer el contraste entre la civilización Occidental Industrializada y el Colonialismo occidental medioeval. El Proyecto Perú–Cornell ha considerado los cambios que ocurren en la cultura y en la sociedad de Vicos como un proceso de 'modernización' u 'occidentalización'" (Holmberg, Dobyns, and Vázquez, "Método para el análisis de los cambios culturales", *Vicos: Método y práctica de antropología aplicada* 57).

36 Holmberg and Dobyns, "El proceso de acelerar cambio cultural", *Vicos: Método y práctica de antropología aplicada*, 69–70.

37 "La introducción de modernos 'postulados fundamentales' dentro de las culturas que carecen de ellos" (Holmberg, Dobyns, and Vázquez, "Método para el análisis de los cambios culturales", *Vicos: Método y práctica de antropología aplicada* 59).

38 "El indio se diluye en el Perú con una lentitud pavorosa. En México es ya una figura pequeña y pronto se habrá confundido con la gran nacionalidad. El caso del indio se ha convertido en el Perú en un problema de creciente gravedad. El proceso del mestizaje es, como ya dijimos, de una lentitud pavorosa" (Arguedas, *Formación de una cultura nacional indoamericana* 8).

39 Arguedas, *Formación de una cultura nacional indoamericana*, 9–27.

40 *Ibid.*, 12.

41 "La influencia de estos complejos factores transformaron al indio del valle en el mestizo actual de habla española, sin desarraigarlo y sin destruir su personalidad. Se produjo un proceso de transculturación en masa bajo el impulso de los más poderosos factores transformantes que en esta zona actuaron simultáneamente. . . . Sin la aparición del caso del Alto Mantaro nuestra visión del Peru andino sería aún amarga" (Arguedas, *Formación de una cultura nacional indoamericana* 12).

42 "El peruano antiguo no concebía la posesión de la tierra como fuente de enriquecimiento individual ilimitado; este concepto estaba directamente vinculado con la concepción religiosa que tenía de la tierra y del trabajo" (Arguedas, *Formación de una cultura nacional indoamericana* 25).

43 "El indio no ha alcanzado todavía a comprender y asimilar, por entero, el concepto occidental de la propiedad y del trabajo" (Arguedas, *Formación de una cultura nacional indoamericana* 25).

44 Arguedas, *Formación de una cultura nacional indoamericana*, 25–26.

45 "En cuanto el indio, por circunstancias especiales, consigue comprender este aspecto de la cultura occidental, en cuanto se arma de ella, procede como nosotros; se convierte en mestizo y en un factor de producción económica positiva. Toda su estructura cultural logra un reajuste completo sobre una base, un "eje." Al cambiar, no uno "de los elementos superficiales de su cultura" sino el fundamento mismo, el desconcierto que observamos en su cultura se nos presenta como ordenado, claro y lógico: es decir que *su conducta se identifica con la nuestra.* ¡Por haberse convertido en un individuo que realmente participa de nuestra cultura! Una conversión total, en la cual, naturalmente, algunos de los antiguos elementos seguirán influyendo como simples términos especificativos de su personalidad que en lo sustancial estará movida por incentivos, *por ideales,* semejantes a los nuestros. Tal el caso de los ex indios del valle del Mantaro . . . primer caso de transculturación en masa que estudiamos someramente en las páginas iniciales del presente trabajo" (Arguedas, *Formación de una cultura nacional indoamericana* 26).

46 Arguedas, *Formación de una cultura nacional indoamericana*, 80–147.

47 "Esta integración pacífica de las castas y culturas en el valle del Mantaro es, como ya dijimos, un hecho excepcional en la historia de las comunidades indígenas del Perú. Se explica por la ausencia del factor que la ha hecho imposible en las otras provincias con densa población indígena . . . Tal factor es el latifundista, el tradicionalmente llamado 'gamonal'" (Arguedas, *Formación de una cultura nacional indoamericana* 87).

48 "Tanto las comunidades de alta población mestiza del valle como las tradicionalmente indígenas, han demostrado tener una mayor aptitud para la integración de nuevas técnicas y normas que las comunidades de las provincias donde fue implantada la servidumbre feudal" (Arguedas, *Formación de una cultura nacional indoamericana* 103–104).

49 Flores Galindo, *Dos ensayos sobre José María Arguedas*, 21–22

50 "Como el horizonte de la redención del mundo indígena" (Manrique, *La pluma y la piel* 95).

51 "El mestizo y el indio, o el hombre de abolengo de provincias, que llega a esta ciudad, no se encuentra en conflicto con ella; porque la masa indígena que allí acude o vive es autóctona en el fondo y no en lo exótico de los signos externos; y está, además, movida por el impulso de la actividad, del negocio, del espíritu moderno, que trasciende y estimula" (Arguedas, *Formación de una cultura nacional indoamericana* 139).

52 "Y llegada la oportunidad revivirá en la ciudad, sin vergüenza y pública-mente, las fiestas de su pueblo, y podrá bailar en las calles a la usanza de su ayllu nativo o sumarse a las fiestas y bailes indígenas de la propia ciudad, pues no será extraña a ellas. Y será un ciudadano, aun a la manera todavía ínfima, pero real, de los barredores municipales que chacchan coca y conversan en quechua, a la madrugada, tendidos en las aceras de las calles; pero con la seguridad de que ha de recibir un salario que le permitirá, si lo deciden, entrar al restaurante "El Olímpico", y sentarse a la mesa, cerca o al lado de un alto funcionario oficial, de un agente viajero o del propio prefecto del departamento, y libres, en todo momento, del temor de que alguien blanda un látigo sobre sus cabezas. Y podrán esperar, sin duda, cambiar de condición, para mejorar, porque la ciudad ofrece perspectivas para todos, sin exigir a nadie que reniegue de sus dioses para ser admitido en su recinto" (Arguedas, *Formación de una cultura nacional indoamericana* 139).

53 "La promesa que ofrecía el desarrollismo imperante a inicios de los cincuenta" and "mundo de las oportunidades abiertas para todos" (Manrique, *La pluma y la piel* 96).

54 "Un intelectual culturalmente colonizado" (Manrique, *La pluma y la piel* 97).

55 Archibald, "Andean Anthropology in the Era of Development Theory", 5.

56 Arguedas, *Formación de una cultura nacional indoamericana*, 34–79.

57 "Se ha convertido en un centro comercial de economía activa, de haber sido la capital de una zona agropecuaria anticuada, de tipo predominantemente colonial" (Arguedas, *Formación de una cultura nacional indoamericana*, 78).

58 "Un cabecilla de Pichqachuri nos dijo, muy seriamente, que su comunidad no progresaba mucho porque tenía pocos mistis y mestizos, y que por eso, ellos, los mayores, estaban empeñados en que sus hijos se convirtieran en mestizos. Esta declaración es importante porque muestra la posibilidad de que los mestizos surjan en las comunidades de Pichqachuri y Qayao por obra de la transformación conscientemente impulsada por los indios y no según el proceso tradicional inverso de empobrecimiento de mistis" (Arguedas, *Formación de una cultura nacional indoamericana* 37).

59 "En lo que se refiere a los naturales, observamos que este proceso va encam-inado a la independencia respecto del despotismo tradicional que sobre ellos ejercían y aún ejercen las clases señorial y mestiza; pero, al mismo tiempo, el proceso está descarnando a los naturales de las bases en que se sustenta su cultura tradicional, sin que los elementos que han de sustituirlos aparezcan aún con nitidez" (Arguedas, *Formación de una cultura nacional indoameri-cana* 78).

60 "Inkarrí vuelve, y no podemos menos que sentir temor ante su posible impo-

tencia para ensamblar individualismos quizá irremediablemente desarrollados. Salvo que detenga al Sol, amarrándolo de nuevo, con cinchos de hierro, sobre la cima de Osqonta, y modifique a los hombres; que todo es posible tratándose de una criatura tan sabia y resistente" (Arguedas, *Formación de una cultura nacional indoamericana* 79).

61 "Su condición de creador literario, que le permitió no renunciar a su intuición, su sensibilidad y su afectividad, elementos reñidos con una concepción positivista del "trabajo científico" . . . pero que, en un país tan desafiante como es el Perú, debido a su enorme complejidad, le permitió no encerrarse en los rígidos esquemas del funcionalismo norteamericano, en la década del cincuenta, ni limitarse a reemplazarlos por los del marxismo imitativo servil, en los hechos similarmente colonial, de la década siguiente" (Manrique, *La pluma y la piel* 98).

62 Rama, *Transculturación narrativa en América Latina*, 194, Flores Galindo, *Dos ensayos sobre José María Arguedas*, 17.

63 "Las potencias que dominan económica y políticamente a los países débiles intentan consolidar tal dominio mediante la aplicación de un proceso de colonización cultural. Por medio del cine, de la televisión, de la radiodifusión, de millones de publicaciones, se trata de condicionar la mentalidad del pueblo latinoamericano. Esta gran empresa tiene auxiliares influyentes y poderosos entre los socios latinoamericanos de los grandes consorcios, porque tales socios están ya, no diremos "colonizados", sino identificados con los intereses, y por tanto, con el tipo de vida, con las preferencias y conceptos respecto del bien y del mal" (Arguedas, *Formación de una cultura nacional indoamericana* 186).

64 "Los propios instrumentos que fortalecen la dominación económica y política determinan inevitablemente la apertura de nuevos canales para la difusión más vasta de las expresiones de la cultura tradicional" (Arguedas, *Formación de una cultura nacional indoamericana* 187).

65 "El camino no tenía por qué ser, ni era posible que fuera únicamente el que se exigía con imperio de vencedores exploiadores, o sea: que la nación vencida renuncie a su alma . . . y tome la de los vencedores, es decir, que se aculture. Yo no soy un aculturado" (Arguedas, "No soy un aculturado" 257).

66 "Un proceso en el cual ha de ser posible la conservación o intervención de algunos de los rasgos característicos no ya de la tradición incaica, muy lejana, sino de la viviente hispano-quechua, que conservó muchos rasgos de la incaica" (Arguedas, *Indios, mestizos y señores* 18).

67 "Así creemos en la pervivencia de las formas comunitarias de trabajo y vinculación social que se han puesto en práctica . . . entre las grandes masas no sólo de origen andino sino muy heterogéneas de las '*barriadas*' que han participado y participan con entusiasmo en prácticas comunitarias que constituían formas exclusivas de la comunidad indígena andina" (Arguedas, *Indios, mestizos y señores* 18–19).

68 Arguedas, *Deep Rivers*, 38.

69 Dorfman, *Some Write to the Future*, 41.

70 *Ibid.*, 41.

71 *Ibid.*, 41.

72 *Ibid.*, 50.

73 "Se suceden como núcleos independientes con poca hilación causal" (Rama, *Transculturación narrativa* 286).

74 Spitta, *Between Two Waters*, 152.

75 "Supuesta falta de unidad orgánica" (González Vigil, "Introducción" 79).

76 In addition to Dorfman's excellent essay, see Ortega, *Texto, comunicación y cultura* and the appropriate chapters in Cornejo Polar, *Los universos narrativos de José María Arguedas*; Rowe, *Mito e ideología en la obra de José María Arguedas*; Castro Klarén, *El mundo mágico de José María Arguedas*; and Vargas Llosa, *La utopía arcaica*. See also González Vigil's exceptionally lucid introduction to the Cátedra edition of *Los ríos profundos*.

77 Arguedas, *Deep Rivers*, 3.

78 "Toda la novela está ya en ese primer capítulo" (Rama, *Transculturación narrativa* 225).

79 Arguedas, *Deep Rivers*, 14.

80 *Ibid.*, 20.

81 *Ibid.*, 22.

82 *Ibid.*, 6–7. I have modified the translation slightly to more accurately reflect the original Spanish: "Eran más grandes y extrañas de cuanto había imaginado las piedras del muro incaico; bullían bajo el segundo piso encalado que por el lado de la calle angosta, era ciego. Me acordé, entonces, de las canciones quechuas que repiten una frase patética constante: *yawar mayu*, río de sangre; *yawar unu*, agua sangrienta; *puk'tik' yawar k'ocha*, lago de sangre que hierve; *yawar wek'e*, lágrimas de sangre. ¿Acaso no podría decirse *yawar rumi*, piedra de sangre, o *puk'ik' yawar rumi*, piedra de sangre hirviente? Era estático el muro, pero hervía por todas sus líneas y la superficie era cambiante, como la de los ríos en el verano, que tienen una cima así, hacia el centro del caudal, que es la zona temible, la más poderosa. Los indios llaman *yawar mayu* a esos ríos turbios, porque muestran con el sol un brillo en movimiento, semejante al de la sangre. También llaman *yawar mayu* al tiempo violento de las danzas guerreras, al momento en que los bailarines luchan" (*Los ríos profundos* 144).

83 Arguedas, *Deep Rivers*, 9.

84 See also Cornejo Polar's penetrating analysis of this passage in *Escribir en el aire*, 213–219.

85 Arguedas, *Deep Rivers*, 18.

86 *Ibid.*, 15.

87 *Ibid.*, 15, 20.

88 On the importance of religion in Arguedas's novels, and the parallels in them with the tenets of liberation theology, see Trigo, *Arguedas: mito, historia y religión*.

89 Arguedas, *Deep Rivers*, 13. I have changed the initial "on" of this passage to "in" in order to more accurately reflect the original Spanish: "En los grandes lagos, especialmente los que tienen islas y bosques de totora, hay campanas que tocan a la medianoche. A su canto triste salen del agua toros

de fuego, o de oro, arrastrando cadenas; suben a las cumbres y mugen en la helada; porque en el Perú los lagos están en la altura. Pensé que esas campanas debían de ser *illas*, reflejos de la María Angola, que convertiría a los *amarus* en toros. Desde el centro del mundo, la voz de la campana, hundiéndose en los lagos, habría transformado a las antiguas criaturas" (*Los ríos profundos* 155–156).

90 Arguedas, *Deep Rivers*, 13.
91 *Ibid.*, 14.
92 *Ibid.*, 158.
93 *Ibid.*, 22.
94 *Ibid.*, 23.
95 *Ibid.*, 90.
96 *Ibid.*, 92.
97 *Ibid.*, 92–93.
98 *Ibid.*, 233.
99 Trigo argues that "in *Deep Rivers* . . . social consciousness and the transformative action derived from it spring precisely from this magical or supernatural, that is, sacred, conception of existence. Such a conception postulates the preservation and restoration of this sacred harmony as humanity's mission, to be carried out not only through ritual but also historical acts / en *Los ríos profundos* . . . la conciencia social y la acción transformadora que de ella se derivan brotan precisamente de esta concepción mágica o sobrenatural, es decir sagrada, de la existencia, que postula como misión humana la preservación y restauración de esta armonía sagrada y no sólo mediante actos rituales sino también mediante actos históricos" (*Arguedas: mito, historia y religión* 84).
100 Arguedas, et al., *Primer encuentro de narradores peruanos*, 239. See also Arguedas's correspondence with the imprisoned Hugo Blanco, reproduced in *El zorro de arriba y el zorro de abajo*, 434–35.
101 Cornejo Polar, *Los universos narrativos de José María Arguedas*, 108.
102 Handelman, *Struggle in the Andes*, 70–76.

Chapter 3   Between Feudalism and Imperialism

1 Flores Galindo, *Buscando un Inca*, 304.
2 On the Peruvian guerrilla movements of the 1960s, see Béjar, *Peru 1965: Apuntes sobre una experiencia guerrillera* and Rénique, "De la 'traición aprista' al 'gesto heróico'. Luis de la Puente Uceda y la guerrilla del MIR."
3 Castañeda, *Compañero: The Life and Death of Che Guevara*, 331–332; Taibo II, *Ernesto Guevara, también conocido como el Che*, 679.
4 Vargas Llosa, *La utopía arcaica*, 233.
5 For more biographical information on Scorza, see Aldaz, *The Past of the Future*, 15–34, and the brief summary in Moraña, "Función ideológica de la fantasia en las las novelas de Manuel Scorza", 171.
6 "Tal vez mañana los poetas pregunten/por qué nuestros poemas / eran largas avenidas / por donde venía la ardiente cólera. / Yo respondo: / por todas

partes oíamos el llanto . . . / Hay cosas más altas / que llorar amores perdidos: / el rumor de un pueblo que despierta / ¡es más bello que el rocío!" (Scorza, *Obra poética* 17).

7   "Yo soy la boca de quien no tiene boca" (Scorza, *Obra poética* 36).

8   "Está todo el Perú envuelto en esta lucha, y no solamente está el Perú sino un poco los grandes poderes que manejan al Perú y a todos los países pequeños en todas las partes del mundo" (*Primer encuentro de narradores peruanos* 240).

9   Rochabrún, *La mesa redonda sobre Todas las sangres del 23 de junio de 1965.*

10 Spitta, *Between Two Waters*, 156. Suleiman defines the thesis or ideological novel as one "written in the realistic mode (that is, based on an aesthetic of verisimilitude and representation), which signals itself to the reader as primarily didactic in intent, seeking to demonstrate the validity of a political, philosophical, or religious doctrine" (*Authoritarian Fictions* 7).

11 "Novela frustrada" (Vargas Llosa, *La utopía arcaica* 254).

12 Spitta, *Between Two Waters*, 152.

13 *Ibid.*, 156.

14 "Al mismo tiempo que sucumbe al ideologismo, internamente lo contesta, con una visión mágico-religiosa opuesta a la ideológica. Y esta contradicción le da una curiosa tirantez, a pesar de sus defectos" (Vargas Llosa, *La utopía arcaica* 254).

15 "Las clases sociales tienen también un fundamento cultural especialmente grave en el Perú andino; cuando ellas luchan . . . la lucha no es sólo impulsada por el interés económico; otras fuerzas espirituales profundas y violentas enardecen a los bandos; los agitan con implacable fuerza" (Arguedas, "La novela y el problema de la expresión literaria en el Perú" 9).

16 See for example, Flores Galindo, *Buscando un Inca*, Portocarrero, *Racismo y mestizaje*, Nelson Manrique, *La piel y la pluma.*

17 Spitta, *Between Two Waters*, 155.

18 "Los vecinos del pueblo, es decir, los señores, se habían empobrecido lentamente en más de un siglo" (Arguedas, *Todas las sangres* 51).

19 Cornejo Polar, *Los universos narrativos de José María Arguedas*; Spitta, *Between Two Waters*; Rochabrún, *La mesa redonda sobre Todas las sangres.*

20 "Bruno quiere una república de indios, manejada por señores caritativos" (Arguedas, *Todas las sangres* 435). Fermín's vision of Peru's future is remarkably similar to the one Mario Vargas Llosa would espouse in his 1990 presidential campaign. See chapter 5.

21 "Comunero leído" (Arguedas, *Todas las sangres* 30); "siempre, pues, comunero" (Arguedas, *Todas las sangres* 32).

22 Rochabrún, *La mesa redonda sobre Todas las sangres*, 27. For an even harsher assessment of the novel, see Gutiérrez, "Estructura e ideología de *Todas las sangres.*" Gutiérrez concludes that "the tragic view of 'the human condition' evident in *All the Worlds* expresses the despair of the Peruvian landowning class / el sentimiento trágico sobre 'la condición humana' que se respira en *Todas las sangres* es la desesperación de la clase terrateniente peruana" (176).

23 Rochabrún, *La mesa redonda sobre Todas las sangres*, 34.

24 "Políticamente sostenible y científicamente válida" (Rochabrún, *La mesa redonda sobre Todas las sangres* 40).

25 Rochabrún, *La mesa redonda sobre Todas las sangres*, 59.

26 *Ibid.*, 59.

27 "Las vacilaciones ideológicas del autor respecto del problema campesino" (Rochabrún, *La mesa redonda sobre Todas las sangres* 59).

28 "Un individuo quechua moderno" (Arguedas, "Yo no soy un aculturado" 256).

29 "Visión patricia . . . subrepticia y no querida atracción por las permanencias aristocráticas" (Rama, *Transculturación narrativa* 98).

30 For more on the parallels between *All the Worlds* and liberation theology, see Trigo, *Arguedas: mito, historia y religión*, 108–96.

31 Arguedas, *Todas las sangres*, 307.

32 For Cornejo Polar, "Demetrio [Rendón Willka] has a historical perspective, which permits him to link his life to a collective process . . . don Bruno, by contrast, lacks a historical consciousness, confuses the future with a past that never was . . . and is unable to separate social destiny from that of concrete individuals. He confuses his salvation with that of the world (or the inverse) and believes that the destruction of individuals . . . is the same as the destruction of the social and ethical systems that those individuals represent / Demetrio se sitúa en una perspectiva histórica, lo que le permite engarzar su vida en un proceso colectivo . . . don Bruno, en cambio, carece de conciencia histórica, confunde el futuro con un pasado nunca realizado . . . y no puede separar el destino social del individuo más concreto: confunde su salvación con la del mundo (o a la inversa) y cree que la destrucción de las personas . . . equivale a la destrucción de los sistemas sociales y éticos que representan" (*Los universos narrativos* 212).

33 As Cornejo Polar notes, "destroyed by his own innumerable contradictions, incapable of effective action, Bruno has recourse only to his useless revenge, and this more as a banner than a weapon / destruido por sus propias e innumerables contradicciones, incapaz de toda acción eficaz, don Bruno sólo puede enristrar, más como bandera que como arma, su inútil venganza" (*Los universos narrativos* 200–201).

34 "Se está tratando de leer el significado de Bruno, con el significado de Fermín, con el significado de Rendón Willka, y yo creo que en esta forma no sale el significado simbólico . . . . lo que yo quiero decir es que la novela corre en dos niveles; y uno es el conflicto económico-social en esta pugna entre una visión de un feudalismo decadente, que trata de renovarse, o que trata de defenderse, o que trata de reconcentrarse en una visión paternalista-mágica; y la otra, que es el conflicto invívito en toda la obra de Arguedas: es el conflicto entre el punto de vista occidental y el punto de vista aborigen. Entonces esos dos conflictos no aparecen linealmente, sino que aparecen mezclados, confundidos, resquebrajados" (Rochabrún, *La mesa redonda sobre Todas las sangres* 35).

35 "Grandes torrentes que sacudían el subsuelo, como que si las montañas

empezaran a caminar. . . . como si un río subterráneo empezara su creciente" (Arguedas, *Todas las sangres* 447–448).

36 Arguedas, *The Fox from up Above and the Fox from Down Below*, 83.

37 "Tras de la iglesia, el cerro protector del pueblo aparecía rojo, cubierto a mantos por las flores del k'antu" (Arguedas, *Todas las sangres* 9).

38 "Es la única flor del invierno; abre sus campanillas que tienen no sólo el color sino el brillo de la sangre, precisamente cuando la superficie de la tierra parece muerta. . . . En el mundo así quemado, las manchas de flor del k'antu aparecen como el pozo o lago de sangre del que hablan los himnos de las corridas de toros, pozo de sangre al que se lanzan para ahogarse los cóndores desengañados" (Arguedas, *Todas las sangres* 18).

39 See, for example, the *comuneros*' reaction to the subsequent appearance of a condor in San Pedro (*Todas las sangres*, 362, 364).

40 Arguedas, *Todas las sangres*, 16.

41 "¡Yo te prefiero, 'Apukintu!'" (Arguedas, *Todas las sangres* 9).

42 "El canto del río va primero a las estrellas y de allí a nuestro corazón" (Arguedas, *Todas las sangres* 374).

43 Arguedas, *Todas las sangres*, 401.

44 "Un río de sangre le brota del corazón a esta elegida del Señor" (Arguedas, *Todas las sangres* 402).

45 "Cómo un río lejano" (Arguedas, *Todas las sangres* 421).

46 Arguedas, *Todas las sangres*, 36.

47 *Ibid.*, 37–38.

48 *Ibid.*, 424, 429, 432.

49 "El río de sangre, tantas horas contenido en el pecho de Bruno, se desbordó. Ya había arrasado a quienes debía arrasar; ahora tenía que salir al mundo o matarlo, por dentro" (Arguedas, *Todas las sangres* 433).

50 "Se hizo alto y corpulento, más rojizo" (Arguedas, *Todas las sangres* 442).

51 "Los fusiles no van a apagar el sol, ni secar los ríos, ni menos quitar la vida a todos los indios. Siga fusilando. Nosotros no tenemos armas de fábrica, que no valen. Nuestro corazón está de fuego. ¡Aquí, en todas partes! Hemos conocido la patria al fin. Y usted no va a matar la patria señor. Ahí está; parece muerta. ¡No! El pisonay llora; derramará sus flores por la eternidad de la eternidad, creciendo. Ahora de pena, mañana de alegría. El fusíl de fábrica es sordo, es como palo; no entiende. Si quieres, si te provoca, dame la muertecita, la pequeña muerte, capitán" (Arguedas, *Todas las sangres* 442).

52 Spitta, *Between Two Waters*, 160.

53 "El individualismo agresivo no es el que va a impulsar bien a la Humanidad sino que la va a destruir, es la fraternidad humana la que hará posible la grandeza no solamente del Perú sino de la Humanidad. Y ésa es la que practican los indios y la practican con un orden, con un sistema, con una tradición . . . que es la que está más o menos mostrada en *Todas las sangres*" (*Primer encuentro de narradores peruanos* 240).

54 "Uno de los fenómenos de la narrativa peruana de nuestro siglo de la mayor importancia" (Escajadillo, *La narrativa indigenista* 108).

55 Escajadillo, *La narrativa indigenista*, 104.

56 "Asistí a una de las grandes rebeliones campesinas que ha habido en el Perú. ... Primero como miembro, después como secretario general del Movimiento Comunal. . . . recogí todos los testimonios que pude" (Osorio, "Conversación con Manuel Scorza" 56–57).

57 "Vi, al redactarlo, que le faltaba esa dimensión fulgurante de los hechos, no había manera de meterlos en un informe racional" (quoted in Moraña, "Función ideológica" 175).

58 "Estos hechos que yo había conocido en el arrabal de la historia peruana me hicieron concebir *Redoble por Rancas*. Un día lo escribí de la primera a la última línea" (quoted in Moraña, "Función ideológica" 175).

59 Scorza, *Drums for Rancas*, ix-x. I have modified the translation slightly. The original reads: "Este libro es la crónica exasperantemente real de una lucha solitaria: la que en los Andes Centrales libraron, entre 1950 y 1962, los hombres de algunas aldeas sólo visibles en las cartas militares de los destacamentos que las arrasaron. Los protagonistas, los crímenes, la traición y la grandeza, casi tienen aquí sus nombres verdaderos. . . . Más que un novelista, el autor es un testigo. Las fotografías que se publicarán en un volumen aparte y las grabaciones magnetofónicas donde constan estas atrocidades, demuestran que los excesos de este libro son desvaídas descripciones de la verdad. Ciertos hechos y su ubicación cronológica, ciertos nombres, han sido excepcionalmente modificados para proteger a los justos de la justicia" (*Redoble por Rancas* 11).

60 See for example Kapsoli, *Los movimientos campesinos en Cerro de Pasco*, 91–113, and Handelman, *Struggle in the Andes: Peasant Political Mobilization in Peru*, 62–70. For a detailed discussion of the correspondence between *Drums for Rancas* and actual historical events, see Kapsoli, "Redoble por Rancas: historia y ficción" in his *Literatura e historia del Perú*, 91–117.

61 Scorza, "Epílogo" to *Redoble por Rancas*, 236.

62 "'Conspiración del silencio' en torno a la obra de Scorza" (Escajadillo, *La narrativa indigenista* 120). Scorza's novels were far more widely read and received more critical attention in Europe than in Peru. Forgues attributes this to the financial fallout from Scorza's failed 1950s publishing venture, the Populibros Peruanos, which sought to make works of classic and contemporary literature available to a popular readership in affordable editions: "perhaps the failure of the publishing enterprise, with all the ill will and resentment it generated against its founder, explains at least in part the unjust silencing of his work in Peru and in Latin America / quizá el fracaso de la empresa editorial con los odios y rencores que desencadenó contra su fundador, nos explique, en parte por lo menos, que su obra haya sido injustamente silenciada en el Perú y en América Latina" (*La estrategia mítica de Manuel Scorza* 16).

63 "La palabra libertó a Chacón. Once años estuvo sepultado en una cárcel sudamericana hasta que una novela lo rescató del olvido" (quoted in Moraña, "Función ideológica" 176). See also Scorza, "Epílogo" to *Redoble por Rancas*, 235 and Peralta, "Liberar lo imaginario: entrevista a Manuel Scorza", 28.

64 *Redoble por Rancas*, for example, has been translated into thirty languages.

65 "Se instala, pues, en un espacio literario doble: de una parte está obviamente condicionado por la nueva narrativa hispanoamericana; de otra, se refiere a una tradición anterior, en gran parte discutida y negada por el boom, como es la novela indigenista" (Cornejo Polar, "Sobre el neoindigenismo y las novelas de Manuel Scorza" 553).

66 "Esquema básico de *El mundo es ancho y ajeno*; lucha, primero legal y luego armada, entre una o varias comunidades y un poderoso gamonal local, batalla que termina en el exterminio de los indios" (Escajadillo, *La narrativa indigenista* 112).

67 "In Scorza's work, the indigenous communities of the Central Andes struggle against gamonales (as in *Broad and Alien is the World*), but also, and above all, against the Cerro de Pasco Corporation (which is not an invented institution like 'the Consortium' of *All the Worlds*) / En la obra de Scorza . . . las luchas de las comunidades del centro es contra los gamonales (como en *El mundo es ancho y ajeno*), pero también, y sobre todo, contra la Cerro de Pasco Corporation (que no es una institución inventada como 'el Consorcio' de *Todas las sangres*)" (Cornejo Polar, "Sobre el neoindigenismo y las novelas de Manuel Scorza" 554).

68 Scorza, *Drums for Rancas*, 64. I have modified the translation slightly. The original reads: "¿a quién se le ocurre acudir a una oficina pública para un asunto relacionado con la colectividad?" (*Redoble por Rancas* 81).

69 Scorza, *Drums for Rancas*, 123.

70 *Ibid.*, 159.

71 *Ibid.*, 159–160.

72 For more on the narrative structure of *Drums for Rancas*, see Oscar Rodríguez Ortiz, *Sobre narradores y héroes*, 95–98.

73 "En los Andes las masacres se suceden con el ritmo de las estaciones. En el mundo hay cuatro; en los Andes cinco: primavera, verano, otoño, invierno, y masacre." (Scorza, *Cantar de Agapito Robles* 21). Curiously, *The Ballad of Agapito Robles* is the only novel of *The Silent War* that does not conclude with a massacre.

74 Scorza, *Drums for Rancas*, 93.

75 Scorza's positive portrayal of Father Chasán, likely influenced by the changes occurring in the Catholic Church during the 1960s and 1970s, is yet another departure from the *indigenista* tradition, in which the priest, along with the governor and the judge, invariably forms part of what González Prada called "the Indian's trinity of brutalizers / la trinidad embrutecedora del indio." Scorza's Father Chasán, by contrast, sides with the indigenous community and blesses Rancas's struggle against the Cerro de Pasco Corporation (*Drums for Rancas* 133). For more on González Prada, see Efraín Kristal, *Una visión urbana de los Andes*, 95–122.

76 Aldaz, *The Past of the Future*, 41.

77 "Mi experiencia personal impedía mostrar el verdadero mundo de los comuneros. Decidí, pues, eliminarme del relato y escribir el libro desde el punto de vista de los protagonistas. Necesariamente era un punto de vista legendario porque los acontecimientos se ofrecían como mito. . . . Recurrir

al mito era en este caso la única forma de ser realista" (Bensoussan, "Entrevista con Manuel Scorza" 3).

78 On Scorza's version of magical realism, see Aldaz, *The Past of the Future*, xi, Escajadillo, "Scorza antes del último combate", 54, Tamayo Vargas, "Manuel Scorza y un neoindigenismo", 689, and Teja *"El mito en Redoble por Rancas"*, 258.

79 See for example Spreen, who observes that "Manuel Scorza almost never bases his work on actually existing myths collected by anthropologists or even by him . . . Rather, he created literary myths to insert into the text / Manuel Scorza casi nunca se basa en los mitos realmente existentes, recopilados por antropólogos o de repente por él mismo . .. Más bien creaba mitos literarios para intercalarlos en el texto" ("Manuel Scorza como fenómeno literario" 123).

80 Scorza, *Drums for Rancas*, 49. I have modified the translation slightly. The original reads: "En una de las paredes del cementerio, un jueves, la noche parió al Cerco. . . . el Cerco circundó el cementerio y descendió a la carretera. Es la hora en que los camiones jadean hacia Huánuco, felices de bajar a tierras arboladas. En el borde de la carretera, el Cerco se detuvo, meditó una hora y se dividió en dos. El camino a Huánuco comenzó a correr entre dos alambrados. El Cerco reptó tres kilómetros y enfiló hacia las oscuras tierras de Cafepampa" (*Redoble por Rancas* 65).

81 Bensoussan, "Entrevista a Manuel Scorza", 4.

82 Scorza, *Drums for Rancas*, 1.

83 *Ibid.*, 1–3. I have modified the translation slightly. The original reads: "Como todos los atardeceres de los últimos treinta años, el traje descendió a la plaza para iniciar los sesenta minutos de su imperturbable paseo. . . . A las cuatro, la plaza hierve, a las cinco todavía es un lugar público, pero a las seis es un desierto. Ninguna ley prohíbe caminar a esa hora, pero sea porque el cansancio acomete a los paseantes, sea porque sus estómagos reclaman la cena, a las seis la plaza se deshabita. . . . Hasta los perros saben que de seis a siete no se ladra allí" (*Redoble por Rancas* 15–16).

84 Scorza, *Drums for Rancas*, 2.

85 *Ibid.*, 47.

86 *Ibid.*, 129.

87 The passage also alludes to Scorza's rather idealized conception of the antagonistic relationship of literature to power.

88 "Muestra como la disposición mental del indio a convivir con el mito puede ser utilizada por la burguesía feudal y por el imperialismo como elemento que infunde respeto, que paraliza la función liberadora, en beneficio del status quo" (Teja, "El mito en *Redoble por Rancas*: su función social" 260).

89 "En los Andes, en esas alturas remotas en el espacio y el tiempo, el mito es natural. . . . El mundo indígena siempre ha sido mágico. Aun hoy se expresa mágicamente" (Bensoussan, "Manuel Scorza: yo viajo del mito a la realidad" 40).

90 "La única posibilidad de existir que les quedaba a los pueblos conquistados. A estos pueblos se les ofrecía una historia insoportable, en la cual *ellos no tenían lugar*. La Conquista sometió a los sobrevivientes de las culturas amer-

91 "La respuesta simplemente mítica es ingenua y peligrosa . . . el mito es también una forma de impotencia" (Osorio, "Conversación con Manuel Scorza" 59).

92 "En mis cinco libros he intentado, y creo que logrado, el pasaje de la sociedad mítica a la sociedad actual" (Osorio, "Conversación con Manuel Scorza" 59).

93 Garabombo, the narrator explains, "was as invisible as all the protests, abuses, and complaints" (Scorza, *Garabombo, el invisible* 176). Scorza, *Cantar de Agapito Robles*, 212–213.

94 "Una cierta ambigüedad en lo que toca a la racionalidad indígena, que tanto es recusada cuanto reivindicada." (Cornejo Polar, "Sobre el 'neoindigenismo' y las novelas de Manuel Scorza" 556). For an extended discussion of the dual function of myth in *La guerra silenciosa*, see Forgues, *La estrategia mítica de Manuel Scorza*.

95 See for example Scorza's comments in an interview with Escajadillo: "I think that *Requiem for a Lightning Bolt* is my best novel; I think that in it I reached a new stage in my creative work. The characters in this novel, like those in the rest of my works, are real and at the same time mythical, but this time the mythical characters become aware of their ambivalent nature and, above all, realize that instead of myths they should be simply men. Myth reflects upon itself and resolves to become clarity / Yo pienso que *La tumba del relámpago* es mi mejor novela; creo haber logrado en ella una nueva etapa en mi creación. Sus personajes son, como todos los de mis novelas, reales y al mismo tiempo míticos, pero esta vez los personajes míticos *se percatan* de su ambivalencia y, sobre todo, comprenden que en vez de mitos deben ser, simplemente, hombres. El mito se reflexiona a sí mismo y resuelve ser la Lucidez" (Escajadillo, "Scorza antes del último combate" 66).

96 "Pretexto necesario pero ya no primordial para la situación narrada" (Bradu, "Scorza: entre la desilusión y la polémica" 50).

97 "Scorza centra todo el interés final de esta serie en el destino de los líderes intelectuales de la rebelión, entre los cuales se presenta a sí mismo como uno de los protagonistas principales" (Bradu, "Scorza: entre la desilusión y la polémica" 50).

98 "No lo hicieron por un sueño o un signo sobrenatural sino como protesta espontánea contra un juicio que perjudicaba a la comunidad" (Spreen, "Manuel Scorza como fenómeno literario en la sociedad peruana" 131). Spreen visited the Department of Cerro de Pasco and interviewed some of the participants in the uprising Scorza chronicles: "we had the opportunity to speak with some of the peasants who participated in the land invasions described in the novels. One of them was Agapito Robles / tuvimos la oportunidad de conversar con algunos campesinos que participaron en las invasiones de tierras descritas en las novelas, uno de ellos ha sido Agapito Robles" (117).

99 "La dolorosa negación de la capacidad movilizadora del mito y la convic-

ción de que la revolución necesita el soporte de una racionalidad moderna y pragmática" (Cornejo Polar, "Sobre el 'neoindigenismo' y las novelas de Manuel Scorza" 554).

100 "En la oleada de tomas de tierras entre 1972–1980 los patrones habían perdido la batalla" (Montoya, *Lucha por la tierra* 40).

101 Scorza, *Requiem for a Lightning Bolt*, 208. I have modified the translation slightly. The original reads: "Sobre la lápida de esa sublevación, nadie borronearía el más pobrísimo epitafio. ¡Ninguna mano arrojaría ninguna flor sobre la tumba de ese relámpago!" (*La tumba del relámpago* 267).

102 "El interés fundamental de Scorza fue . . . determinar de qué manera el pensamiento mítico y el pensamiento histórico moderno podían ser materia de un complejo proceso de transculturación que confiriera eficiencia a los movimientos campesinos del futuro, lo que evidentemente se asocia . . . al gran tema del mejor indigenismo: la contradicción irresuelta entre el deber de preservar la identidad del pueblo indígena y el derecho de conquistar la modernidad. En este sentido, pese a las obvias y esenciales diferencias que hay entre ellas, las obras de José María Arguedas y de Manuel Scorza coinciden en el examen de un mismo espacio problemático. Para Arguedas el valor supremo es el de la identidad, aunque acepte hasta con entusiasmo la modernidad que pueda desarrollarse a partir de esa matriz, mientras que para Scorza, mucho más político, las proporciones son casi inversas" (Cornejo Polar, "Manuel Scorza: señas para trazar un contexto" 106).

103 Escajadillo, *La narrativa indigenista*, 23.

Chapter 4   The *Criollo* City Transformed

1 Klarén, *Peru: Society and Nationhood in the Andes*, 434. See also José Matos Mar, *Desborde popular y crisis del estado*, 70–73.

2 Sheahan, *Searching for a Better Society: The Peruvian Economy from 1950*, 18–19, 59.

3 According to Matos Mar, in 1984 *barriadas* accounted for 37 percent of Lima's population (*Desborde popular y crisis del estado* 70).

4 Matos Mar, *Desborde popular y crisis del estado*, 81–82.

5 The classic studies of *barriadas* are Degregori, Blondet and Lynch, *Conquistadores de un nuevo mundo*, and Golte and Adams, *Los caballos de Troya de los invasores*.

6 Matos Mar, *Desborde popular y crisis del estado*, 19.

7 According to Nugent, "the poverty of the slums, intimately related to decay, to who is worth more and who is worth less, can not be considered the same as the poverty of the *barriada*, the very existence of which would be inexplicable without the idea of progress / no puede considerarse igual la pobreza del tugurio, intímamente ligada a la decadencia, de quien vale más o menos, que la pobreza de la barriada, cuya sola existencia sería inexplicable sin el significado del progreso" (*El laberinto de la choledad* 31).

8 "La creación de las *barriadas* y la perspectiva del progreso resultan inseparables" (Nugent, *El laberinto de la choledad* 31–32).

9 Nugent, *El laberinto de la choledad*, 35.

10 "El aspecto que aporta la barriada al espacio urbano ha sido de tal fuerza que simplemente transformó *el rostro* de la ciudad. . . . El territorio de la barriada no es producto de ninguna decadencia urbana. Se trata, más bien, de la renovación del espacio urbano a través de la pobreza. . . . En sentido estricto, caracterizar las *barriadas* como población marginal, carece de sentido y no sólo por motivos cuantitativos. No se trata de gente que está "en las afueras" o en los "márgenes" de la ciudad. Por el contrario, se trata de una brusca redefinición del espacio urbano. La ciudad se renueva, pero esa nueva piel está abrumadoramente marcada por la pobreza" (Nugent, *El laberinto de la choledad* 30–31).

11 These are still referred to by their well-off residents as "residential neighborhoods / barrios residenciales" or "centrally-located neighborhoods / barrios céntricos." The former term would seem to imply that the rest of the city is not "residential", perhaps not even fit for human habitation, despite the fact that the vast majority of Limeños reside outside of "barrios residenciales" like Miraflores and San Isidro. The term "barrios céntricos", for its part, leads one to wonder from whose perspective these neighborhoods, located as far from the old city center as are some *barriadas*, could possibly be imagined as central.

12 Not counting, of course, Arguedas's exceptionally early treatment of the topic in *Yawar Fiesta* (1941), discussed in chapter 1.

13 "No es posible explicar la transición del indigenismo a la narrativa urbana en términos de un rechazo de lo local o regional . . . la transición obedece a un momento en la historia del Perú durante el cual la llegada masiva del indio a las grandes ciudades elimina una de las razones de ser del indigenismo: la curiosidad que el lector urbano había tenido por aquella población que conforma la mayoría en su país, pero cuya cultura y modo de vida ignoraba porque vivía en otra región geográfica. Cuando el indio llega a la ciudad, la curiosidad que se tenía sobre él se reduce considerablemente porque por primera vez en la historia del Perú los habitantes urbanos se ven obligados a convivir con los indios" (Kristal, "Del indigenismo a la narrativa urbana" 58).

14 I refer, of course, to Kristal's useful study of early *indigenista* narrative, *Una visión urbana de los Andes*.

15 Manuel Scorza's five-novel cycle would seem to be a major exception. However, Scorza's novel's were first published outside of Peru and were far more popular and widely read in Europe and in other parts of Latin America than in his native country.

16 "De alguna manera esta literatura, como la del indigenismo, le proporciona a la clase acomodada información sobre las clases bajas. Las descripciones de las *barriadas* y de la llegada del indio están destinadas a los lectores urbanos ya establecidos en la ciudad que observan la llegada del indio y la formación de estas poblaciones marginales" (Kristal, "Del indigenismo a la narrativa urbana" 69).

17 "Mientras que en un primer momento se podía leer estos relatos como se leían los indigenistas, es decir, como historias sobre poblaciones que los lectores probablemente desconocen, en un segundo momento eso va a ser

imposible ya que el indio se habrá integrado cabalmente a una ciudad profundamente transformada por su presencia. Es entonces que la narrativa va a empezar a explorar personajes y situaciones inherentes a la nueva ciudad" (Kristal, "Del indigenismo a la narrativa urbana" 69).

18 "Esquematizando bastante, podríamos resumir la configuración del nuevo sector dominante en tres grupos: 1) la oligarquía en decadencia que tenía el poder de las tierras y que cayó con el apogeo de industriales y de exportadores; 2) una nueva clase media que se beneficia con la llegada del indio, constituida por grupos que por primera vez pueden tener sirvientas, cocineras, choferes, mano de obra barata para construcciones y otros proyectos de escala menor; y 3) un nuevo sector dominante vinculado al comercio internacional que participa y se beneficia directamente en los amplios proyectos de exportación importación y a veces industrialización" (Kristal, "Del indigenismo a la narrativa urbana" 69).

19 Miguel Gutiérrez, *La generación del 50: un mundo dividido*.

20 "Renovar y actualizar la narrativa peruana incorporando a ella los avances expresivos alcanzados por la narrativa occidental" (Higgins, *Cambio social y constantes humanas* 9).

21 "Oligarquía caída que mantiene su nombre pero que ha perdido su poder y está obligada a convivir con los sectores bajos o marginados de la región urbana" (Kristal, "Del indigenismo a la narrativa urbana" 69–70).

22 "¿En qué momento se había jodido el Perú?" (Vargas Llosa, *Conversación en La Catedral* 13). In *Conversación en La Catedral*, notes Peter Elmore, "the immersion in mediocrity, in unease, appears to be the only ethical refuge from a defective and unjust reality / la inmersión en la mediocridad, en el malestar, aparece como el único refugio ético ante una realidad defectiva, injusta" ("Imágenes literarias de la modernidad" 39).

23 Julio Ortega, for example, notes of Ribeyro that "his neutral writing seeks precisely to erase all evidence of form and all traces of style / su escritura neutral busca precisamente borrar las evidencias formales y las marcas de estilo" ("Los cuentos de Ribeyro" 128).

24 Among Ribeyro's nineteenth-century ancestors, for example, are two Supreme Court Justices and Foreign Ministers (Julio Ramón Ribeyro, "Ancestros" 22).

25 "Acusa una conciencia aguda del cambio histórico y el Peru retratado en sus relatos es una sociedad en vías de transformarse" (Higgins, *Cambio social y constantes humanas* 15).

26 Higgins, *Cambio social y constantes humanas*, 61.

27 "Plantean situaciones que tipifican el conflicto de una clase media moviéndose en el modesto infierno de una sociedad precapitalista que se moderniza sin democratizarse" (Ortega, "Los cuentos de Ribeyro" 130).

28 "Una visión de las clases medias y populares peruanas, y limeñas en particular, en que la mediocridad, la desilusión y la impotencia son las normas que rigen el destino de los 'excluidos del festín de la vida,' esos seres alienados por una sociedad que los atrapa y destruye inexorablemente" (Márquez and Ferreira, "Presentación" 16). Losada has taken this to mean that Ribeyro denies the possibility of social transformation (*Creación y praxis* 87, 90–92).

Ribeyro, however, did not consider his attitude regarding social change pessimistic: "I do not really consider myself a pessimist but rather a skeptical optimist, which may seem contradictory. This species, more numerous than is supposed, holds onto some hope that things might be resolved, that not everything can go badly in this world, that man, obliged to suffer and perish, will eventually find a form of life compatible with his essential aspirations and that he will finally invent a viable society. Which one? As a skeptic I can not provide a recipe; as an optimist I believe that the recipe exists. / Yo no me considero realmente como un pesimista, sino como un escéptico optimista. Lo que puede parecer contradictorio. Esta especie, más numerosa de lo que se cree, conserva cierta esperanza en que las cosas se arreglen, en que todo no puede ir para mal en este mundo, en que el hombre a fuerza de padecer y perecer, terminará por encontrar una forma de vida compatible con sus anhelos esenciales y que inventará finalmente una sociedad viable. ¿Cuál? Como escéptico no puedo indicar ninguna receta, como optimista creo que la receta existe" (*La caza sutil* 144).

29   The evidence Andreu presents for the Andean identity of the migrant protagonists of "Al pie del acantilado" is unconvincing. See Andreu, "Legitimidad literaria y legitimidad socio-económica en el relato de Julio Ramón Ribeyro."

30   Cornejo Polar, "El indigenismo y las literaturas heterogéneas" 11.

31   "Traigo buenas noticias para tu marido . . . Ahora, durante el almuerzo, hemos decidido construir un nuevo bar, al lado de la piscina. Los socios quieren algo moderno, ¿sabes? Hemos acordado que Miguel haga los planos" (Ribeyro, *Cuentos* 155).

32   Ribeyro, *Cuentos*, 161.

33   "Del accidente no quedaba ni un solo rastro ni un alambre fuera de lugar, ni siquiera el eco de un grito" (Ribeyro, *Cuentos*, 161).

34   As Elmore puts it, "the good faith of a liberal man is turned into the guilty conscience of a petit bourgeois who betrays his own principles / la buena fe de un hombre liberal se muda en la mala conciencia de un pequeño burgués que traiciona sus principios" (*El perfil de la palabra* 93).

35   "En estos asuntos lo que valen son las pruebas escritas" (Ribeyro, *Cuentos*, 160).

36   "¿Piensas quedarte con él?" (Ribeyro, *Cuentos*, 154).

37   "Algo podemos hacer por este muchacho. Me cae simpático" (Ribeyro, *Cuentos*, 154).

38   Bryce Echenique has on more than one occasion compared his work to that of Arguedas, noting that both he and Arguedas confronted the problem of writing across a deep social divide, though the nature of that divide is different for each, as is the problem of how to represent orality in written form. For Arguedas, this meant finding a means for representing the spoken form of one language, Quechua, in the written form of another, Spanish (see chapter 1). Bryce Echenique, meanwhile faced the somewhat less daunting challenge of developing a written form of Spanish capable of producing the effect of orality in the *same* language. See Bryce Echenique, *La historia personal de mis libros*, 39–40, and Julio Ortega, *El hilo del habla: la narrativa de Alfredo Bryce Echenique*, 119–120.

39   "Los profundos cambios sociológicos de la capital peruana durante los años
     1945–70" (Soubeyroux, "Rapports sociaux et niveaux de discours dans *Un
     mundo para Julius*" 84, quoted in Wood, *The Fictions of Alfredo Bryce
     Echenique* 35). For more on the geographical and historical setting of the
     novel, see de la Fuente, *Cómo leer a Alfredo Bryce Echenique*, 55, and Roffé
     "Entrevista a Alfredo Bryce Echenique", 107.

40   Critics have not failed to note the parallels between the character Julius's
     upbringing in the novel and the author's own genteel family origins.
     Luchting, for example, notes that "*A World for Julius* contains a certain
     amount of autobiographical material / *Un mundo* contiene cierta cantidad
     de material autobiográfico" (*Alfredo Bryce: humores y malhumores* 45).
     Bryce Echenique himself admits that *A World for Julius* is "a portrait of the
     oligarchy of the world in which I had lived, more or less / un retrato de la
     oligarquía del mundo en que yo había vivido más o menos" ("Confesiones"
     67). The novelist's father was an influential banker and his mother a direct
     descendant of a colonial Viceroy and a nineteenth-century president of Peru
     (de la Fuente, *Cómo leer a Alfredo Bryce Echenique* 9). As Bryce Echenique
     puts it, "I was born and lived a good part of my life in the midst of a fam-
     ily in which someone had always been something important (Viceroy,
     President of the Republic, Mayor, Chairman of the Board, etc.) / nací y he
     vivido, una buena parte de mi vida, en medio de una familia en la cual
     siempre alguien había sido algo importante (virrey, presidente de la
     República, alcalde, presidente del directorio, etc.)" (quoted in Ortega, *El
     hilo del habla* 105).

41   "*Un mundo para Julius* reproduce, con rara imparcialidad, la vida privile-
     giada de los señores y la precaria de los siervos; compendia la injusticia social
     en un hogar de familia, simplificante espejo de un sistema económico en cuyo
     centro se coloca, como una acusación, la perpleja inocencia de Julius, el niño
     sensible y solitario que va descubriendo una realidad cruel que no comprende
     pero que aprende con tristeza y pesar" (Oquendo, "El largo salto de Bryce"
     125).

42   The comparison to the fate of the landowning elite becomes even more
     explicit if one also interprets cancer as a "modern" disease.

43   "The servants are responsible for Julius's initial upbringing, with the conse-
     quence that from his most tender infancy he finds it natural to treat and love
     the servants like human beings. . . . In effect, Julius grows up convinced that
     the values of the servants' world are real values whose social functioning he
     perceives with sympathy, in open contrast to the degraded values of his
     parents' world. / La educación inicial de Julius queda en manos de la
     servidumbre, con la consecuencia de que desde su más tierna infancia
     encuentra que es natural tratar y querer a los criados como a seres humanos.
     . . . En efecto, Julius crece con el convencimiento de que los valores que
     informan el mundo de los sirvientes, son valores reales cuyo funcionamiento
     social él percibe con simpatía, en abierto contraste con los valores
     degradados del mundo de sus padres" (Mejía, "Veinticinco años de *Un
     mundo para Julius*" 169).

44   "Terminarán por desarrollar en él las contradicciones entre el conjunto de

valores que él asume y los que predominan en la sociedad" (Mejía, "Veinticinco años de *Un mundo para Julius*" 169).

45 Rodríguez-Peralta, "Narrative Access to *Un mundo para Julius*", 415.

46 On the novel's initial reception, see Wood, *The Fictions of Alfredo Bryce Echenique*, 32, and Escajadillo, "Bryce: Elogios varios y una objeción", 137.

47 "El general Velasco, presidente de la República, y Alfredo Bryce habían destruido a la oligarquía peruana" (Bryce Echenique, "Confesiones" 67).

48 "Hay en Bryce, pues, junto con la sátira por momentos mordaz, una suerte de simpatía . . . por el mundo de la burguesía. *Un mundo para Julius* es una parodia de la oligarquía, pero tiene hacia ella algunas notas de ambigua fascinación; hasta cierto punto constituye un canto . . . de un mundo que se va" (Escajadillo, "Bryce" 143). For Rodríguez Peralta, "there is no overt social protest in *Un mundo para Julius*" ("Narrative access to *Un mundo para Julius*" 415). Wood, for his part, adds that "while the oligarchy's existence is depicted in all its injustice, stagnation and futility, mentions of social movements are limited to fleeting references to strikes and workers' rights, and there is certainly no proposal for a revolution of the kind that was actually taking place" (*The Fictions of Alfredo Bryce Echenique* 32).

49 On the orality of the narrative and the use of free indirect discourse, see Bryce Echenique, "Confesiones sobre el arte de vivir y escribir novelas" 68, Duncan "Language as Protagonist" 121, Luchting, *Alfredo Bryce*, 48, Rodríguez-Peralta "Narrative Access to *Un mundo para Julius*" 409–412, Roffé "Entrevista a Alfredo Byce Echenique" 108–109, and Wood, *The fictions of Alfredo Bryce Echenique*, 37.

50 See, for example, Duncan, "Language as Protagonist" 122–123, 127, and López-Baralt, "Otra forma de complicidad", 53–54.

51 Duncan, "Language as Protagonist: Tradition and Innovation in *Un mundo para Julius*", 123.

52 "Un narrador muy vivaz, dispuesto en cualquier momento . . . a imitar la *manera* de hablar de otro, a asumir las *palabras* de otra persona, en breve, a apropiarse, fugazmente o a través de largos pasajes, el *punto de vista* de algún otro personaje en la novela" (Luchting, *Alfredo Bryce: humores y malhumores* 48).

53 Bryce Echenique, *A World for Julius*, 193. I have modified the translation slightly. The original reads: "La señora [Susan] les anunció meses pagados de vacaciones y Celso y Daniel se entregaron a su felicidad, porque ahora podrían edificar. Edificar. Esa es la palabra que utilizaban y para qué ingenieros ni arquitectos, mi brazo. El diccionario debe dar tanto sobre la palabra edificar, la etimología, el latín y todo, pero para qué mierda cuando ellos ya se iban a edificar y te enseñaban los dientes al sonreír y tú ya andabas en plena asociación edificar edificio grande departamentos hoteles suites y ellos seguían sonriéndote con una miga de pan pegada entre los dientes enormes y vacaciones largas pagadas y se iban a edificar pues. Cuando mojaban el pan en el café con leche sobre la mesa de la repostería la asociación avanzaba y el color del café con leche te arrojaba de bruces contra la casucha de barro y lo de edificar perdía lo edificante y la cara de ellos mojando los panes ya qué diablos sería lo que te hacía pensar que el diccionario no da la pena

la caricatura de la palabra lo chiquito de la palabra... Si los hubieras visto edificando en el sentido de miga de pan entre dientes en sonrisa, con las tazas ahí adelante, Celso y Daniel momentos antes de abandonar el viejo palacio para irse a ed... en el terrenito de la barriada" (*Un mundo para Julius* 184).

54   Bryce Echenique, *A World for Julius*, 196. I have modified the translation somewhat. The original reads: "Se quedó ahí parada, toda de negro y la melena azabache, mirando la ciudad y sintiendo que la ciudad era mala porque no tenía bancas y ella necesitaba sentarse. Cómo era la ciudad, ¿no?, tan llena de edificios enormes, altísimos desde donde la gente se suicida, amarillos, sucios, más altos, más bajos, más modernos, casa viejas y luego puro cemento y sin bancas y ella necesitaba tanto sentarse, un ministerio tan grande y ninguna banca y los pies cómo le dolían, donde mi comadre el piso es de tierra tan húmeda que me duelen los riñones, puro cemento y de nuevo ninguna banca, cómo es la ciudad, ¿no?, cómo será, pues, la gente camina, no descansa nunca, faltaban bancas y ella no tardaba en caerse sentada, tal vez podría dejar el paquete sobre el motor de un auto estacionado, recostarse un poquito sobre un guardabarro" (*Un mundo para Julius* 187).

55   Bryce Echenique, *A World for Julius*, 202–203. I have modified the translation somewhat. The original reads: "Arminda dio tres pasos tímidos y ya estaba en la suite, absurda. Susan notó que empezaba a oscurecer lastimosamente, cosa que podría deprimirla y corrió a cerrar todas las cortinas, para acercar la noche y con ella el cóctel. . . . Arminda continuaba parada, tres pasos adentro y de pronto también sucia y había murmurado algo. . . . para Susan todo andaba un poco en el subconsciente otro poco por ahí atrás, hasta que bebió una pizca de jerez, dejó nuevamente la copita sobre la mesa y ahora sí ya no tardaba en ver a Arminda, en ocuparse de ella, por alguna parte debe haber dinero, hay que cogerlo, entregárselo, pagarle y quedarse con el paquete de camisas, Arminda ya, ahora sí: darling, *can you give me some money please?* Juan Lucas, sentado e improvisando una profunda lectura de Time, extrajo la billetera y alargó el brazo hacia Susan, sin mirar porque el artículo se ponía cada vez más interesante" (*Un mundo para Julius* 192).

56   Bryce Echenique, *A World for Julius*, 203. I have modified the translation somewhat. The original reads: "En seguida avanzó hasta la copita de jerez y bebió nuevamente una pizca, a ver si de ahí surgía algo porque la mujer continuaba en la suite, y qué se iban a hacer con ella, a lo mejor Julius se demora horas en venir. Se conversa o no se conversa, parecía pensar la pobre Susan, porque la presencia de Arminda como que iba creciendo y ni avanzaba ni retrocedía ni se marchaba ni nada y el jerez ya no tardaba en terminarse y ella tampoco ni se sentaba ni se iba a cambiar y Juan Lucas era capaz de pedirle unos anteojos que no tenía, tan interesado seguía en su Time, ya sólo faltaba que la revista esté al revés para que la suite estalle" (*Un mundo para Julius* 193).

57   Bryce Echenique, *A World for Julius*, 205. I have modified the translation slightly. The original reads: "Susan, interesadísima . . . seguía la apertura del paquete con un delicioso y falso entusiasmo. Lo que no era muy seguro es que pudiera mantenerlo, porque el paquetito la verdad es que iba perdiendo lo de te traigo un regalito y se iba convirtiendo en lo que era: el regalo de una

mujer pobre a un niño millonario, y en pena . . . . . . En la pena que tú nunca olvidarás, Julius" (*Un mundo para Julius* 194).

58 Bryce Echenique, *A World for Julius*, 208. I have modified the translation slightly. The original reads: "Con la oscuridad de la noche los contrastes dormían un poco, pero ello no le impedía observar todas las Limas que el Mercedes iba atravesando, la Lima de hoy, la de ayer, la que se fue, la que debió irse, la que ya es hora de se vaya, en fin Lima. Lo cierto es que de día o de noche las casas dejaron de ser palacios o castillos y de pronto ya no tenían esos jardines enormes, la cosa como que iba disminuyendo poco a poco. Había cada vez menos árboles y las casas se iban poniendo cada vez más feas, menos bonitas en todo caso porque acababan de salir de tenemos los barrios residenciales más bonitos del mundo, pregúntale a cualquier extranjero que haya estado en Lima, y empezaba a verse edificiotes esos cuadrados donde siempre lo que falla [sic] es la pintura de la fachada" (*Un mundo para Julius* 197).

59 Bryce Echenique, *A World for Julius*, 209.

60 Bryce Echenique, *A World for Julius*, 209. I have modified the translation slightly. The original reads: "Por primera vez en una casa, en pleno comedor y la sala no está por ninguna parte, una gallina lo estaba mirando de reojo, nerviosísima, y bajo la media luz de una bombilla colgando de un techo húmedo, todo al borde del corto circuito y el incendio, familia en la calle. Y él ya no sabía hacia dónde mirar y es que miraba ahí para no mirar allá y sentía que continuaba insultando a Guadalupe, a Arminda, tal vez hasta a Carlos" (*Un mundo para Julius* 198).

61 Ortega, "Introduction", *The Fox from up Above and the Fox from Down Below*, xi. For more on the anchovy boom in Chimbote, see Flores Galindo and Sulmont, *El movimiento obrero en la industria pesquera. El caso de Chimbote.*

62 See Arguedas's letter of 1 February 1967, to North American anthropologist John Murra, in which he describes his ongoing research in Chimbote (*Las cartas de Arguedas* 140–143).

63 See for example the fragments of interviews reproduced as an appendix to Lienhard's *Cultura andina y forma novelesca*, 199–205.

64 *Las cartas de Arguedas*, 141.

65 *Ibid.*, 142.

66 Arguedas, *The Fox from up Above and the Fox from Down Below*, 43. I have modified the translation slightly. The original reads: "El olor de los desperdicios, de la sangre, de las pequeñas entrañas pisoteadas en las bolicheras y lanzadas sobre el mar a manguerazos, y el olor del agua que borbotaba de las fábricas a la playa hacía brotar de la arena gusanos gelatinosos; esa fetidez avanzaba a ras del suelo y elevándose" (*El zorro de arriba y el zorro de abajo* 40).

67 Arguedas, *The Fox from up Above and the Fox from Down Below*, 97.

68 *Ibid.*, 97.

69 *Ibid.*, 243. I have modified the translation slightly. The original reads: "Nos hemos igualado en la miseria miserableza . . . aquí está reunido la gente desabandonada del Dios y mismo de la tierra, porque ya nadies es de ninguna

parte-pueblo en *barriadas* de Chimbote. . . . aquí no hay desprecios de unos apellidazos, más grandes más chicos, contra los homildes cholos que dicen. Poca ayuda habrá entre vecinos y más bien hasta se roban; por desventuranza, se pelean su poco; pero desprecio mismo no hay y cuando llega el oportunidad de fuerza levantamos uno a otro, como yo a me compadre y sobrinos. Así es. El miseria en la barriada que decimos es gusanera que hace levantarse al desabandonado" (*El zorro de arriba y el zorro de abajo* 229–230).

70 "El Mal . . . que contamina el mundo de la novela se enraíza en la esencia del sistema industrial . . . la noción misma de desarrollo, de modernización, de adelanto tecnológico, es exorcizada en el libro" (Vargas Llosa, *La utopía arcaica* 46).

71 "Hostil al desarrollo industrial, antiurbano, pasadista. Con todas las injusticias y crueldades de que puede ser víctima en sus comunidades de las alturas andinas, el indio está allí mejor que en Chimbote. Ésa es la moraleja del libro" (Vargas Llosa, *La utopía arcaica* 307).

72 The fish-meal plant manager Ángel Rincón, for example, notes of his Andean migrant workers that "when they're taught to run machinery, and what's more, when the engineers explain the workings of the most complicated key parts and tell how the machines function as a whole, these animals learn – rather slowly – but I would say they have a deeper understanding than the gringos themselves. . . . sometimes they're delighted with the tubing and the gears, the nozzles, the twists and turnings of the parts; they guess how they work instead of learning about them; they'll stay here for hours without claiming overtime, just looking to see how the parts are linked together and what effect they have; they get happy and make a fuss over the machines" (*The Fox from up Above and the Fox from Down Below* 124).

73 Arguedas, *The Fox from up Above and the Fox from Down Below*, 86.

74 William Rowe, for example, notes that "*The Fox* constituted a new phase for which the previous vision and methods were inadequate / *El zorro* constituía una etapa nueva para la cual la visión y los métodos anteriores no podían servir" (*Mito e ideología* 192).

75 Franco, "From Modernization to Resistance: Latin American Literature, 1959–1976", 287–289.

76 In the first diary of *The Fox from up Above and the Fox from Down Below*, for example, he writes that "if I don't write and publish, I'll shoot myself" (17). I have modified the translation slightly. The original reads: "Si no escribo y publico, me pego un tiro" (*El zorro* 14). He opens the final diary with an admission of defeat: "Either I have been struggling with death or else I think I have been struggling with death at quite close quarters while writing this intermittent, painful tale. The few allies I had were weak and uncertain; death's have won" (*The Fox from up Above and the Fox from Down Below* 256).

77 Arguedas, *The Fox from up Above and the Fox from Down Below*, 263.

78 "En una novela en la que dijo que se mataba porque se sentía sin fuerzas para seguir creando, Arguedas dio la prueba más convincente de que era un creador" (Vargas Llosa, *La utopía arcaica* 326).

79 "La dolorosa novedad de la vida urbana moderna", "una estética narrativa que traduce el desarraigo, la frustración, la falta de perspectivas personales e históricas de los individuos" (Lienhard, "La 'andinización' del vanguardismo urbano" 324).

80 Lienhard, "La 'andinización' del vanguardismo urbano", 323–326.

81 For Cornejo Polar, such fragmentation "is the only viable narrative technique for the chaotic and atomized universe of Chimbote / es la única técnica narrativa viable frente al atomizado y caótico universo de Chimbote" (*Los universos narrativos* 243).

82 "La cultura quechua se puede considerar como un 'texto' o conjunto de 'textos,' que desempeña, dentro de *El zorro*, la función que tienen en general los textos del pasado dentro de las obras literarias: materia prima que se destruye y reelabora. El texto, en este caso, no es un producto predominantemente verbal, sino un complejo sistema compuesto por signos verbales, musicales, gestuales, etc." (Lienhard, *Cultura andina y forma novelesca* 139).

83 Lienhard, *Cultura andina y forma novelesca*, 85–90.

84 Duviols, "Francisco de Ávila, extirpador de la idolatría: Estudio biobibliográfico", included as an appendix to Arguedas's translation of de Ávila's manuscript, *Dioses y hombres de Huarochirí*, 151–175.

85 "Una especie de *Popol Vuh* de la antigüedad peruana" (Arguedas, *Dioses y hombres de Huarochirí* 9).

86 "La alusión al pasado pre-hispánico no pretende ser una evocación melancólica de algo que ya no existe, de lo que se ha perdido irremediablemente, sino que el pensamiento que creó esos mitos sigue vigente y tiene futuro, y ha traspasado ahora las barreras de lo andino" (Gazzolo, "La corriente mítica en *El zorro de arriba y el zorro de abajo*" 45).

87 Vargas Llosa, *La utopía arcaica*, 297.

88 Arguedas, *The Fox from up Above and the Fox from Down Below*, 88, 189. I have modified the translation slightly. The original reads: "¿A qué habré metido estos zorros tan difíciles en la novela?" (83) and "estos 'Zorros' se han puesto fuera de mi alcance: corren mucho o están muy lejos. Quizá apunté a un blanco demasiado largo o, de repente, alcanzo a los 'Zorros' y ya no los suelto más" (179).

89 Arguedas, *The Fox from up Above and the Fox from Down Below*, 26, 52–55.

90 "Nombres atribuidos a una función, la de narrar hechos de arriba y de abajo" (Lienhard, "La última novela de Arguedas" 187–188).

91 Salomon and Urioste, *The Huarochirí Manuscript*, 83. Arguedas's Spanish translation reads: "Ella . . . esperó en su chacra a Tutayquiri, para hacerlo caer en la mentira. Y, mostrándole su parte vergonzosa y también los senos, le dijo: "Padre, descansa un poco; bebe siquiera algo de esta chicha, come de este potaje." Y él se quedó. Y viéndolo descansar y quedarse, unos y otros también se quedaron en aquel lugar. Por esa causa, sólo conquistaron hasta el pueblo Alloca de Abajo (Ura Alloca). Si Tutayquiri no hubiera sido engañado por esa mujer, entonces, hasta Caracu de Abajo habría pertenecido

a los de Huarochirí y Quinti, todas las chacras" (*Dioses y hombres de Huarochirí* 69).

92 Lienhard, "La 'andinización' del vanguardismo urbano" 328. See also Lienhard, *Cultura andina y forma novelesca*, 136–140.

93 On the Andean symbolism in this chapter, see also Gazzolo, "La corriente mítica en *El zorro de arriba y el zorro de abajo*", 60–66.

94 Early analyses of *The Fox from Up Above and the Fox from Down Below* may be found in the appropriate chapters of Cornejo Polar's *Los universos narrativos de José María Arguedas* and Rowe's *Mito e ideología en la obra de José María Arguedas*. More recent studies include, in addition to Lienhard's *Cultura popular andina y forma novelesca*; Lindstrom, "*El zorro de arriba y el zorro de abajo*: una marginación al nivel del discurso"; Elmore, "Imágenes literarias de la modernidad, entre *Conversación en la Catedral* de Vargas Llosa y *El zorro de arriba y el zorro de abajo de Arguedas*"; Portocarrero, "Las últimas reflexiones de José María Arguedas"; Gazzolo, "La corriente mítica en *El zorro de arriba y el zorro de abajo de José María Arguedas*"; and "Lo femenino en *El zorro de arriba y el zorro de abajo*", Lambright, "Losing Ground: Some Notes on the Feminine in *El zorro de arriba y el zorro de abajo*", as well as the essays that accompany the critical edition of the novel edited by Fell.

95 Arguedas, *The Fox from Up Above and the Fox from Down Below*, 45.

96 *Ibid.*, 45.

97 *Ibid.*, 45.

98 *Ibid.*, 54. I have modified the translation slightly. The original reads: "Fue detenido por una virgen ramera que lo esperó con las piernas desnudas, abiertas, los senos descubiertos y un cántaro de chicha" (*El zorro de arriba y el zorro de abajo* 50).

99 Arguedas, *The Fox from Up Above and the Fox from Down Below*, 41. I have modified the translation somewhat. The original reads: "Tú, puta, blancona, huivona. Ahistá, carajo. Toma, carajo. Doscientos soles nada para mí. Puta, putaza" (*El zorro de arriba y el zorro de abajo* 38).

100 Arguedas, *The Fox from Up Above and the Fox from Down Below*, 42.

101 *Ibid.*, 42.

102 *Ibid.*, 43.

103 *Ibid.*, 46. I have modified the translation slightly. The original reads: "A poco de arrancar el automóvil, el chofer oyó que el pasajero hablaba en quechua, fuerte, casi gritando ya. La mujer le contestaba igual. Hablaron, después, juntos, al mismo tiempo. Parecía un duo alegre y desesperado" (*El zorro de arriba y el zorro de abajo* 42).

104 My interpretation of this episode draws on Cornejo Polar, *Los universos narrativos de José María Arguedas*, 235–239, and Portocarrero "Las últimas reflexiones de José María Arguedas", 242–243.

105 Franco, "Self-Destructing Heroines", 366. Fore more on the role of women in *The Fox from Up Above and the Fox from Down Below*, see Gazzolo, "Lo femenino en *El zorro de arriba y el zorro de abajo*", and Lambright, "Losing Ground: Some Notes on the Feminine in *El zorro de arriba y el zorro de abajo*."

106 It should be noted, nonetheless, that Arguedas's fiction almost invariably represents sexuality of any kind, male or female, as malevolent and degrading. This is due at least in part to the multiple traumas he suffered as a small child in his stepmother's house, including, apparently, sexual abuse. In the first diary of *The Fox from Up Above and the Fox from Down Below*, for example, Arguedas recalls how a female visitor to his stepmother's house engaged him in sexual relations at a time when he would have been less than ten years old (24). In addition, his much older stepbrother apparently forced the young Arguedas to witness his sexual relations with local women (Vargas Llosa, *La utopía arcaica* 50–51).

107 Arguedas, *The Fox from Up Above and the Fox from Down Below*, 48.

108 *Ibid.*, 50–51. I have modified the translation slightly, The original reads: "Se sacó el sombrero, enarcó el brazo como para bailar, hizo brillar la cinta del sombrero, moviéndolo, y con la melodía de un carnaval muy antiguo, cantó, bailando: Culebra Tinoco / culebra Chimbote / culebra asfalto / culebra Zavala / culebra Braschi / cerro arena culebra / juábrica harina culebra" (*El zorro de arriba y el zorro de abajo* 47).

109 Arguedas, *The Fox from Up Above and the Fox from Down Below*, 51.

110 "Canto monorrítmico lento . . . a menudo caracterizado por la evocación de un universo de sombría violencia" (Lienhard, "Glosario" 261).

111 Rowe, *Mito e ideología*, 193.

112 "Es uno de los motivos más emocionantes de la novela" (Rowe, *Mito e ideología* 207). Cornejo Polar, too, admires the chapter as "perhaps the most accomplished in the entire novel and one of the most striking in Arguedas's narrative fiction / tal vez el mejor logrado de toda la novela y uno de los más sobrecogedores en la narrativa de Arguedas" (*Los universos narrativos* 248).

113 Cornejo Polar considers him a central character. In Cornejo Polar's view, Moncada's sermons "represent a kind of mirror in which the reality of the port is reflected / representan una suerte de espejo en el que la realidad del puerto se refleja" (*Los universos narrativos* 254). Moncada's insanity, Cornejo Polar suggests, is a product of Chimbote's chaotic modernization, such that "Moncada knows all of the port's secrets, and does not keep them to himself. For this reason, his demented sermons are, paradoxically, the verbalized consciousness of Chimbote / Moncada no desconoce ningún secreto del puerto. Tampoco los calla. Sus demenciales sermones son por esto, paradójicamente, la verbalizada conciencia de Chimbote" (*Los universos narrativos* 255).

114 Arguedas, *The Fox from Up Above and the Fox from Down Below*, 143.

115 "Aunque costeño, es receptivo a la sensibilidad serrana y capaz de incorporarla dentro de su propia visión de las cosas" (Rowe, *Mito e ideología* 207).

116 My argument here is indebted to Shea's very suggestive reading of this chapter in "*El zorro de arriba y el zorro de abajo*: Las cinco onzas que mataron a José María Arguedas", a paper presented at the Jornadas Andinas de Literatura Latinoamericana, Cusco, Peru, 9–13 August 1999.

117 Arguedas, *The Fox from Up Above and the Fox from Down Below*, 151.

118 *Ibid.*, 151.

119 *Ibid.*, 229.

120 *Ibid.*, 234.
121 *Ibid.*, 231.
122 *Ibid.*, 251.
123 *Ibid.*, 251.
124 *Ibid.*, 253.
125 *Ibid.*, 254.
126 *Ibid.*, 55.
127 See Lienhard, "La última novela de Arguedas: Imagen de un lector futuro", 190–196.
128 Recall, for example, his account of the effects of Andean migration on Lima in chapter 7 of *Yawar Fiesta.*
129 "Se han ido formando dos circuitos económicos: uno, oficial, constituido por el universo registrado de personas que operan en el comercio, la producción, transporte y servicios al amparo de las leyes civiles; y otro, contestatario y popular en el que opera un universo de empresas y actividades no registradas, que se mueven fuera de la legalidad o en sus fronteras, frecuentemente adaptando al nuevo medio las estrategias, normas y costumbres inmemoriales de la sociedad andina" (Matos Mar, *Desborde popular* 58).
130 "Particularmente importantes, entre las formas nuevas de organización social urbana que surgen del aporte serrano, son las asociaciones de migrantes, que combinan formas de organización gremial con sistemas andinos comunales de reciprocidad y agrupación" (Matos Mar, *Desborde popular* 81–82).
131 "Encuentra sus modos en las tradiciones de adaptabilidad ecológica y ayuda mutua andina y termina irrumpiendo a través de la costra formal de la sociedad tradicional criolla" (Matos Mar, *Desborde popular* 89).
132 de Soto, *The Other Path*, 236.
133 *Ibid.*, 209.
134 *Ibid.*, 243.
135 "Es inexacto imaginar que la migración opera como fuerza imbatible y todopoderosa que reconstruye desde sus raíces la identidad del migrante campesino, convirtiéndolo, por ejemplo, en protagonista de la "larga marcha"—supuestamente casi siempre exitosa—hacia la propiedad privada y el capitalismo (De Soto, 1986), entre otras muchas razones porque el migrante tiende a repetir en la ciudad modos de producción y de relaciones sociales—como la reciprocidad, la operatividad económica de la familia ampliada o el simple padrinazgo—que difícilmente se incorporan a las normas del capitalismo moderno" (Cornejo Polar, "Una heterogeneidad no dialéctica" 840).
136 Degregori, for example, notes that "an indication of this blind spot in Mario Vargas Llosa's current vision of Peru is to be found in his prologue to *The Other Path*, in which he welcomes those in the informal economy as the primary supporters of the struggle for economic liberty and against mercantilism and statism, but *says not a single word that might serve to acknowledge them as the bearers of a culture and builders of a nation* / Un anuncio de este punto ciego en la visión del Perú que hoy exhibe MVLl se encuentra en su prólogo a *El otro sendero*, donde saluda a los informales como puntales en la lucha por la libertad económica contra el mercantilismo

y el estatismo, pero *no dice una sola palabra en que los reconozca como portadores de cultura y constructores de nación*" (*Elecciones* 1990 121).

Chapter 5   Mario Vargas Llosa Writes Of(f) the Native

1   See for example, Degregori, Blondet, and Lynch, *Conquistadores de un nuevo mundo: De invasores a ciudadanos en San Martín de Porres*, Golte and Adams, *Los caballos de troya de los invasores: Estrategias campesinas en la conquista de la gran Lima*, and Matos Mar, *Desborde popular y crisis del estado: El nuevo rostro del Perú en la década de 1980*.

2   On the Shining Path and the violence and terror of the 1980s and early 1990s, see Bonilla, *Perú en el fin del milenio*; Degregori, *Ayacucho 1969–1979: el surgimiento de Sendero Luminoso* and *Qué difícil es ser dios: ideología y violencia política en Sendero Luminoso*; Gorriti, *The Shining Path: A History of the Millenarian War in Peru*; Manrique, *El tiempo del miedo: la violencia política en el Perú, 1980–1996*; Montoya, *Al borde del naufragio: democracia, violencia y problema étnico en el Perú*; Palmer, *Shining Path of Peru*; Poole and Rénique, *Peru: Time of Fear*; Stern, *Shining and Other Paths*.

3   Palmer, "La rebelión de Sendero Luminoso en el Perú rural", 334, 348.

4   "El elemento modernizador no fue un agente económico (mina, industria, cultivo comercial), sino fundamentalmente ideológico: una universidad . . . podríamos decir que en Ayacucho el proceso se invierte y no es el cambio económico el que conduce a transformaciones sociales y culturales, sino que primero llega la *idea*" (Degregori, *Qué difícil es ser Dios* 18).

5   "Contraste, que con los años sería explosivo, entre la expansión del horizonte intelectual y el atraso económico" (Flores Galindo, *Buscando un Inca* 308–309).

6   Degregori, *Qué difícil es ser Dios*, 23, and Mayer, "Peru in Deep Trouble", 196.

7   "Surgió del encuentro . . . entre una élite intelectual provinciana mestiza y una juventud universitaria también provinciana, andina y mestiza" (Degregori, *Qué difícil es ser Dios* 7).

8   "Jóvenes que se encuentran en una tierra de nadie ubicada entre dos mundos: el tradicional andino de sus padres, cuyos mitos, ritos y costumbres, al menos parcialmente ya no comparten; y el mundo occidental o, más precisamente, urbano-criollo, que los rechaza por provincianos, mestizos, quechua-hablantes. Los jóvenes exigen *coherencia*, una "visión del mundo" que sustituya a la andina tradicional, que ya no es más la suya . . . . Y creen encontrar lo que buscan en esa ideología rígida que se presenta como verdad única y les da la ilusión de coherencia absoluta: el marxismo-leninismo-maoísmo" (Degregori, *Qué difícil es ser Dios* 18–19).

9   According to Degregori, "a vision that pretends to be absolutely scientific becomes tremendously affective and ends up offering its members a strong, quasi religious, fundamentalist identity. / una visión que se pretende absolutamente científica se convierte en tremendamente afectiva y termina ofreciendo a sus miembros una fortísima identidad cuasi religiosa, fundamentalista" (*Qué difícil es ser Dios* 23).

10 Manrique argues in a similar vein that the Shining Path's rise was facilitated by the failures of Velasco's modernizing initiatives: "the social sectors most affected by the failure of this project were basically those that had not had access to social mobility before, due to ethnic and racial in addition to social and economic obstacles. These sectors had an opportunity then [under Velasco] to learn of the rights they had formally but which were denied them in practice. It was these same sectors that would later constitute the backbone of the Shining Path. . . . The mid-level cadre of the Shining Path are not peasants, properly speaking, but rather the youth produced by recent processes of de-peasantization: the children of peasants or ex-peasants who no longer fit into the traditional world in which their parents lived but who are also unable to integrate themselves into the system once they have migrated. / Los sectores sociales más afectados por el fracaso de este proyecto fueron básicamente aquéllos que anteriormente no habían tenido acceso a la movilidad social, por trabas no sólo sociales y económicas sino también étnico raciales, que tuvieron entonces la oportunidad de conocer los derechos que formalmente tenían y les eran negados en la realidad cotidiana, en buena medida los mismos que después constituirían la columna vertebral de Sendero Luminoso. . . . Los mandos de Sendero no son propiamente campesinos sino más bien jóvenes procedentes de procesos de descampesinización recientes: hijos de campesinos o ex campesinos, que ya no pueden insertarse más en el mundo tradicional en el que vivieron sus padres pero que tampoco tienen cómo integrarse en el sistema una vez que migran" (*El tiempo del miedo* 55).

11 Manrique, *El tiempo del miedo*, 54.

12 "La nueva Reforma Agraria no otorgó el poder a los campesinos. Emprendida desde el estado y bloqueando cualquier posibilidad de movilización autónoma, debió reemplazar el deteriorado poder de los hacendados por el de los funcionarios estatales" (Flores Galindo, *Buscando un Inca* 305).

13 As Manrique observes, "the disappearance of the landowners produced a power vacuum in the countryside that merchants and the state agrarian reform bureaucracy unsuccessfully attempted to fill. In addition to exploitation and oppression, landowners had performed functions necessary for the social reproduction of the peasantry: mediating peasants' relationships with the state, the church, the judicial apparatus, military conscription, the market, etc. The Shining Path filled this vacuum by resorting to methods similar to those once used by landowners to assure their hegemony: a vertical authoritarianism backed up by the extensive use of violence. . . . Clearly the Shining Path's social project was radically different than that of traditional landowners, but the two groups shared a vertical and authoritarian character. / la desaparición de los terratenientes produjo un vacío de poder en el campo que intentaron llenar sin éxito los comerciantes y la burocracia estatal creada por la reforma agraria. Los hacendados, además de la expoliación y la opresión, cumplían un conjunto de funciones necesarias para la reproducción social del campesinado: intermediar su relación con el Estado, la Iglesia, el aparato judicial, la conscripción militar, el mercado, etcétera. Sendero cubriría este vacío recurriendo a métodos similares a los empleados por los

terratenientes para asegurar su hegemonía: un autoritarismo vertical apoyado en el recurso extensivo de la violencia. . . . Evidentemente el proyecto social de Sendero tenía radicales diferencias con el de los terratenientes tradicionales, pero compartía con éste su carácter vertical y autoritario" (*El tiempo del miedo* 110–112).

14 "Nueva forma de ser *misti*" (Degregori, *Qué difícil es ser Dios* 26).

15 "30 mil muertos, 600 mil desplazados, 40 mil huérfanos, 20 mil viudas, 4 mil desaparecidos, 500 mil menores de 18 años con estrés postraumático y 435 comunidades arrasadas" (Manrique, *El tiempo del miedo* 21). The final report of the Comisión de la Verdad y Reconciliación / Truth and Reconciliation Commission, issued the year after the publication of Manrique's book, estimates 69,280 dead and disappeared between 1980 and 2000 as a result of the war.

16 Rowe gives a lucid summary of this trajectory in "Liberalism and Authority." See also Kristal's account in *Temptation of the Word: The Novels of Mario Vargas Llosa*, 69–81, 99–123.

17 For Vargas Llosa's account of his disillusionment with the Cuban revolution, written shortly before his definitive break with Cuba and with socialism, see "Un francotirador tranquilo", in *Contra viento y marea I (1962–1982)*, 201–212.

18 On Sartre, see "Sartre, veinte años después" (1978) and "El mandarín" (1980) in Mario Vargas Llosa, *Contra viento y marea I*, 324–327 and 387–401, respectively. On Camus, see "Albert Camus y la moral de los límites" (1975), *Contra viento y marea I*, 231–253. On Isaiah Berlin, see "Isaiah Berlin, un héroe de nuestro tiempo" (1980), *Contra viento y marea I*, 406–424. On Hayek, see "Muerte y resurrección de Hayek" (1992), in *Desafíos a la libertad*, 110–114.

19 See Rowe, "Liberalism and Authority", and Degregori, "El aprendiz de brujo y el curandero chino: Etnicidad, modernidad y ciudadanía", in Degregori and Grompone, *Elecciones 1990*, 73.

20 For an insightful reading of this novel in its Peruvian context, see Cornejo Polar, *La novela peruana*, 243–256. See also Zapata, "Las trampas de la ficción en *La historia de Mayta*."

21 See Vargas Llosa, *La utopía arcaica: José María Arguedas y las ficciones del indigenismo*. It should be noted that this work does not represent a sudden break in Vargas Llosa's thinking about Arguedas. Rather, his view of Arguedas's work has evolved from enthusiastic support in the 1960s, through a gradual distancing over the next two decades, to the more open criticism of *La utopía arcaica*, which casts Arguedas as an occasionally brilliant, but politically misguided, even manipulated, novelist.

22 For an illuminating analysis of the Uchuraccay report as well as its political and economic context, see Mayer, "Peru in Deep Trouble: Mario Vargas Llosa's 'Inquest in the Andes' Reexamined."

23 On Belaúnde's offer, see Lauer, *El sitio de la literatura: Escritores y política en el Perú del siglo xx*, 98, and Klarén, *Peru: Society and Nationhood in the Andes*, 399–400.

24 Vargas Llosa, "El nacimiento del Perú", "Latin America: Fiction and

Reality", "Novels Disguised as History: The Chronicles of the Birth of Peru", and "Questions of Conquest: What Columbus Wrought, and What He Did Not."

25 Vargas Llosa notes that in July of 1987 he was correcting the page proofs of *The Storyteller* on a beach in northern Peru when he heard of the government plan to nationalize the banks. He rushed back to Lima to organize opposition to the bank nationalization, and his leadership of this movement served as a prelude to his campaign for the presidency (*A Fish in the Water*, 27–28).

26 Degregori, *Elecciones 1990*, 71–132.

27 The other Commission members were jurist Abraham Guzmán Figueroa and journalist Mario Castro Arenas. They were advised by a team of anthropologists and linguists, as well as a psychoanalyst and another jurist. On the Commission's team of advisers see "Informe sobre Uchuraccay", 87–88.

28 A version of the report was published in English by the *New York Times* as "Inquest in the Andes."

29 On the Commission's visit to Uchuraccay, see Flores Galindo, *Buscando un Inca: Identidad y utopía en los Andes*, 329n and Mayer, "Peru in Deep Trouble", 205–206.

30 "La Comisión ha llegado a la *convicción absoluta* de que los comuneros . . . confundieron a los nueve forasteros que se aproximaban con un destacamento senderista" (Vargas Llosa, "Informe sobre Uchuraccay" 100).

31 "La Comisión tiene la *convicción relativa* de que los periodistas debieron ser atacados de improviso, masivamente, sin que mediara un diálogo previo" (Vargas Llosa, "Informe sobre Uchuraccay" 101).

32 Flores Galindo, *Buscando un Inca*, 329n. Mayer claims that the Commission was given only some of the photographs captured by the police, and that others, the ones which created problems for the Commission's mistaken identity theory, were leaked later ("Peru in Deep Trouble" 184). He does not, however, explain why and by whom (presumably the police) the photos were first withheld and then leaked.

33 Vargas Llosa, "Historia de una matanza", *Contra viento y marea III*, 187–188.

34 "Ciertos indicios, por las características de las heridas sufridas por las víctimas y la manera como éstas fueron enteradas, de un crimen que a la vez que político-social, pudo encerrar matices mágico-religiosos" (Vargas Llosa, "Informe sobre Uchuraccay" 125).

35 "Las lesiones de los cadáveres descritas por la autopsia apuntan a *una cierta coincidencia* con estas creencias" (Vargas Llosa, "Informe sobre Uchuraccay" 126, my emphasis).

36 Vargas Llosa, "Informe sobre Uchuraccay", 124.

37 Mayer, "Peru in Deep Trouble", 205.

38 See the discussion of the two Peru theory in Mayer, "Peru in Deep Trouble", 191–194. Mayer argues that Vargas Llosa misappropriates the term deep Peru, coined in the 1940s by historian Jorge Basadre. Basadre made a distinction between legal Peru, consisting of the state, and deep Peru, which referred to the nation composed of its people. As Mayer notes, "For Basadre, profound aspects of a people's sense of nationhood are present among all sectors of the

population" (192). The distinction is akin to the more contemporary one between the state and civil society. Vargas Llosa, on the other hand, reserves the term deep Peru for indigenous peoples exclusively, while official Peru encompasses everyone else, that is, all non-indigenous Spanish-speaking citizens.

39 For a lucid account of such participation in the nineteenth century, see Mallon, *Peasant and Nation*.

40 Mayer, "Peru in Deep Trouble", 187.

41 *Ibid.*, 193.

42 Vargas Llosa, "Questions of Conquest", 48.

43 *Ibid.*, 49.

44 *Ibid.*, 51.

45 Mariscal, *Contradictory Subjects*, 67.

46 *Ibid.*, 96.

47 Vargas Llosa, "Questions of Conquest", 51.

48 *Ibid.*, 52–53.

49 Vilas, "Participation, Inequality, and the Whereabouts of Democracy", 21–22. See also Robinson, who notes that "with few exceptions, neoliberal adjustment results in a fall in popular consumption and social conditions, a rise in poverty, immiseration, and insecurity, 'food riots,' heightened inequalities, social polarization and resultant political conflict" (*A Theory of Global Capitalism* 80).

50 Degregori, *Elecciones 1990*, 126.

51 Doris Sommer, "About-Face: The Talker Turns", 127.

52 Degregori, *Elecciones 1990*, 116.

53 See Fins, "Missionization and the Machiguenga", 24–27.

54 Vargas Llosa, *The Storyteller*, 26.

55 Vargas Llosa opens and closes "Questions of Conquest" by fondly remembering his teacher Porras Barrenechea.

56 "In the new Peru, infused with the science of Marx and Mariátegui, the Amazonian tribes would, at one and the same time, be able to adopt modern ways and to preserve their essential traditions and customs within the mosaic of cultures that would go to make up the future civilization of Peru. Did we really believe that socialism would insure the integrity of our magico-religious cultures? Wasn't there already sufficient evidence that industrial development, whether capitalist or communist, inevitably meant the annihilation of those cultures? Was there one exception anywhere in the world to this terrible, inexorable law? Thinking it over – in the light of the years that have since gone by, and from the vantage point of this broiling-hot Firenze – we were as unrealistic and romantic as Mascarita with his archaic, anti-historical utopia" (Vargas Llosa, *The Storyteller* 78).

57 Joaquín Barriales, *Matsigenka* and Vicente de Cenitagoya, *Los machiguengas*.

58 Rowe, "Liberalism and Authority", 60.

59 "Ever since my unsuccessful attempts in the early sixties at writing about the Machiguenga storytellers, the subject had never been far from my mind. . . . Why, in the course of all those years, had I been unable to write my story

about the storytellers? The answer I used to offer myself, each time I threw the half-finished manuscript of that elusive story into the wastebasket, was the difficulty of inventing, in Spanish and within a logically consistent intellectual framework, a literary form that would suggest, with any reasonable degree of credibility, how a primitive man with a magico-religious mentality would go about telling a story. All my attempts led each time to the impasse of a style that struck me as glaringly false" (Vargas Llosa, *The Storyteller* 156–158).

60   Davis, "Mario Vargas Llosa and Reality's Revolution: *El hablador*", 141, Snook, "Reading and Writing for Meaning: Narrative and Biography in *El hablador*", 68.
61   Vargas Llosa, *The Storyteller*, 240.
62   Fornet, "Dos novelas peruanas", 61–62.
63   Calabrese argues that "the mediation of the anthropologist/*hablador* is a fundamental strategy to keep the reader from questioning this appropriation of the voice of the 'other'" ("*El hablador* de Vargas Llosa: o, La imposibilidad de la utopía" 57).
64   Booker, Vargas Llosa Among the Postmodernists, 132.
65   *Ibid.*, 138.
66   Volek, "*El hablador* de Vargas Llosa: Del realismo mágico a la postmodernidad", 96.
67   Vargas Llosa, *The Storyteller*, 151.
68   O'Bryan-Knight, *The Story of the Storyteller* 134.
69   For more on Machiguenga ethnographic sources and Vargas Llosa's use of them, see Sá, "Perverse Tribute: Mario Vargas Llosa's *El hablador* and its Machiguenga Sources."
70   Vargas Llosa, *The Storyteller*, 94.
71   Miller argues that twentieth-century Latin American intellectuals have rarely lived up to this self-image and have generally played a more marginal role in their societies (*In the Shadow of the State: Intellectuals and the Quest for National Identity in Twentieth Century Spanish America* 43–94).
72   On the traditional role of the *letrado*, see Rama, *La ciudad letrada*. Note, however, that Miller argues that Rama exaggerates the role of twentieth-century Latin American intellectuals (*In the Shadow of the State* 134). On the erosion of the *letrado*'s authority in the late twentieth century, especially the changes experienced by the authors of the 1960s "Boom" in Latin American literature, including Vargas Llosa, see Franco, "What's Left of the Intelligentsia? The Uncertain Future of the Printed Word."
73   Fornet, "Dos novelas peruanas", 62.
74   Since losing the 1990 elections, Vargas Llosa has withdrawn from formal participation in the political arena (though he still writes political essays) and has become "more pessimistic about the possibilities of political action" (Kristal, *Temptation of the Word* 186).
75   For Vargas Llosa's response to the proposed bank nationalization, which he considered a threat to freedom, see his "Hacia el Perú totalitario" and "Frente a la amenaza totalitaria" in *Contra viento y marea III (1964–1988)*, 417–422.
76   See Bulmer Thomas, *The New Economic Model in Latin America and its*

Impact on Income Distribution and Poverty. See also Vilas, "Participation, Inequality, and the Whereabouts of Democracy."

77 For the campaign slogan, see Degregori, *Elecciones 1990*, 75. On the unregulated, "informal" black market economy as a free-market model for the national economy, see Vargas Llosa's foreword to de Soto's *The Other Path*, xiii–xxvii.

78 Degregori, *Elecciones 1990*, 73–74.

79 Vargas Llosa, *A Fish in the Water*, 514.

80 Richmond Ellis, "The Inscription of Masculinity and Whiteness in the Autobiography of Mario Vargas Llosa", 233.

81 Sarlo, "Aesthetics and Postpolitics: From Fujimori to the Gulf War", 251–252.

82 Degregori, *Elecciones 1990*, 111, 118.

83 Rosaldo, *Culture and Truth*, 70.

84 Steele, "*El hablador*, reseña", 365–366.

85 Vargas Llosa, *Contra viento y marea* III, 231.

86 For the argument that the Shining Path was not an indigenous movement, see Degregori, *Qué difícil es ser Dios: Ideología y violencia política en Sendero Luminoso.* On the Shining Path's hostility to indigenous Andean culture, see Mayer, "Peru in Deep Trouble", 196.

87 Vargas Llosa, *Death in the Andes*, 5.

88 See, for example, his *¿Quién mató a Palomino Molero? / Who Killed Palomino Molero?*

89 Vargas Llosa, *Death in the Andes*, 45.

90 Figueroa, "El regreso del Cabo Lituma", 42.

91 Vargas Llosa, *Death in the Andes*, 155.

92 Figueroa, "El regreso del Cabo Lituma", 42; Kristal, *Temptation of the Word*, 194; Penuel, "Intertextuality and the Theme of Violence in Vargas Llosa's *Lituma en los Andes*", 443.

93 For more on *pishtaco* tales, particularly contemporary versions, see Ansión, *Pishtacos: De verdugos a sacaojos.* On the resurgence of the belief in *pishtacos* during the Shining Path war, see Manrique, *El tiempo del miedo: La violencia política en el Perú 1980–1996*, 293–303. For a particularly illuminating interpretation of the meanings and significance of the *pishtaco* figure in the Andean region, see Weismantel, *Cholas and Pishtacos*, 4–16, 193–213.

94 Vargas Llosa, *Death in the Andes*, 158.

95 *Ibid.*, 153.

96 *Ibid.*, 176.

97 Sommer, *Foundational Fictions.*

98 While the Shining Path's political program and ideology have little or nothing in common with indigenous cultures, with the group's top leadership made up of *mestizo* intellectuals, still the guerrilla group attracted the support of thousands of indigenous men and women who fought in its ranks.

99 Figueroa, "El regreso del Cabo Lituma",41.

100 Penuel, "Intertextuality and the Theme of Violence in Vargas Llosa's *Lituma en los Andes*", 458; Figueroa, "El regreso del Cabo Lituma", 41; Kristal, *Temptation of the Word*, 188–189.

101 My translation of "¿En que momento se había jodido el Perú?", *Conversación en La Catedral*, 13. Rabassa's version is "At what precise moment had Peru fucked itself up?" *Conversation in The Cathedral*, 3.

Epilogue   More than Skin Deep? Social Change in Contemporary Peru

1 Roncalla, "¿Hablan los Apus?" 1.

2 Silverman, "Touring Ancient Times", 882. See also the report of the event in *Caretas*, "¡Apúrate! Decían los Apus", 2 de agosto de 2001.

3 De la Cadena, *Indigenous Mestizos*, 29–34. See also de la Cadena, "Reconstructing Race", 22–23.

4 Though de la Cadena does not note the parallel, this attitude seems to echo Arguedas's comments about the *mestizo* in his 1939 article "Entre el kechwa y el castellano, la angustia del mestizo", quoted above in chapter 2.

5 De la Cadena, "The Marketing of *El Cholo* Toledo", 20.

6 *Ibid.*, 21.

7 Again, though de la Cadena does not note it, Toledo's image seems to echo Arguedas's enthusiasm for capitalist modernization in some of his anthropological articles of the 1950s, particularly "Evolución de las comunidades indígenas. El Valle del Mantaro y la ciudad de Huancayo" (1957).

8 *Notisur*, "Peru: Unions Protest Economic Policies of President Alejandro Toledo." Ratings – June 2004, 7%; August 2004, 12%; September 2004, 15%. Results from Datum(www.datum.com) and CPI (Compañía Peruana de Estudios de Mercados y Opinión Públicia, www.cdi.com).

9 Toledo Brückmann, "El 94% contra Alejandro Toledo."

10 *Notisur*, "Peru: Critics Call for Action as President Alejandro Toledo Completes First 100 Days in Office" and "Peru: Unions Protest Economic Policies of President Alejandro Toledo." Forero, "President of Peru is Dogged by Scandals as Calls to Resign Grow", A9. *BBC News*, "Peru's Leader Slashes Salary."

11 *Notisur*, "Peru: Vice President Raúl Diez Canseco Resigns" and "Peru: President Alejandro [sic] Marks First Anniversary."

12 The most notable of these have been repeated strikes by peasant farmers, health care workers, and teachers demanding the pay raises Toledo had promised during his presidential campaign, as well as the June 2002 popular uprising in Arequipa provoked by the president's attempt to privatize two electric power companies that he had promised to keep public during his presidential campaign. The government's heavy-handed attempts to deal with such energetic opposition have included declarations of states emergency and suspensions of constitutional protections and have led to the death of several protesters. *Notisur*, "Peru: Unions Protest Economic Policies of President Alejandro Toledo." *Caretas*, "Escuchando con ira", "Lecciones de una huelga", and "Estado de emergencia. Lo que se veía venir." Forero, "Peruvians Riot Over Planned Sale of 2 Regional Power Plants", A3. *The New York Times*, "Troops and Police Clash With Protesters as Unrest Grows in Peru", A9.

13 *Notisur*, "Peru: Cabinet Resignations Continue, New Prime Minister Appointed." Forero, "President of Peru is Dogged by Scandals as Calls to

Resign Grow", A9. *The New York Times*, "Peru Leader Voices 'Disappointment' in Scandal; Not Enough, Opponents Say", A8. *Caretas*, "Operación Wantan."

14 Wurgaft, "Eliane Karp, el 'talón de Aquiles' de Alejandro Toledo; La esposa del presidente está acusada de tráfico de influencias y enriquecimiento ilícito."

15 *The Washington Post*, "Peruvian President Defends Wife's Bank Contract", A24. *El mundo*, "La primera dama de Perú deja su trabajo en un banco vinculado a Vladimiro Montesinos."

16 Forero, "President of Peru is Dogged by Scandals as Calls to Resign Grow", A9. *Caretas*, "¿El último 28?" and "Examen de Resonancia – Patética."

17 María Elena García and José Antonio Lucero, "*Un País Sin Indígenas?*: Rethinking Indigenous Politics in Peru."

18 Manrique, "Modernity and Alternative Development in the Andes", 239.

19 This idea of Manrique's appears to bear some resemblance to de la Cadena's theorization of the indigenous *mestizo*.

20 Manrique, "Modernity and Alternative Development in the Andes", 240.

21 Manrique's explanations in many respects echo those suggested by Montoya, *Multiculturalidad y política*, 155–160.

22 Gelles, "Andean Culture, Indigenous Identity, and the State in Peru," 249–250.

23 De la Cadena, *Indigenous Mestizos*, 325; García, "The Politics of Community", 73; Gelles, "Andean Culture, Indigenous Identity, and the State in Peru," 247.

24 Montoya, *Multiculturalidad y política*, 171.

25 "Pueden haber excelentes proyectos de revaloración y afirmación cultural indígenas, pero si no se cuestiona el poder, si no se ofrece una alternativa a la política de reestructuración del capitalismo de hoy, los problemas de fondo no se resolverán" (Montoya, *Multiculturalidad y política* 173).

26 "Obviamente no es Arguedas quien puede poner en práctica la transculturación peruana; ... la literatura operó para él como *el modelo reducido de la transculturación*, donde se podía mostrar y probar la eventualidad de su realización de tal modo que si era posible en la literatura también podía ser posible en el resto de la cultura. Arguedas, por no ser gobierno, ni poder político, ni revolución, no puede ubicar en su mejor vía al proceso de la transculturación; en cambio hace lo que sí puede o cree poder hacer, apelando a todas sus energías: mostrar la transculturación en la literatura narrativa" (Rama, *Transculturación narrativa* 202).

27 Franco, "What's Left of the Intelligentsia?" 198.

28 *Ibid.*, 197.

29 *Ibid.*, 203.

30 See for example the novels *La otra cara* (1992) and *El retorno de los Mayas* (1998) by Mayan author Gaspar Pedro González. For more on the Maya cultural rights movement in Guatemala, see Kay Warren, *Indigenous Movements and Their Critics: Pan-Maya Activism in Guatemala* and Edward F. Fischer and R. Mckenna Brown, eds. *Maya Cultural Activism in Guatemala*.

BIBLIOGRAPHY

Adorno, Rolena. *Guaman Poma: Writing and Resistance in Colonial Peru*. Second edition. Austin: University of Texas Press, 2000.

Aldaz, Anna-Marie. *The Past of the Future: The Novelistic Cycle of Manuel Scorza*. New York: Peter Lang, 1990.

Alegría, Ciro. *Broad and Alien is the World*. New York: Farrar & Rinehart, 1941.

———. *El mundo es ancho y ajeno*. Caracas: Biblioteca Ayacucho, 1978 [1941].

———. *Mucha suerte con harto palo: memorias*. Ordenamiento, prólogo y notas de Dora Varona. Buenos Aires: Editorial Losada, 1976.

Alonso, Carlos. "*Rama y sus retoños*: Figuring the Nineteenth Century in Spanish America." *Revista de Estudios Hispánicos* 28 (1994): 283–292.

Andreu, Alicia. "Legitimidad literaria y legitimidad socio-económica en el relato de Julio Ramón Ribeyro." *Revista de Crítica Literaria Latinoamericana* 20.39 (1994): 169–176.

Ansión, Juan, ed. *Pishtacos: De verdugos a sacaojos*. Lima: Tarea, 1989.

Archibald, Priscilla. "Andean Anthropology in the Era of Development Theory," in *José María Arguedas: Reconsiderations for Latin American Cultural Studies*. Eds. Ciro A. Sandoval and Sandra M. Boschetto-Sandoval. Athens, OH: Ohio University Center for International Studies, 1998. 3–34.

Arguedas, José María. *The Fox from Up Above and the Fox from Down Below*. Trans. Frances Horning Barraclough. Pittsburgh: University of Pittsburgh Press, 2000.

———. *El zorro de arriba y el zorro de abajo*. Edición crítica de Eve-Marie Fell. México, D.F.: Colección Archivos, 1992 [1971].

———. "No soy un aculturado." *El zorro de arriba y el zorro de abajo*. México: Colección Archivos, 1992. 256–258.

———. *Indios, mestizos y señores*. Ed. Sybila Arredondo de Arguedas. Lima: Editorial Horizonte, 1989.

———. *Señores e indios: acerca de la cultura quechua*. Ed. Angel Rama. Montevideo: Arca/Calicanto, 1976.

———. "Conversando con Arguedas." *Recopilación de textos sobre José María Arguedas*. Juan Larco, ed. Havana: Casa de las Américas, 1976. 21–30.

———. *Formación de una cultura nacional indoamericana*. Ed. Angel Rama. México: Siglo XXI, 1989 [1975].

Bibliography

———. Trans. *Dioses y hombres de Huarochirí*. México, D.F.: Siglo XXI, 1975.

———. *Todas las sangres*. Buenos Aires: Editorial Losada, 1973 [1964].

———. *Los ríos profundos*. Edición de Ricardo González Vigíl. Madrid: Cátedra, 1995 [1958].

———. *Deep Rivers*. Trans. Frances Horning Barraclough. Austin: University of Texas Press, 1978.

———. No title. *Cultura y pueblo* 1.1 (enero-marzo 1964): 1.

———. *El Sexto*. Lima: Editorial Mejía Baca, 1961.

———. "Incorporación del toro a la cultura indígena. El interesante caso de la conversión del amaru," *Trilce* (Quincenario cultural peruano), Lima, Vol. 1 (2a quincena VI-1951): 3–4, 10.

———. "La novela y el problema de la expresión literaria en el Perú," in *Yawar fiesta*. Lima: Editorial Horizonte (1980) 7–17. Originally published in *Mar del sur 9*, Lima (enero-febrero de 1950): 66–72.

———. "Los ríos profundos. Novela inédita." *Tradición* año II, vol. III, núms. 7–10 (enero-agosto 1951): 83–86

———. "El zumbayllu." *Letras Peruanas* año I, núm. 1 (junio 1951): 4–5, 29.

———. "Los ríos profundos." *Las Moradas* vol. II, núm. 4 (1948): 53–59.

———. *Yawar Fiesta*. Trans. Frances Horning Barraclough. Austin: University of Texas Press, 1985.

———. *Yawar fiesta*. Lima: Editorial Horizonte, 1980 [1941].

———. *Canto kechwa. Con un ensayo sobre la capacidad de creación artística del pueblo indio y mestizo*. Lima: Ediciones "Club del Libro Peruano," 1938.

Arguedas, José María, and Francisco Izquierdo Ríos. *Mitos, leyendas y cuentos peruanos*. Lima: Ministerio de Educación Pública, 1947.

Barriales, Joaquín. *Matsigenka*. Lima: Secretariado de Misiones Dominicanas, 1977.

Basadre, Jorge. *Perú: problema y posibilidad*. Segunda edición. Lima: Banco Internacional del Perú, 1978 [1931].

BBC News. "Peru's Leader Slashes Salary." July 7, 2003. <http://news.bbc.co.uk/go/pr/fr/-/1/hi/world/americas/3051689.stm>.

Béjar, Héctor. *Peru 1965: Apuntes sobre una experiencia guerrillera*. La Habana: Casa de las Américas, 1969.

Bensoussan, Albert. "Entrevista con Manuel Scorza." *Insula* 30.340 (1975): 1–4.

———. "Manuel Scorza: 'Yo viajo del mito a la realidad.'" *Crisis* 1.12 (1974): 40–42.

Beverley, John. *Subalternity and Representation: Arguments in Cultural Theory*. Durham: Duke University Press, 1999.

———. *Against Literature*. Minneapolis: University of Minnesota Press, 1993.

Beverley, John and Marc Zimmerman. *Literature and Politics in the Central American Revolutions*. Austin: University of Texas Press, 1990.

Blanco, Hugo. *Tierra o muerte: Las luchas campesinas en Perú*. 2ª edición. México, D.F.: Siglo Veintiuno, 1974.

Bonilla, Heraclio, ed. *Perú en el fin del milenio*. México, D.F.: Consejo Nacional para la Cultura y las Artes, 1994.

Booker, M. Keith. *Vargas Llosa Among the Postmodernists*. Gainesville: University Press of Florida, 1994.

Bibliography

Bradu, Fabienne. "Scorza: entre la desilusión y la polémica." *Revista de la Universidad de México* 33.8 (1979): 49–51.

Bryce Echenique, Alfredo. *La historia personal de mis libros.* Lima: Fondo Editorial del Congreso del Perú, 2000.

———. *Un mundo para Julius.* Lima: PEISA, 1997 [1970].

———. *A World for Julius.* Trans. Dick Gerdes. Austin: University of Texas Press, 1994.

———. "Confesiones sobre el arte de vivir y escribir novelas." *Cuadernos Hispanoamericanos* 417 (1985): 65–76.

Bueno, Raúl. "Sobre la heterogeneidad literaria y cultural de América Latina,"in *Asedios a la heterogeneidad: Libro de homenaje a Antonio Cornejo Polar.* Eds. José Antonio Mazzotti y U. Juan Zevallos Aguilar. Philadelphia: Asociación Internacional de Peruanistas, 1996. 21–36.

Bulmer Thomas, Victor, ed. *The New Economic Model in Latin America and its Impact on Income Distribution and Poverty.* New York: St. Martin's Press, 1996.

Calabrese, Elisa. "El hablador de Vargas Llosa: o, la imposibilidad de la utopía." *Discurso Literario: Revista de Estudios Iberoamericanos* 10.2 (1993): 53–62.

Cardoso, Fernando Henrique and Enzo Faletto. *Dependency and Development in Latin America.* Berkeley: University of California Press, 1979.

Caretas. "¿El último 28?" Edición Nº 1833. 26 de julio de 2004. <http://www.caretas.com.pe/2004/1833/articulos/toledo.html>

———. "Examen de resonancia – Patética." Edición Nº 1833. 26 de julio de 2004. <http://www.caretas.com.pe/2004/1833/articulos/editorial.html>

———. "Operación Wantan." Edición Nº 1807. 22 de enero de 2004. <http://www.caretas.com.pe/2004/1807/articulos/almeyda.html>

———. "Estado de emergencia. Lo que se veía venir." Edición Nº 1774. 29 de mayo de 2003. <http://www.caretas.com.pe/2003/1774/ articulos/ mensaje. html>

———. "Lecciones de una huelga." Edición Nº 1772. 15 de mayo de 2003. <http://www.caretas.com.pe/2003/1772/articulos/ayzanoa.html>

———. "¡Apúrate! Decían los Apus." Edición Nº 1681. 2 de agosto de 2001. <http://www.caretas.com.pe/2001/1681/articulos/toledo.html>

Castañeda, Jorge. *Compañero: The Life and Death of Che Guevara.* New York: Alfred A. Knopf, 1997.

Castro Klarén, Sara. *El mundo mágico de José María Arguedas.* Lima: IEP, 1973.

Castro Pozo, Hildebrando. *Nuestra comunidad indígena.* Lima: Perugraph Editores, 1979 [1924].

Cenitagoya, Vicente de. *Los machiguengas.* Lima: Sanmarti y Cia., [1944?]

Comisión de la Verdad y Reconciliación. *Informe final.* 2003. <http://www. cverdad.org.pe/pagina01.php>

Congrains Martín, Enrique. *No una sino muchas muertes.* Barcelona: Planeta, 1975 [1958].

Contreras, Carlos, and Marcos Cueto. *Historia del Perú contemporáneo.* Lima: Red para el Desarrollo de las Ciencias Sociales en el Perú, 1999.

Cornejo Polar, Antonio. *Los universos narrativos de José María Arguedas.* Segunda edición. Lima: Editorial Horizonte, 1997 [1973].

Bibliography

———. "Mestizaje e hibridez: los riesgos de las metáforas." *Revista Iberoamericana*. 63.180 (1997): 341–344.

———. "Una heterogeneidad no dialéctica: sujeto y discurso migrantes en el Perú moderno." *Revista Iberoamericana*. 62.176–177 (1996): 837–844.

———. "Estudio preliminar." *José María Arguedas: antología comentada*. Ed. Antonio Cornejo Polar. Lima: Biblioteca Nacional del Peru, 1996. 11–44.

———. *Escribir en el aire: ensayo sobre la heterogeneidad socio-cultural en las literaturas andinas*. Lima: Editorial Horizonte, 1994.

———. *La novela peruana*. Lima: Editorial Horizonte, 1989.

———. "Sobre el 'neoindigenismo' y las novelas de Manuel Scorza." *Revista Iberoamericana* 50.127 (1984): 549–557.

———. "Manuel Scorza: señas para trazar un contexto." *Quehacer* 28 (1984): 104–107.

———. *La cultura nacional: Problema y posibilidad*. Lima: Lluvia editores, 1981.

———. "El indigenismo y las literaturas heterogéneas: su doble estatuto socio-cultural." *Revista de Crítica Literaria Latinoamericana* 4.7–8 (1978): 7–21.

Coronil, Fernando. "Transculturation and the Politics of Theory: Countering the Center, Cuban Counterpoint." Fernando Ortiz. *Cuban Counterpoint: Tobacco and Sugar*. Trans. Harriet de Onís. Durham: Duke University Press, 1995.

Cotler, Julio. *Clases, estado y nación en el Perú*. Lima: Instituto de Estudios Peruanos, 1978.

D'Allemand, Patricia. *Latin American Cultural Criticism: Re-Interpreting a Continent*. Lewiston, NY: The Edwin Mellen Press, 2000.

Davis, Mary E. "Mario Vargas Llosa and Reality's Revolution: El hablador." *Literature and Revolution*. Ed. David Bevan. Amsterdam: Rodopi, 1989. 135-144.

Degregori, Carlos Iván. "El aprendiz de brujo y el curandero chino: etnicidad, modernidad y ciudadanía," in *Elecciones 1990, demonios y redentores en el nuevo Perú: una tragedia en dos vueltas*. Ed. Carlos Iván Degregori y Romeo Grompone. Lima: IEP, 1991. 70–132.

———. *El surgimiento de Sendero Luminoso : Ayacucho 1969–1979*. Lima: Instituto de Estudios Peruanos, 1990.

———. *Qué difícil es ser Dios : ideología y violencia política en Sendero Luminoso*. Lima: El Zorro de Abajo Ediciones, 1989.

Degregori, Carlos Iván, and Romeo Grompone, eds. *Elecciones 1990, demonios y redentores en el nuevo Perú: una tragedia en dos vueltas*. Lima: IEP, 1991.

Degregori, Carlos Iván, Cecilia Blondet y Nicolás Lynch. *Conquistadores de un nuevo mundo: de invasores a ciudadanos en San Martín de Porres*. Lima: Instituto de Estudios Peruanos, 1986.

De la Cadena, Marisol. "Reconstructing Race: Racism, Culture and Mestizaje in Latin America." *NACLA Report on the Americas* 34.6 (May/June 2001): 16–23.

———. "The Marketing of *El Cholo* Toledo." *NACLA Report on the Americas* 34.6 (May/June 2001): 20–21.

———. *Indigenous Mestizos: The Politics of Race and Culture in Cuzco, Peru, 1919–1991*. Durham: Duke University Press, 2000.

Bibliography

De la Fuente, José Luis. *Cómo leer a Alfredo Bryce Echenique*. Madrid: Ediciones Júcar, 1994.

De Soto, Hernando. *El otro sendero*. Lima: Editorial El Barranco, 1986.

Dorfman, Ariel. *Some Write to the Future: Essays on Contemporary Latin American Fiction*. Durham: Duke University Press, 1991.

Duncan, J. Ann. "Language as Protagonist: Tradition and Innovation in *Un mundo para Julius*." *Forum for Modern Language Studies* 16.2 (1980): 120–135.

Duviols, Pierre. "Francisco de Ávila, extirpador de la idolatría: Estudio biobibliográfico." José Maria Arguedas. Trans. *Dioses y hombres de Huarochirí*. México, D.F.: Siglo XXI, 1975. 151–175.

Ellis, Robert Richmond. "The Inscription of Masculinity and Whiteness in the Autobiography of Mario Vargas Llosa." *Bulletin of Latin American Research* 17.2 (1998): 223–236.

Elmore, Peter. *El perfil de la palabra: La obra de Julio Ramón Ribeyro*. Lima: Fondo Editorial de la Pontificia Universidad Católica del Perú, 2002.

———. *Los muros invisibles: Lima y la modernidad en la novela del siglo XX*. Lima: Mosca Azul Editores, 1993.

———. "Imágenes literarias de la modernidad, entre *Conversación en la Catedral* de Vargas Llosa y *El zorro de arriba y el zorro de abajo* de Arguedas." *Márgenes* 2 (1987): 23–42.

Escajadillo, Tomás G. *La narrativa indigenista peruana*. Lima: Amaru Editores, 1994.

———. "Scorza antes del ultimo combate." *Hispamérica* 19.55 (1990): 50–72.

———. *Alegría y El mundo es ancho y ajeno*. Lima, Perú : Instituto de Investigaciones Humanísticas, Universidad Nacional Mayor de San Marcos, 1983.

Escobar, Alberto. *Arguedas o la utopía de la lengua*. Lima: IEP, 1984.

Escobar, Arturo. *Encountering Development: The Making and Unmaking of the Third World*. Princeton: Princeton University Press, 1995.

Figueroa, Armando. "El regreso del Cabo Lituma: Dos mundos andinos vistos por Mario Vargas Llosa." *Quimera* 122 (1994): 40–44.

Fins, Stephanie. "Missionization and the Machiguenga." *Cultural Survival Quarterly* 7.3 (1983): 24–27.

Fischer, Edward F. and R. McKenna Brown, eds. *Maya Cultural Activism in Guatemala*. Austin University of Texas Press, 1996.

Flores Galindo, Alberto. *Buscando un Inca: Identidad y utopía en los Andes*. 4ª edición. Lima: Editorial Horizonte, 1994 [1986].

———. *Obras completas*. Lima: SUR, 1994.

———. *Dos ensayos sobre José María Arguedas*. Lima: SUR, 1992.

Flores Galindo, Alberto and Manuel Burga. *Apogeo y crisis de la República Aristocrática*. In Alberto Flores Galindo, *Obras completas II*. Lima: SUR, 1994. 15–364.

Flores Galindo, Alberto and Denis Sulmont. *El movimiento obrero en la industria pesquera. El caso de Chimbote*. Lima: Programa Académico de Ciencias Sociales de la Pontificia Universidad Católica del Perú, Taller Urbano Industrial, 1972.

Forero, Juan. "President of Peru is Dogged by Scandals as Calls to Resign Grow." *New York Times*, February 12, 2004. A9.

———. "Peruvians Riot Over Planned Sale of 2 Regional Power Plants." *New York Times*, June 18, 2002. A3.

Forgues, Roland, ed. *José María Arguedas, La letra inmortal. Correspondencia con Manuel Moreno Jimeno*. Lima: Ediciones de Los Ríos Profundos, 1993.

———. *La estrategia mítica de Manuel Scorza*. Lima: CEDEP, 1991.

Fornet, Jorge. "Dos novelas peruanas: entre sapos y halcones." *Plural* 22.263 (1993): 57–62.

Franco, Jean. *The Decline and Fall of the Lettered City: Latin America in the Cold War*. Cambridge, MA: Harvard University Press, 2002.

———. *Critical Passions: Selected Essays*. Ed. Mary Louise Pratt and Kathleen Newman. Durham: Duke University Press, 1999.

———. "What's Left of the Intelligentsia? The Uncertain Future of the Printed Word." *Critical Passions: Selected Essays*. Ed. Mary Louise Pratt and Kathleen Newman. Durham: Duke University Press, 1999. 196–207.

———. "From Modernization to Resistance: Latin American Literature, 1959–1976." *Critical Passions: Selected Essays*. Ed. Mary Louise Pratt and Kathleen Newman. Durham: Duke University Press, 1999. 285–310.

———. "Self-Destructing Heroines." *Critical Passions: Selected Essays*. Ed. Mary Louise Pratt and Kathleen Newman. Durham: Duke University Press, 1999. 366–378.

———. "¿La historia de quién? La piratería postmoderna." *Revista de Crítica Literaria Latinoamericana* 33 (1991): 11–20.

García, María Elena. "The Politics of Community: Education, Indigenous Rights, and Ethnic Mobilization in Peru." *Latin American Perspectives* 30.1 (January 2003): 70–95.

García, María Elena and José Antonio Lucero. "*Un País Sin Indígenas?*: Re-thinking Indigenous Politics in Peru," in *The Struggle for Indigenous Rights in Latin America*. Eds. Nancy Grey Postero and Leon Zamosc. Brighton and Portland: Sussex Academic Press, 2004. 158–188.

Gazzolo, Ana María. "La corriente mítica en *El zorro de arriba y el zorro de abajo* de José María Arguedas." *Cuadernos Hispanoamericanos* 469–70 (1989): 43–72.

———. "Lo femenino en *El zorro de arriba y el zorro de abajo*." *Cuadernos Hispanoamericanos* 536 (1995): 93–101.

Gelles, Paul H. "Andean Culture, Indigenous Identity, and the State in Peru," in *The Politics of Ethnicity: Indigenous Peoples in Latin American States*. Ed. David Maybury-Lewis. Cambridge, MA: Harvard University David Rockefeller Center for Latin American Studies, 2002. 239–266.

Golte, Jürgen y Norma Adams. *Los caballos de Troya de los invasores: estrategias campesinas en la conquista de la gran Lima*. Lima: Instituto de Estudios Peruanos, 1987.

González, Gaspar Pedro. *La otra cara (La vida de un Maya)*. Rancho Palos Verdes, CA: Fundación Yax Te', 1998 [1992].

———. *El retorno de los Mayas*. Ciudad de Guatemala: Fundación Myrna Mack, 1998.

Bibliography

González Prada, Manuel. *Páginas libres / Horas de lucha*. Caracas: Biblioteca Ayacucho, 1976.

González Vigíl, Ricardo. "Introducción." *Los ríos profundos*. Madrid: Cátedra, 1995 [1958]. 9–108.

Gorriti, Gustavo. *The Shining Path: a history of the millenarian war in Peru*. Trans. Robin Kirk. Chapel Hill: University of North Carolina Press, 1999.

Gunder Frank, Andre. *Capitalism and Underdevelopment in Latin America: Historical Studies of Chile and Brazil*. New York: Monthly Review Press, 1967.

Gutiérrez, Miguel. *La generación del 50: un mundo dividido*. Lima: Labrusa, 1988.

———. "Estructura e ideología de *Todas las sangres*." *Revista de Crítica Literaria Latinoamericana* 6.12 (1980): 139–176.

Handelman, Howard. *Struggle in the Andes: Peasant Political Mobilization in Peru*. Austin: University of Texas Press, 1975.

Haya de la Torre, Víctor Raúl. *El antimperialismo y el APRA*. 4ta edición. Lima: Biblioteca Amauta, 1982 [1936].

Herskovits, Melville J. *Acculturation: The Study of Culture Contact*. New York: J.J. Augustin Publisher, 1938.

———. *Man and His Works: The Science of Cultural Anthropology*. New York: Alfred A. Knopf, 1948.

Higgins, James. *Cambio social y constantes humanas: La narrativa corta de Ribeyro*. Lima: Fondo Editorial de la Pontificia Universidad Católica del Perú, 1991.

Holmberg, Allan R., ed. *Vicos: Método y práctica de antropología aplicada*. Lima: Editorial Estudios Andinos, 1966.

Jacobsen, Nils. *Mirages of Transition: The Peruvian Altiplano, 1780–1930*. Berkeley: University of California Press, 1993.

Kapsoli, Wilfredo. *Los movimientos campesinos en el Perú*. Tercera edición. Lima: Ediciones Atusparia, 1987.

———. *Literatura e historia del Perú*. Lima: Editorial Lumen, 1986.

———. *El pensamiento de la Asociación Pro Indígena*. Cusco: Centro Las Casas, 1980.

———. *Los movimientos campesinos en Cerro de Pasco*. Huancayo: Instituto de Estudios Andinos, 1975.

Kay, Cristóbal. *Latin American Theories of Development and Under-development*. New York : Routledge, 1989.

Kirk, Robin. *Grabado en piedra : las mujeres de Sendero Luminoso*. Lima: Instituto de Estudios Peruanos, 1993.

Klarén, Peter. *Peru: Society and Nationhood in the Andes*. Oxford: Oxford University Press, 2000.

Kristal, Efraín. *Temptation of the Word: The Novels of Mario Vargas Llosa*. Nashville: Vanderbilt University Press, 1999.

———. *Una visión urbana de los Andes: Génesis y desarrollo del indigenismo en el Perú 1848–1930*. Lima: Instituto de Apoyo Agrario, 1991 [1989].

———. "Del indigenismo a la narrativa urbana en el Perú." *Revista de Crítica Literaria Latinoamericana* 14.27 (1988): 57–74.

Bibliography

Lambright, Anne. "Losing Ground: Some Notes on the Feminine in *El zorro de arriba y el zorro de abajo*." *Hispanófila* 122 (1998): 71–84.

Larco, Juan, ed. *Recopilación de textos sobre José María Arguedas*. Havana: Casa de las Américas, 1976.

Larson, Brooke. *Indígenas, élites y estado en la formación de las repúblicas andinas*. Lima: IEP, 2002.

Latham, Michael E. *Modernization as Ideology: American Social Science and "Nation Building" in the Kennedy Era*. Chapel Hill: The University of North Carolina Press, 2000.

Lauer, Mirko. *El sitio de la literatura: Escritores y política en el Perú del siglo xx*. Lima: Mosca Azul, 1989.

Lévano, César. *Arguedas: un sentimiento trágico de la vida*. Lima: Editorial Gráfica Labor, 1969.

Lienhard, Martin. "Voces marginadas y poder discursivo en América Latina." *Revista Iberoamericana* 66.193 (2000): 785–798.

———. *La voz y su huella: escritura y conflicto étnico-social en América Latina 1492–1988*. Hanover, NH: Ediciones del Norte, 1991.

———. "La 'andinización' del vanguardismo urbano," in José María Arguedas. *El zorro de arriba y el zorro de abajo*. Edición crítica de Eve-Marie Fell. Madrid: Colección Archivos, 1990. 321–332.

———. *Cultura andina y forma novelesca: zorros y danzantes en la última novela de Arguedas*. Segunda edición. Lima: Editorial Horizonte, 1990 [1981].

———. "La última novela de Arguedas: Imagen de un lector futuro." *Revista de Crítica Literaria Latinoamericana* 6.12 (1980): 177–96.

Linton, Ralph. *The Study of Man: An Introduction*. New York: Appleton-Century-Crofts, 1936.

López Albújar, Enrique. *Cuentos andinos*. Lima: Peisa, 1995 [1920].

López-Baralt, Mercedes. *Guaman Poma: autor y artista*. Lima: Pontificia Universidad Católica del Perú, 1993.

Losada Guido, Alejandro. *Creación y praxis: la producción literaria como praxis social en Hispanoamérica y el Perú*. Lima: Universidad Nacional Mayor de San Marcos, Dirección Universitaria de Biblioteca y Publicaciones, 1976.

Luchting, Wolfgang A. *Alfredo Bryce: humores y malhumores*. Lima: Milla Batres, 1975.

Mallon, Florencia. *Peasant and Nation: The Making of Postcolonial Mexico and Peru*. Berkeley: University of California Press, 1995.

Manrique, Nelson. *El tiempo del miedo: la violencia política en el Perú 1980–1996*. Lima: Fondo Editorial del Congreso del Perú, 2002.

———. "Modernity and Alternative Development in the Andes," in *Through the Kaleidoscope: The Experience of Modernity in Latin America*. Ed. Vivian Schelling. London: Verso, 2000. 219–47.

———. *La piel y la pluma: escritos sobre literatura, etnicidad y racismo*. Lima: SUR, 1999.

———. *Yawar mayu: sociedades terratenientes serranas 1879–1910*. Lima; DESCO, 1988.

Mariátegui, José Carlos. *7 ensayos de interpretación de la realidad peruana*. Sexagésima segunda edición. Lima: Biblioteca Amauta, 1995 [1928].

——. *Seven Interpretive Essays on Peruvian Reality*. Trans. Marjory Urquidi. Austin: University of Texas Press, 1988.

——. *Peruanicemos al Perú*. Lima: Biblioteca Amauta, 1988.

Mariscal, George. *Contradictory Subjects: Quevedo, Cervantes and Seventeenth Century Spanish Culture*. Ithaca: Cornell University Press, 1991.

Márquez, Ismael P. and César Ferreira, eds. *Asedios a Julio Ramón Ribeyro*. Lima: Fondo Editorial de la Pontificia Universidad Católica del Perú, 1996.

——. "Presentación," in *Asedios a Julio Ramón Ribeyro*. Eds. Ismael P. Márquez and César Ferreira. Lima: Fondo Editorial de la Pontificia Universidad Católica del Perú, 1996. 21–29.

——. *Los mundos de Alfredo Bryce Echenique*. Lima: Fondo Editorial de la Pontificia Universidad Católica del Perú, 1994.

Martin, Gerald. *Journeys Through the Labyrinth: Latin American Ficiton in the Twentieth Century*. New York: Verso, 1989.

——. "Mario Vargas Llosa: Errant Knight of the Liberal Imagination." *Modern Latin American Fiction: A Survey*. Ed. John King. London: Faber and Faber, 1987. 205–233.

Matos Mar, José. *Desborde popular y crisis del estado: el nuevo rostro del Perú en la década de 1980*. 7ta. edición. Lima: CONCYTEC, 1988.

Matos Mar, José y José Manuel Mejía. *La reforma agraria en el Perú*. Lima: Instituto de Estudios Peruanos, 1980.

Matto de Turner, Clorinda. *Aves sin nido*. México, D.F.: Editorial Oasis, 1981 [1889].

Maybury-Lewis, David, Ed. *The Politics of Ethnicity: Indigenous Peoples in Latin American States*. Cambridge, MA: Harvard University David Rockefeller Center for Latin American Studies, 2002.

Mayer, Enrique. "Peru in Deep Trouble: Mario Vargas Llosa's 'Inquest in the Andes' Reexamined." *Rereading Cultural Anthropology*. Ed. George E. Marcus. Durham: Duke University Press, 1992. 181–219.

Mejía, Gustavo. "Veinticinco años de *Un mundo para Julius*." *Cuadernos Hispanoamericanos* 548 (1996): 167–171.

Melis, Antonio. *Leyendo Mariátegui, 1967–1998*. Lima: Biblioteca Amauta, 1999.

Miller, Nicola. *In the Shadow of the State: Intellectuals and the Quest for National Identity in Twentieth Century Spanish America*. London: Verso, 1999.

Montoya, Rodrigo. *Multiculturalidad y política: Derechos indígenas, ciudadanos y humanos*. Lima: SUR, 1998.

——. *Al borde del naufragio: democracia, violencia y problema étnico en el Perú*. Lima: SUR, 1992.

——. *Lucha por la tierra, reformas agrarias, y capitalismo en el Perú del siglo XX*. Lima: Mosca Azul, 1989.

——. "*Yawar fiesta*: una lectura antropológica." *Revista de Crítica Literaria Latinoamericana* 6.12 (1980): 55–68.

Moraña, Mabel. "Función ideológica de la fantasia en las novelas de Manuel Scorza." *Revista de Crítica Literarira Latinoamericana*. 9.17 (1983): 171–192.

El mundo. "La primera dama del Perú deja su trabajo en un banco vinculado a

Vladimiro Montesinos." 16 de agosto de 2002. <http://www.elmundo.es/elmundo/2002/08/16/internacional/1029478412.html>

Muñoz, Fanni. "La fiesta del turupukllay en el mundo andino." *Márgenes* 4.10/11 (1993): 211–231.

Muñoz, Silverio. *José María Arguedas y el mito de la salvación por la cultura.* Lima: Editorial Horizonte, 1987.

Murra, John V. and Mercedes López-Baralt, eds. *Las cartas de Arguedas.* Lima: Fondo Editorial de la Pontificia Universidad Católica del Perú, 1996.

The New York Times. "Peru Leader Voices 'Disappointment in Scandal; Not Enough, Opponents Say." February 2, 2004. A8.

———. "Troops and Police Clash With Protesters as Unrest Grows in Peru." May 29, 2003. A9.

Notisur. "Peru: Vice President Raúl Diez Canseco Resigns." February 13, 2004. <http://ladb.unm.edu/prot/search/retrieve.php3?ID[0]=25565>

———. "Peru: Cabinet Resignations Continue, New Prime Minister Appointed." January 9, 2004. <http://ladb.unm.edu/prot/search/retrieve. php3? ID[0] =25533>

———. "Peru: President Alejandro [sic] Marks First Anniversary." August 2, 2002. <http://ladb.unm.edu/prot/search/retrieve.php3?ID[0]=25048>

———. "Peru: Unions Protest Economic Policies of President Alejandro Toledo." May 17, 2002. <http://ladb.unm.edu/prot/search/retrieve.php3?ID[0]=24954>

———. "Peru: Critics Call for Action as President Alejandro Toledo Completes First 100 Days in Office." November 9, 2001. <http://ladb.unm.edu/prot/search/retrieve.php3?ID[0]=24773>

Nugent, José Guillermo. *El laberinto de la choledad.* Lima: Fundación Friedrich Ebert, 1992.

O'Brien, Pablo. "Escuchando con ira." *Caretas.* Edición N° 1726. 20 de junio de 2002. <http://www.caretas.com.pe/2002/1726/articulos/arequipa.html>

O'Bryan-Knight, Jean. *The Story of the Storyteller: La tia Julia y el escribidor, Historia de Mayta, and El hablador by Mario Vargas Llosa.* Amsterdam: Rodopi, 1995.

Oquendo, Abelardo. "El largo salto de Bryce." *Los mundos de Alfredo Bryce Echenique.* César Ferreira e Ismael P. Márquez, Eds. Lima: Pontificia Universidad Católica del Peru, 1994. 123–128.

Ortega, Julio. "Introduction." *The Fox from Up Above and the Fox from Down Below.* José María Arguedas. Trans. Frances Horning Barraclough. Pittsburgh: University of Pittsburgh Press, 2000. xi-xxii.

———. *El hilo del habla: la narrativa de Alfredo Bryce Echenique.* Guadalajara: Universidad de Guadalajara, 1994.

———. "Los cuentos de Ribeyro." *Cuadernos Hispanoamericanos* 417 (1985): 128–145.

———. *Texto, comunicación y cultura: Los ríos profundos de José María Arguedas.* Lima: CEDEP, 1982.

Ortiz, Fernando. *Contrapunteo cubano del tabaco y el azúcar.* Caracas: Biblioteca Ayacucho, 1987 [1941].

Ortiz Rescaniere, Alejandro, ed. *José María Arguedas, recuerdos de una amistad.* Lima: Fondo Editorial de la Pontificia Universidad Católica del Perú, 1996.

Bibliography

Osorio, Manuel. "Conversación con Manuel Scorza: América Latina, los fantasmas de la historia." *Plural* 151 (1984): 56–59.

Palmer, David Scott, ed. *The Shining Path of Peru*. 2nd ed. New York: St. Martin's Press, 1994.

———. "La rebelión de Sendero Luminoso en el Perú rural." *Perú en el fin del milenio*. Heraclio Bonilla, compilador. México, D.F.: Consejo Nacional para la Cultura y las Artes, 1994. 333–362.

Penuel, Arnold M. "Intertextuality and the Theme of Violence in Vargas Llosa's *Lituma en los Andes*." *Revista de Estudios Hispánicos* 29 (1995): 441–60.

Peralta, Elda. "Liberar lo imaginario: entrevista a Manuel Scorza." *Plural* 10.114 (1981): 26–30.

Perus, Françoise. "A propósito de las propuestas historiográficas de Ángel Rama." *Ángel Rama y los estudios latinoamericanos*. Ed. Mabel Moraña. Pittsburgh: IILI, 1997. 55–70.

———. "El dialogismo y la poética histórica bajtinianos en la perspectiva de la heterogeneidad cultural y la transculturación narrativa en América Latina." *Revista de Crítica Literaria Latinoamericana*. 21.42 (1995): 29–44.

Pinilla, Carmen María, ed. *Arguedas en familia: cartas de José María Arguedas a Arístides y Nelly Arguedas, a Rosa Pozo Navarro y Yolanda López Pozo*. Lima: Fondo Editorial de la Pontificia Universidad Católica del Perú, 1999.

Poole, Deborah and Gerardo Rénique. *Peru: Time of Fear*. London: Latin America Bureau, 1992.

Portocarrero, Gonzalo. "Las últimas reflexiones de José María Arguedas." *Márgenes* 4.8 (1991): 231–267.

Postero, Nancy Grey, and Leon Zamosc, eds. *The Struggle for Indigenous Rights in Latin America*. Brighton & Portland: Sussex Academic Press, 2004.

Pratt, Mary Louise. "La modernidad desde las Américas." *Revista Ibero-americana* 66.193 (2000): 831–840.

———. "Transculturation and autoethnography: Peru, 1615/1980." *Colonial discourse / postcolonial theory*. Eds. Francis Barker, Peter Hulme, and Margaret Iversen. Manchester: Manchester University Press, 1994. 25–46.

———. *Imperial Eyes: Travel Writing and Transculturation*. New York: Routledge, 1992.

Primer encuentro de narradores peruanos. Segunda edición. Lima: Latino-americana Editores, 1986.

Quijano, Aníbal. *Dominación y cultura: lo cholo y el conflicto cultural en el Perú*. Lima: Mosca Azul, 1980.

Rama Angel. *La ciudad letrada*. Hanover, NH: Ediciones del Norte, 1984.

———. *La novela en América Latina: Panoramas 1920–1980*. México, D.F.: Fundación Angel Rama y Universidad Veracruzana, 1986.

———. "Medio siglo de narrativa latinoamericana (1922–1972)." *La novela en América Latina: Panoramas 1920–1980*. México, D.F.: Fundación Angel Rama y Universidad Veracruzana, 1986. 99–202.

———. *Transculturación narrativa en América Latina*. México, D.F.: Siglo XXI, 1982.

Redfield, Robert, Ralph Linton and Melville H. Herskovits. "Memorandum for the Study of Acculturation." *American Anthropologist* 38 (1936): 149–52.

Bibliography

Rénique, Jose Luis. "De la 'traición aprista' al 'gesto heróico'. Luis de la Puente Uceda y la guerrilla del MIR." *Ciberayllu*. 11 junio 2004. <http://www.andes.missouri.edu/andes/Especiales/JLRLaPuente/JLR_LaPuente1.html>

Reynoso, Oswaldo. *En octubre no hay milagros*. Lima: PEISA, 1994 [1965].

Ribeyro, Julio Ramón. "Ancestros," in *Asedios a Julio Ramón Ribeyro*. Eds. Ismael P. Márquez and César Ferreira. Lima: Fondo Editorial de la Pontificia Universidad Católica del Perú, 1996. 21–29.

———. *Cuentos Completos*. Madrid: Alfaguara, 1994.

———. *La caza sutil*. Lima: Milla Batres, 1976.

———. *Los geniecillos dominicales*. Lima: Milla Batres, 1973.

Robinson, William I. A *Theory of Global Capitalism: Production, Class, and State in a Transnational World*. Baltimore: The Johns Hopkins University Press, 2004.

Rochabrún, Guillermo, ed. *La mesa redonda sobre Todas las sangres del 23 de junio de 1965*. Segunda edición. Lima: IEP, 2000.

Rodríguez Ortiz, Oscar. *Sobre narradores y héroes: A propósito de Arenas, Scorza, y Adoum*. Caracas: Monte Avila, 1980.

Rodríguez-Peralta, Phyllis. "Narrative Access to *Un mundo para Julius*." *Revista de Estudios Hispánicos* 17.3 (1983): 407–418.

Roffé, Reina. "Entrevista a Alfredo Bryce Echenique." *Cuadernos Hispanoamericanos* 611 (2001): 107–121.

Roncalla, Fredy Amílcar. "¿Hablan los Apus?" *Quehacer* 137. Septiembre-Octubre 2002. <http://www.desco.org.pe/publicaciones/QH/QH/ qh137fr.htm>

Rosaldo, Renato. *Culture and Truth: The Remaking of Social Analysis*. Boston: Beacon Press, 1989.

Rowe, William. "Liberalism and Authority: The Case of Mario Vargas Llosa." *On Edge: The Crisis of Contemporary Latin American Culture*. Eds. George Yúdice, Jean Franco, and Juan Flores. Minneapolis: University of Minnesota Press, 1992. 45–64.

———. *Mito e ideología en la obra de José María Arguedas*. Lima: Instituto Nacional de Cultura, 1979.

Sá, Lucia. "Perverse Tribute: Mario Vargas Llosa's *El hablador* and its Machiguenga Sources." *Journal of Iberian and Latin American Studies* 4.2 (1998): 145–164.

Salazar Bondy, Sebastián. *Lima la horrible*. México, D.F.: Ediciones Era, 1964.

Salomon, Frank and George Urioste, trans. *The Huarochirí Manuscript: A Testament of Ancient and Colonial Andean Religion*. Austin: University of Texas Press, 1991.

Sarlo, Beatriz. "Estética y pospolítica: Un recorrido de Fujimori a la Guerra del Golfo." *Cultura y pospolítica: el debate sobre la modernidad an América Latina*. Ed. Néstor García Canclini. México: Consejo Nacional para la Cultura y las Artes, 1995. 309–324.

Schmidt, Friedhelm. "¿Literaturas heterogéneas o literatura de la transculturación?" *Nuevo Texto Crítico*. 7.14–15 (1994–1995): 193–198.

Scorza, Manuel. *Drums for Rancas*. Trans. Edith Grossman. New York: Harper & Row, 1977.

———. *Redoble por Rancas. Obras completas de Manuel Scorza: Volumen 2.* México, D.F.: 1991 [1970].

———. *Garabombo, el invisible. Obras completas de Manuel Scorza: Volumen 3.* México, D.F.: 1991 [1972].

———. *El jinete insomne. Obras completas de Manuel Scorza: Volumen 4.* México, D.F.: 1991 [1977].

———. *Cantar de Agapito Robles. Obras completas de Manuel Scorza: Volumen 5.* México, D.F.: 1991 [1977].

———. *La tumba del relámpago. Obras completas de Manuel Scorza: Volumen 6.* México, D.F.: 1991 [1979].

———. *Obra poética.* Lima: Peisa, 1990.

Shea, Maureen. "*El zorro de arriba y el zorro de abajo:* Las cinco onzas que mataron a José Mariá Arguedas." Paper presented at the Jornadas Andinas de Literatura Latinoamericana, Cusco, Peru, 9–13 August 1999.

Sheahan, John. *Searching for a Better Society: The Peruvian Economy since 1950.* University Park, PA: The Pennsylvania State University Press, 1999.

Silverman, Helaine. "Touring Ancient Times: The Present and Presented Past in Contemporary Peru." *American Anthropologist* 104.3 (2002): 881–902.

Snook, Margaret L. "Reading and Writing for Meaning: Narrative and Biography in El hablador." *Mester* 20.1 (1991): 6371.

Sommer, Doris. "About Face: The Talker Turns." *boundary 2* 23.1 (1996): 91–133.

———. *Foundational Fictions: The National Romances of Latin America.* Berkeley: University of California Press, 1991.

Soubeyroux, Jacques. "Rapports sociaux et niveaux de discours dans *Un mundo para Julius.*" *Co-textes 9: Alfredo Bryce Echenique.* Montpellier: Centre d'Études et Recherches Sociocritiques, 1985. 83–99.

Spitta, Sylvia. *Between Two Waters: Narratives of Transculturation in Latin America.* Houston: Rice University Press, 1995.

Spreen, Heike. "Manuel Scorza como fenómeno literario en la sociedad peruana: *La guerra silenciosa* en el proceso sociocultural del Peru." *La literatura en la sociedad de América latina. Homenaje a Alejandro Losada.* Ed. Jose Morales Saravia. Lima: Latinoamericana, 1986. 117–137.

Steele, Cynthia. "Reseña de *El hablador* de Mario Vargas Llosa." *Revista de Crítica Literaria Latinoamericana* 15.30 (1989): 365–367.

Stern, Steve, ed. *Shining and Other Paths: War and Society in Peru, 1980–1995.* Durham: Duke University Press, 1998.

Suleiman, Susan Rubin. *Authoritarian Fictions: The Ideological Novel as a Literary Genre.* New York: Columbia University Press, 1983.

Taibo II, Paco Ignacio. *Ernesto Guevara, también conocido como el Che.* México, D.F.: Planeta, 1996.

Tamayo Vargas, Augusto. "Manuel Scorza y un neoindigenismo." *Cuadernos Hispanoamericanos* 300 (1975): 689–693.

Teja, Ada María. "El mito en *Redoble por Rancas:* su función social." *Annali, Istituto Universitario Orientale, Napoli, Sezione Romanica* 20 (1978): 257–278.

Toledo Brückman, Ernesto. "El 94% contra Alejandro Toledo. El rechazo al mandatario peruano reúne a la oposición y genera disturbios interminables en su país." *La Opinión*. 24 de mayo de 2004. <http://www.laopinion.com /archivo/index.html?START=1&RESULTSTART=1&DISPLAYTYPE=single &FREETEXT=toledo&FDATEd12=this+year&FDATEd13=20040524&BO OLp00=latinoamerica&SORT_MODE=Relevancia>

Trigo, Pedro. *Arguedas: mito, historia y religión*. Lima: CEP, 1982.

Valcárcel, Luis E. *Tempestad en los Andes*. Lima: Editorial Universo, 1972 [1927].

Vargas Llosa, Mario. *La utopía arcaica: José María Arguedas y las ficciones del indigenismo*. México, D.F.: FCE, 1996.

———. *Death in the Andes*. New York: Farrar, Straus, Giroux, 1996.

———. *Desafíos a la libertad*. Lima: Peisa, 1994.

———. *A Fish in the Water: A Memoir*. Trans. Helen Lane. New York: Farrar, Straus, Giroux, 1994.

———. *Lituma en los Andes*. Barcelona: Planeta, 1993.

———. *El pez en el agua: memorias*. Barcelona: Seix Barral, 1993.

———. "Cabezazos con la Madre Patria." *El País*, Madrid (26 de enero de 1992): 11–12.

———. *Mario Vargas Llosa: A Writer's Reality*. Syracuse: Syracuse University Press, 1991.

———. "Novels Disguised as History: The Chronicles of the Birth of Peru." *Mario Vargas Llosa: A Writer's Reality*. Syracuse, NY: Syracuse University Press, 1991. 21–38.

———. "Questions of Conquest: What Columbus Wrought, and What He Did Not." *Harper's* 281 (December 1990): 45–53.

———. *Contra viento y marea III: 1964–1988*. Barcelona: Seix Barral, 1990.

———. *The Storyteller*. New York: Farrar, Straus, Giroux, 1989.

———. "Latin America: Fiction and Reality." *Modern Latin American Fiction: A Survey*. Ed. John King. London: Faber and Faber, 1987. 1–17.

———. *El hablador*. Barcelona: Seix Barral, 1987.

———. *¿Quién mató a Palomino Molero?*. Barcelona: Seix Barral, 1986.

———. "El nacimiento del Perú." *El País*. Suplemento "Domingo," Año II, Número 26 (13 de abril de 1986): 16–17.

———. *Historia de Mayta*. Barcelona: Seix Barral, 1984.

———. "Inquest in the Andes" (*New York Times Magazine*, July 31, 1983): 18–23.

———. *Contra viento y marea I: 1962–1982*. Barcelona: Seix Barral, 1983.

———. *La tía Julia y el escribidor*. Barcelona: Seix Barral, 1977.

———. *Conversation in the Cathedral*. New York: Harpers Row, 1975.

———. "Ciro Alegría según Mario Vargas Llosa." Dora Varona, ed. *Ciro Alegría: trayectoria y mensaje*. [Compilación]. Lima: Ediciones Varona, 1972. 200–205.

———. *Conversación en La Catedral*. Barcelona: Seix Barral, 1969.

———. *La Casa Verde*. Barcelona: Seix Barral, 1965.

Varona, Dora. *La sombra del condor: biografía ilustrada de Ciro Alegría*. Lima: DISELPESA, 1993.

———, ed. *Ciro Alegría: trayectoria y mensaje*. [Compilación]. Lima: Ediciones Varona, 1972.

Vilas, Carlos. "Participation, Inequality, and the Whereabouts of Democracy."

Bibliography

The New Politics of Inequality in Latin America. Ed. Douglas Chalmers, Carlos Vilas, *et al.* New York: Oxford University Press, 1997.

Volek, Emil. "El hablador de Vargas Llosa: del realismo mágico a la postmodernidad." *Cuadernos Hispanoamericanos: Revista Mensual de Cultura Hispánica* 509 (1992): 95–102.

Warren, Kay. *Indigenous Movements and Their Critics: Pan-Maya Activism in Guatemala.* Princeton: Princeton University Press, 1998.

The Washington Post. "Peruvian President Defends Wife's Bank Contract." August 14, 2002. A24.

Weismantel, Mary J. *Cholas and Pishtacos: Stories of Race and Sex in the Andes.* Chicago: The University of Chicago Press, 2001.

———. *Food, Gender, and Poverty in the Ecuadorian Andes.* Philapdelphia: University of Pennsylvania Press, 1988.

Williams, Raymond L. "Los niveles de la realidad, la función de lo racional y los demonios: *El hablador* y *Lituma en los Andes.*" *Explicación de textos literarios* 25.2 (1996–97): 141–154.

Wise, David. "Indigenismo de izquierda y de derecha: dos planteamientos de los años 1920." *Revista iberoamericana.* 49.122 (1983): 159–169.

———. "A Peruvian *Indigenista* Forum of the 1920s: José Carlos Mariátegui's *Amauta.*" *Ideologies and Literature.* 3.13 (1980): 70–104.

Wood, David. *The Fictions of Alfredo Bryce Echenique.* London: King's College Department of Spanish & Spanish American Studies, 2000.

Wurgaft, Ramy. "Eliane Karp, el 'talón de Aquiles' de Alejandro Toledo. La esposa del presidente de Perú está acusada de tráfico de influencias y enriquecimiento ilícito." *El mundo.* 30 de julio de 2004. <http://www.elmundo.es/papel/2004/07/30/mundo/1672845.html>

Zapata, Roger. *Guamán Poma, indigenismo y estética de la dependencia en la cultura peruana.* Minneapolis: Institute for the Study of Ideologies and Literature, 1989.

———. "Las trampas de la ficción en *La historia de Mayta.*" *La historia en la literatura iberoamericana: Textos del XXVI Congreso del Instituto Internacional de la Literatura Iberomericana.* Eds. Raquel Chang-Rodriguez and Gabriella de Beer. New York: Ediciones del Norte / City University of New York, 1989. 189–197.

Index

7 ensayos de interpretación de la real-idad peruana (Mariátegui), 4, 21

Abancay, *Deep Rivers* (Arguedas), 85, 86, 88, 92–3, 94, 142
acculturation, 1–2, 7–8, 178
  Arguedas's anthropological articles, 26, 71–3, 83, 84
  development theory, 26
  The Fox from up Above and the Fox from Down Below (Arguedas), 153
  see also transculturation
'Adriana' (*Death in the Andes*), 189, 190, 191, 192, 193
Afro-Peruvian culture, 134, 202n
agrarian reform, 24, 74, 122, 164, 249n
  gamonales, 28, 96, 165
  implementation of, 165
  pressure on government, 28, 96
Agua (Arguedas), 70
"Al pie del acantilado" (Ribeyro), 130
'Albert' (*Death in the Andes*), 191
Alegría, Ciro, 3, 17
  American Popular Revolutionary Alliance (APRA), 25, 36, 98, 212n, 215n
  as *aprista*, 212n
  background, 34, 35–7
  Broad and Alien is the World, 25–6, 32–43, 45, 46, 64, 114
  as *indigenista* author, 25
  as *mestizo* intellectual, 25, 36
  Mucha suerte con harto palo, 35
  socialist *indigenismo*, 25
Alianza Popular Revolucionaria Americana (APRA) *see* American Popular Revolutionary Alliance (APRA)
All the Worlds (Arguedas), 97, 100–12, 148, 153, 158
  Andean cosmology, 99, 100

Andean myths, 27, 99, 100, 107, 108, 109
Andean oral tradition, 87, 101
  capitalism, 27, 99, 100, 101–2, 103, 104, 110, 111
  cholo social group, 103–4
  colonos, 102, 103, 109, 110, 111
  comuneros, 102, 103–4, 110, 111
  Cornejo Polar on, 229n
  costeños, 108, 110
  critical reception, 27, 99, 100–1, 103–4
  feudalism, 27, 99, 101, 102, 103, 104–5, 107, 110, 111, 112, 116
  gamonales, 101, 105, 108, 109, 110
  imperialism, 27, 103, 109, 111, 112, 114, 116
  indigenous Andean culture, 27, 99, 100–4, 106–12, 123
  mistis, 102, 107–8
  modernity, 99, 102, 104, 105, 107, 110, 111, 112
  modernization, 27, 99, 100, 101–3, 104, 111
  social analysis, 100–2
  social realism, 27, 99
  yawar mayu, 90, 106–12
Amaru Cancha, *Deep Rivers* (Arguedas), 90, 92
amarus
  Deep Rivers (Arguedas), 90, 91–2, 93, 154
  Drums for Rancas (Scorza), 118
  Yawar Fiesta (Arguedas), 48, 60, 61, 62, 63, 154
Amauta, 23, 24
'Amenábar, Alvaro' (*Broad and Alien is the World*), 38, 40, 41, 42
American Popular Revolutionary Alliance (APRA), 22, 23, 24–5, 37
  and Alegría, 25, 36, 98, 212n, 215n

and Cornejo Polar, 71
and Mariátegui, 212*n*
and Scorza, 98
Andamarca, *Death in the Andes* (Vargas Llosa), 190, 191
"The Andean Highlands in the Process of Peruvian Culture" (Arguedas), 76, 77, 84, 221*n*
Andean social narrative, 33
Andean Stories (López Albújar), 21, 213*n*
'don Andrés Aragón de Peralta' (*All the Worlds*), 102, 107–8, 110
'don Antenor, Mayor' (*Yawar Fiesta*), 52, 53, 54–5
Antes o mundo não existia, 11
anthropology, 7–8, 68
   Arguedas's articles, 26, 66–84, 94, 95, 144
anti-colonialism, 5, 81, 192
'Anto' (*All the Worlds*), 109, 110, 111
applied anthropology *see* anthropology
APRA *see* American Popular Revolutionary Alliance (APRA)
Apukintu, *All the Worlds* (Arguedas), 107, 108
Apurímac River, *Deep Rivers* (Arguedas), 92
apus
   Death in the Andes (Vargas Llosa), 191
   Deep Rivers (Arguedas), 92
   Toledo's presidential campaign, 196
   Yawar Fiesta (Arguedas), 49
'Arangüena, don Julián' (*Yawar Fiesta*), 51, 52–3, 59, 61, 62, 63
Archibald, Priscilla, 73
Arequipa uprising, 255*n*
Arguedas, Arístides, 70–1
Arguedas, don Víctor Manuel, 35
Arguedas, José María
   Agua, 70
   All the Worlds, 27, 87, 90, 97, 99, 100–12, 114, 116, 123, 148, 153, 158, 229*n*
   amarus, 48, 60, 61, 62, 63, 90, 91–2, 93, 118, 154
   "The Andean Highlands in the Process of Peruvian Culture", 76, 77, 84, 221*n*
   anthropological articles, 26, 66–84, 94, 95, 144
   background, 16, 34, 35–7, 214*n*, 245–6*n*

collectivism, 76, 160
contrast between novels and anthropological articles, 69–71
Cornejo Polar on, 47, 71, 123, 216*n*, 229*n*, 246*n*
"The Cultural Complex in Peru", 72, 73, 75
"Culture: A Heritage Not Easily Colonized", 83
Deep Rivers, 26–7, 33, 34, 66, 67, 68–9, 70–1, 84–95, 97, 106, 142, 148, 153, 154, 158, 213*n*
depression, 71, 146, 209*n*, 220–1*n*
development theory, 26, 67–9, 80, 82, 83, 84
"Diamantes y pedernales", 70, 213*n*
"Entre el kechwa y el castellano", 216*n*
"The Evolution of Indigenous Communities", 77–9
The Fox from up Above and the Fox from Down Below, 28–9, 68–9, 70, 143–58
"Hijo Solo", 70
"I Am Not Acculturated" acceptance speech, 208*n*
Inca Garcilaso prize, 84
"Indigenismo in Peru", 84
influence of Vallejo's *El tungsteno*, 213*n*
linguistic differentiation, 46–7, 148, 216*n*, 238*n*
literary heterogeneity, 9
as *mestizo* intellectual, 16, 25, 36
modernity, 34, 83, 123, 159, 200
"La muerte de los Arango", 70
narrative transculturation, 8–9, 10, 13, 16–17, 26–7, 31, 199–201
"La novela y el problema de la expresión literaria en el Perú", 46
"Orovilca", 70
Peru–Cornell project, 73, 75
Peruvian Communist Party, 25, 36–7
posts during the 1960s, 97–8
"Puquio, a Changing Culture", 80–4
as Quechua speaker, 7, 16, 34, 35, 97
radicalization, 26–7, 67, 68, 82, 83, 84, 95, 98
relation to indigenous movements, 97–8
rural to urban migration, 158–9
sexuality in fiction, 245–6*n*
social class, 101

Index

Arguedas, José María (continued)
  socialism, 66, 82, 83, 99
  socialist indigenismo, 25
  suicide, 16, 146, 208–9n, 221n
  transculturation, 26, 68, 71–3, 76, 77, 83, 123, 178, 199
  Vargas Llosa on, 167, 250n
  violence in novels, 69
  Yawar Fiesta, 25, 26, 32–7, 44–64, 70, 80, 91, 124, 148, 151, 154, 188
Ariadne, 192
Aristocratic Republic, 17–19, 24
'Arminda' A World for Julius, 137, 138–40, 141–2
Asian-Peruvian culture, 202n
Asociación Pro Indígena, 20–1, 41
assimilation see cultural assimilation
'Asto' (The Fox from up Above and the Fox from Down Below), 152–3
Asturias, Miguel Ángel, 16–17
'Asunta de la Torre' (All the Worlds), 108, 110, 111, 153
"At the Foot of the Cliff" (Ribeyro), 130
Atahualpa, 81, 174, 175
Atusparia rebellion, 41
auki, 61, 63
aukillu, The Fox from up Above and the Fox from Down Below (Arguedas), 155
Aunt Julia and the Scriptwriter (Vargas Llosa), 178
Autonomía, 41
Aves sin nido (Matto de Turner), 20
Ayacucho region, 163–4, 169
ayllus
  "Puquio, a Changing Culture" (Arguedas), 80, 81
  Yawar Fiesta (Arguedas), 44, 45, 46, 48, 51, 52, 53–5, 56, 57, 60, 61, 63, 188

The Ballad of Agapito Robles (Scorza), 97, 116, 121, 232n
barriadas
  Arguedas's anthropological articles, 84
  Chimbote, 143, 145, 156
  Lima, 124, 125, 126, 128, 136, 137, 138, 140–2, 186, 235n
Barriales, Joaquín, 180
barrios céntricos, 236n
barrios residenciales, 236n
Bartolomé de las Casas, 174

Basadre, Jorge, 1, 17, 251n
Belaúnde Terry, Fernando, 28, 167, 168, 169, 170
Benavides, General Oscar, 36
Berlin, Isaiah, 166
Beverley, John, 11, 12–13, 15
biennio rosso, 22
Bildungsroman, 68
Birds Without a Nest (Matto de Turner), 20
Blanco, Hugo, 94, 95
Boletín Titikaka, 21
Bolivia, 198
Bolshevik revolution, 22, 23
Booker, M. Keith, 182
Boom novels, 3–4, 9, 11, 13, 32
  Arguedas's diaries, 147
  compared to All the Worlds (Arguedas), 27, 99
  Scorza's writings, 27, 99, 114, 115, 117
bourgeois realism, 6
Broad and Alien is the World (Alegría), 33
Britain
  imperialism, 24
  as model for Vargas Llosa, 166, 167
Broad and Alien is the World (Alegría), 32–43, 45, 114
  capitalism, 25, 38, 42
  collectivism, 25, 41, 42–3
  commercial success, 33–4
  comuneros, 38, 39, 40, 41, 42, 43
  critical reception, 33–4
  Escajadillo on, 39, 114, 212–13n
  Farrar & Rinehart prize, 33
  gamonales, 38, 40, 114
  indigenous Andean culture, 35, 37, 42
  lack of linguistic differentiation, 46
  main themes, 25–6, 32–3
  modernity, 25, 38, 39, 42
  narrative form, 37–9, 46, 64
  Rama on, 32–3
  regional context, 34–5
  translations, 33, 213n
'Bruno Aragón de Peralta' (All the Worlds), 102, 103, 104–5, 108, 109–10, 111, 229n
Bryce Echenique, Alfredo, 3, 17, 238n
  background, 239n
  urban narratives, 127, 158
  A World for Julius, 28–9, 128, 129, 133–43, 239n

Index

Bueno, Raúl, 9, 207n
bullfights, *Yawar Fiesta* (Arguedas), 44, 45, 46, 48, 49–53, 54–6, 63–4
bulls, *Deep Rivers* (Arguedas), 91–2
Burga, Manuel, 18, 23, 210n
Bush, George H.W., 162
Bustamante y Rivera, José, 65

Calabrese, Elisa, 253n
Camus, Albert, 166
Cantar de Agapito Robles (Scorza) *see The Ballad of Agapito Robles* (Scorza)
capitalism, 4, 23–4, 162, 212n
   All the Worlds (Arguedas), 27, 99, 100, 101–2, 103, 104, 110, 111
   Arguedas's anthropological articles, 66–7, 69, 76–7, 78–9, 82, 84, 95
   Broad and Alien is the World (Alegría), 25, 38, 42
   Deep Rivers (Arguedas), 27
   The Fox from up Above and the Fox from Down Below (Arguedas), 144–5, 146, 152
   The Green House (Vargas Llosa), 29
   Vargas Llosa, 29
   A World for Julius (Bryce Echenique), 135
'Cardozo, Michael' (*The Fox from up Above and the Fox from Down Below*), 156–7
'Carlos' *A World for Julius*, 134, 140, 141
Casa de la Cultura, 97
La casa verde (Vargas Llosa) *see The Green House* (Vargas Llosa)
Castro Arenas, Mario, 251n
'Castro, Benito' (*Broad and Alien is the World*), 39, 40–2
Castro Klarén, Sara, 218n
Castro Pozo, Hildebrando, 21, 211n
Catholicism, 91, 93
'Cecilio Encarnación' (*The Fox from up Above and the Fox from Down Below*), 145
'Celso' *A World for Julius*, 134, 137–8, 141, 142
Cenitagoya, Vicente de, 180
Centro Unión Lucanas, *Yawar Fiesta* (Arguedas), 53, 54, 55, 56–7, 62–3, 124
Cerro de Pasco Copper Corporation, 98, 114–15, 116–17
Cerro de Pasco indigenous movement,

27, 28, 98, 112–13
Chacón, Héctor, 113–14, 115–16, 118, 119, 120, 121
'Chasán, Father' (*Drums for Rancas*), 117, 118, 120, 232n
Chaupi, *Yawar Fiesta* (Arguedas), 51
chicheras' rebellion, *Deep Rivers* (Arguedas), 86–7, 93, 153
Chile, US-sponsored 1973 coup, 204n
Chimbote, 29, 143–6, 148, 150, 151–6, 158
cholo social group, 2, 203n
   All the Worlds (Arguedas), 103–4
   change in Indian identity, 198
   Toledo's presidential campaign, 195–6, 197
   A World for Julius (Bryce Echenique), 134
La ciudad letrada see The Lettered City (Rama)
Civilista Party, 18, 19
class conflict, Peru, 1, 3, 14, 30, 95, 133, 168
collectivism
   All the Worlds (Arguedas), 102, 103
   Arguedas, 160
   Arguedas's anthropological articles, 67, 82
   Broad and Alien is the World (Alegría), 25, 41, 42–3
   Mariátegui, 23, 160
   Yawar Fiesta (Arguedas), 45, 54, 55, 56–7, 58
colonial heritage, Peru, 202n
colonos
   All the Worlds (Arguedas), 102, 103, 109, 110, 111
   Deep Rivers (Arguedas), 85, 86–7, 93, 94, 142
   indigenous land movements, 94
coming of age novel, 68–9
   see also Deep Rivers (Arguedas); *A World for Julius* (Bryce Echenique)
Comisión Nacional de Pueblos Indígenas, Amazónicos y Afroperuanos, 197
Comité Pro Derecho Indígena Tahuantinsuyu, 21
"El complejo cultural el Perú" (Arguedas) *see* "The Cultural Complex in Peru" (Arguedas)

comuneros
  All the Worlds (Arguedas), 102,
    103–4, 110, 111
  Broad and Alien is the World
    (Alegría), 38, 39, 40, 41, 42, 43
  Drums for Rancas (Scorza), 114–15,
    116–18, 119, 120
  indigenous land movements, 95, 96
  "Puquio, a Changing Culture"
    (Arguedas), 81
  Requiem for a Lightning Bolt
    (Scorza), 121, 122
  Uchuraccay, 167, 170–2, 173, 177
  Yawar Fiesta (Arguedas), 44, 45, 47,
    48, 50–2, 53–5, 57, 58, 59, 61, 62,
    63
CONAIE, 12
CONAPA, 197
Condorcanqui, José Gabriel, 81
condors
  All the Worlds (Arguedas), 107
  Yawar Fiesta (Arguedas), 49, 50
conflicts *see* class conflict; ethnic
    conflict; social conflicts
Congrains Martin, Enrique, 128
Conquest, chronicles of, 5, 6, 174–5
consumption system, as element of
    literary process, 4, 5
Contreras, Carlos, 18, 202*n*
Convención Valley, 94–5
Conversation in the Cathedral (Vargas
    Llosa), 65, 128, 193, 194
Cornejo Polar, Antonio
  All the Worlds (Arguedas), 229*n*
  Arguedas and indigenous identity,
    123
  Arguedas's disillusionment, 71
  Arguedas's literary language, 47
  *The Fox from up Above and the Fox
    from Down Below* (Arguedas),
    246*n*
  heterogeneous literatures, 3–7, 9–10,
    13, 43
  homogeneous literatures, 4–5
  independence era poetry, 5–6
  "An Indian's Hide is Cheap"
    (Ribeyro), 130, 158
  indigenista literature, 6–7, 43, 44, 47
  Scorza's writings, 114, 121, 122–3
  transculturation, 10
  Yawar Fiesta (Arguedas), 47, 216*n*
Cornell University, 73–5
Cortázar, Julio, 3
cosmology, Andean, 9

  All the Worlds (Arguedas), 99, 100
  Deep Rivers (Arguedas), 68–9, 86, 87
  Drums for Rancas (Scorza), 99
  *The Fox from up Above and the Fox
    from Down Below* (Arguedas),
    68–9
  Yawar Fiesta (Arguedas), 26, 47, 48
costeños
  All the Worlds (Arguedas), 108, 110
  Death in the Andes (Vargas Llosa),
    189
  *The Fox from up Above and the Fox
    from Down Below* (Arguedas), 29
  Yawar Fiesta (Arguedas), 52, 54
Cotler, Julio, 20, 210*n*
criollo elite
  critique of, 2
  *The Fox from up Above and the Fox
    from Down Below* (Arguedas), 144,
    152–3
  "An Indian's Hide is Cheap"
    (Ribeyro), 28, 129, 130–3
  indigenista literature, 6
  indigenous–*criollo* divide, 1–3, 29,
    164, 166, 198, 202–3*n*
  Lima as stronghold of, 28, 59, 125–6
  literary forms, 16
  and *mestizaje*, 203*n*
  mestizo intellectuals, 21
  monopolization of cities, 125
  perpetuation of dominance, 30–1
  rural to urban migration, 158–9
  and Shining Path, 29, 198
  The Storyteller (Vargas Llosa),
    179
  support for Toledo, 196
  urban narratives, 127–9
  and Vargas Llosa, 184
  A World for Julius (Bryce Echenique),
    29, 128, 129, 133–43
  Yawar Fiesta (Arguedas), 59
Cuba, transculturation, 8
Cuban revolution, 66, 97
  and Arguedas, 26, 68, 82, 83
  and Rama, 32
  and Vargas Llosa, 166
Cuentos andinos (López Albújar), 21,
    213*n*
Cueto, Marcos, 18, 202*n*
"La cultura: patrimonio difícil de colo-
    nizar" (Arguedas), 83
*Cultura popular andina y forma novel-
    esca* (Lienhard), 151
cultural assimilation, 1–2, 7–8, 158

Index

Arguedas's anthropological articles, 66, 68, 72, 76, 77, 84
and Vargas Llosa, 30, 168, 176, 187, 190
cultural colonization, 83
"The Cultural Complex in Peru" (Arguedas), 72, 73, 75
cultural criticisms, Latin American traditions, 4
cultural heterogeneity, 1, 3, 9, 14
and Cornejo Polar, 4, 6, 10
"An Indian's Hide is Cheap" (Ribeyro), 133
and Vargas Llosa, 168, 175–6
cultural homogeneity, 12, 187
cultural imperialism, 83
cultural influence
acculturation, 7
Arguedas's anthropological articles, 72, 73, 75
The Fox from up Above and the Fox from Down Below (Arguedas), 148, 156
Peru–Cornell project, 73, 75
"Culture: A Heritage Not Easily Colonized" (Arguedas), 83
culture
harmonious fusion of, 70, 76, 77, 83
Mantaro Valley, 76–9
mestizo in Arguedas's writings, 71–3
role in social conflicts, 24
see also acculturation; indigenous Andean culture; regional cultures; transculturation
culture change
Arguedas's anthropological articles, 67, 68, 71–3, 75, 76
The Fox from up Above and the Fox from Down Below (Arguedas), 29
Rama's narrative transculturation, 9
Cusco, *Deep Rivers* (Arguedas), 87–92, 94
Cuzco, 22, 196

D'Allemand, Patricia, 10
'Daniel' (*A World for Julius*), 134, 137–8, 141, 142
De Ávila, Francisco, 149
de la Cadena, Marisol, 196
de Soto, Hernando, 159, 160–2
Death in the Andes (Vargas Llosa), 30, 168–9, 187–94, 198
narrative structure, 189–90

The Death of Artemio Cruz (Fuentes), 115
Deep Rivers (Arguedas), 33, 34, 66, 67, 84–95, 148, 158, 213n
amarus, 90, 91–2, 93, 154
Andean cosmology, 68–9, 86, 87
Andean oral tradition, 67, 86, 87, 89–90, 91
bulls, 91–2
chicheras' rebellion, 86–7, 93, 153
colonos, 85, 86–7, 93, 94, 142
critical acclaim, 68, 97
feudalism, 67, 69, 94, 95
gamonales, 88
hacienda peons, 85, 86–7, 88
Inca walls, 88–90, 93
indigenous Andean culture, 26–7, 84–7, 88–90, 91, 94, 142
mestizos, 85, 86
mistis, 84–6, 88, 89, 90, 91, 92
pachakutiy, 90, 91, 92
pongos, 85, 88, 89, 91, 92, 93
social change, 84, 86, 87, 94, 99
women, 86, 153
writing of, 70–1, 220n
yawar mayu, 89, 90, 93, 106
Degregori, Carlos Iván, 177, 178, 248n
1990 elections, 30, 168, 247n
The Green House (Vargas Llosa), 185
Shining Path, 163–4, 165
"Del paternalismo a la democracia" (Holmberg), 74
Democracia y Trabajo, 36
democracy
Bustamante y Rivera government, 65
Melgar's *yaraví*, 6
Peru–Cornell project, 75
urban migrants, 159, 160–1
and Vargas Llosa, 166
Yawar Fiesta (Arguedas), 58, 59
democratization, 31, 163, 198, 199, 200
barriadas, 124
"An Indian's Hide is Cheap" (Ribeyro), 133
"lettered city", 13, 16–17
Oncenio, 20
Ribeyro's short stories, 129
A World for Julius (Bryce Echenique), 135
dependency theory, 3
Desâna indigenous group, 11
Desborde popular y crisis del estado (Matos Mar), 159

development theory, 26, 67–9, 80, 82, 83, 84
'd'Harcourt, Hortensia' (*Death in the Andes*), 190, 191
"Diamantes y pedernales" (Arguedas), 70, 213*n*
'Dionisio' (*Death in the Andes*), 189, 190, 191, 192, 193
Dionysius, 192
discursive heterogeneity, 207*n*
distribution system, as element of literary process, 4
Dominican missionaries, 182
Don Quiote, 114
Donoso, José, 4
'Dora' ("An Indian's Hide is Cheap"), 130–3
Dorfman, Ariel, 85, 86
Dos Passos, John, 147
Drums for Rancas (Scorza), 27–8, 97, 112–23
    Andean cosmology, 99
    Andean myths, 27, 99, 117–21
    comuneros, 114–15, 116–18, 119–20
    imperialism, 115, 116, 120
    indigenous Andean culture, 27–8, 99, 115–21
    modernity, 27, 99
    narrative structure, 115–17
dualism, Peru, 4, 202*n*

Ecuador, 12, 198
Edwards, Jorge, 4
elites
    Aristocratic Republic, 18, 24
    impact of modernization, 127
    "An Indian's Hide is Cheap" (Ribeyro), 28, 129
    indigenismo, 22
    urban narratives, 127–9
    A World for Julius (Bryce Echenique), 133–43, 158
    see also criollo elite; *gamonales*; *mistis*
Ellis, Robert Richmond, 186
Elmore, Peter, 37, 44, 55–6, 58, 237*n*, 238*n*
ELN guerrilla group, 97
En octubre no hay Milagros (Reynoso), 128
"Entre el kechwa y el castellano" (Arguedas), 216*n*
entrepreneurialism, 79, 82, 159, 160–1, 184

"Epístola a los poetas que vendrán" (Scorza), 98
'Ernesto' (*Deep Rivers*), 84–93, 142
Escajadillo, Tomàs G.
    Broad and Alien is the World (Alegría), 39, 114, 212–13*n*
    Retablo ayacuchano (Scorza), 123
    The Silent War (Scorza), 112, 113, 114
    A World for Julius (Bryce Echenique), 136
    Yawar Fiesta (Arguedas), 212–13*n*
Escobar, Alberto, 105–6, 111
Escobar, Arturo, 67
'Esteban de la Cruz' (*The Fox from up Above and the Fox from Down Below*), 154–5, 156
ethnic conflict, Peru, 1, 3, 14, 30, 95, 133, 168
ethnocentrism, 8
ethnopoetics, 15–16
"The Evolution of Indigenous Communities" (Arguedas), 77–9

Farrar & Rinehart, 33
fascism, 22
Faulkner, William, 117
Favre, Henri, 103–4
"The Featherless Vultures" (Ribeyro), 130
'Felipa' (*Deep Rivers*), 86
'Fermín Aragón de Peralta' (*All the Worlds*), 102, 103, 104, 105, 109, 110, 111
Ferreira, César, 129
feudalism, 3, 18, 23, 65–6
    All the Worlds (Arguedas), 27, 99, 101, 102, 103, 104–5, 107, 110, 111, 112, 116
    Deep Rivers (Arguedas), 67, 69, 94, 95
    Drums for Rancas (Scorza), 115, 116, 120
    Mantaro River valley, 69, 76, 78, 79
    Peru–Cornell project, 73–5
    Requiem for a Lightning Bolt (Scorza), 122
    A Fish in the Water (Vargas Llosa), 30, 168–9
Flaubert, Gustave, 117
Flores Galindo, Alberto
    agrarian reform, 165
    Arguedas's writings, 16, 69–70
    Aristocratic Republic, 18

Index

gamonal, 204*n*
  indigenous rebellions, 210*n*, 211–12*n*
  Mantaro Valley, 78
  on Mariátegui, 23
  Western-Andean cultural confrontation, 202–3*n*
FOCEP, 122
Forgues, Roland, 231*n*
Fornet, Jorge, 181
The Fox from up Above and the Fox from Down Below (Arguedas), 28–9, 70, 143–58
  Andean cosmology, 68–9
  Andean migrants, 28–9, 129, 143–6, 148, 150, 152, 154–8
  Andean myth, 29, 129, 146, 148, 149–50, 151, 152, 154, 157, 158
  Andean oral tradition, 149
  Arguedas's diaries, 146–7, 150, 243*n*, 246*n*
  capitalism, 144–5, 146, 152
  criollo elite, 144, 152–3
  indigenous Andean culture, 29, 144, 145–6, 147, 148, 151–8
  narrative techniques, 147–8
Franco, Jean, 13, 15–16, 146, 153, 200
Frente Obrero, Campesino, Estudiantil y Popular (FOCEP), 122
"From Paternalism to Democracy" (Holmberg), 74
Fuentes, Carlos, 4, 115
Fujimori, Alberto, 30–1, 186–7, 195, 197
Fundación Pacha para el Cambio, 197

'Gabriel' (*Deep Rivers*), 87–8, 90–1, 93
"Los gallinazos sin plumas" (Ribeyro), 130
gamonales, 18, 24, 204*n*, 209*n*
  agrarian reform, 28, 96, 165
  All the Worlds (Arguedas), 101, 103, 105, 108, 109, 110
  Arguedas's anthropological writings, 78, 81
  Broad and Alien is the World (Alegría), 38, 40, 114
  Deep Rivers (Arguedas), 88
  Drums for Rancas (Scorza), 116
  impoverishment of, 127
  indigenous land movements, 96
  Odría government, 65–6
  The Silent War (Scorza), 114
  Yawar Fiesta (Arguedas), 44, 52, 53, 61

gamonalismo, 3, 27, 78, 96
  All the Worlds (Arguedas), 102, 103, 104, 111
  Broad and Alien is the World (Alegría), 25
Garabombo, the Invisible (Scorza), 97, 121
García, Alan, 166–7, 168
García Marquez, Gabriel, 3–4, 8, 9
Gazzolo, Ana María, 149
Los geniecillos dominicales (Ribeyro), 128
'Gertrudis' (*All the Worlds*), 109, 110
González Prada, Manuel, 20, 22, 232*n*
González Vigíl, Ricardo, 60, 87
The Green House (Vargas Llosa), 29, 115, 166, 185, 189, 193, 194
'Guadalupe' (*A World for Julius*), 141
Guaman Poma de Ayala, Felipe, 5
Guatemala, 12, 200
La guerra silenciosa (Scorza) *see The Silent War* (Scorza)
guerrilla movements, 28, 97
  see also Shining Path
Guevara, Che, 97, 156
Guimarães Rosa, João, 8, 9
Gutiérrez, Miguel, 228*n*
Guzmán, Abimael, 164, 165
Guzmán Figueroa, Abraham, 251*n*

hablador, The Storyteller (Vargas Llosa), 178, 180–3
El hablador, (Vargas Llosa) *see The Storyteller* (Vargas Llosa)
hacienda peons *see* peons
haciendas, expansion of, 18, 38
Harper's, 168, 174, 179
Haya de la Torre, Víctor Raúl, 22, 23–4, 25, 37, 98, 212*n*, 215*n*
Hayek, Frederick von, 166
Herskovits, Melville J., 7–8, 71, 83
heterogeneous literatures, 3–7, 9–10, 13–14, 16, 43
"Hijo Solo" (Arguedas), 70
Historia de Mayta (Vargas Llosa) *see The Real Life of Alejandro Mayta* (Vargas Llosa)
Historia del Perú contemporáneo (Contreras and Cueto), 202*n*
Holmberg, Allan, 73, 74, 75
homogeneous literatures, 4–5, 6
'Horse Thief' (*Drums for Rancas*), 121
Huancayo, 78, 79–80

Index

'Huarcaya, Casimiro' (*Death in the Andes*), 190, 191
Huarochirí manuscript, 149–51, 152
Huasipungo (Icaza), 33, 38, 42
'Huatyacuri' (*The Fox from up Above and the Fox from Down Below*), 149, 151, 154, 157
Huaychao, 169
Huayna Capac, 90, 92
Hugo, Victor, 37

"I am the voice of those who have no voice" (Scorza), 98
Icaza, Jorge, 46
  Huasipungo, 33, 38, 42
imperialism, 3, 23–4, 212n
  All the Worlds (Arguedas), 27, 103, 109, 111, 112, 114, 116
  Aristocratic Republic, 18
  Drums for Rancas (Scorza), 115, 116, 120
  Requiem for a Lightning Bolt (Scorza), 122
imperialist nostalgia, 187
Las imprecaciones (Scorza), 98
Inca empire, 174–5
Inca Garcilaso prize, 84
"An Indian's Hide is Cheap" (Ribeyro), 28, 129, 130–3, 142
indigenismo, 20–2, 25, 28, 53
"Indigenismo in Peru" (Arguedas), 84
indigenista intellectuals, 21, 23
indigenista literature, 5, 6–7, 21, 25, 199, 206n
  decline of, 126
  Escajadillo on, 212–13n
  as heterogeneous literature, 43
  linguistic differentiation, 46, 47
  shift to urban narrative, 126
  see also *All the Worlds* (Arguedas); *Broad and Alien is the World* (Alegría); *Deep Rivers* (Arguedas); *Drums for Rancas* (Scorza); *The Silent War* (Scorza); *Yawar Fiesta* (Arguedas)
indigenous Andean culture, 14
  All the Worlds (Arguedas), 27, 99, 100–4, 106–12, 123
  Arguedas's anthropological articles, 26, 66, 68, 69, 71–3, 75, 77, 78, 79, 80, 81, 82, 83
  Arguedas's upbringing, 16, 35
  Arguedas's writings, 7, 8, 10, 16–17, 34, 117, 199–201

Broad and Alien is the World (Alegría), 35, 37, 42
  de Soto on, 161–2
Death in the Andes (Vargas Llosa), 30, 168–9, 187–94
Deep Rivers (Arguedas), 26–7, 84–7, 88–90, 91, 94, 142
Drums for Rancas (Scorza), 27–8, 99, 115–21
The Fox from up Above and the Fox from Down Below (Arguedas), 29, 144, 145–6, 147, 148, 151–8
Guaman Poma's chronicle, 5
Haya de la Torre, 24
"indigenous *mestizo*", 196
  as obstacle to capitalist modernization, 29
"Questions of Conquest" (Vargas Llosa), 30, 168, 174–8, 187
"Report on Uchuraccay" (Vargas Llosa), 30, 167–8, 170–4, 194
Requiem for a Lightning Bolt (Scorza), 121–2
Seven Interpretive Essays on Peruvian Reality (Mariátegui), 4, 21
Shining Path, 164, 188
  and socialism, 99
The Storyteller (Vargas Llosa), 30, 168, 178–84, 187, 188
Vargas Llosa, 29, 30, 166, 167, 170–4, 175–94, 251–2n
Yawar Fiesta (Arguedas), 26, 37, 47, 48, 49, 51, 54, 56, 57, 64
  see also cosmology, Andean; myth, Andean; oral tradition, Andean
indigenous Andeans
  All the Worlds (Arguedas), 101, 107, 109, 110
  Arguedas's anthropological articles, 26, 66–84, 94, 95, 144
  Aristocratic Republic, 18–19, 24
  Atusparia rebellion, 41
  Death in the Andes (Vargas Llosa), 188, 192, 194
  Deep Rivers (Arguedas), 85, 90, 92, 94
  destruction of elite, 198
  "An Indian's Hide is Cheap" (Ribeyro), 132
  indigenous–*criollo* divide, 1–3, 29, 164, 166, 198, 202–3n
  influence on intellectuals, 14–17
  Mantaro River valley, 69, 76–9
  narrative transculturation, 15

280

Index

Oncenio period, 19–20, 24
Peru–Cornell project, 73–5
popular mobilizations, 160
rural rebellions, 18–19, 210*n*,
  211–12*n*
and Shining Path, 159
The Storyteller (Vargas Llosa), 188
struggles of, 1, 3
Toledo's presidential campaign,
  195–6
urban narratives, 126–7, 128–9
A World for Julius (Bryce Echenique),
  138
Yawar Fiesta (Arguedas), 26
see also acculturation; *ayllus*; collectivism; *comuneros*; cultural
  assimilation; feudalism; migrants,
  Andean; modernization;
  Westernization
indigenous land movements, 3, 24, 26,
  27–8, 66, 68, 74, 82, 96–8
Arguedas's anticipation of, 90, 94
Convención Valley, 94–5
Scorza's activism, 112
see also *All the Worlds* (Arguedas);
  Broad and Alien is the World
  (Alegría); Cerro de Pasco indigenous movement; *Drums for Rancas*
  (Scorza); *Requiem for a Lightning
  Bolt* (Scorza)
indigenous movements, 11–12, 14, 37,
  163
Aristocratic Republic, 18–19
lack of nationwide body, 198–9
see also Cerro de Pasco indigenous
  movement
individualism, 43, 76, 77, 82, 112,
  174–5
industrialization, 65, 66, 125, 127
"Informe sobre Uchuraccay" (Vargas
  Llosa) see "Report on Uchuraccay"
  (Vargas Llosa)
Inkarrí myth, 81–2
Instituto de Estudios Peruanos, 100,
  103–4
integration, 1, 11
Arguedas's anthropological articles,
  83, 84
Mantaro Valley, 78
Peru–Cornell project, 73
Vargas Llosa, 173, 175–6
intellectuals, 14–17, 159
and Rama, 8, 10, 11, 21
see also *letrados*

Inti Cancha, 91
Italian Communist Party, 22
Izquierdo Ríos, Francisco, 60

'Jiménez, don Pancho' (*Yawar Fiesta*),
  52–3
El jinete insomne (Scorza), 97
Joyce, James, 117, 147
'Juan Lucas' (*A World for Julius*), 135,
  137, 139, 140, 142
'Julius' (*A World for Julius*), 133–5,
  136, 137, 138, 140–2

Kafka, Franz, 178, 180
Karp, Eliane, 195–6, 197
K'ayau, *Yawar Fiesta* (Arguedas), 51–2,
  55, 56, 59, 61, 62, 63
Kenhíri, Tomalãn, 11
Klarén, Peter, 65
K'ollana, *Yawar Fiesta* (Arguedas), 51
K'oñani, 59–60, 61, 62, 63
Kosko, 21
Kristal, Efraín, 126, 127
Kumu, Umúsin Panlõn, 11
Kuntur, 21

labor movements, 13, 19, 22, 23, 37, 41
land conflicts see agrarian reform;
  indigenous land movements
Larson, Brooke, 203*n*
Ledesma, Genaro, 122
'Ledesma' (*Requiem for a Lightning
  Bolt*), 121
Leguía, Augusto B.
  fall of (1930), 24
  and Haya de la Torre, 23
  indigenous population, 19–20, 21
  Ley de Conscripción Vial, 20, 58
  and Mariátegui, 22
  middle class, 19, 210*n*
  modernization project, 19, 37
  populism, 19–20, 37, 210*n*
  road construction projects, 20, 28,
    58
Lenin, Vladimir Ilyich, 212*n*
letrados, 183, 187, 253*n*
"lettered city", 12, 13, 16, 200
The Lettered City (Rama), 12, 13
Lévano, César, 214–15*n*
Ley de Conscripción Vial, 20, 58
liberalism, 187, 203*n*
liberation theology, 91, 104, 117, 156
Lienhard, Martin, 15, 60, 147, 148,
  151, 158

Index

Lima
  barriadas, 124, 125, 126, 128, 136, 137, 138, 140–2, 186, 235*n*
  as *criollo* elite stronghold, 28, 59, 125–6
  labor movements, 41
  migrants, 44, 56, 58–9, 124, 125, 144, 159
  modernization during *Oncenio*, 19
  Ribeyro's short stories, 129–30
  transformation of, 3, 28
  tugurios, 125
  worker's movement, 22
  Yawar Fiesta (Arguedas), 44, 48, 53, 56, 58–9
  see also San Marcos University; *A World for Julius* (Bryce Echenique)
Lima the Horrible (Salazar Bondy), 128
Linton, Ralph, 7, 71, 83
literacy, 12, 183
literary criticism, independent Latin American, 3–4
literary heterogeneity, 9, 43, 207*n*
literary process, elements of, 4, 5
literary representation, 14–17
literature
  diminished status of, 200
  and power, 12, 17
'Lituma' (*Death in the Andes*), 189, 190, 191–3, 194
Lituma en los Andes (Vargas Llosa) *see Death in the Andes* (Vargas Llosa)
'Llantac, Medardo' (*Death in the Andes*), 191
López Albújar, Enrique, 21, 46, 213*n*
Lucanas province *see* Centro Unión Lucanas
Luchting, Wolfgang A., 136, 239*n*

Machiguenga, 30, 168, 178–84
Machu Picchu, 196
magical realism, 27, 99, 117
Malloch Brown, Mark, 187
Manhattan Transfer (Dos Passos), 147
Manrique, Nelson, 205–6*n*, 209*n*
  Arguedas's literary sensibility, 82
  Arguedas's radicalization, 82, 83
  Arguedas's treatment of capitalism, 79
  colonized aspects of Arguedas's works, 80, 82
  development theory, 80
  emergence of Shining Path, 248–9*n*

nationwide indigenous movement, 198
Mantaro River valley, 69, 76–9, 94
'Maqui, Rosendo' (*Broad and Alien is the World*), 39–40, 41, 42, 45
María Angola, *Deep Rivers* (Arguedas), 90–2, 93
Mariátegui, José Carlos, 6, 205*n*
  aestheticism, 22, 211*n*
  collectivism, 23, 160
  as critic of Peruvian society, 22–3, 24
  imperialism, 23, 212*n*
  indigenismo, 21, 22, 25, 53
  indigenista literature, 6, 206*n*
  indigenous Andean culture, 112
  indigenous rebellions, 211–12*n*
  in Italy, 22–3, 211*n*
  lasting presence, 25
  Marxist *indigenismo*, 22
  Peruvian Communist Party, 22, 24, 36
  Peruvian Socialist Party, 4, 22, 23, 37
  Seven Interpretive Essays on Peruvian Reality, 4, 21
Mariscal, George, 175
Márquez, Ismael, 129
Martin, Gerald, 38
Marx, Karl, 21
Marxism, 4, 22–3, 164–5
  All the Worlds (Arguedas), 100–1, 112
mass media, 16–17, 183, 197, 200
Matos Mar, José, 159–60, 179
Matto de Turner, Clorinda, 20
'Maxwell' (*The Fox from up Above and the Fox from Down Below*), 156, 157
Maya cultural rights movement, 12
Mayer de Zulén, Dora, 20–1
Mayer, Enrique, 172, 173, 251*n*
'Mayta, Alejandro' (*The Real Life of Alejandro Mayta*), 167
Melgar, Mariano, 5–6
Melis, Antonio, 211*n*, 212*n*
mercantilism, 161
'Mercedes' (*Death in the Andes*), 189–90, 193, 194
mestizaje
  Arguedas's writings, 72, 73, 75, 80, 83
  and *criollo* elite, 203*n*
  The Fox from up Above and the Fox from Down Below (Arguedas), 156
  myths of, 203*n*

Index

Peru–Cornell project, 73, 75
"Puquio, a Changing Culture"
  (Arguedas), 80, 81
Scorza's writings, 123
transculturation, 10–11, 72, 73
mestizo intellectuals, 18–19, 21, 23, 25,
  36, 121, 122, 164
mestizos, 2
  Alegría as, 25, 36
  "The Andean Highlands in the
    Process of Peruvian Culture"
    (Arguedas), 76, 77
  Arguedas as, 16, 25, 36
  Arguedas's anthropological articles,
    70, 71–3, 76, 77, 78, 79, 80–1
  Broad and Alien is the World
    (Alegría), 40, 41, 42, 43
  "The Cultural Complex in Peru"
    (Arguedas), 72, 73
  Deep Rivers (Arguedas), 85, 86
  democratization, 31
  Fujimori's campaign, 186–7
  indigenista literature, 5, 6, 21, 25,
    206*n*
  indigenous rebellions, 18–19
  Mantaro valley, 76, 77, 78, 79
  "Puquio, a Changing Culture"
    (Arguedas), 80–1
  as Quechua speakers, 34
  Requiem for a Lightning Bolt
    (Scorza), 121, 122
  revolutionary role, 23
  Shining Path, 164
  support for Toledo, 196
  Vargas Llosa's presidential campaign,
    30, 185, 187
  Yawar Fiesta (Arguedas), 44, 49–50,
    51, 53, 59, 63
Metamorphosis (Kafka), 180
Mexican revolution, 22, 23
Mexico, Indians, 75
'Michèle' *Death in the Andes*, 191
middle class
  Aristocratic Republic, 18
  Conversation in the Cathedral
    (Vargas Llosa), 128
  growth of, 18, 19, 20, 24, 127
  guerrilla groups, 97
  "An Indian's Hide is Cheap"
    (Ribeyro), 129, 130–3
  Oncenio, 19, 20
  Ribeyro's short stories, 129
  There Are No Miracles in October
    (Reynoso), 128

urban narratives, 128
migrant associations, 160
migrants, Andean
  *The Fox from up Above and the Fox
    from Down Below* (Arguedas),
    28–9, 129, 143–6, 148, 150, 152,
    154–8
  "An Indian's Hide is Cheap"
    (Ribeyro), 28, 129, 130–3, 158
  Lima, 44, 56, 58–9, 124, 125, 144,
    159
  rural-to-urban, 1–2, 14, 20, 28–9,
    124–9, 158–62, 177
  A World for Julius (Bryce Echenique),
    28–9, 129, 134, 136–43, 158
  see also barriadas; *cholo* social group
'Miguel' ("An Indian's Hide is Cheap"),
  130–3, 142
military dictatorships, 204*n*
  Odría government, 3, 26, 65–6, 68,
    95, 98, 128
  Velasco Alvarado government, 24,
    28, 96, 135–6, 165, 198, 248–9*n*
Miller, Nicola, 253*n*
minga, *Yawar Fiesta* (Arguedas), 57
MIR guerrilla group, 97
Miraflores, 126, 236*n*
Misitu, *Yawar Fiesta* (Arguedas), 48,
  51–2, 54, 55, 56, 59–60, 61–3, 91
mistis, 18
  agrarian reform, 165
  All the Worlds (Arguedas), 102,
    107–8
  Deep Rivers (Arguedas), 84–6, 88,
    89, 90, 91, 92
  "Puquio, a Changing Culture"
    (Arguedas), 80–1
  as Quechua speakers, 34, 51
  Yawar Fiesta (Arguedas), 44, 45, 47,
    48, 50, 51–5, 57, 58, 59, 60–1, 62,
    63, 151
modernity, 3, 11, 14, 15, 36, 164
  All the Worlds (Arguedas), 99, 102,
    104, 105, 107, 110, 111, 112
  Arguedas, 34, 83, 123, 159, 200
  Broad and Alien is the World
    (Alegría), 25, 38, 39, 42
  criollo elite, 2, 59, 135
  Death in the Andes (Vargas Llosa),
    188, 189
  Drums for Rancas (Scorza), 27, 99
  *The Fox from up Above and the Fox
    from Down Below* (Arguedas), 144,
    146, 147

Index

modernity *(continued)*
  "An Indian's Hide is Cheap"
    (Ribeyro), 131, 132
  "Report on Uchuraccay" (Vargas
    Llosa), 171, 172
  urban narratives, 128
  Vargas Llosa, 30, 166, 167, 168,
    173–4, 175, 177, 178
  A World for Julius (Bryce Echenique),
    134, 135
  Yawar Fiesta (Arguedas), 26, 47,
    48–9, 59, 63, 188
modernization, 17–20
  All the Worlds (Arguedas), 27, 99,
    100, 101–3, 104, 111
  Arguedas's anthropological articles,
    26, 66–7, 68, 69, 76–84
  barriadas, 125
  Death in the Andes (Vargas Llosa),
    188
  emergence and growth of Shining
    Path, 163–4
  *The Fox from up Above and the Fox
    from Down Below* (Arguedas), 144,
    145
  The Green House (Vargas Llosa), 29,
    185
  "An Indian's Hide is Cheap"
    (Ribeyro), 133
  indigenous–*criollo* divide, 1, 3, 29
  Mantaro River valley, 69, 76–80
  narrative transculturation, 11, 14, 17
  Odría government, 26, 65–6, 68
  Oncenio, 19, 37
  Peru–Cornell project, 73–5
  Puquio, 80–4
  rural migrants, 125, 127
  social conflicts, 14, 16, 47, 50, 64,
    117
  The Storyteller (Vargas Llosa), 168,
    178, 182–3, 187
  Vargas Llosa, 29, 30, 166, 167,
    176–7, 187
  A World for Julius (Bryce Echenique),
    135
  see also Broad and Alien is the World
    (Alegría); *Yawar Fiesta* (Arguedas)
'Moncada' (*The Fox from up Above and
  the Fox from Down Below*), 154,
  155–6, 246n
Montenegro, Francisco, 115–16,
  118–20, 121
Montoya, Rodrigo, 51, 122, 198, 199
Moreno Jimeno, Manuel, 214–15n

Movimiento Comunal del Perú, 98
Mucha suerte con harto palo (Alegría),
  35
"La muerte de los Arango" (Arguedas),
  70
El Mundo es ancho y ajeno (Alegría) *see
  Broad and Alien is the World*
  (Alegría)
Un mundo para Julius (Bryce
  Echenique) *see A World for Julius*
  (Bryce Echenique)
Muñoz, Fanni, 49, 50, 60
Museo Nacional de Historia, 97
Mussolini, Benito, 36
myth, Andean
  All the Worlds (Arguedas), 27, 99,
    100, 107, 108, 109
  Death in the Andes (Vargas Llosa),
    192
  Deep Rivers (Arguedas), 93, 154
  Drums for Rancas (Scorza), 27, 99,
    117–21
  *The Fox from up Above and the Fox
    from Down Below* (Arguedas), 29,
    129, 146, 148, 149–50, 151, 152,
    154, 157, 158
  Inkarrí myth, 81–2
  "Puquio, a Changing Culture"
    (Arguedas), 84
  Requiem for a Lightning Bolt
    (Scorza), 121, 122
  The Storyteller (Vargas Llosa), 178
  Yawar Fiesta (Arguedas), 48, 51–2,
    54, 55, 56, 59–60, 61, 63, 91, 154

Naccos, *Death in the Andes* (Vargas
  Llosa), 188–9
narrative acculturation, 33
narrative transculturation, 7–9, 10–17,
  199–201, 207n
  Arguedas, 8–9, 10, 13, 16–17, 26–7,
    31, 199–201
  Rama, 3, 7, 8, 9, 10–12, 13, 14, 15,
    69, 106, 199
  see also All the Worlds (Arguedas);
    Deep Rivers (Arguedas); *The Fox
    from up Above and the Fox from
    Down Below* (Arguedas); *Yawar
    Fiesta* (Arguedas)
National Commission of Indigenous,
  Amazonian, and Afroperuvian
  Peoples, 197
national liberation movements, 3
Nazca, *Yawar Fiesta* (Arguedas), 55–6

neoclassicism, 6
neoindigenista literature, 213n
neoliberalism, 3, 160–2, 166, 176, 183, 184, 196–7
'Nilda' (A World for Julius), 134
Not Just One but Rather Many Deaths (Congrains Martin), 128
"La novela y el problema de la expresión literaria en el Perú" (Arguedas), 46
Nuestra comunidad indígena (Castro Pozo), 21
Nueva Corónica y Buen Gobierno (Guaman Poma), 5
Nugent, José Guillermo, 59, 125, 235n

Odría, General Manuel, 3, 26, 65–6, 68, 95, 98, 128
'Old Man' (Deep Rivers), 87, 88, 90, 92, 93
Oncenio, 19–20, 24, 37
Oquendo, Abelardo, 134
oral tradition, Andean, 11, 16, 117
   All the Worlds (Arguedas), 87, 101
   Broad and Alien is the World (Alegría), 43
   Deep Rivers (Arguedas), 67, 86, 87, 89–90, 91
   Drums for Rancas (Scorza), 118
   The Fox from up Above and the Fox from Down Below (Arguedas), 149
   "Puquio, a Changing Culture" (Arguedas), 81
   Yawar Fiesta (Arguedas), 47, 48, 56, 60, 64, 87
"Orovilca" (Arguedas), 70
Ortega, Julio, 129, 237n
Ortiz, Fernando, 7, 8, 11, 33
The Other Path (de Soto), 159, 162, 247n
Our Indigenous Community (Castro Pozo), 21
Oviedo, José Miguel, 103

Pacha Foundation for Change, 197
pachakutiy
   Deep Rivers (Arguedas), 90, 91, 92
   The Fox from up Above and the Fox from Down Below (Arguedas), 154
   Yawar Fiesta (Arguedas), 60
pachamama, Yawar Fiesta (Arguedas), 49
painting, 21

'Pancho' ("An Indian's Hide is Cheap"), 130–3
'Pariacaca' (The Fox from up Above and the Fox from Down Below), 149
Partido Comunista del Perú "Sendero Luminoso" see Shining Path
Partido Nacionalista Libertador, 24
paternalism, 74, 172
La Patria Nueva, 19
PCP-SL see Shining Path
peons
   agrarian reform, 165
   Broad and Alien is the World (Alegría), 40
   Deep Rivers (Arguedas), 85, 86–7, 88
   indigenous land movements, 66, 94, 95, 96
   Peru–Cornell project, 73–4
   Yawar Fiesta (Arguedas), 53, 62
Peru
   Aristocratic Republic, 17–19, 24
   Bustamante y Rivera government, 65
   colonial divide, 1–3, 202–3n
   colonial heritage, 202n
   dependence on US, 26, 65, 68
   dualism, 4, 202n
   expansion of public education, 164
   Fujimori government, 30–1, 186–7, 195, 197
   Odría government, 3, 26, 65–6, 68, 95, 98, 128
   Oncenio, 19–20, 24, 37
   political power, 17–20
   radicalization of politics, 66, 97
   rise of New Left, 97
   Toledo government, 30–1, 195–8, 255n
   Velasco Alvarado government, 24, 28, 96, 135–6, 165, 198, 248–9n
   see also agrarian reform; modernization
Peru–Cornell project, 73–5
Perus, Françoise, 13–14
Peruvian Communist Party, 24, 25, 71
   and Arguedas, 25, 36–7
   change of name, 22, 211n
   and Shining Path, 163
Peruvian Socialist Party, 4, 22, 23, 37
El pez en el agua (Vargas Llosa) see A Fish in the Water (Vargas Llosa)
Pichqachuri
   "Puquio, a Changing Culture" (Arguedas), 80–1
   Yawar Fiesta (Arguedas), 51

Index

"La piel de un indio no cuesta caro" (Ribeyro) *see* " An Indian's Hide is Cheap" (Ribeyro)
pishtacos, *Death in the Andes* (Vargas Llosa), 192
'Pisser' (*Drums for Rancas*), 121
Piura, 185
Pizarro, Francisco, 174, 175
poetry, 5–6
pongos, *Deep Rivers* (Arguedas), 85, 88, 89, 91, 92, 93
Popper, Karl, 166
Popular Culture and Novelistic Form (Lienhard), 151
Populibros Peruanos, 231*n*
Porras Barrenechea, Raúl, 179
Portocarrero, Julio, 215*n*
postcolonialism, Peru, 202*n*
poverty
    Death in the Andes (Vargas Llosa), 194
    The Fox from up Above and the Fox from Down Below (Arguedas), 145
    neoliberalism, 176
    urban narratives, 125
    A World for Julius (Bryce Echenique), 139, 140–1, 143
Pratt, Mary Louise, 14, 15
Premio Nacional de Poesía, 98
principales, *Yawar Fiesta* (Arguedas), 44
production, as element of literary process, 4, 5
pueblos jóvenes, 124
punarunas, 59–60, 61, 62, 63
Puquio
    Arguedas's anthropological articles, 69, 80–4, 94
    mestizos, 80–1
    modernization, 80–4
    Yawar Fiesta (Arguedas), 34, 44–6, 48, 51–4, 55–6, 60–1, 80
"Puquio, a Changing Culture" (Arguedas), 80–4

Qayao, 81
Quechua language
    Alegría, 34, 35
    All the Worlds (Arguedas), 108
    Arguedas, 7, 16, 34, 35, 97
    Death in the Andes (Vargas Llosa), 189
    Deep Rivers (Arguedas), 85, 92
    *The Fox from up Above and the Fox

from Down Below (Arguedas), 148, 153
mestizos, 34
mistis, 34, 51
"Report on Uchuraccay" (Vargas Llosa), 170
Yawar Fiesta (Arguedas), 35, 46–7, 57, 58
"Questions of Conquest" (Vargas Llosa), 30, 168, 174–8, 184, 187
Quijano, Aníbal, 104, 203*n*

Rama, Ángel
    All the Worlds (Arguedas), 104
    Andean social narrative, 33
    Arguedas's anthropological articles, 72
    Broad and Alien is the World (Alegría), 32–3
    Deep Rivers (Arguedas), 88
    The Fox from up Above and the Fox from Down Below (Arguedas), 69
    intellectuals, 8, 10, 11, 21
    lettered city, 12, 13, 200
    mestizo, 72
    narrative acculturation, 33
    narrative transculturation, 3, 7, 8, 9, 10–12, 13, 14, 15, 69, 106, 199
    significance of 1941 in Latin American literature, 32
    Transculturación narrativa en América Latina, 8, 9, 11, 13, 34
    Yawar Fiesta (Arguedas), 32–3, 34
Ravines, Eudocio, 211*n*, 215*n*
The Real Life of Alejandro Mayta (Vargas Llosa), 167, 178
Redfield, Robert, 7, 71
Redoble por Rancas (Scorza) *see Drums for Rancas* (Scorza)
referents, as element of literary process, 4, 5, 6, 9
regional cultures
    All the Worlds (Arguedas), 104
    feudal power relations, 78
    Mantaro Valley, 76–9
    narrative transculturation, 7, 8–9, 10
    Yawar Fiesta (Arguedas), 52
'Rendón Willka, Demetrio' (*All the Worlds*), 102–4, 105, 106, 110, 111, 229*n*
"Report on Uchuraccay" (Vargas Llosa), 30, 167–8, 169–74, 194
Requiem for a Lightning Bolt (Scorza), 97, 99, 121–2, 234*n*

Index

Retablo ayacuchano (Scorza), 123
Reynoso, Oswaldo, 128
Ribeyro, Julio Ramón, 3, 4, 17, 158
  "At the Foot of the Cliff", 130
  "The Featherless Vultures", 130
  "An Indian's Hide is Cheap", 28,
    129, 130–3, 142
  short stories, 129–30
  skeptical optimism, 237–8n
  The Weekend Geniuses, 128
Los ríos profundos (Arguedas) *see Deep
  Rivers* (Arguedas)
*The Rise of the Popular and the Crisis
  of the State* (Matos Mar), 159
romanticism, 6
Rosaldo, Renato, 187
Rowe, William, 154, 155, 181, 243n
Rulfo, Juan, 8, 10, 13
Rumi, *Broad and Alien is the World*
  (Alegría), 34, 38, 39–40, 41–3, 45
'Rustler' (*Drums for Rancas*), 121

Sabogal, José, 21
Salazar Bondy, Sebastián, 4, 103, 128
San Isidro, 126, 236n
San Marcos University, 36, 68, 97
'Santa Maca' (*Requiem for a Lightning
  Bolt*), 121
Sarlo, Beatriz, 186
Sartre, Jean Paul, 166
Schmidt, Friedhelm, 10
Scorza, Manuel, 3, 17
  American Popular Revolutionary
    Alliance (APRA), 98
  as *aprista*, 212n
  The Ballad of Agapito Robles, 97,
    116, 121, 232n
  Boom narrative techniques, 27, 99,
    114, 115, 117
  Cerro de Pasco indigenous movement,
    98, 112–13
  Drums for Rancas, 27–8, 97, 99,
    112–23
  "Epístola a los poetas que vendrán",
    98
  Garabombo, the Invisible, 97, 121
  "I am the voice of those who have no
    voice", 98
  Las imprecaciones, 98
  literary innovations, 114
  magical realism, 27, 99, 117
  poetry, 98
  political activities, 98
  relation to indigenous movements, 98

Requiem for a Lightning Bolt, 97, 99,
  121–2, 234n
Retablo ayacuchano, 123
The Silent War, 97, 98, 99, 112, 114,
  122, 236n
The Sleepless Rider, 97
socialism, 99
socialist *indigenismo*, 25
transculturation, 123
semi-feudal landowners *see* feudalism;
  gamonales; *mistis*
Sendero Luminoso see Shining Path
serranos, 96
  Yawar Fiesta (Arguedas), 46, 52, 59
*Seven Interpretive Essays on Peruvian
  Reality* (Mariátegui), 4, 21
El Sexto, 36
Shining Path, 1, 3, 63, 123, 159, 160
  Ayacucho department, 169
  criollo elite, 29, 198
  Death in the Andes (Vargas Llosa),
    30, 188, 189, 190–1, 193, 198
  emergence and growth, 163–6,
    248–9n
  human costs of conflict, 165–6
  indigenous Andean culture, 164, 188
  indigenous support for, 254n
La Sierra, 21
sierra, *Yawar Fiesta* (Arguedas), 52, 54
"La sierra en el proceso de la cultura
  peruana" (Arguedas) *see* "The
  Andean Highlands in the Process of
  Peruvian Culture" (Arguedas)
sierra landowners, Odría government,
  65–6, 96
sierra population, 124
The Silent War (Scorza), 97, 98, 99,
  112, 114, 122, 236n
The Sleepless Rider (Scorza), 97
social change, 24, 26, 65, 95, 200
  Alegría, 37
  All the Worlds (Arguedas), 101, 104,
    105
  Arguedas, 37
  Arguedas's anthropological articles,
    67, 69, 71, 84
  Broad and Alien is the World
    (Alegría), 32, 37
  criollo elite, 128
  Deep Rivers (Arguedas), 84, 86, 87,
    94, 99
  impossibility of, 70
  "An Indian's Hide is Cheap"
    (Ribeyro), 132

Index

social change *(continued)*
North American anthropology, 71
Requiem for a Lightning Bolt
(Scorza), 99
Scorza's commitment to, 98
Yawar Fiesta (Arguedas), 32, 37, 55,
56, 58, 64
social class
All the Worlds (Arguedas), 111
Arguedas on, 101
changing relations in Peru, 1
see also middle class; working class
social conflicts
All the Worlds (Arguedas), 101
Andean social narrative, 33
Deep Rivers (Arguedas), 70
of modernization, 14, 16, 47, 50, 64,
117
and narrative form, 1–31
role of culture, 34
Scorza's novels, 114, 117
see also Broad and Alien is the World
(Alegría); *Yawar Fiesta* (Arguedas)
social realism, 5, 6
All the Worlds (Arguedas), 27, 99,
108
development theory, 67
*The Fox from up Above and the Fox
from Down Below* (Arguedas), 146,
147
Huasipungo (Icaza), 33
"An Indian's Hide is Cheap"
(Ribeyro), 28, 129
Scorza's writings, 27, 98, 114
El tungsteno (Vallejo), 33, 106
Yawar Fiesta (Arguedas), 47, 51
socialism, 23, 24, 159
All the Worlds (Arguedas), 112
Arguedas, 66, 82, 83, 99
Scorza, 99
Vargas Llosa, 29
see also Peruvian Socialist Party
socialist *indigenismo*, 25, 53
socialist realism, 33
Sommer, Doris, 177, 193
Spitta, Sylvia, 46–7, 62, 100, 102, 111
Spreen, Heike, 233*n*
Steele, Cynthia, 188
'Stirmsson, Paul' (*Death in the Andes*),
191–2
Storm in the Andes (Valcárcel), 21
The Storyteller (Vargas Llosa), 30, 168,
178–84, 187, 188
student movement, 19, 36

subaltern studies, 15
'Subprefect' (*Yawar Fiesta*), 52, 53, 54
Suleiman, Susan Rubin, 228*n*
'Susan' (*A World for Julius*), 134, 135,
136–7, 139–40, 142

Tasurinchi, *The Storyteller* (Vargas
Llosa), 180, 182
Teja, Ada María, 120
Tello, Julio C., 21
Tempestad en los Andes (Valcárcel), 21
text, as element of literary process, 4, 5
There Are No Miracles in October
(Reynoso), 128
Theseus, 192
La tía Julia y el escribidor (Vargas
Llosa), 178
Tierra o muerte (Blanco), 94
'Timoteo' (*Death in the Andes*), 192
'Tinoco, Pedrito' (*Death in the Andes*),
190, 191
Todas las sangres (Arguedas) *see All the
Worlds* (Arguedas)
Toledo, Alejandro, 30–1, 195–8, 255*n*
'Tomás' (*Death in the Andes*), 189–90,
193, 194
*Transculturación narrativa en América
Latina* (Rama), 8, 9, 11, 13, 34
transculturation, 7–9, 10–14, 207*n*
Arguedas's writings, 26, 68, 71–3, 76,
77, 83, 123, 178, 199
mestizaje, 10–11, 72, 73
Peru–Cornell project, 73
Scorza's writings, 123
Vargas Llosa, 178
Trigo, Pedro, 227*n*
Trujillo, 24, 36
tugurios, 125
La tumba del relámpago (Scorza) *see
Requiem for a Lightning Bolt*
(Scorza)
El tungsteno (Vallejo), 33, 38, 42, 106,
152, 213*n*
Túpac Amaru, 81
Túpac Amaru II, 81, 198
turupukllay, Yawar Fiesta (Arguedas),
44, 45, 49–53, 54–6, 63–4
'Tutaykire' (*The Fox from up Above
and the Fox from Down Below*),
150, 152

Uchuraccay Commission, 30, 167–8,
169–74, 194
Ulysses (Joyce), 147

Index

United States
  counter-revolutionary movements, 204*n*
  coup in Chile 1973, 204*n*
  imperialism, 3, 23–4
  Peru's dependence on, 26, 65, 68
  Peruvian Aristocratic Republic, 18
  Peruvian *Oncenio* period, 19
Universidad Agraria La Molina, 97
Universidad Nacional Mayor de San Marcos, 36, 68, 97
Universidad Nacional San Cristóbal de Huamanga, 163–4
urban narratives, 4, 126–9
  see also The Fox from up Above and the Fox from Down Below (Arguedas); "An Indian's Hide is Cheap" (Ribeyro); *A World for Julius* (Bryce Echenique)
urbanization, 1–2, 14, 20, 28–9, 66, 124–9, 158–62, 177
  see also cholo social group
USAID, 195

Valcárcel, Luis E., 21
Valdelomar, Abraham, 211
Vallejo, César, *El tungsteno*, 33, 38, 42, 106, 152, 213*n*
Vargas Llosa, Mario, 3, 4, 17
  All the Worlds (Arguedas), 100–1
  on Arguedas, 167, 250*n*
  Aunt Julia and the Scriptwriter, 178
  bank nationalization, 168, 251*n*
  Broad and Alien is the World (Alegría), 37
  changing ideology, 166–7
  Conversation in the Cathedral, 65, 128, 193, 194
  Death in the Andes, 30, 168–9, 187–94, 198
  A Fish in the Water, 30, 168–9
  The Fox from up Above and the Fox from Down Below (Arguedas), 145, 146
  The Green House, 29, 115, 166, 185, 189, 193, 194
  indigenous Andean culture, 29, 30, 166, 167, 170–4, 175–94, 251–2*n*
  modernization, 29, 30, 166, 167, 176–7, 187
  presidential campaign, 29–30, 162, 166, 184–7
  prologue to *The Other Path*, 162, 247*n*

"Questions of Conquest", 30, 168, 174–8, 184, 187
  The Real Life of Alejandro Mayta, 167, 178
  The Storyteller, 30, 168, 178–84, 187, 188
  transculturation, 178
  Uchuraccay Commission, 30, 167–8, 169–74, 194
  urban narratives, 127
  Yawar Fiesta (Arguedas), 46, 54, 64
Vasconcelos, José, 23
Velasco Alvarado, Juan, 24, 28, 96, 135–6, 165, 198, 248–9*n*
Vicos hacienda, 73–5, 82, 83
Vilas, Carlos, 176
'Vilma' *A World for Julius*, 134, 142

The Weekend Geniuses (Ribeyro), 128
Weismantel, Mary J., 202*n*, 217*n*, 254*n*
Western literary forms, 6, 7, 117
Westernization, 14, 68, 80, 82, 123, 127
  Peru–Cornell project, 73–5
  Vargas Llosa campaign, 187
Westernized culture *see* acculturation; *criollo* elite
women
  Deep Rivers (Arguedas), 86, 153
  The Fox from up Above and the Fox from Down Below (Arguedas), 153–4
  Yawar Fiesta (Arguedas), 45, 64
working class, 23
  growth of, 18, 19
World Bank, 195
A World for Julius (Bryce Echenique), 28–9, 128, 129, 133–43, 239*n*
  oral, conversational style, 136

Yanacocha, *Drums for Rancas* (Scorza), 115
Yanahuanca, *Drums for Rancas* (Scorza), 115, 118–19
yaraví, 6
Yarusyacán, *Requiem for a Lightning Bolt* (Scorza), 121, 122
Yawar Fiesta (Arguedas), 25, 44–64, 70
  amarus, 48, 60, 61, 62, 63, 154
  Andean cosmology, 26, 47, 48
  Andean myth, 48, 51–2, 54, 55, 56, 59–60, 61, 63, 91, 154
  Andean oral tradition, 47, 48, 56, 60, 64, 87

Index

Yawar Fiesta (Arguedas) *(continued)*
  ayllus, 44, 45, 46, 48, 51, 52, 53–5,
    56, 57, 60, 61, 63, 188
  bullfight, 44, 45, 46, 48, 49–53,
    54–6, 63–4
  collectivism, 45, 54, 55, 56–7, 58
  commercial success, 33–4
  comuneros, 44, 45, 47, 48, 50–2,
    53–5, 57, 58, 59, 61, 62, 63
  critical reception, 33–4
  Escajadillo on, 212–13*n*
  Farrar & Rinehart prize, 33
  gamonales, 44, 52, 53, 61
  indigenous Andean culture, 26, 37,
    47, 48, 49, 51, 54, 56, 57, 64
  linguistic differentiation, 46–7, 148
  main themes, 26, 32–3
  mestizos, 44, 49–50, 51, 53, 59, 63
  Misitu, 48, 51–2, 54, 55, 56, 59–60,
    61–3, 91
  mistis, 44, 45, 47, 48, 50, 51–5, 57,
    58, 59, 60–1, 62, 63, 151
  modernity, 26, 47, 48–9, 59, 63, 188
  narrative form, 45–6

Rama on, 32–3, 34
regional context, 34–5
road construction episode, 48, 55–8,
  64, 80, 188
social change, 32, 37, 55, 56, 58, 64
structure of, 47–8
turupukllay, 44, 45, 49–53, 54–6,
  63–4
women, 45, 64
yawar mayu
  All the Worlds (Arguedas), 90,
    106–12
  Deep Rivers (Arguedas), 89, 90, 93,
    106

Zola, Emile, 37
El zorro de arriba y el zorro de abajo
  (Arguedas) *see The Fox from up
  Above and the Fox from Down
  Below* (Arguedas)
Zulén, Pedro, 20–1, 41
Zumbagua fiesta, 217*n*
'Zuratas, Saúl' *The Storyteller* (Vargas
  Llosa), 178, 179, 180–2